Teacher Education Through Distance Learning

ABOUT THE AUTHOR

Dr. Surendra Kumar (Born on January 2, 1978) has done his schooling from Ambedkar Nagar. He obtained his M.A. (Economics, Ancient History and Education) from Dr. Ram Manohar Lohia Avadh University, Faizabad (U.P.). He obtained his M.Ed. Degree from University of Allahabad, Allahabad.

He completed his D.Phil. in Education from University of Allahabad, Allahabad.

Surendra Kumar joined in teaching profession in the year 2005as Assistant Professor in the Department of B.Ed., S.S. Khanna Girls' Degree College, Allahabad (Constituent College, University of Allahabad, Allahabad).

Dr. S. Kumar has published around 26 research papers in reputed national and international journals and 04 chapters in books. His areas of interest are Distance Education and Teacher Education.

Teacher Education Through Distance Learning

Surendra Kumar
M.A. (Economics, Ancient History & Education), M.Ed., D.Phil.
in Education, UGC-NET (Education)
Assistant Professor
B.Ed. Faculty
S.S. Khanna Girls' Degree College
(Constituent College of University of Allahabad, Allahabad

CONCEPT PUBLISHING COMPANY PVT. LTD.
NEW DELHI-110059

ISBN-13: 978-93-88937-41-2

First Published 2021

Published and Printed by

Concept Since 1974

Concept Publishing Company Pvt. Ltd.
A/15-16, Commercial Block, Mohan Garden,
New Delhi-110059 (INDIA)
T : 91 11 25351460, 91 11 25351794
E : publishing@conceptpub.com; *W* : www.conceptpub.com

Cataloging in Publication Data--Courtesy: D.K. Agencies (P) Ltd. <docinfo@dkagencies.com>

Kumar, Surendra, 1978- author.
Teacher education through distance learning / Surendra Kumar, Dr. Madhu Tandon.
pages cm
Includes bibliographical references and index.
ISBN 9789388937412

1. Teachers—Training of—India. 2. Distance education—India. I. Tandon, Madhu, author. II. Title.

LCC LB1727.I5K86 2021 | DDC 370.71154 23

Prof. P.K. Sahoo
Vice-Chancellor
University of Allahabad
Allahabad-211002

प्रो. पी. के. साहू
कुलपति
इलाहाबाद विश्वविद्यालय
इलाहाबाद - 211002

Foreword

Teacher education through Open Distance Learning Mode has its genesis in India since early sixties, when NCERT introduced correspondence-*cum*-contact programme based B.Ed. programme in Regional Colleges of Education for catering to the backlog of pre-service trained teachers in the Indian schools. The growth of ODL mode teacher education programme witnessed country wide appreciation through initiatives of open university system in the country. The instructional inputs along with professional development processes matter a lot in making ODL mode teacher education programmes relevant and effective. It requires suitable curriculum design and management of instructional system employing human resources and technological inputs. Even though traditional mode teacher education paradigm dominate instructional process, ODL mode teaching learning process proves its worth through suitable blending of ICT based instruction with hands on experience of student teachers in development of professional skills in real school situation. This book contains data based revealation of teacher education practices promoted through Open University programmes. Dr. Surendra Kumar has done as systematic fieldwork of instructional processes of B.Ed. Programme of IGNOW and UPRT open university and has portrayed the status of operation of teacher development activities at institutional level. The perception of student teachers and teacher educators throw light on quality dimensions of such processes. The work is worthy of critically analysing the relevance and utility of various processes of development of professional skills and attitudes through ODL mode teacher education programme in the country. The empirical study presented in the form of a book is a volunerable piece of reference for teacher education students, experts and researchers. Dr. Surendra Kumar's effort is commendable in bringing out such piece of research on alternative mode of teacher development programme.

Date: 7.11.2019
Allahabad

P. K. Sahoo

Mobile : 9452229765 # Email : pksahooald@rediffmail.com

Acknowledgements

This research study is an effort to deepen our understanding about teacher education of open universities. Distance education for teacher training is widely used around the world, in both small and large countries and in a variety of contexts. In fact, open and distance education is more than an alternative delivery system and operational concerns, its planning must confront fundamental issues of teacher education like integration of theory and practice and ask what kind of teacher development results in better student learning. It can be concluded that improvement on quality and competency is related with in-service and pre-service training which in turn related with process dynamics of such training programme. Therefore, there exists a strong need to understand and analyze the processes involved in teacher training programme.

This study would not have been possible without the cooperation of number of persons, first and foremost I would like to convey my heartfelt gratitude and express pride in having worked under the benign guidance of my supervisor Prof. P.K. Sahoo, Vice-Chancellor, University of Allahabad, Allahabad, who with an indulgent understanding attuned and guided my curiosity to analyse minutely various aspects of the present study.

I extend my special thanks to Dr. (Mrs.) Namita Sahoo (Assistant Professor, K.P. B.Ed. Training College, Allahabad, University of Allahabad) for her concern, care and encouragement for my work.

I offer my heartfelt thanks to Prof. Dhananjai Yadav, Head, Education Department, University of Allahabad. Special thanks to Prof. Vidya Agarwal and Prof. Pratibha Upadhyay for providing continuous support and guidance.

I am highly grateful to Dr. Jaipal Singh Vyast, MLC and Former Associate Professor, Hindu College, Moradabad, Dr. B.C. Das, Asst. Professor, Ravenshaw University, Cuttack, Dr. Basant Bahadur Singh,

Reader, R.B.S. College, Agra and Dr. M.K. Muchhal, Reader, D.J.P.G. College, Baraut, Baghpat for their cooperation throughout my research work.

I am equally grateful to all the experts of IGNOU as well as UPRTOU who readily rendered all possible help and cooperation in the collection of data. I would also like to extend special thanks to all B.Ed. trainees of IGNOU and UPRTOU who patiently have given entire details required.

Special thanks to all the scholars whose works have been reviewed for taking timely help and direction for the completion of the study. I am indebted to all the authors whose books have been consulted to get a better horizon for the framework of the study.

I am grateful to all my seniors and friends Dr. Dinesh Kumar, Dr. G.N. Tiwari, Dr. Reena Singh and Dr. Rama Gupta for their support. I have absolutely no words to express my deep sense of gratitude to them.

I am also thankful to my parents, younger brother Virendra Kumar and cousin Sri Ram Narayan and my thanks are to my wife Mrs. Anita for rendering all possible support and help towards the completion of this work.

Last but not the least, I am thankful to Concept Publishing Company Pvt. Ltd., New Delhi for undertaking publication of this and materialising it meticulously in the present form.

18th January, 2020 **Surendra Kumar**
295-D, Sector-D
Shantipuram Aawas Yojana,
Phaphamau, Prayagraj.

Contents

List of Tables

Abbreviations

AIOU	:	Allama Iqbal Open University
B.Ed.	:	Bachelor of Education
B.T.C.	:	Basic Teaching Certificate
CIET	:	Central Institute of Educational Technology
CIG	:	Certificate in Guidance
DEC	:	Distance Education Council
DEP-DPEP	:	Distance Education Project-District Primary Education Programme
DPE	:	Diploma in Primary Education
EMPC	:	Electronic Media Production Centre
ICT	:	Information and Communication Technology
IGNOU	:	Indira Gandhi National Open University
UPRTOU	:	Uttar Pradesh Rajarshi Tondon Open University
KOU	:	Kota Open University
KSOU	:	Karnataka State Open University
M.Ed.	:	Master of Education
NCERT	:	National Council of Educational Research and Training
NCTE	:	National Council for Teacher Education
NUEPA	:	National University of Educational Planning and Administration
SLM	:	Self-Learning Materials

1

Introduction

1.0 Introduction

India is a country of the largest teacher training systems of the world. A large number of teacher educators are engaged in teacher training at different levels. The role, function, competence and preparation of teachers have no doubt undergone a change from time to time but the need for a teacher has been imperative in all times. The role of the teacher is changing so fast that no amount of pre-service or in-service teacher education through traditional mode can probably cope with the expectations of the society. The preparation of teachers has changed with the change of times and with the expectations of the society.

The following observation in the Year book of education (1963) is pertinent. "The strength of an educational system largely depends upon the quality of its teachers." Therefore, no more important matter than that of securing a sufficient supply of the right kind of people to the profession, providing them with the best possible training and ensuring them a status and esteem commensurate with the importance and responsibility of their work. With the rapid expansion of schooling, these problems have acquired importance and urgency.

Thus in the context of the argument placed in favours of education for teachers, it is apparent that the teaching depends upon the quality of teachers who to a great extent depend upon the quality of professional training, hence the training of teachers should be accorded top most considerations in chalking out any programme of educational reconstruction.

In India at present, about 5 million teachers are working in education system. For the dream of tomorrow to be realized, where all the children and eligible youth of the country attend the system, India would require another set of 5 million teachers. For a school with five grades, we have merely two teachers on average (approximately) (Passi, 1998).

Present training institutions are not enough for this target. There is still very shortage of teachers and still large number of under-qualified teachers work in the school system. Further professional education and training are always a way behind the reality. There is an urgent need to overcome such impediments. All our teachers need updated training at varying levels of varying types and at different stages of their career. Many of our teachers including women teachers, are handicapped to attend programmes organized beyond their place of stay. In such cases what will happen to the studies of children of under-staffed or untrained or under-qualified single teacher schools is a big challenge for us. Solution to this problem lies in distance education. Therefore, it has enlarged the scope of education. Coupled with open learning, it provides structural flexibility. It has an important tool for teacher training at the initial. Training stage as well as for further upgradation of the knowledge and skills of the trained teachers without removing them from their work place.

1.1 Need for Open and Distance Teacher Education

The Secondary Education Commission (1952-53) said that "*We are, however, convinced that the most important factor in the contemplated educational reconstruction is the teacher, his personal qualities, his educational qualification, his professional training and the place that he occupies in the school as well as in the community. The reputation of a school and its influence on the life of community invariably depends on the kind of teachers working in it.*" The Education Commission (1964-66) stated "*of all the different factors which influence the quality of education and its contribution to national development, the quality, competency, and character of teachers are undoubtly the most significant. Nothing is more important than securing a sufficient supply of high quality recruits to the teaching profession, providing them with the best possible professional preparation and creating satisfactory conditions of work in which they can be fully effective.*" Realizing the importance of teacher in the educational system, the National Policy on Education 1986, as revised in the year 1992, has observed that—"*The status of the teacher reflects the socio-cultural ethos of a society; it is said that no people can rise above the level of its teachers... Teacher education is a continuous process, and its pre-service and in-service components are inseparable. As the first step, the system of teacher education will be overhauled.*" Teachers are the largest professional groups in human development sector, and their nature is ever-changing in size and character.

No system of Education can rise above the levels of its teachers. If education is the fundamental institution of any society the teachers are centre to any school, college and university. No programme of educational reforms can be implemented without the willingness and active co-operation of teachers. Teachers could be the most powerful agents of social regeneration, because the whole edifice of educational system is based upon the teachers. The impact of teachers on upcoming generation that is on the students is very subtle and long lasting.

Teacher education system is an important vehicle to improve the quality of school education. The revitalization and strengthening of the teacher education system is, therefore, a powerful means for the upliftment of educational standards in the country. It inculcates the necessary pedagogical skill and competencies among the teachers and makes them professionally competent to meet the demands of the society. They are expected to be leading catalysts of the information society. Teacher preparation needs to give more thinking into the different roles a teacher is to play to meet the new challenges in the information society and to help the young learners learn how to learn.

Distance education for teacher training is widely used around the world, in both small and large countries and in a variety of contexts. In fact, open and distance education is more than an alternative delivery system and operational concerns, its planning must confront fundamental issues of teacher education like integration of theory and practice and ask what kind of teacher development results in better student learning, because:

- The planning of teacher training and development needs to be tied more effectively into issues of supply, demand and retention. Traditional training forms and practices may lack the capacity to be sufficiently responsive to a changing environment.
- A solution frequently offered, as a first response to perceived teacher shortage, especially in the absence of reliable data or careful analysis of the problem, is to train more teachers and distance education is proposed as the means of doing this rapidly and on a large scale.
- The growing needs for professional development require more flexible forms of provision and more channels for reaching teachers, to offer them more access and choice.
- The increasing mobility of teachers is likely to require more attention in future, together with problems of qualifications, international accreditation and possible course provision.

Distance education as an educational process in which teachers and learners are separated in space and/or time for some or all of the time of study and in which the learning materials takeover some of the traditional roles of the teacher.

Learning materials play a central role, incorporating a variety of media and, in most systems, provision is made for students to interact with tutors and other students as a means of support. Many distance education programmes include some face-to-face contact; either at local centre in weekend or residential schools, and the balance of time between face-to-face contact and self-study in programmes vary widely. Open learning is an organized educational activity where learners also study themselves for some or all the time. It is based on a set of values in which constraints on study are minimized in the time of access, time, pace and method of study. Translated into concrete terms providing learners with access to learning resources, advice, support and, in many cases, assessment of learning. Distance teacher education programmes may not incorporate some of the values, which characterize open learning. As per professional education norms conditions for teacher preparation through distance mode are of structured nature. Access to teacher education programmes is restricted by entrance qualification or examination and by the requirements of programmes of study for recognition by teacher accreditation authorities like NCTE and DEC.

1.2 Meaning of Distance Education

Distance Education is sometimes taken to mean the use of television and at some other times the use of Internet. The word *Distance* implies that the student are always remote, only exceptionally meeting each other and/or with their teachers. UNESCO (2002) has defined *distance education as an educational process in which a significant proportion of the teaching is conducted by someone removed in space and/or time from the learner.* The gap between the learners and the institution is minimized through media and materials—print and non-print (audio-video and digital), radio programme, TV programme, audioconfrencing, teleconferencing and Internet. Learners also learn through occasional meeting with tutors and with peer group. The constraints on the study are minimized in terms either of access, or of time and place, pace, methods of study and/or any of these combinations. Distance education has the potentiality to reach large number of learners at a time in their work place, provide learning resources for them and enable them to qualify without attending school/college in person. It also opens up new opportunities to the learners for keeping up-to-date no matter where or when they want to study. In terms of cost per student, distance education programme has often shown advantages over conventional programmes.

1.3 The Concept of Open University

An open learning system may be defined as one in which the focus of learning is primarily on the students. The Open University represents an alternative approach to higher learning. It stands distinctively away from a highly formal, institutionalised and centrally administered system of education. Its philosophy is built around the principles of university, flexibility and innovativeness. Its ideas and institutions, its methods and procedures are all shaped accordingly. Conceptually, it can be viewed as a system drawing upon the best elements in formal and non-formal education. The 'openness' consists of a variety of features:

First, the entry requirements are not too exacting. A genuine interest in picking up knowledge is all that it expects. Consequently, it would try to embrace as many learners as possible.

Second, its territorial reach is visibly wide. It aims at carrying education to true doorstep of the learners.

Third, the open-university is learner-oriented. It devises its courses and methods of teaching to suit the needs of the learners.

Fourth, it believes in fair delivery of quality education materials including, study material, assignments, media and technology, counselling services etc.

Fifth, its administration is decentralised. In promoting distance education, the university creates a wide network of study centres. Students need only to come to the nearest available centre for collecting information, completing the formalities, discussing their academic issued and appearing for evaluation of their work at intervals chosen by them.

Sixth, student assessment under Open University is based on the principle of continuous assessment and credit system. It does not require to get bogged down in one final examination. One can study at one's own pace.

1.4 B.Ed. Programmes of Open Universities

The B.Ed. programme is training programme for professional development of untrained experienced teachers working in government or government recognised schools. The B.Ed. programme was launched by Kota Open University first time in the country. IGNOU launched B.Ed. programme in 2001 and UPRTOU in 2003. Nowadays there are many open universities organising B.Ed. programmes for above said purpose. In following Table 19 universities are offering distance mode B.Ed. programme. The requirement of teaching experience for B.Ed. are given in Table 1.0 along with course duration.

Table 1.0: List of Open Universities Offering B.Ed. Programme in India

Sl. No.	*Universities*	*Required Teaching Experience (in years)*	*Maximum Duration of Course (in years)*
1.	Andhra University — School of Distance Education	2	1
2.	Annamalai University—Directorate of Distance Education	-	-
3.	Bangalore University — Directorate of Correspondence Courses and Distance Education	3	2
4.	Bharathidasan University — Centre for Distance Education	3	2
5.	Himachal Pradesh University—International Centre For Distance Education and Open Learning	-	2
6.	Indira Gandhi National Open University	2	2-4
7.	Jamia Millia Islamia—Dr. A.S. Centre for Distance and Open Learning	2	2-6
8.	Kakatiya University—School of Distance Learning and Continuing Education	3	2
9.	Karnataka State Open University	2	2
10.	Kota Open University (V.M. Open University)	3	2
11.	Madhya Pradesh Bhoj (Open) University	2	2
12.	Maharshi Dayanand University—Directorate of Distance Education	2	2
13.	Panjab University—Department of Correspondence Studies	-	-
14.	Tamil Nadu Open University	2	-
15.	Sri Padmavati Mahila Visvavidyalayam Distance Education Centre	2	2
16.	Shri Venkateswara University—Directorate of Distance Education	2	2
17.	University of Jammu—Directorate of Distance Education	2	2
18.	Uttar Pradesh Rajarshi Tondon Open University	2	2-4
19.	Yashwantrao Chavan Mahrashtra Open University	2	2

1.5 Objectives of the Distance Mode B.Ed. Programme

This programme is meant to systematize and give a method and structure to the experiences of B.Ed. trainees. Specifically, this programme aims at enhancing the professional competencies and skills of the teachers working in elementary, secondary and senior secondary schools. Thus, it enables B.Ed. trainees for development of following competencies:

(i) Competence to teach the subject(s) of specialization of B.Ed. trainees on the basis of the accepted principles of teaching and learning.
(ii) Skills, understanding, interests and attitudes which would enable B.Ed. trainees to foster all-round growth and development of their students.
(iii) Skills in identifying, selecting, innovating and organizing learning experiences for teaching school subjects.
(iv) Understanding of psychological principles of growth and development, individual differences and cognitive, psychomotor and attitudinal learning.
(v) Skills in guiding their students in order to enable them to solve their personal as well as academic problems.
(vi) Understanding the role of home, school and community in shaping the personality of the child, and help to develop an amicable home-school relationship for mutual benefit.
(vii) Understanding the role of school in a changing society.
(viii) Ability to undertake investigatory projects and action research to improve the school system.

1.6 Instructional System

The instructional system of the B.Ed. programme of Open University is carried out through DE system. The major components of instructional activities of DE system are:

- Study of open learning print based course materials by distance learners.
- Attempting self-assessment questions incorporated in the course materials.
- Getting in touch with counsellors during workshop at study centres located in teacher training colleges.

- Getting opportunity for group interaction with peers and tutors during workshops at the study centres.
- Viewing TV lessons/Video lessons and listening to radio lessons/ audio cassette based lessons.
- Having opportunity for group interaction through teleconferencing during contact sessions.
- Training in simulated situations.
- Conducting practice teaching activities in schools under supervision of teacher educators and mentors.
- Conducting projects and school experience-based activities under supervision of teacher educators.
- Doing assignments prescribed for each course.
- Exposure to counsellors feedbacks on assignments, project and school experience activities.
- Exposure to peer trainees feedbacks on various occasions of group learning situations and practicals.

IGNOU and other Open Universities adopt above stated instructional processes for B.Ed. programme in principle. Specific provisions are made for operation of instructional system through involvement of various organs of the university at headquarters level, at regional centre level, at study centre level and at practice teaching school level.

1.7 Phases of Assessment in Distance B.Ed. Programme

The Open University assesses pupil-teachers in two phases:

1. Theory
2. Practical; this unit is further divided into four sub-areas:
   (i) ***Practical/Application-oriented assignment:*** It includes questions in the concerned areas, project work, model lesson plan/unit plan, case studies, action research etc. The assignments responses commented upon and evaluated within specified time and feedback provided to the B.Ed. trainees promptly. The evaluation of these assignments would be part of the evaluation of the concerned theory courses.
   (ii) ***School-based Practical work:*** This activity includes administration of psychological test/tools, organizing health education activities, participation in sports and games,

conducting debates, preparation of school time-table construction of question papers together with scoring procedures, selection and use of different resources such as libraries, laboratories, media and materials, participation in class activities related to the teaching subjects etc.

(iii) ***Workshop-based practical work:*** The workshop is conducted by the resource persons/experts in education. Audio-video programmes are used as support materials. In the workshop the trainees perform various activities for improving their teaching competencies.

(iv) ***Practice Teaching:*** To improve skills in teaching, the B.Ed. trainees are required to undertake pre-planned teaching under the supervision of teacher educators engaged by the study centre concern with the universities. Every trainee presents 40 model lessons (20 in each of the two teaching subjects).

1.8 Inputs of the Programme

In order to achieve the objectives, the programme is offered through study centres various media, which includes print material, counselling sessions, Audio-video, telecast, broadcast, teleconferencing, interactive radio counselling and learning resource centres.

1.8.1 Micro-teaching

Micro-teaching is a very important and useful training technique to train our student-teachers and orient teacher-educators by conducting workshop on micro-teaching.

According to Buch (1968) "Microteaching is a teacher education technique which allows teachers to apply clearly defined teaching skill to carefully prepared lessons in a planned series of five to ten minutes encounters with a small group of five to ten pupils, often within an opportunity to observe the results on videotape."

Passi (1976) defined Microteaching as "a training technique which requires student teachers to teach a single concept using specified teaching skill to a small number of pupils in a short duration of time.

Microteaching is a training technique aimed at simplifying the complexities of normal classroom teaching. It is described as a "Scaled down teaching encounter in class size and class time" (Allen and Ryan,

1969). In microteaching, attention is focused on specific teaching skills, i.e., lecturing, questioning, explaining, demonstrating etc. which the student-teacher practices for short periods (5-10 minutes) with a small group of pupils (usually 5-10). The practice session is recorded usually on videotape and is then played back to the student teacher in order to obtain immediate feedback. The resulting feedback together with the supervisor's comments and observations made by the pupils helps the student-teacher to analyse his performance and thus restructure the lesson in order to teach it to a different group of pupils. Again, this is followed by immediate refeedback, so that further analysis and evaluation can take place in order to identify any areas where further improvement could be made. By employing this 'Plan-Teach-Feedback-Replan-Refeedback' cycle.

It is possible to give the student teacher the opportunity to put into immediate practice what he has learned from the video replay and from the peer group and other feedback on the previous attempt" (Percival and Ellington, 1984).

However, there can be many variations in terms of class size and class time. For instance, "the size of the class may vary from 3 to 10 pupils and time may vary from 3 to 20 minutes. The pupils may be either real or peers acting as pupils; the source of feedback may be one or many like self, pupils, peers acting and supervisors, teacher educators, audiotape recording, videotape recording etc. The feedback can be immediate or delayed, prescriptive or descriptive, qualitative or quantitative, and variations may be made in length of time devoted to any phase of the microteaching cycle" (Das *et al.*, 1980).

1.8.2 Feedback

Feedback is being used widely in modifying human behaviour. Feedback means knowledge of results. It refers to providing information to an individual about his behaviour/performance with a view to modifying it in the desired direction. It includes points of strengths as well as weaknesses relating to the behaviour/performance. The systematic feedback provided to an individual on his performance/behaviour helps him to improve upon it in the desired direction.

In the micro-teaching approach, the B.Ed. trainees are provided feedback on his teaching performance on the basis of the observations. The feedback is provided in terms of the use of the component behaviours comprising the skill under practice. There is a provision for immediate and specific feedback to be provided to a trainee undergoing practice for attaining mastery over a teaching skill. The specific immediate feedback helps a trainee to modify his behaviour in the desired direction, and thus, facilitates acquisition of the teaching skills.

Feedback can be provided either individually or in a group. Decision about the conditions in which feedback is to be provided depends on the availability of the facility, the type of feedback and the type of student-teacher who is to be provided with the feedback.

1.8.3 Teaching Skills

Teaching is a set of interrelated activities a teacher performs in the classroom with a view to facilitate learning in students. Teaching activities can be analyzed in terms of teachers' behaviour. Teacher behaviour may be considered as a set of activities of the teacher which are observable. The various set of activities related to behaviours included in teaching are: introducing, explaining, demonstrating, questioning, maintaining classroom discipline, illustrating, encouraging students to answer questions, posing problems for students to solve etc. which may be described as teaching skills.

Gage (1968) defines teaching skills as "specific instructional techniques and procedures that a teacher may use in the classroom. They represent an analysis of the teaching process into relatively descrete components that can be used in different combination in the continuous flow of the teacher's performance."

Passi (1976) has defined teaching skill as "a group of teaching acts of behaviours intended to facilitate pupil's learning directly or indirectly."

Thus micro-teaching is used for developing certain teaching skills. A teaching skill is defined as a set of teachers' behaviour which are especially effective in bringing about desired changes in pupil-teachers. For convenience and behavioural adaptation the researcher has clubbed different teaching skills given by Passi and associates into the following categories that find mass acceptability.

Skill of Introductory the Lesson: It refers to the development of cognitive rapport between pupils and teacher. Generally introducing a lesson includes what the teacher does with or without the help of the pupils before stating the aim of the lesson. It requires a skill on the part of the teacher to introduce a lesson.

In order to develop the skill of introducing the lesson, pupils have to practice using more of desirable behaviours (using previous knowledge, using appropriate devices) and avoiding undesirable ones (lacking in continuity, uttering irrelevant statement and questions).

Skill of Questioning: Skill of questioning refers to the formulation of relevant, precise, conscise, clear, specific and grammatically correct questions. These properties are also known as the components of the questioning skill.

Questioning means art of getting informations from the students. Purpose of questioning may be — to test the previous knowledge of the students, to keep the student alert and attentive, to know whether the students know what is meaningful, to stimulate thinking etc. A question is said to be meaningful if it has good—(i) structure, (ii) process, and (iii) Product.

Skill of explaining: Explanation is defined as an activity to bring about an understanding in someone about a concept, principle or phenomenon while giving explanation, causes for the phenomenon, reasons behind the action and various logical steps involved in arriving at inferences are given. A good explanation is one which is understood by the pupils. Therefore, a teacher must try to explain the concepts, thoughts, ideas etc. in such a way that it is understandable by the pupils for whom it is concerned.

Skill of explaining has got following teacher behaviours which can be broadly divided into desirable behaviour (use of introducing statements, use of concluding statements, use of explaining links, use of visual techniques, technical words defined, interesting to pupils, covering essential points, questions to test pupils understanding) and undesirable behaviours (irrelevant statements, lack of continuity, lack of fluency, vague words or phrases).

Skill of illustration with examples: Many a time when a teacher teaches an abstract concept ideas or some mathematical concept, only explanation does not meet requirements of the pupils. They require something more than mere explanation. This demand of the pupils is fulfilled when a skilful teacher uses some examples to illustrate the idea, concept or principle under study. This behaviour of the teacher makes them easy to understand the content under study.

From the above description it can be concluded that examples are the observation or situations of occurrence of a concept or generalization. The skill of illustration can be defined as the selection of the examples relevant to the concept or the generalization to be taught to pupils, so that the content under study may be clear and understandable to the pupils. It will be much better if these examples are taken from pupils' daily life.

Skill of reinforcement: There are various ways in which the teacher can reinforce (strengthen) the pupil's desirable behaviour. But one thing must be clear in the mind of the teacher that while using positive reinforcer, reinforces or strengthens desirable pupil responses and while using negative reinforcer negatively reinforces pupil's responses. This implies that the teacher has to practice using positive reinforcers and avoid the use of negative reinforces in the classroom, so that the pupils participate more and more in classroom activities. That is why this skill is named as skill of reinforcement.

Skill of blackboard writing: In all the tasks like drawing of diagrams and figures, giving definitions, writing the language of the problems and their solutions, drawing generalizations, giving principles and formulae and assigning home work, blackboard proves a good helping hand to the teacher.

Blackboards are widely used in all sectors of education and training and are most suitable for giving a holistic picture of the lesson. A good blackboard work brings clearness in perception and concepts being taught, and adds variety to the lesson. Blackboards can be suitably used for displaying notes and diagrams during a lesson and for working through calculations or similar exercise in front of a class.

Skills of demonstration: Demonstration is a process of describing and explaining the concept, idea, teaching point etc. with the help of specimens or experiments as way of teaching. It makes the subject matter concrete and teaching more simpler and meaningful as it helps the teacher to link learning with the real life situations of the learner.

Skill of lesson closure: Lesson closure is similar to achieving closure which is a process of determining the extent to which the objectives have been achieved; teaching has been successful and learning experiences have been provided. It is process of summing up main points covered during the lesson taking learners' response into account. Achieving closure refers to the summary of what the learners should now know and able to do.

"Achieving closure is similar to a state known as recapitulation in the Herbartian steps, according to which it is a process of associating new facts with the old knowledge, applying new knowledge in various situations, and ensuring repetition of the facts in the best possible way" (Passi, 1981).

1.8.4 Lesson Planning

Any activity well planned in advance comes out to be successfully is classroom teaching. If a teacher plans his lesson before hand, he knows what he is going to teach, how he is going to teach, what teaching aids he is going to use, what questions he is going to ask, what questions students might ask, what objectives he is going to achieve and how he is going to evaluate that he has achieved his identified objectives. The answers of such questions make a lesson plan.

For a new teacher, lesson plan may be a detailed script and for an experienced teacher it may be a small package of some teaching points in the written form or just in his mind. For any teacher a lesson plan comes out to be very effective.

It is advisable for a teacher to select and organize in a logical sequence the suitable material for classroom instruction. From where should he start today's lesson with respect to where he ended yesterday. If yesterday's lesson ended with the completion of a part of sub-unit or lesson, then it pays way to develop his lesson. Should the part of the lesson be repeated at the very beginning of the lesson? Should the students be asked to tell what they learnt yesterday? Should the basic generalizations be asked from the students? Teacher should give serious thought to such questions in order to arrive at efficient teaching.

1.8.5 Unit Planning

Planning a unit is similar to lesson planning. A unit may have several lessons. Therefore, it may not be complete in one class period. It may take several class periods to complete a unit. If unit plans are given in teacher's guides they might be very useful for the teachers specially the new teachers. A new teacher feels difficulty in teaching a topic in his class not because he does not know the subject matter, but because he does not know exactly how much subject matter in a certain topic suits the varying age levels of the students. Again he faces the difficulty in selecting the teaching material. He also finds it difficult to decide what activities should be undertaken to cast a lasting impression on the minds of the students. Very often the teachers, specially the new ones do not have enough practice of how to evaluate, how far the students have followed what they have been taught. But for many experienced teachers it may be quite easy. Thus, a new teacher may take advantage of their experiences, but they are not always available to him.

1.8.6 Practice Teaching

Practice teaching is the period of practical teaching experience in school, which forms one of the major parts of the training for teacher trainees. More practice-based teacher education have been encouraged internationally and become part of the common discourse about education. The distance teacher education programmes handled the management of teaching practice in different ways, reflecting the regulations and norms of the different countries and the importance placed on it within different teacher education systems. In India NCTE advocates for an internship of 4 weeks duration, during which the teacher trainees deliver at least 40 lessons, 20 in each subject in the school they are serving. NCTE also mentioned that the field practicum centres will be the selected school where teacher trainees are working for the organization of practice teaching, work experience, action research studies and innovative curricular practices. The selected schools where teacher trainees are working. Again, most teacher trainees need support, guidance, and feedback on their work are treated as practicum centres. NCTE advocates supervising ten lessons out of forty lessons by the specified teacher educators of training colleges/university departments. In order to make supervision effective, supervisors need orientation. Perraton and Potashnik (1997) felt the need of training of supervisors in how to work with teachers in their classroom to support what was learned in training.

1.8.7 Training Personnel

According to the norms formulated both by NCTE and UGC-NCTE-DEC joint committee, each university offering B.Ed. through distance mode will admit only those candidates who are currently working in the school system located in the territorial jurisdiction assigned to it by its Act/State governments. Regarding qualification, they mentioned that a candidate should be at least a graduate for taking admission to B.Ed. course.

About the teaching experience, according to the proposal of UGC-NCTE-DEC joint committee, teaching experience and age of the candidates should be considered priority criteria for admission. The candidate should have two years teaching experience in recognized schools and be a working teacher at senior secondary, secondary, upper primary and primary levels and remains so during the total period of the B.Ed. programme. NCTE also motioned about the same thing but the school it mentioned that the school should be a recognized one. Further NCTE has mentioned that admission will be based on the length of service and preference to be given to secondary school teachers.

1.8.8 Programme Study Centre

NCTE has mentioned that only teacher education institutions offering regular B.Ed. programme recognized by the NCTE shall be designated as study centres for B.Ed. programme and those teacher education institutions which are offering B.Ed. programme. Maximum number of teacher trainees in a study centre shall not exceed 100 per batch in case of B.Ed. course. These centres will be equipped with adequate audio-visual equipment. Staff for these centres may include one coordinator, ten teacher educators and one technical support personnel on part-time basis. Adequate facilities for coordinator's room, classroom and store room, display of audio-video gadgets, library books and other learning materials etc. should be made available. Part-time teachers may be selected depending upon the requirements of electives offered.

At present, there are approximately 21 programme study centres all over U.P. of IGNOU and 10 of UPRTOU. The list of programme study centres are given in the appendix. These centres are established in conventional B.Ed. colleges recognised by NCTE. The faculties of these colleges serve as extended faculty of IGNOU as well as UPRTOU. Academic counsellors provide counselling, guidance and supervision in these centres. Universities provide equipments and other facilities to be utilized by programme study centres. Support materials are made available through Regional Centres of concerned open universities. These resource centres function under the direct control of the concerned Regional Director of the region.

In the Programme Study Centres, the Programme incharge carries the responsibility of implementing the programme and management of the centre with the help of identified academic counsellors, and part-time staff. All the Programme incharge, counsellors and part-time staff are paid honorarium as per University norms.

A study centre has a lot of activities perform such as to arrange counseling session, group activities, workshop, providing laboratory, library, computer and other facilities, evaluation of assignments etc. Teacher trainees benefit significantly from their involvement in various activities.

1.8.9 Counsellor

According to NCTE norm, the person from education discipline with the qualification as laid down by UGC should be appointed as counsellors.

UGC-NCTE-DEC joint committee advocated for inducting experts drawn from conventional institutions to be appointed as counsellors into the philosophy, possibilities and competencies specific to distance education. There are various activities to be performed by counsellors. The counsellor has to perform ......*to motivate and encourage the remote site students, keep up their enthusiasm, and maintain discipline in the classroom. He is also responsible for smooth running of equipment, helping students with interaction, handing out, collecting, and grading papers, guiding collaborative groups who are working with manipulative, answering questions when necessary and assisting the studio teacher when asked. The site facilitator also carries out the assessment procedure defined by the teacher, via print, portfolios, on-line communications, or FAX* (Sherry, 1996).

1.8.10 Evaluation Process/Assessment Strategy

Evaluation is one of the most important components of any programme on the basis of which the extent of achievement of instructional objectives are measured, and the institution gets feedback for further improvement. Perraton and Potashnik (1997) mentioned that the effectiveness of Distance Education Programme can be measured in at least five ways: (a) looking at its success in reaching audiences, (b) in completion rates of those following distance education courses, (c) in their examination results, (d) in their learning gains, and (e) in the effects on teachers' classroom practice. But the list is incomplete and does not talk about the process of evaluating such components. NCTE advocated for comprehensive and continuous, with formative evaluation for B.Ed. course through distance mode. It says:

> Formative and summative evaluation will be conducted in all curricular and co-curricular areas of the courses. The university will ensure continuous and comprehensive evaluation as per the guidelines. The written, practical, oral and other innovative forms of evaluation will be employed as and when necessary. The institution will ensure continuity of feedback on the basis of evaluation of assignments, practical and other activities. The overall framework of marks, marking/grading shall be comparable to those in the regular programme. Formative (internal) evaluation shall have a minimum of 30 per cent weightage for theory courses. There shall be separate pass marks

for both formative (internal) and summative (external) evaluation. Practical components shall be internally evaluated in terms of grades.

NCTE has created norms to evaluate the teacher trainees as well as teacher education institutions for recognition. NCTE and DEC constitute a joint standing committee to periodically assess the performance of the institutions offering or proposing to offer B.Ed. through distance mode, based on which granting/continuance of recognition/accreditation could be considered. It should also create norms and procedure to evaluate the distance teacher education programme.

The assessment strategy is designed to provide support to trainees and to help them to maximize their potential as well as to evaluate their performance. The learning style in materials, encompass opportunities for self-assessment, which help trainees to develop the habit of evaluation and independent learning.

1.8.11 Media and Technology

Media and materials are one of the major parts of distance education course. Quality of the teaching and learning process is dependent upon the quality of the study materials (Naidu, 1994). Media and materials include study materials—print, audio, video and digital materials. It also includes interactive media such as teleconferencing, audio-conferencing and online education.

Print material is a backbone for open and distance learning system and it serves as an effective teaching tool. The courses for delivery by open and distance education has been prepared by leading experts in various specializations in teacher education from across the country. The programme includes a wide range of subjects. The main aim is to provide learners an in-depth understanding of teaching profession, administrative and behavioural aspects of teacher.

The learning activities within the materials focus on professional experience and the new expected knowledge and practical experience of learners.

The main learning materials in the form of printed are dispatched to students at the beginning of each year. These instructional materials have been prepared in simple and interactive language. The conversational style is enhanced by relevant illustrations. Learners are provided with study and tutorial guides also known as student teachers' handbook and academic counsellor manuals. The programme guide provide the student with a plan of whole course, the content of each Unit along with corresponding objectives, the learning activities and the instructions about how they should approach their study on a continuous basis. The tutorial guide (counsellors' manual) provides guidance to both the learner and teacher about suggested activities for their counselling and self and supervised activities.

1.8.12 Counselling Session

Print materials are used for transmission of subject matter, because it serves as a tool of teaching. As open and distance education is more about learning than teaching and that the human element only can adopt to provide an individualized structure for students' needs. Therefore, in addition of being provided with reading/study materials, students are also given an opportunity to meet with the counsellors and other participants of the programme at specifically designated times and places during face to face counselling sessions. The counselling sessions provide the trainees with an opportunity to interact with fellow learners and tutors and clarify the problem areas that trainees may have encountered with the print materials during self-study and during teaching in the class. Each of these academic counsellors is a specialist in particular subject area working in conventional B.Ed. college/s. An academic counsellor is not expected to teach but to facilitate learning. In counselling sessions the academic counsellor informs, advises or counsels. In a tutorial he/she primarily teaches or discusses course content. These two activities are combined together during workshops.

1.8.13 Workshops

Organisation of workshops are the most important function of study centres/programme study centres. The workshops are held on weekends or public holidays or as per convenience of Programme Study Centres when their regular students are on vacation. Workshop schedules are prepared on the basis of guidelines developed by the open universities and is dispatched to learners soon after they receive the self-instructional print material. Attendance requirement of 75 per cent is compulsory in workshops.

1.9 Operation of the Programme

Operation of the Programme involves a central system of management by the University combined with a network of approved programmed study centres throughout the country that provide support and facilities to the trainees. Network of approved centres comprises B.Ed. colleges which are recognised by National Council of Teacher Education (NCTE).

1.10 Scheme of Monitoring of Practical Activities

The reports along with the mentor's authentication and comments submitted to the workshops facilitator in the first or the second workshops as specified the followings:

1.10.1 Report of the Activities which are to be Submitted in Workshop I

Report of the following four activities are to be submitted in workshop I:

1. Maintenance of register and records
2. Addressing the school assembly.
3. Conducting a sociometric test in the classroom.
4. Content Analysis exercise.

1.10.2 Report of the Activities which are to be Submitted in Workshop II

Report of the following seven activities are to be submitted in workshop II:

1. Administration of intelligence test, personality test and aptitude test on one student and analysis of results.
2. Preparation of cumulative records.
3. Preparation of school time-table.
4. Organising Career Talk/ PTA Meeting/ Debate/ Panel Discussion/ Quiz Programme.
5. Action Research.
6. Field Trip.
7. Organisation of a campaign.

1.11 Organisation of Workshop-based Practical Activities

Classroom instruction requires mastery of various methods and modes of communication with the students. Instruction includes proper planning of instruction, special techniques associated with teaching specific subjects and also general management strategies needed for organising teaching in a classroom. Apart from this, the teacher also has a multifaceted role of the manager, the researcher and the social welfare individual. To prepare to effectively fit in all these roles of B.Ed. trainees two workshops of 12 days each have been planned. Workshop I is conducted before the commencement of practice teaching and workshop II after a large portion of practice teaching is over.

To successfully complete the B.Ed. programme, B.Ed. trainees have to participate in all the activities of the workshops. The workshop facilitators and workshop directors specially oriented for the purpose will conduct the workshops. In the workshops B.Ed. trainees participate individually as well as in groups, in various activities and sharpen their teaching competence. Only those topics/activities which need guided experiences are included in the workshop. B.Ed. trainees work on their activities under the direct supervision/guidance of teacher educators and the workshop also give them an opportunity to work with their fellow student teachers. The quality and extent of participation and the progress made by B.Ed. trainees monitored and evaluated by the facilitators. Therefore, it is expected that they come to participate in the workshops with prior preparation. This preparatory phase has been called the pre-workshop activity. The tasks performed during the workshop are referred to as during workshop activity. All tasks done during workshop have to be followed up in teaching/learning situations and the descriptions of all these constitute the post-workshop activities. It is to be noted here that the first workshop corresponds to the first year theory courses and most of the school based activities to be carried out during practice teaching. Apart from these, the first workshop orients B.Ed. trainees to all aspects of practice teaching. The second workshop corresponds to the second year theory courses and some more school-based activities. It also provides the final polish to their teaching and management skills inside and outside the classroom. Table I and Table II provide a cursory overview of the activities of the two workshops. The details of these activities are presented in the *appendix*.

1.12 Instructional Organisation/Delivery

A few instructional inputs are delivered to B.Ed. trainees by Post such as Programme guide, printed course material, assignments and supplementary materials. Counselling services are made available to the students at study centres/programme study centres. Counselling is provided through workshops at programme study centres. Teleconferencing is delivered from IGNOU Headquarters through satellite for all the programmes. In the delivery process mainly one-way communication takes place between faculty of headquarters and students. In case of teleconferencing and assignment evaluation two-way communication takes place between students and faculty, between students and counsellors and among students themselves.

1.12.1 Assignments

Written assignments are a crucial part of interactive process and a tool of continuous evaluation. Significant resources are committed to it both by providers and by the trainees. The purpose of assignments is not only to enhance trainees writing ability, but also to make them go through whole course in order to find the relevant answers after understanding the course.

Trainees must complete the assignments to progress from one year to another, as the submission of assignments is compulsory for the successful completion of the programme.

The assignments are corrected by counsellors who provide feedback in the form of grades and tutor comments for a two-way communication. The corrected and graded assignments are returned to the trainees to get feedback. In calculating the final grade, assignments are given weightage.

1.12.2 Examination

Examination includes assessment of knowledge and competency in the particular course. This helps ensure that trainees have understood the course material, identify points for further study and assess progress.

A panel examiners in each course sets papers. The question papers are moderated by faculty and outside experts. Registration and Evaluation Division of the University manages this process. The Term End Examination is held at the end of each year/session in the central places known as examination centres which are mostly the Study Centres/ Programme Study Centres of the Universities.

If a student fails the examination in one or more subjects but passes the assignments the student is deemed to have failed in that particular course/courses and the students have to rewrite the examination for that course only, but not the assignment. However, they are allowed to proceed to next session/year of the study. Trainees can complete the programme in a stipulated period of minimum two years but they have the flexibility to complete the programme in a maximum period of four years.

1.12.3 Practical Examination

Practical examination is conducted to assess the competency in teaching skills, administrative and research skills etc. The practical examination is held at the end of practical experience at Programme study Centre in depending upon the feasibility of the programme study centres. If a student fails in practical examination in a particular subject, he/she is allowed to re-appear in the examination of specific practical course only during next session. Learners are expected to pass in theory activities and practical examination separately. The self and supervised activities are counted towards the assignment and/or continuous evaluation of the practical courses.

1.13 Programme Monitoring

An essential component of supporting the delivery of a open and distance learning B.Ed. programme is its monitoring. The programme is monitored in various ways.

1.13.1 Records of B.Ed. Trainees

The Programme Incharge maintains an attendance register of the trainees keep a record of their attendance during workshops. Programme Incharge sends these records to programme coordinator for onward transmission of these records to the Central Office, i.e. the Regional Director and/or Student Registration and Evaluation Division (SRED) for scrutiny.

Counsellors/Programme Incharge keep a record of assignments and self-activities and send the grades and marks to Programme Incharge who in turn submits the records to the concerned division and officers viz., Student Registration and Evaluation Division and Regional Director/ Regional Services Division. The Programme Incharge also issues a certificate of attendance in theory and practical sessions and completion of self-activities to trainees for onward submission to the University.

1.13.2 Records of Counsellors

Programme Incharge keep record of work at the face to face sessions, i.e.

number of counselling sessions self and supervised practical sessions conducted by academic counsellors and record of evaluated assignments and practical activities. These records are submitted to the Regional Director on a quarterly basis.

1.13.3 Submission of Reports

The report of activities and problems faced by the programme Incharge is submitted to the concerned programme coordinator at the headquarters. This helps the faculty to monitor the programme.

1.13.4 Review Meetings

Review meetings are held with programme incharges periodically to collect feedback. Similarly, periodic orientation is also organized to keep the counsellors informed about the changes and to review the programme.

1.14 Rationale of the Study

The teacher education programme carried out by many formal teacher education universities/institution is not sufficient to fulfil the requirements of school system. Many Universities are providing preservice teacher education programmes through 'Distance Mode'. According to U.G.C., near about 70 lakh teachers are required for better and efficient functioning of '*Sarva Siksha Abhiyan*' and other educational plans. The formal Teacher educational institution/ Universities are unable to fulfil these requirements of teachers for achieving educational goals of the country. At the same time Distance Mode will be boon for us, because it offers teacher education programme for the untrained in-service teachers. Efficient functioning of educational institutions depend upon the quality of teachers, which in turn linked with the improvement in the quality of in-service and pre-service teacher training to a great extent. Research evidences on teacher preparation, its curriculum, delivery mechanism and process dimensions are very much significant to develop clear understanding about teacher education modes. More specifically, open distance mode of teacher education programme which incorporates specific paradigm of teacher preparation need to be analysed with research evidences.

In this context studies carried out by Sabharwal (1999) and Singh and Singh (1999) presented conceptual analysis of teacher education programme, its relevance and scope inside DE System, implication of formal teacher education programme on DE based teacher education etc. in the country. Exploring training needs for in-service elementary teacher for professional development have been attempted by independent studies of Arora and Singh (1999). Kapoor (1998), Sahoo (1999), Senapathi (1999), Shastri and Aiholi (1996) and Benakanal (1996). The researcher conducted studies on exploring in-service education needs of secondary and college level teachers respectively through distance education mode.

Besides these studies a number of studies have aimed at identifying background of learners of various kinds of D.E. based teacher education programmes. Such attempts have been made by Sahoo (1985), Kamar *et al.* (1985), Upreti (1988), Khan (1991), Pugazenthi (1992), Patil (1996), Patri (1996) and Khan (1999). Mukhopadhyay (1999) has attempted to design different models for imparting teacher education through DE mode.

A number of studies have been conducted to explore the nature of Media and its utilisation in various kinds of teacher education programmes. Such attempts have been made by Nagaraju (1982), Sahoo (1985), Rathore (1991), Pugazenthi (1992), Phutela (1996), SRRI (1994) etc. The studies which focused on teacher evaluation programme as one of the components of DE read as Sahoo (1985), Kumar *et al.* (1986), Upreti (1988), Khan (1991), Patil (1996), Bhusan and Bhusan (1999), Khan (1999), Sahoo and Khan (1999), Singh and Rana (1999) and Sahoo *et al.* (1999). These evaluations either focus on any one aspect or more than one aspects of teacher education programme.

There exists a strong need to understand and analyze the processes involved in teacher training programme through distance mode. Different questions are raised in this context. What are the activities carried out for development of teachers competencies? What are its relevance for training activities? And what is the level effectiveness of nature and organization of various kinds of activities for teachers competency development?

In order to find answers to above kind of questions the investigator intends to analyze the process of B.Ed. programme offered by Distance Education Mode and its relevance. Keeping these points in mind the investigator perceive that there exists a strong need to study the utility and effectiveness of processes of B.Ed. programme offered through Distance Education Mode by the open universities. Since, open distance mode B.Ed. programme integrates distance mode as well as supervised mode of development of teacher competencies, the study will be considered more meaningful to evaluate the existing processes adopted at different levels of training through different means.

1.15 Research Questions

(1) What are the various processes adopted for development of teacher competencies among B.Ed. trainees of open universities?
(2) To what extent the processes are relevant in relation to development of teacher competencies among B.Ed. trainees of open universities?
(3) To what extent the nature and organization of various processes are effective in development of teacher competencies among B.Ed. trainees of open universities?

1.16 Statement of the Problem

B.Ed. programme of open universities is an academic programme, offered at a distance, which involves various inputs such as print material, audio video materials, assignments with counsellors commenting and grading, face-to-face academic counselling session, practical contact session, workshops, seminars, resource centre, term end examination and academic experiences. Keeping in view the functionality costs, feasibility and compatibility of inputs, it become imperative to assets whether the inputs fulfil the objectives of B.Ed. programmes or not. For this propose above three questions are also relevant. In order to find answer of the above raised questions the problem undertaken for the study has been stated as follows:

"A Study of Processes of B.Ed. Programmes in Open Universities."

1.17 Objectives of the Study

1. To explore various processes adopted for development of teacher competencies among B.Ed. students of Open Universities.
2. To study the relevance of such processes in relation to development of teacher competencies among B.Ed. students of Open Universities as per perception, statements of the teacher, counsellors and the mentors.
3. To study the effectiveness of the nature and organisation of various kinds of activities involved in development of teacher competencies among B.Ed. students of Open Universities as per perception of the students, counsellors and the mentors.

1.18 Hypotheses

The hypothesis of the study in the context of objectives read as:

1. The response patterns of B.Ed. trainees and the university background are not independent from each other.
2. The response patterns of counsellors and the university background are not independent from each other.

1.19 Operational Definition

Processes: Process is defined as implementation of inputs adopting appropriate methods and procedures to realize the specified objectives. Processes in ODL based teacher education indicate the materialization and internationalization of relevant inputs through appropriate methods and procedures adopted by the teaching learning and managing groups involved in the programme.

Processes are the primitive unit for allocation of system resources. Each process has its own address space and one thread of control. A process executes a programme, but each process has its own copy of the programme within its own address, space and executes it independently of other copies.

1.20 Delimitation of the Study

The present study will be delimited to the B.Ed. Programme offered by IGNOU and UPRTOU in U.P.

2

Review of Related Literature

2.0 Introduction

This chapter deals with review of related literature. It presents a broad overview of the research in various aspects. Review of related literature and research studies is an essential step towards completion of any research study.

The review of related literature involves the systematic identification, location and analysis of documents, containing information related to the research problem. Written literature reviews are critical summaries of what is known about a particular topic. It serves an integrative function and facilitates the accumulation of knowledge (Polit and Hngler, 1989).

Research cannot be conducted in vacuum or isolation. Review of research literature enables the researcher to juxtapose one's research study with those conducted by others. Fourth, review of related literature enables a researcher to become aware of further developments in terms of concepts and constructs related to theories in an area of research and lastly review of research enables a researcher to learn about the latest tools of data collection, techniques of data analysis and methods of interpretation and presentation of date analysis.

Chapter 2 discuss the review of related literature has been divided into two parts. First part of the review focus on study related open and distance education, whereas second part of the review focuses on the study related open and distance teacher education.

2.1 Studies Conducted on Open and Distance Learning

A few studies have been conducted on distance education in India and abroad.

Meierhenry's (1955) study involved two groups of students in which both groups saw 28 filmed lecture demonstration of 30-minute duration, read the same assignment in the text book, and took the same final examination. The on-campus group held discussion for 20 minutes after each film and the off-campus group turned in written assignments. There was no significant difference between the scores of two groups on the final examinations. Retention rates for both the groups were 100 per cent.

Parson (1957) divided 40 university upper class men into two groups. 20 enrolled in developmental psychology and 20 enrolled in an unrelated course in the psychology department to serve as controls. The 20 subjects in experimental group were then randomly assigned to one of the three groups: correspondence study, kinescope (TV) study and regular instruction. All groups were taught by Parsons. Borderline significant differences favouring correspondence study over the other two methods in terms of academic achievement were reported both at the end of the course and as a result of follow up testing 4 months later.

Lepore and Wilson (1958) compared the performance of 3 groups of students––those watching television at home, those watching television in classroom and those receiving conventional instruction (who were taught by the same instructor in six college credit courses at San Francisco State College). The students in both groups watching television compared favourably with the conventional students in 5 of the 6 subjects. Students of high, low and average ability learnt equally well when taught by television or conventional method.

Grant and Merrill (1963) in their study divided 40 nurses in each of the 3 cities into groups of 20 homes and 20 hospital classroom viewers. Each group watched 2 programmes on 3 medical topics. Each broadcast was of 28 minutes in length and included 10 questions. All the nurses were equated in terms of age, number of children and hospital work shift. Dropout rates were 92 per cent for hospital group and 90 per cent for home group. An evaluation session held during the seventh week in each city revealed that learning was greater for those in the home-viewing group than those who watched as a group in the hospital.

Janes and McIntyre (1964) in their study found that students undergoing a social science tele-course performed significantly better in only one of the 12 tests. On all other tests no significant difference was found in their performance.

Spencer (1965) evaluated the grades received in all credit and non-credit courses by all correspondence students (a total of 3,303 grades) at the Pennsylvania State University between July 1, 1962 and June 30, 1963. The grades earned by correspondence students in credit course were better than those earned by the full-time students during spring term of 1963.

Childs (1966) summarized the results of some American studies comparing distance higher education with the conventional study.

Crissy (1966) evaluated the effectiveness of correspondence course entitled "Security of Classified Matter." An experimental group of 115 naval officers taking the course by correspondence was tested for the knowledge of course content immediately after and 4 months after completing the three assignment courses. Similar tests were administered to 475 officers who had completed the course through regular classroom study and 472 officers who had recent security experience related to the course content. Two control groups of 115 and 128 officers with no knowledge of contents of the course were also tested. The subjects learning in classrooms or by experimental means had scores not higher on an average than those who studied by correspondence.

Sehwartz and Haskell (1966) compared the academic performance of 25 electronic technicians who learned from a remotely located computer with the achievement of 79 control students who studied programmed texts. No significant difference in examination scores was observed although the distance group (computer group) had slightly higher scores.

Walsh (1966) reported two experiments, which combined programmed instruction with correspondence instruction. The first involved 1500 correspondence students and the second involved 5000 students. In both the cases the students' achievement was essentially the same regardless of whether programmed instruction was added to correspondence instruction. However, the use of programmed instruction did improve student motivation as measured by the number of assignments completed.

Schwartz and Long (1967) in their study found that the control group performed significantly better but as in the 1966 study the distance group working on computer took 30 per cent less time to complete the course.

Willingham (1967) compared the academic achievement of two control groups and an external group of students in a freshman English class at the University of Kansas—each semester during 1963 through 1967. The experimental group met with an instructor once a week for tutoring and otherwise studied mainly by correspondence. One control group followed the traditional classroom method, meeting three times a week an instructor using lectures and discussion groups, while the other control group was exempted from freshman composition that semester and studied literature instead. 40 students were involved in the first year,

80 in the second and 160 in each of the last 2 years. Numbers in the control group were comparable. Based on final examinations, papers and other measures of achievement, the author concluded that there was no significant difference among the groups involved and that the students in freshman composition learnt equally well in all the three groups.

Glatter and Wedell (1971) conducted a retrospective survey comparing 960 correspondence and 840 part-time conventional students who sat for post-secondary qualification examinations in English in 1963. Of the correspondence students 23.96 per cent and of the part-time students 28.21 per cent passed both parts of their examinations. Glatter and Wedell concluded that there was "little difference in examination performance and the incidence of dropout between students whose main study method was correspondence and those who were following mainly a part-time oral course.

Goodman (1972) surveyed the past rates of internal (day and evening) and external students in 7 subjects at the University of Queensland (Australia) in 1965. On an average the day students had a pass rate of 82 per cent; the evening students 76.6 per cent and the external students 80 per cent. When the rates of the day and evening students (without knowing the exact number of students) were averaged to get one internal pass rate, this rate 79.3 per cent, was slightly lower than the pass rate of the external students, i.e. 80 per cent.

According to **Dysinger and Bridgeman's (1975)** study an instructor in 1955 taught introductory psychology to 167 conventional and 41 correspondence students using the same text and giving certain multiple choice questions to both groups of students on the final examination. No significant difference was found between the achievements of two groups on those final examination questions even when the students were compared on the basis of age of ability.

Grimmet (1975) compared the achievement of 177 students who watched introductory course in television at off-campus group viewing sites at the University of Newfoundland in Canada. The students were compared with 124 days and 78 evening students who took the same course in conventional on-campus classes during the same (1969-70) year. In all the cases the dropout rare was extremely low (5 per cent or less). In the final marks there was no significant difference between the performances of the various groups.

Harris (1975) completed a survey of 569 faculty (tutors) from 7 representatively sized correspondence institutions in England. He discovered that 99 per cent of the faculty worked part-time, with 55 per cent handling only one course. Three-fourth of the tutors were men and one-tenth were retired from full-time work elsewhere. Although only 15 per cent of tutors were under 30 years of age; 28 per cent had no previous teaching experience. Wide variation was noticed in how often individual faculty members communicated with the students. Although one-quarter of the faculty had written comments to 40 to 200 students on an average two-week period, one-third of the faculty had written to fewer than five students during this period.

Medsker and others (1975) surveyed faculty at 18 California universities across the state with special degree programmes and found that the participation and experience in programme was linked to a positive attitude about the programme.

Agler (1976) compared the academic achievement of all tele-course learners and 12 representatives on-campus classes taking English in the Dallas Community College District, during spring semester of 1976. No significant difference was found in the grades of the two groups.

Agler and Linn (1976) in their study of 8 tele-courses in the Dallas County Community College District from 1972 to 1975 found that the students in equivalent on-campus classes performed better in all 8 subjects. Overall classroom student pass out rates were significantly higher than the tale-course students passed rates. In one course only 40 per cent of tale-course students passed. This study portrayed achievement through distance education as highly inferior.

Brown (1976) compared the final grades of tele-course students enrolled in an introductory accounting course at the State University of Nebraska/University of Mid America during the fall of 1974 with the grades of 61 University of Nebraska, Lincoln, students taking the same course and using the same course material in conventional classes during the spring semester of 1975. 96 per cent of the students in both groups passed and tele-course students averaged B grade while classroom students averaged C+ grade.

Dutt (1976) conducted a study on the trend of the enrolment in correspondence courses from 1971 to 1976 taking into consideration, the nature of courses offered and enrolment into these courses. He found that 55 per cent to 56 per cent students did not submit any assignment.

Macken (1976) conducted a comprehensive survey the finding of which is 67 American studies of the effectiveness of correspondence education at the college, technical and high school level. Macken concluded that there was no significant difference in learning outcomes between the two methods.

McIntyre and Wales (1976) compared the effectiveness and costs of the non-campus Community College in Washington State with three similarly sized campus based colleges. They found that Community College (i) performed no better in assessing and meeting the needs of target groups and (ii) spent 10 per cent less money per student and 6 per cent less per course.

Biswal's (1979) study revealed that enrolment was higher in Arts, Commerce and Education in comparison to others. Admission procedures were found to be liberal in nature in all correspondence institutions. Study indicated that the students who received the evaluated assignment responses in time appreciated the compulsory submission of assignments. They found the tutor-marked assignments useful to some extent for their studies.

Horwitz (1979) identified about 200 empirical studies to evaluate the significant Open Education programmes. He investigated the impact of Open Education and traditional education programmes on various student outcome variables such as achievement, self-concept, attitude towards school, creativity correspondence and conformity, curiosity, anxiety, adjustment, locus of control and cooperation. In several instances the studies showed no significant difference in Open school learners on the above mentioned variables.

McIntosh and Rigg (1979) found that about 50 per cent of the British employers surveyed felt that the degree from the Open University of United Kingdom was equivalent to that of other British Universities.

Orlansky and String (1979) reviewed the 48 evaluation studies of computer based education (computer based education is apparently the same as computer based instruction) in military training finding it significantly superior in 15 of 48 and inferior in only one. Orlansky and String felt that overall difference in achievement was found in 32 studies. They reported a 30 per cent saving in instructional time.

Peterson (1979) performed a meta-analysis of studies by Horwitz to find the effect size (mean and standard deviation of open and traditional education groups). Peterson noticed that for most student outcomes effect sizes were small indicating little advantage for either open or traditional education groups. Average effect size for locus of control and anxiety were '0' indicating thereby no advantage for either open or traditional education. However, for student outcomes creativity, attitude towards school and curiosity, average effect sizes were positive and indicated a slight advantage for open education students.

Hult (1980) in his study divided 96 students enrolled in a graduate level course in human development at the University of Southern California into three groups. The first group watched a tele-course version of the course with no instructor contact. The second group also watched the tele-course but had instructor. The third group attended a regular class in the subject. Hult maintained high control over variables such as instruction, course material, course content and final examination. However, the examination result did not differ significantly among the three groups.

Mount and Walter (1980) compared the academic performance of students watching a tele-course and students in the classroom taking an introductory psychology course at Mountain View College (Texas). Tele-course students achieved significantly higher test scores. Information on variables affecting achievement was not available.

Panday (1980) found no significant difference between the achievement of under-graduate students of correspondence and regular streams. The achievement of under-graduate students of correspondence course was lower than that of the regular students at the pre-university level and B.A. part-I level. The findings were just the reverse at B.A. part II and III level.

Singh (1980) found that they were employed and belonged to different vocations: teachers, administrators, clerks, sales workers, farmers, mechanics and labourers with major concentration in teaching and clerical jobs.

Tianjing & Jingtao (1980) had studied on "Exploration of Instructional Staff Training Model in Rural Distance Education case study of Instructional Staff Training of TCP Project" and they found that Central Agricultural Broadcasting and Television School (CABTS) is a specialized school carrying out rural distance education. At present, it has become a distance training system covering the vast rural areas of the country. In recent years, along with the wide application of modern educational technologies in distance education and the ever-maturing learner-centred educational rationale the instructional and administrative staff who accustomed to the use of the traditional approaches in delivering distance education faces new challenges.

With the technical support of the Food and Agriculture Organization of the United Nations CABTS conducted training to over 3,500 senior management staff, management and administrative staff, learning material designers and production technicians as well as instructional staff, through different models and approaches, in such aspects in modern distance education which is based in digital environment as management, instructional capacity, instructional approaches, design and development of digital teaching materials and delivery approaches. Training approaches were advanced combining face-to-face instruction with distance education, which had strong interactivity and achieved good results. It improved the capacity of CABTS in managing modern distance education school, the capacity of designing and producing digital new type instructional materials as well as the capacity of implementing rural distance education using new type of digital instructional materials.

Agbola (1981) carried out a study on an assessment of what took place at the contact sessions also revealed a mixture of desirable and undesirable trends. In some classes, lecturers distributed handouts without explaining them; while in some they dictated lecture notes without allowing for explanations on these notes.

Hedges *et al.* (1981) concluded that open education did not produce consistent results for different student outcomes. Open education made its strongest results in favour of student outcomes such as creativity, cooperativeness, self-reliance, attitude towards school, curiosity and adjustment. Open education made weakest results in favour of student outcomes pertaining to reading mathematics and language achievement.

Lewis (1981) revealed that National Extension Colleges were concerned as students failed to complete correspondence courses because of isolation. To overcome this, they allocated to all 53 students living in Leeds, a counsellor to help them with general problem of isolation or study skills not specific to a subject. Passout rate was compared and improvement was seen.

Moss and Brew (1981) found that most conventional higher education staff at three English universities were familiar with UKOU's text and television programme although less than 50 per cent recommended them.

Khan (1982) in a study of dropouts from distance education courses pointed out a number of reasons for students to join higher education and particularly distance education. As regards higher education in general, the respondents to his questionnaire gave the following reasons: to improve qualifications (34.98%); to increase knowledge (24.95%); for promotional prospects (19.89%) and to pass time (5.33%). Other reasons cited for distance education were: lack of time to pursue full time education (46.91%); not getting admission in a regular college (36.19%); and remoteness from colleges (4.14%).

He found that most of the institutions made use of lesson scripts, assignments and personal contact programmes. The major share of instructional activities especially the production of instructional texts and teaching during the personal contact programmes was performed by the part-time teachers. Quite a large number of teachers were senior and experienced. In comparison to part-time staff, the full-time staff of correspondence teaching institutions was found to be less experienced. None of the teachers were formally trained in performing instructional activities through distance education.

Freeman (1982) noted a problem associated with the tutorial centres in borrowed premises was the unwillingness of some of these institutions to provide further services for students of other institutions.

Keegan (1982) noted that Fern University found it difficult to establish study centres outside its home state of North-Rhine Westphalia, as the other states did not favour the establishment of the university.

Rumble and Harry (1982) found that six of the nine Distance Teaching Universities used telephone tuition. The three universities that did not use the telephone were located in three developing nations—Venezuela, Pakistan and People's Republic of China.

Tight (1982) studied the part-time degree level study in the United Kingdom. For this, survey was made of provision existing (in 1980-81) for part-time first degree and post-graduate study at universities/polytechnics, colleges and institutes and extra-mural departments in the United Kingdom. Institutional constraints were examined but they did not place substantial restriction on development. An attempt was made to estimate demand from existing Open University, national and local surveys. A potential market of 1,000,000 people was suggested on the basis of the surveys.

Broussard (1983) conducted a comparative study of three one year phases of computer assisted instruction at home with those undergoing a conventional education programme. Traditional students outperformed those using computer assisted instruction in 1980-81, but the group using computers significantly outperformed the control group in the second phase, 1981-82 and also exceeded the control group by a borderline significant amount in last year of the project. Overall the computer assisted group performed somewhat better than the control group.

Pillai and Mohan (1983) studied the issues on the impact of correspondence education. They found that the maximum impact was on social well-being, as it enabled the learners to improve their social status and they could utilize their leisure time with advantage. However, the impact on occupational betterment in terms of better job opportunities and business improvement was found among 18 per cent of the respondents who had undergone education through the correspondence courses. Only 11 per cent students were financially better off after passing out of the system. Thus only a small percentage of students could achieve better financial status and occupational improvements as a result of correspondence education.

Smith (1983) in his study compared 120 tele-course students taking the same four-hour courses on campus in terms of scores in the final examinations. The same instructor taught both the tele-course and classroom students in the study conducted during the spring semester of 1983 at Saddleback Community College. There was no significant difference in the final examination scores of the two groups of students in any of the courses studied. Completion rates of tele-course students were lower.

Brey and Grigsby (1984) the Annenberg/CPB PROJECT funded in a study documented in which 8,000 tele-courses were surveyed. According to the resulting data, most of the students were women (68%), employed (80%), white (84%) and married (84%). 60 per cent students lived within a 30 minute drive from a college and only 7 per cent lived at an hour's drive away from campus. But the majority of tele-course students also said that no travel time and no conflict with the work schedule were motivation for enrolling. The most important reason for enrolling was that on-campus classes conflicted with work (41%) of with the leisure time (12%). Twelve per cent of the students gave preference for learning at home as their most important reason.

Perry (1984) surveyed 304 institutions offering 468 programmes in eighty countries and found that the television was used at all levels. The telephone was employed more in developed regions such as Europe and North America, where the institutions surveyed used telephone at 29 per cent and 49 per cent respectively. Only 5 per cent of the Asian programmes and no African programmes used it. Overall use of telephone was about 22 per cent.

Rachel (1984) reviewed studies of computer assisted instruction in the ABE and GED classroom of seven studies including comparison of achievement between computer assisted instruction and traditional instruction. The results showed strong effect sizes for computer assisted instruction and the other three also favoured computer assisted instruction but not by significant amounts.

Siyaram (1984) found that the students and teachers had favourable attitude towards correspondence education. The attitude of teachers was more favourable than that of the students. The quality of academic performance of correspondence education students in Meerut University was slightly superior to the average quality of those of Indian universities. The academic performance of correspondence education in different Indian universities differed significantly. The academic performance of various correspondence education programmes was not higher than that of regular education except for Meerut University.

Vydehi and Sarwal (1984) told that most of the studies conducted on the instructional process have attempted to describe the instructional process and the reactions of the participants of the system; only two studies attempted at developing the teaching materials and examining their effectiveness.

Chander *et al.* (1985) have a study in the Institute Of Correspondence Courses, University of Kerala, on the students of two year pre-degree and three-year degree programmes to identify the reasons for dropout. Incidentally this resulted in a comparison between dropouts and persisters and highlighted the factors motivating the students. 18.5 per cent of the total students dropped out during 1983-84. There was no significant difference between the persisters and dropouts with regard to their age and marital status. The proportion of single or married students among the dropouts was the same as that among the persisters. Proportion of male and female students was more or less the same among the dropouts and the persisters except in the case of degree students where the proportion of females was slightly more among the dropouts. The unemployed students tended to drop out more than the employed students among those pursuing the degree course. However, an opposite tendency was seen among the pre-degree students. In general, it was observed that employment was a factor, which had a positive influence on the tendency to persist.

They analyzed the study habits of dropouts and persisters of the Institute of Correspondence Courses of Kerala. In the study habits were included such factors as a fixed time for study, disturbance during studies, discussion of lesson with others, submission of assignments, attending contact programmes and attending classes other than the contact programmes. Two of the habits, viz. following a fixed time for study and disturbance during study did not influence the dropout behaviour as the percentage of respondents with these habits was more or less the same among the dropouts and the persisters. But, the other habits had a significant impact upon the dropout behaviour. While, 41 per cent of the persisters discussed their lessons with their friends and/or neighbours, only 25 per cent of the dropouts held any such discussion. The persisters who had not sent any assignments constituted only 49 per cent of the total; their percentage among the dropouts was 64. Similarly, while 38 per cent of the persisters attended contact programmes regularly, only 16 per cent of dropouts did so. The percentage of dropouts who never attended the contact programmes constituted 55 per cent of the total, while the percentage of such respondents among the persisters was only 24. About 18 per cent of the persisters also attended the coaching classes other than the contact programmes of the institutes. Only 8 per cent of the dropouts attended the classes. Thus, it can be seen that dropouts experience a sort of academic isolation. They did not discuss their lessons and study problems with others. They did not submit the assignments for evaluation. They did not attend contact programmes of the institutes nor did they attend coaching classes elsewhere.

Sahoo (1985) in his study of "Distance Education in Himachal Pradesh University" found that the annual enrolment figure during 1972 and 1988 varied from 3,418 to 7,586 which is almost one-third of the total enrolment figures of all the higher education institutes and colleges of the University in that state. At the post-graduate level, the total enrolment was as high as about 15 times that of the similar courses of formal university system. The total enrolment in undergraduate and +2 pre-university courses increased from 933 to 2332 during 1971 to 1984. Towards 1987-88, it came down to 1527 because of change over to 10+2+3 pattern. Among all the M.A. courses, the highest rates of enrolment were seen in Economics and English with 736 to 924 students on the average year. On the other hand, only 47 students on an average per year enrolled themselves for M.A. (Sanskrit). A course-wise analysis of the Directorate of Correspondence Courses revealed a curvilinear trend of growth with regard to M.A., M.Ed. and M.Com. courses. Research studies revealed that the distance education system had high rate of dropouts which was 32 per cent to 85 per cent at post-graduate level. Especially after the first semesters, the percentage of the dropouts varied from 50 per cent to 75 per cent. Mostly, the dropouts belonged to the upper age groups with a larger gap of time between their last qualifying examination and admission to the present courses. The dropouts were from rural background, had poor academic family background and employment status. The ration of women dropping out of the system was higher than that of men.

He found that major causes of dropping out of the system were non-attendance of personal contact programmes, lack of proper student-teacher contact, lack of library facilities, non-availability of reference materials, not submitting the required number of assignments and difficulty in studying the lesson scripts. Quite a large number of dropouts (69%) aspired for continuing their studies further provided improvements were brought about in the system.

He found that correspondence courses conducted by Himachal Pradesh University found that most of the students felt the assignment system to be useful. In the case of Himachal Pradesh University no uniform policy was maintained regarding teaching during the contact sessions; the usual methods adopted were lecture and question-answer. Because of paucity of time, most of the teachers covered selected topics through delivery of lectures.

Bahuguna (1986) in his study of three universities (Delhi University, Delhi; Kurukshetra University, Haryana and Meerut University, U.P.) found that the results and achievement of the formal education students were better due to provision of better teaching facilities and full-time learning. The correspondence students had mostly poor academic background and were also part-time learners. The problems relating to receiving the required course material and proper contact programmes were also the cause of lower achievement of the correspondence stream students. He found that there was a need for greater motivation among the distance learners and for attitudinal change by enhancing the image of correspondence education. Motivation could be created by developing high quality self-instructional material and by interaction through assignments. Creation of more useful courses by correspondence course directorates could reduce the negative attitude towards correspondence education.

Balasubramanium (1986) found that submission of assignments was treated as a mere formality. Most of the teachers, students, dropouts and pass-outs of the correspondence system of education felt that assignments covered the syllabus only partially. The students reported a considerable time lag between sending the assignments and receiving them after evaluation.

Mulay (1986) found that the media chosen by most of the correspondence institutions was print with some exceptions where radio and television were used.

Panda and Panda (1987) confirm in their studies that as a whole regular students scored higher in social and total adjustment than the correspondence students. The study, however, shows that SES (especially low SES) caused low social and total adjustment among students pursuing courses through correspondence education.

Whittington (1987) reviewed over 100 studies of tele-course *versus* conventional achievement, practically all of which showed equal or superior cognitive outcome on the part of tele-course achievement. Synthesized the result of three reviews and thirteen meta-analysis of kindergarten through college. They concluded that computer-assisted instruction raised student achievement on examination from the 50th to the 60th percentile, meaning that on an average students in the computer assisted instruction section scored a full grade better than did the control groups.

Chib (1988) reported attendance have been rather discouraging especially when contact sessions play a supplementary role and attendance is optional. For instance, Panjab University had 20 per cent attendance.

Holm (1988) studying the retention rates of Minnesota's college programme of individualized learning found that just under half of the 1983-84 enrollees were active in the programme or graduated in the fall of 1987. Factors such as proximity of residence, previous post-secondary education and length of professional experience were correlated with persistence.

Schumer (1988) conduct a survey on the use of face-to-face contact by distance teaching institutes reported that out of 166 institutions which responded, 127 (76.5%) organized face-to-face contact sessions to support student learning. The group approach dominated the practice in contact sessions. The traditional tutorial approach of teacher learner and one-to-one contact made possible to look into individual student's problems.

Vydehi (1988) evaluated the presentation of first year degree level English course of S.V. University with regard to satisfaction of the needs of the students, attainment of objectives of the course and the nature of instructional process. Analysis of aims of teaching English, methods of instruction, reaction of students and teachers as well as observation of personal contact programmes was done to locate the weaknesses of the curriculum. On the basis of these findings distance teaching material was prepared. This alternative distance teaching material was based on 'student active format'. The achievement of students using modified approach (based on student active format and conventional approach) were compared. The results of students using modified approach were found to be comparatively better.

Keegan (1990) reported that some institutions did not provide for contact teaching at all because they believed that the students wanted to be left alone, as any provision for it would infringe on learner's autonomy or curb the independence of the learner. Their view was that the sessions should remain peripheral, as their use would be tantamount to watering down of the purity of distance teaching.

Harichandan (1991) reported that most of the students of Y.B. Chavan Maharashtra Open University and Indira Gandhi National Open University were aware of the availability of facilities in study centres. Most of the facilities available at the study centres were grossly under-utilised. Only 52 per cent and 32 per cent of the students sought the advice of co-ordinator and expert counsellor respectively. He found that 46 per cent of the students strongly agreed that self-instructional material was the most appropriate medium for study. 32 per cent strongly favoured listening to the expert and 22 per cent reported that writing notes was the most appropriate medium for study. Discussion with peers and friends did not seem to be very appropriate medium for study. He found that most of the facilities available at Indira Gandhi National Open University study centres were relatively adequate. The study centres of Y.B. Chavan Maharashtra Open University did not provide any computer facilities, nor small cubicles for listening and viewing of audio and video programmes. However, the Y.B. Chavan Maharashtra Open University study centres had a small theatre like room for viewing video programmes and lectures by experts from outside were not arranged. Most co-ordinators faced problems in the following areas: (i) paucity of funds, (ii) lack of co-operation from the institutes where the study centres were located, (iii) adequate classroom facilities, (iv) adequate teaching materials, (v) printed study materials not reaching in time from the Head/Regional office, and (vi) non-availability of resource persons.

Rathore (1991) revealed that correspondence institutes in India relied more on face to face teaching during the personal contact programmes than on tutoring through written correspondence initiated by students using the means of assignments. The submission of assignments is a compulsory condition for appearing in final examinations in many correspondence institutions in India. Thus these institutions were making only a half-hearted use of assignments as a learning strategy in distance teaching.

Mason and Miller (1992) told that it is also becoming a common practice to mix non-residential compulsory attendance at contact sessions with shorter and optional contact sessions. This helps retain a lot of face-to-face teaching at a cheaper cost.

Srinivasacharyulu and Ramiah (1992) in their investigation into the students' response towards face to face services at the B.R. Ambedkar Open University found that among the students of this university, the majority belonged to the non-formal stream. "Distance" played an important role in the enrolment and attendance of the students. Among the learners' difficulties, lack of provision for individual meetings with the counsellor and hesitation among the students ranked at the top. All the students sought the help of friends/relatives in their studies. Employed students in particular liked to have two time schedules for counselling and practical classes so that they could choose convenient dates. They also concluded that face-to-face support facilities, though minimal, should be on the basis of learner's needs, problems and quality of the progress of his/her work throughout the period of studies.

Rathore (1993) in his study of the Directorates/Institutes of Correspondence Course and Departments of Distance Education of India found that about 56 per cent students neither got model solutions nor their assignments with comments by tutors. This means that non-contiguous two-way communication potential that tutor-marked assignments offer in distance education is not being fully exploited.

Singh (1993) found that total enrolment of 41 Correspondence Institutes and 4 Open Universities in India in 1989-90 was 4,87,000 out of the overall enrolment of 42,50,000. The coverage of higher education through correspondence/distance mode was about 10 per cent in 1989-90. The concentration of distance learners in South, North, Western and Central and East zones was 66 per cent, 27 per cent, 5 per cent and 2 per cent respectively. He found that increase in female enrolment from 31 per cent to 39.6 per cent in Correspondence Course Institutes and a corresponding decrease in Open Universities from (30% to 21%). In Correspondence Course Institutes; 39 per cent learners were from rural background. Study confirmed these findings and revealed that 50 per cent of the learners in Open Universities were employed. The percentage of employed learners was 42 per cent in Correspondence Course Institutes. A sizeable number of them (30%) were first generation learners in higher education.

He also found that as far as teaching learning methodology was concerned, most of the Correspondence Course Institutes depended on printed lessons for imparting instruction. Only 6 Correspondence Course Institutions had some radio talks for their students. On the academic side it was felt that there was a need to adopt the distance education teaching-learning methodology by making their course material self-instructional and in the distance education format, introducing electronic media to supplement instruction, providing well-equipped study centres for face-to-face counselling and evaluation of students' assignments and at the same time improving their delivery system. He found that most of the

Correspondence Course Institutes depended on printed lessons for imparting instruction and only 6 Correspondence Course Institutes had arranged some radio talks for their students. Student support facilities in the form of study centres were provided by 50 per cent correspondence course institutes, but most of the centres were not properly organized and offered very little facilities to the learners.

Black (1994) in his study addressed the controversy among academics in conventional university over the credibility of distance education despite increased demand for it. It was found that in general the faculty were not familiar with or supportive of distance education except for undergraduate courses. This was very little support for a graduate programme by distance education.

Hussain and Sahoo (1994) found that majority of Indira Gandhi National Open University learners agreed with the comments and grades awarded; nearly 32 per cent sought clarification in the comments and grades. About one-third of learners found the comments inadequate, had difficulty in understanding them and did not appreciate the placement of comments on assignment responses. While 22 per cent of assignment responses had positive reinforcements, 28 per cent contained negative reinforcement and only 10 per cent comments were exclusively related to the subject.

Murali Manohar (1994) conducted a study of the academic counsellors and course writers of B.R. Ambedkar Open University. He found that a large number of them had experience in formal institutions of learning and they considered their experience as relevant and useful to some extent but they still believed that some specialization or skill was required to be more effective in discharging their duties. The existing training facilities were too inadequate, and scattered in an uneven manner. This is apparent from the fact that while certain staff had received some kind of training, others had either received insufficient training or had undergone no training at all. Those of the staff, who underwent training, were trained for extremely short duration, with no repetition of the same and they had never been sent to any formal training institution. About the attitude of staff towards training a large number of them expressed the need for training and there was almost unanimous opinion that training would improve the efficiency of the staff. This indicates a healthy thinking in organization and readiness of the staff to learn things required for discharging the job efficiently.

Agrawal (2000) conducted a study on Distance Education: Prospects and Problems. The objectives of the study were: (1) to find out the characteristics of distance learner; (2) To ascertain the extent to which the information need perceived by the learners were achieved through distance teaching; (3) To find out the problems on the basis of sex, faculty (arts and commerce) and also the location, i.e. rural-urban; (4) To locate and study the problems of distance learner under categorized personal, social, economic, academic and psychological aspects out of the content method and administration of the programme; (5) To give suggestions for further improvement and advancement in distance teaching with regard to lesson materials, lesson schedule, report sheet, assignments and personal contact programme based on the opinion of distance learners, educators and planners; and (6) To offer suggestions for further research.

The findings of the study were: (1) the chief characteristics of distance education is the physical separation of the learner from the teacher; (2) Personal contact programme and counselling sessions were found to be very useful; (3) Most of the learners were found to be satisfied with the present system of distance education with admission procedure, examination and revaluation, libraries, counselling; (4) Half of the sample was found to be inconvenienced with quality of the learning material as compared to that of regular; (5) No arrangements of practical, teleconferencing and other communication techniques were found there for learners of B.A. and B.Com; (6) Rural learners of both the faculties were found to be more dissatisfied with library, hostel facilities; (7) The learners were of the view that vocational education couldn't be imparted through distance education; (8) The rural urban groups of arts differed significantly regarding the problem related to learning material, and availability of material; (9) The rural learners of both groups had more problems related to social and psychological aspect; (10) The administrators, planners opined that distance education was highly specialized task, so pre-entry and in-service training were essential and experienced counselors were and should be adopted in distance education; (11) The planners/counsellors were of the view that the inhibition of the conventionalists didn't allow distance institution to run laboratory-based course but needed provisions would be made in near future; (12) The administrators were satisfied with the library services of open universities; (13) The planners/counsellors were of the view that the reputation of distance education should be judged by its nature and quality and not by its pass percentage; and (14) They revealed that mostly the newspapers were used for publicity of admission notification but perhaps the IGNOU was only, using all the communication techniques.

Peng & Yanhui (2004) have made a survey on the requirements of the support service for distance learners. Questionnaire was adopted in analyzing and discussing the following aspects in Tianjin, China, as the situation, learning feature, study process, study barrier and the requirement on support service for distance students.

The following conclusions are made through survey: the distance learners in Tianjin are almost "junior adults." At present, the adopted teaching method is mainly face-to-face as well as through Internet supplementarily. More than 90 per cent of the students have the ability to study on the internet. The principal reason for not using Internet as a main method for distance study is that the quality of resources is not suitable for students' requirement. The salient barrier and difficulty throughout the study process is the lack of time. The main method of asking for help in study is to inquire face-to-face and phone the teachers.

Piyuan & Baohong (2004) have a study on "Analysis of Distance Learners' Study Habit." This shows that students prefer face-to-face tutorial and self-directed learning to some other learning models in distance education. The interaction between the teacher and the students and the cooperative learning among students happen less frequently and the percentage of online students is in the minority. Good study habit cannot stem completely from their naturally-developed habit but can be developed with the help of perfectly-designed online learning environment and the high quality and diversity of online learning resources. The improvement of support system and the confirmation of teaching models in distance education will help to reach this goal.

Qianwei, Jingjing, Xiaowen and Jianliang (2004) have a Survey of Information Technology Use in Primary and Middle Education in the Pearl River Delta. The sample consisted of 25 middle schools and 6 primary schools, among them 9 are key schools and 22 are average schools. There were 40 questionnaires sent out and 32 were returned, of which 31 were valid. 500 teachers questionnaires were sent out to teachers in 5 primary schools and 19 middle schools in the Pearl River Delta. 480 were returned, of which 457 were valid, hence the return rate was 92.31 per cent of which 95.21 per cent were valid. In the sample there were 194 teachers (42.5%) with less than 5 years of teaching experience, 104 (22.8%) with 5 to 10 years, 199 (26%) with 10 to 20 years, and 40 (8.7%) with more than 20 years. The students surveyed included junior high 2nd year and senior high 2nd year students from a total of 20 middle schools.

Results of this survey are: 100 per cent of the schools offer information technology as a course. Some primary schools start this from grade one, and most primary schools offer information technology courses for grades 3 to 5. Middle schools mainly offer the courses for the early grades, such as junior high 1st year and senior high 1st year students. 77.4 per cent of the schools surveyed indicated that they had educational technology development plans and in 83.9 per cent of the schools the leaders manage the work related to educational technology and schools attach importance to educational technology.

The schools putting educational technology into practice are doing so comparatively well. 65 per cent of schools said they had courses in which computers and the Internet were used and in 70 per cent of the schools it was reported that at least half of the teachers could use computers or the Internet in their teaching. Most schools reported comparatively less use of multimedia networks in their teaching.

83 per cent of the teachers reported that they own computers, and 65 per cent of teachers' computers connect with the Internet. Most teachers have the basic hardware for managing and obtaining information. The teachers reported that they have had their own computers and Internet connections for a relatively short time, mostly 1 to 3 years. Only 79 (18%) said they had owned computers for 5 years or longer. Interestingly, 29 (72.8%) of this group were teachers with more than 20 years of teaching experience. 34.6 per cent of the teachers said that they had attended training to study computer and Internet knowledge, 53.2 per cent learn by themselves, and 43.3 per cent learn from colleagues or friends. 69.1 per cent and 26.9 per cent of the teachers select the purpose for applying modern educational technology as to "make the teaching results better: promote students to study" and to "let students completely develop, and lay foundations for them to become citizens of the information society." 28.4 per cent of the teachers choose "for the inspection or attending the demonstration lesson." A large number of teachers said that the purpose for applying modern educational technology is right on the whole, but if it is used just for inspection or attending the demonstration lesson it will lost its true meaning. 28 per cent of the teachers think that the teaching results of applying modern educational technology is great, while at the same time 2.3 per cent think it is not effective. The other 69.2 per cent gave an average rating for this item.

Rahayu, Ratnanigsih and Iryani (2004) have a study on "The Study of Learning Materials and the Implementation of Practical Work of Biology in Indonesian Open University." The purposes of this study were: (1) to review printed and non-printed learning material of Practicum Biology III, and (2) to evaluate the implementation of partnership in laboratory work, especially for Biology III. The results of this study show that (i) in general printed material of practicum Biology III is adequate. However, revision and modification to follow competence-based curriculum is needed, (ii) the non-printed material (video) of practicum Biology III is essential in assisting students in doing practical work, however, technical aspects of the video still needs improvement, and (iii) there are still some important factors to be considered in carrying out partnership for laboratory work with other universities.

Songbin (2004) has worked on A Survey of Autonomous Learning Conditions in Open and Distance Education. He found that only about 38.5 per cent of the learners have the time to come to school for tutorials at weekends, while the other 61.5 per cent cannot. The 29.2 per cent of respondents who have access to online learning at home and the 1.6 per cent having access to online learning at their working units, we find that only 30.8 per cent of the learners have access to conditions that enable them to learn by network. 14.4 per cent of the learners have computers at home or at their working units and it is quite convenient for them to use these computers. However, even if this percentage is added to the former one, there is still only 45.2 per cent of the learners who have access to conditions suitable for computer-assisted learning, leaving 54.7 per cent who cannot have had access to distance learning through the computer of network. From the statistical data he found that 13 out of 431 of the respondents did not expect to have centralized tutorials, while 418 expressed their wish to have centralized tutorials. This accounted for 97 per cent, among which 354 made definite selections and 64 made repeated selections showing their compliance with the school's arrangements. The survey results indicate that the learning form most expected by the OE learners of the county-level RTVUs is cooperative learning. This accounts for 74.5 per cent of the respondents, 38.5 per cent of whom hope to learn by group cooperation at their location and 36.2 per cent of whom wish to have group cooperative learning at school. The next expectation is the individual autonomous learning guided by the tutors, selected by 56.8 per cent of the respondents. The last one is complete autonomous learning, indicated by 17.9 per cent. The phenomenon calls for manifold individualized needs wants to be catered for by our learning supporting system.

The most commonly rated support item that county-level RTVU learners expect the school to provide is the print media, in which the teaching materials account for 81.2 per cent, the tutorial materials for 79.8 per cent the review guidebooks 81.7 per cent, keys to exercises 78.4 per cent, and the other learning reference materials 53.1 per cent.

Multimedia teaching and tutorship courseware is the second support item expected by the learners, with the teaching and tutorship floppy disks accounting for 52.7 per cent, the CD ROMs 51.3 per cent, the VCD courseware 59.2 per cent, the VCR courseware 44.8 per cent, and the course tutorial contents provided by the tutors that can be copied at any time 68.9 per cent.

Online service is the third supporting item anticipated by OE learners, in which the teaching and tutorial live broadcast classroom accounts for 48.3 per cent, online teaching and tutorship courseware 41.2 per cent, teaching and tutorship VOD courseware 44.8 per cent and teaching and tutorship IP courseware 38.1 per cent. In addition, 40.1 per cent learners indicated they would like the school to specially prepare tutors for each of them.

Yadav & Sahoo (2004) have a study on "University Teachers Perception about Future of ICT in Education." The objectives of the study were: (1) To study the perception pattern of university teachers about the future different dimensions of ICT in education. (2) To compare the perceptions of Traditional University Teachers and Open University Teachers about the future of different dimensions of ICT in education. The study remained confined to Allahabad district. 100 teachers of University of Allahabad and its affiliated colleges and 40 teachers of IGNOU, New Delhi and UPRTOU, Allahabad were sample respondents. Those respondents who had earlier exposures of ICT were contacted for data collection. The data were collected with the help of a five-point scale questionnaire developed by the authors. The data were analyzed with the help of Chi-Square Test of Independence.

Chi-Square analysis of data reveals that in 16 out of 40 items the perception pattern of Traditional and Open University teachers have been found to be independent of each other (i.e. Not significant at.05 level). Both the group of teachers forecasting future of ICT in different aspects of education above 60 per cent ranged from 42 per cent to 85 per cent. In item No. 10 Visual media can adversely affect print media in future, 52 per cent teachers perceived the future of ICT below 40 per cent and in item No. 31-Excessive use of ICT can minimize the importance of teachers, 65 per cent-68 per cent teachers forecasted to be below 40 per cent range.

In the rest of 24 items the perception patterns of Traditional and Open University teachers about the future of ICT in education have been to be significantly different from each other. In 13 items, i.e. 2, 4, 5, 6, 7, 11, 12, 17, 18, 21, 22, 24, 25 the percentage of Open University Teachers forecasting at the level 60 per cent and above have been found to be significantly higher than their Traditional University counterparts. Whereas in 7 items, i.e. 9, 15, 35, 36, 38, 39 and 40 the percentage of Traditional University Teachers forecasting the role of ICT in education at the level 60 per cent and above have been found to be significantly higher than their Open University Counterparts.

In item No. 3—utility of printed materials will be threatened due to ICTs, No. 23 Future centres of education will be Cyber Caffes rather than institutions, No. 32—Students will give more importance to TV/ VCR programmes over their teachers, and No. 33 In labs frogs can be replaced with computer package experiments, 40 per cent-70 per cent teachers of both the groups forecasted the future of ICT below 40 per cent level.

Boondao (2005) conducted a study on "How Assignments Affect Students Studying Mathematics in a distance Education system in Thailand." The population consisted of students who enrolled in the Mathematics for Social Science course. The sample consisted of 691 students who enrolled in the Mathematics for Social Science course in semester one of 2004. All students who enrolled were sent the assignments and asked to submit them within the first two months of the semester. There were 294 (42.5%) who submitted assignments. After the final examination, students who submitted assignments were asked to fill in questionnaires and 176 (59.9%) responded. It was found that students who submitted assignments gained significantly higher marks than those who did not. They found the assignments more difficult than the final examination. Students made some very useful suggestions. They felt that STOU should have assignments for all subjects because assignments encouraged students to study. They suggested that marks from assignments should be 30 per cent or 40 per cent of the total and that the return time for assignments should spread over the four months that it takes to study the 15 units in the course.

Mohamad and Mohamad (2005) made An Analysis of Learning Styles of Distance Learners. Results of the study were used to make comparison and correlation analyses between learning styles and academic achievement, programme of studies, gender and income. 162 students responded to the online questionnaire. The study showed that 35.5 per cent students preferred visual learning style followed by 29.6 per cent sensory, 14.2 per cent active, 0 per cent verbal and 2.5 per cent intuitive. The male students were found dominant in visual learning style as compared to the females who were sensory dominant. The students who were majors in banking tended towards sensory style as compared to finance and business studies students who were inclined towards visual style. While the mass communication and public administration students dominated in visual and sensory styles. The higher income students preferred more visual style as compared to the middle income who were dominant in both visual and sensory. The higher achievers were found to be better disposed towards visual as compared to low achievers who were sensory dominant in style. The learning styles were not significantly different between genders, programme of studies and semesters. It was also found that there was no significant relationship between learning styles and academic achievement.

2.2 Studies Conducted on ODL Based Teacher Education

A few studies have been conducted on teacher education through distance mode in India and abroad.

Green (1967) studied an independent study-style system in Florida State University used to teach in-service teachers both in conventional classes and by correspondence. A pre-test was administered to 142 subjects enrolled in mathematics classes after 4 conventional classroom lessons. On the basis of this, students were labelled low, middle or high achievers. Each of the 5 classes was divided into 2 sections that closely approximated each other in term of previous achievement of its members. 77 subjects completed the next 6 lessons by correspondence while 65 control subjects took the same lessons in class. A common test was administered and a retention test was given 6 weeks later. The difference between the two groups on each test was not statistically significant.

Shankar (1984) detailing the earliest formal attempt at teacher education through correspondence point out the meagre attention given to assignments and recommended regular monitoring of 10-20 per cent of evaluated assignments.

Upreti (1988) studied on the impact of teacher training through correspondence courses (B.Ed. SSCC). Major findings were as follows: Factors like the work place, rural-urban background, family structure, age, sex, religion and caste of the teachers affected the vertical mobility from elementary to secondary level. Regarding the inter-generational occupational mobility it was observed that the main shift has been from cultivation and labour to service category. Teachers from the urban background and working in urban areas were found to have more vertical mobility while most of the elementary teachers had got the vertical mobility after having their B.Ed. degree.

Rastogi (1969) studied the supervision of practice teaching of B.Ed. students through correspondence.

Kumar (1981) and **Kumar *et al.* (1986)** have studied on the motivation of B.Ed. correspondence course students.

Ram (1984) studied on evaluation of correspondence education in terms of cost and academic performance.

Arun, Renu (1990) conducted a study to identify background characteristics of distance learners, reasons behind joining the B.Ed. through correspondence course, delineating of distance learners in terms of key psychological variables, namely self-images, learner orientation, interpersonal relations and learning strategies. To evaluate the effectiveness of institutional components as existing in the institute of Correspondence Education, University of Jammu, comparing distance learners and full-time B.Ed. trainees in terms of completion rate, dropout rate, percentage and quality of results, and studying the attitude of distance learners towards distance education. To study the relationship between learner and institutional variables with respect to success in distance learning, and to predict success of distance learning system on the basis of learner variables.

All 3314-distance learners doing B.Ed. through ICE, University of Jammu were included in the sample. The data were collected by using the five tools, namely Proforma for the identification data (including reasons behind joining the correspondence course); learners' orientation inventory; evaluation scale for instructional material; attitude scale for distance learning system; and proforma for dropouts. All these tools were developed by the researcher. Along with these, some other tools like Interpersonal Relations Inventory, Learning Strategies Inventory and Personality Word List were also used for collection of data.

Information was collected from 630 distance learners regarding background variables. Out of 630 learners, three-fourth were married and those who were above the age of 30 years constituted 60 per cent of sample. 68 per cent of the candidates were from rural background, taking greater advantage of B.Ed. course through correspondence. However, only five per cent candidates had a first division in their previous university examination and 74 per cent distance learners were first generation distance learners.

Khan (1991) studied effectiveness of Distance Education Programme with reference to the teachers training course of Kashmir University. Major findings were—

1. The availability of centres for Practice teaching is increasing year after year in consideration of the interests of the pupil teacher.
2. There is a yearwise increase in the enrolment system from the session 1988-89 and also on increase in the enrolment as compared to the formal system of education.
3. The male and the female ratio shows a substantial increase in the Department of Distance Education.
4. So for as the pass percentage of the results from the year 1977-78 to year 1988-89 is concerned, it goes hand in hand with the formal system of education.
5. During 1977-78 the pass percentage ratio between the non-formal and the formal system was 60 : 63.5 and during 1988-89 it was 62 : 65.
6. The teaching competency of teacher trained through the formal system is higher than that of those trained through DDE.
7. The duration of contact programmes with the pupil teachers in order to have face-to-face learning with tutors is three months.
8. The rate of delivering the general and criticism lesson in the DDE is higher than that needed in the formal system.
9. The per capita cost in the DDE is less than in the college of education run by government (A.G.M. 1863).

Pugazenthi (1991) conducted a study of Teacher Education Programme through correspondence system in Madurai Kamraj University. Major findings were—

1. Only teacher candidates were submitted to the courses initially from 1983-84 graduate as well as postgraduates were also being admitted.
2. The age of the teacher trainees ranged from 25 to 61 years.
3. Thirty eight per cent of the M.Ed. and 49.4 per cent of the B.Ed. candidates belonged to the rural areas.
4. The rate of dropouts was found to be 1.7 per cent to 4.2 per cent at B.Ed. level and 3.2 per cent to 7.4 per cent at M.Ed. level which were very low.
5. The physical facilities provided and the methodology adopted during contact programme were not found to be satisfactory.
6. The teaching community lacked expertise in the writing of scripts.

7. 72 per cent of the B.Ed. and 83 per cent of the M.Ed. students found the functioning of the study centres inadequate and inefficient.
8. The trainees found it difficult to find a place for practice teaching as well as suitable guiding teachers.
9. The per head cost of training through the correspondence system was found to be much lower than that of learning through the formal system.

Chivore (1992) conducted a study about many countries, Zimbabwe faced a demand for teachers that far outstripped the supply from conventional colleges. This example of a pre-service teacher education programme may be useful to educators in other countries.

Since attaining its independence, Zimbabwe has invested heavily in education. In the process of that investment, the government has introduced various types of teacher education programmes. Prominent among them was the ZINTEC Programme, which brought with it distance education as a mode of training pre-service, non-graduate teachers. This innovation affected all forms of pre-service, non-graduate teacher education, in that for the first time in the country's history distance education played a prominent role in teacher education. What is now urgently required is a systematic and thorough impact evaluation of teachers trained since independence to assess their effectiveness. This is crucial because if money spent producing incompetent, inefficient, and ineffective educators it is money wasted.

Prasad and John (1992) conducted a study with the objectives of finding out: Guidance given for practice teaching by teacher educators; self-preparation of the trainees for teaching practice; Supervision of teaching practice; and Achievement of objectives of teaching practice.

A stratified sample of 120 B.Ed. teacher trainees of Kakatiya University was selected. Equal weightage was given to distance and conventional (formal) institutions. An opinionnaire, prepared by observing teaching practice of trainees and informal discussions with the supervisors of teaching practice, was administered in order to collect data.

It was found that the level of perception and performance of the B.Ed. trainees of distance education was same as that of the trainees of conventional institutions. The trainees felt that sufficient guidance had been provided to them regarding teaching practice. But majority of them preferred materials prepared in regional language. The distance trainees were found to have more control over classroom situation so as to make students more disciplined than the trainees of conventional institutions. Majority of the teaching practice classes lacked adequate seating arrangements. Trainees from both conventional and distance institutions could not use sufficient charts and 3-dimensional aids. But, it was remarkable to note that the distance trainees performed better in experimental demonstration in comparison to their counterparts of conventional institutions. The results showed that the trainees of distance education were in no way inferior to their counterparts in conventional institutions with regard to level of perception, self-preparation and achievement of objectives of practice teaching.

Srinivas (1992) conducted a study the major objective of which was to examine the grammar component of the existing materials for high school teachers. The objectives were broken into three stages. In the first stage the trainees and their needs were identified. The views of distance learners were obtained on the appropriateness of the content, format and presentation of the materials. Also the views of subject specialists were obtained on the appropriacy of the content and the format. The learners' needs were identified through three methods—questionnaire, interview and analysis of trainees' own written English.

In stage two, effort was made to find out whether the grammar materials fulfilled the needs of the trainees. Three sample lessons were prepared on the basis of the suggestions made by the analysis. In stage three, the three sample lessons were tested.

The study presented an argument in favour of the teaching of grammar in consonance with the current theories of language learning and advocated a semantic approach to the teaching of grammar. On the basis of the profile of the trainee, his/her real perceived needs, and the semantic approach, the adequacy of the in-service teacher training correspondence course materials was established. The inadequacy was identified in terms of its weakness not merely as distance learning materials but also as teacher training materials. It was, therefore, suggested that the course may be improved by carrying out certain modifications in the existing materials. To demonstrate the feasibility of these modifications, three sample lessons incorporating the suggested modifications were produced as part of the study to investigate the need for further modifications for improvement. A tryout was also conducted. The yielded certain suggestions for further modifications.

Acharya (1995) conducted a study on teacher education programme through distance learning system. Major findings of her study were: Infrastructural facilities of Distance Education cell were inadequate. There was irregularity in the receipt of instructional materials by the students. There was no provision of permanent teaching staff. Duration of contact programme was very short and 74 per cent of the students felt the non-availability of library books. Students should have more practice of practical works as viewed by 63.6 per cent of teachers. Internal examination was suggested by 73 per cent of teachers. The Distance System of teacher education programme was partly successful as opined by 81.8 per cent of teachers and 18.2 per cent of the teachers rated it was a poor system of learning. All the teachers suggested for reducing the sanctioned strength of enrolment in the Distance System of teacher education programme. Teacher education programme should not be imparted through distance mode was suggested by 85 per cent of the educationists.

Murugan (1996) argued that the present system of centralistic training offered to the academic counsellors of IGNOU is inadequate and inappropriate. He suggested an alternative approach where the counsellors would undergo distance training and also have some 'hands-on' experience of a handling a couple of counselling sessions, before they were called for face-to-face training. The distance training could through a set of booklets, each on a topic (the acquaintance with which is considered essential for the prospective counsellor to carry out his tasks), accompanied by some 'reflective sheets' (containing series of questions that prompt trainees to reflect on and respond). The subsequence face to face training would devote a larger share of its time on discussion/sharing of trainees' experiences. This kind of training oriented to inculcation of an approach to reflective practice would help in accommodating the needs of both the trainees and the organization.

Pugalenthi (1998) conducted a study on an evaluation of Distance Education Teaching with specific reference to certain selected Universities in the State of Tamil Nadu. Objectives of this study were:

(1) To analyze the potentialities of educational technology in the teacher education courses of distance education. (2) To survey the different types of media in use, such as print material, contact programmes, radio and television broadcasting, videocassettes and audiocassettes in the teacher education courses of distance education. (3) To measure the distance learners' attitude towards distance education in variety of dimensions. (4) To study the distance learners' perception of the distance teacher education courses in the selected universities of Tamil Nadu. (5) To study the distance learner's perception of the effectiveness of personal contact programmes of the distance teacher education courses in the

selected universities of Tamil Nadu. (6) To offer suggestions and recommendations for the improvement in the use of educational technology in the distance education programmes.

Cluster sampling techniques was adopted in collecting data from all the 51 distance learners of the M.Ed. courses of Alagappa University, Annamalai University, Bharathiyar University, Madurai-Kamaraj University and University of Madras from all the 220 B.Ed. trainees of Sri Ramakrishna Vidhalaya College of Education and Government College for Women, Coimbatore. Regarding the learners of the B.Ed. distance education course, data were obtained from the set of 92 trainees of the two-year B.Ed. distance education course (1997) of University of Madras who attended the PCP classes at Saradha College of Education for Women, Salem and the 130 block of trainees of the first year B.Ed. course of Bharathiyar University for whom special PCP classes were arranged at Coimbatore.

Findings were: (1) Lack of an explanatory introduction about their course, giving details about how to use the course and related non-conventional media for self-learning. (2) Lack of proper advance organizers or pre-activating elements such as objectives, an index of contents with suitable comments, a brief introduction of each unit giving both abstract and general comments to stimulate and involve students' thought process essential for reinforcing the understanding and grasp of the content within the unit and the like. (3) Lack of interactive presentation, i.e. element of non-contagious communication, as suggested by Holmberg and complex presentation of learning materials. (4) Lack of activities that interact with the text and support to transfer knowledge and comprehension of concepts. (5) Improper placement or lack of proper progress indicators for the students (self-check questions). (6) Lack of proper exercises from each taxonomic level of the objectives for the course. The control of the difficulty level of these exercises is essential to sustain student motivation. (7) Lack of sequential and orderly presentation of content. (8) The printing quality is poor. (9) Excessive and repeated delays in the delivery of learning materials. (10) Excessive delay in the answering of queries. (11) Unqualified personnel attending the teaching process or attendance by professionals still unconvinced of the benefits of distance education who unconsciously tend to discredit this teaching method in their mix age. (12) Difficulties in the communication process either by personal enquiries, by telephone, by computer or by other communication devices.

Sahoo *et al.* (1999) conducted case study of B.Ed. programme of Kota

Open University. The findings in the context of achievement of objectives of classroom management (56%) and improvement in evaluation procedures (48%) a large chunk of students found curriculum most effective whereas with regard to other objectives like, to understand learner, to develop teaching skills and following innovations of education. Most of the trainees (51 to 62%) found B.Ed. curriculum effective to some extent.

Most of the trainees (55 to 74%) agreed that utility of course first, second and third (Education is Emerging Indian society, Psychology of learning development and educational management) and optional courses were very high, whereas with regard to course fourth, i.e. curriculum development and educational technology most of the students (54%) found its utility limited.

Majority of students (56 to 57%) were satisfied with contact camps and practice teaching in school situations. 49 per cent of teachers appreciated the guidance of tutors to a large extent.

With regard to developments of teaching skills majority of students (60%) have reported about its usefulness to some extent, 49 per cent reported to large extent and about in terms of new teaching methods. In the case of other areas, viz. taking appropriate decision related to teaching work, development of learning material for school students, development and use of teaching aids and development of good question papers for evaluations, the practical works helped students to a large extent (51 to 79%).

The trainees reported that course duration was very long. They forced problems related to uneven distribution of course activities as conducted by the university.

Around 47 per cent of total student opined that the course materials were sufficient to complete the course. Almost equal number of students opined about its partial contribution to complete the course successfully. The students suggested in open ended form that the radio and T.V. lessons, other means available in market, computer assisted learning material, teleconferencing and video and audio cassette programmes must be added to the existing course material.

Majority of students (57%) had reported about getting sufficient time to study the course materials supplied by KOU whereas 38 per cent students found some time to study material.

A whole majority of students (53 to 78%) found the unit contents appropriate to some extent for theory courses as well as methods of teaching courses. Specially in case of methods of teaching courses only 17 per cent students found them appropriate to large extent. Whereas 78 per cent students found them appropriate to some extent.

Around 89 per cent students found the course content difficult to some extent and only 8 per cent students found it very much difficult.

Majority of students (52%) found the methods of teaching course material useful to a large extent in the completion of practical work. However, significance section of students (48%) found them useful to some extent or least in practical work.

Majority of students (55%) found course materials appropriate to a large extent in getting self-assignment, feedback. While performing learning activities through study of B.Ed. course material were found to be most appropriate by 68 per cent of trainees.

The overall impact of Students Support Services on students is perceived to be positive to some extent by majority of students. With regard to solution of general queries a majority of students (52%) found Students Support Services most useful, whereas 44 per cent students found these useful to some extent.

With regard to organisational aspects of PCP a large number of students (48 to 76%) found PCP organisation satisfactory to some extent. This was noticed in the context of duration, time-table, physical facilities and selection of appropriate counsellors. Around 47 per cent students have expressed high level satisfaction on different other activities.

A large number of students (44 to 68%) found PCP least beneficial in the case of rest of items, viz. to understand theoretical subject, to develop skills and practical work abilities, to develop skills for implementation of group activities, to develop abilities for solving educational problems.

Most of the students expressed dissatisfaction about lack of timely communication from the university regarding different activities. Many a times the Regional Centres were passive in responding to students' queries. They were rude in dealing with students. Ordinary postal correspondence was very poor. Moreover no satisfactory response went from the university offices to the students.

About general guidance the students were dissatisfied with the existing facilities. Neither in postal form nor in face-to-face situation general guidance was found adequate by students. During counselling students problem and interest were not focused by tutors.

Information regarding PCP reaches students at the eleventh hour. There was no tentative schedule for PCP. The students were not provided such schedule in advance. Hence, candidates did not get chance to be academically prepared for PCP activities. They perceived that as if attendance in PCP was a mere formality and the university gave emphasis on attendance.

The PCP classes were held as per Regional Centres and Study Centres discretion which might not suit always to students. Many students found that distance between students working place and PCP centre was quite far. The physical facilities like sitting arrangements, rooms, teaching aids etc. at PCP centre were not conducive for adequate academic activities. Moreover the suitable boarding and lodging facilities were not located by students. Hence, the health and hygine problem occurred during PCP. Some students complained that their PCP centres were changed from one study centre to another at the eleventh hour, hence they found it difficult to cope with the situations. The female students found difficult to adjust with PCPs schedules. The students found it expensive to attend PCPs.

With regard to duration of the programmes the students found it quite short. Because of short duration of PCP lectures were concentrated on a few topics. Practical activities were neglected. Students did not get opportunity to interact with tutors. It happened mainly because of overcrowded classes in appropriate sitting arrangements, short duration of PCP and lack of cooperation from tutors. There was no library facility and laboratory facilities for instruction during PCP.

The students faced a lot of problems with regard to tutors, selection of topics and curricular activities during PCP. Many a times the tutors were not having expertise in specific subjects. Some of them were not trained to deal with different skill based areas. A few tutors managed different subject areas repeatedly. Neither programme coordinators nor tutors encouraged students to raise students queries. The programme co-ordinators remained indifferent to students. Sometimes frequent change of tutors during PCP affected flow of academic activities. More stress was given on lectures.

Practical skill based and group interaction-oriented activities were neglected. It was also noticed that in some centres subject tutors were not available for science, commerce and language subjects. All the subject areas did not get proportionate weightage in PCP time-table. As a whole the PCP management was not systematic keeping in view the interest of students. The PCP activities were not monitored property by centre co-ordinators and principals. Majority of students (59.67%) found assignment useful to some extent.

A large number of students (47%) suggested that 50 to 75 per cent weightage should be given to application-oriented questions in assignments. Moreover majority of students (61%) suggested that 50 per cent weightage should be given to assignments out of the total marks in B.Ed. The existing 30 per cent weightage must be revised.

On examining the system of theory paper and practice teaching most of the students (61 to 74%) expressed their satisfaction to some extent.

The teacher educators' views on assignments have been consolidated read as:

- The existing system of assignment is very formal. Students involvement in preparation of assignments is mainly restricted to reproducing facts from course materials. Most of the students take submission of assignments as a mere formality. The purpose of assignments for maintaining continuity in studies is defeated. Common pattern of questions is followed in all the assignments.
- The time given for submission of assignments is limited. The students submit all the assignments in one go. Many students clear assignments after the final examination of theory papers and practical are over.
- There is no proper provision for giving guidance by counsellors to students on how to prepare assignments.
- Feedback mechanism of assignment evaluation is almost non-existent. The tutors assign marks on assignments. No comment is given on assignments. The university does not have provision for dispatch of evaluated assignments to students. Only in a few cases the students get chance to verify the assignment marks at the Regional Centres. The students do not get feedback on assignments hence formative purpose of assignments is lost.

Gunawardena (2000) conducted a study on Using Technology for quality improvement of Teacher Education in OUSL: Problems and Possibilities. He found that the exposure of the student teachers to technology in their own educational careers is limited. The limited exposure in turn leads to negative attitudes which hinder acquisition of technical skills even when opportunities are provided. The following table (Table 2.1) reveals the poor utilization of educational technology, even to the limited extent to which it is provided, by student teachers, who were resident in remote and distant areas.

Table 2.1: Utilization of Student Support Services

(Percent)

Facility	*Used*	*Not used*	*No response*
Audio cassettes	19.0	71.4	09.6
Video cassettes	49.5	40.0	09.5
Computers	04.8	85.7	09.5

The use of new technologies, especially interactive media, is facilitated if the student teachers have access to the equipment required. In Table 2.2 teachers indicate the situation to be extremely disadvantaged. In the extremely deprived communities which have access only to postal services, all types of electrical and electronic media are beyond the reach of student teachers, in their homes or schools.

Table 2.2: Availability of Facilities to Use Different Media (%)

Medium	*Often*	*Sometimes*	*Rarely*	*Never*	*No Response*
Radio	09.4	21.0	14.3	50.5	04.8
Audio Cassettes	01.09	03.8	09.5	78.6	06.2
Video Cassettes	00.0	01.0	27.8	68.6	07.6
Telephone	01.9	07.7	15.2	69.8	05.4
Postal Services	61.0	13.3	08.6	13.3	03.8
Computers	00.0	00.9	00.9	92.8	05.4

Joshi (2000) conducted a study on In-Service Training of Primary School Teachers through Distance mode: IGNOU Experience. The researcher observed that (from students' enrolments of 1993-1997):

(i) All regional centres have representation in it, in spite of the fact that this programme is offered in two languages only and in India school education, i.e. primary education is imparted in regional languages.

(ii) The number of learners successfully completing the programme has been on the increase except in 1995, in spite of lower enrolment in later years.

(iii) Working people are the major clientele. Teachers represent about half of them and primary teachers have a significant representation, i.e. 204/224.

(iv) Urban/metropolitan cities represent more than three-fourths of the population. The deprived section of the population is very-very meagre.

(v) Three-fourths of the student population is in the age group of 21-35 years which reflects enthusiasm of the young people in the system as well as in the programme.

(vi) About three-fourths of the population is female which shows a positive trend in catering to the female population in spite of under enrolment in the programme.

(vii) More than half of the respondents were teachers and more than one-third were primary school teachers.

(viii) About three-fourths were married and more than 90 per cent were having children in the family.

(ix) More than 50 per cent of the respondents were in the age group 21-35 years, while in the age group 31-35 years has more than one-fourth of respondents.

(x) More than two-thirds were female students.

(xi) More than three-fourth were from urban areas.

(xii) The respondents' representations were from all over the country.

(xiii) The majority of the respondents were satisfied with the programme, but satisfaction varied as per their expectations.

Kabir (2000) conducted a study on Teacher Education in Bangladesh through Distance Mode. He found that programme continued till 1987 with three batches of students totalling 10281 (3211 in 1987, 3287 in 1988 and 3783 in 1989) and of them, 7202 (2506 in 1987, 2299 in 1988 and 2397 in 1989) completed the course successfully. The proportions of male and female students remain by and large similar throughout the years but their age distribution differs significantly. The majority of students of this programme are above 30 years of age and this speaks of the fact that as a teachers' training programme, B.Ed. has attracted the working teachers of the secondary schools. This also reflects the magnitude of untrained teachers in the country's school system.

Tutor training has been a regular feature of almost all the programmes. It will not be out of place to mention here that Bangladesh Open University has recently conducted a survey to obtain students' feedback on its study materials. It came out that more than 477 of rural students and 657 of urban students rated the B.Ed. programmes from very good to excellent when asked to give an overall rating and of them, 44 per cent of female and 54 per cent of male students rated the programme from very good to excellent. When asked specifically about the learning objectives of the programme, more than 66 per cent of the rural and 65 per cent of the urban students rated the B.Ed. Programme from very good to excellent in improving their teaching skills.

The School of Education conducts summer and winter school in which practical lesson planning and teaching are given great emphasis. A sample of 45.5 per cent of rural students and 56.7 per cent of urban students rated B.Ed. tutorial services from good to excellent and most of the students considered problem-solving type of tutorial support as the most effective for their learning. Quality of text materials is also considered an important factor in distance education. On the average, 52.1 per cent rated the learning contents of the books from very good to excellent.

Parajuli (2000) conducted a study on Teacher Training through Distance Teaching. Objectives of this study were: (a) To improve the teaching-learning situation and make it more qualitative through a different type of training procedure. (b) To provide training to the teachers within a short span of time. (c) To facilitate training to both teachers financially capable of supporting themselves and to those who did not. (d) To reduce the cost of the training programme. (e) To eliminate the problems of finding a substitute teacher in place of the teacher sent for training. (f) To provide training while teaching, both Orientation and Intensive Training Programmes were so arranged that they were conducted in the winter and summer vacations of the schools.

Findings of this study were: (a) Trainees were highly satisfied. (b) The result was quite satisfactory. In the beginning the programme was conducted in three districts. The inputs of trainees were 29, 77 and 24 respectively and out of these 22, 65 and 21 passed the programme. Similarly, in the second phase, the programme was launched in 6 other districts of Far Western region and the total output was 78 per cent. Six failed trainees from Baitadi district were permitted to join the programme and repeat the course this time and all six got through in the final evaluation. So the total output was 80 per cent. (c) After the completion of the training, the trainees could take the reading materials with them. This opportunity provided feedback to maintain the knowledge level of the teachers. Similarly in the third phase, the programme was launched in the next 5 districts of the Mid region and the district of the Far Western region and in the fourth phase 4 districts of the Mid region and one district of the Far Western region and the result were 37 and 46 per cent respectively. (d) All the teacher staff including the coordinator itself is not well oriented with this programme. So, visits to observe such programmes, training and other similar programmes would be highly recommended to run this programme more smoothly. (e) These experiences provided ample scope for its expansion in other districts of the country.

Phalachandra and Veena (2000) conducted a study on "Efficacy of Interactive Television Technique in the Training of Primary School

Teachers." Results of this study revealed that in all 847 teachers participated in the training; 54 per cent of them were male teachers and 46 per cent female. The other information collected about participants indicated that 39 per cent of participants were below 30 years of age and 38 per cent were in the age group 30-40 years. Further, 50 per cent of the participants had less than 5 years of teaching experience, another 37 per cent had between 6 and 15 years of experience. Information, which is of utmost importance, is that 74 per cent of the teachers were working in rural schools.

To ascertain the impact of the training on teachers, different approaches were adopted. First, the feedback from the participants was obtained through audio feedback and also through written reports on the training programme and an evaluation of the programme was done adopting pre-test and post-test experimental design. Special tools such as achievement test and observation schedule were developed and administered by specially appointed investigators on a sample of 286 teachers at 8 centres. Further, faculty members of National and State agencies visited the remaining centres and sent their feedback about the effectiveness of the programme.

The overall gain on the achievement test was found to be 1.57 which is significant at .01 level. Seventy two per cent of participants found presentation and demonstration useful; 69 per cent of participants found the panel discussion as useful. Reading materials and telephone service were found useful by 57 per cent and 68 per cent participants respectively. Further, the question-answer session and panel-discussion were found to be interesting and effective.

The methodology used in the experiment was found to be better than the conventional method. The telephone proved very useful. The answers given by the experts were found to be satisfactory, relevant and useful. The conduct of the programme by the panelists and moderator was considered as of a good standard. There was a better understanding among teachers of child-centred and activity-based teaching and of also the significance of minimum levels of learning. The teachers reported that the programme was "effective", "created interest", pepped up their "enthusiasm", "improved their capabilities", and felt "superb."

Pradhan (2000) conducted a study on "Effect of Cooperative Peer Learning Strategies on Attitudes of Student Teachers and Primary School Pupils and their perception towards Teaching and Learning." The objectives of this particular study were to:

1. Demonstrate the process of cooperative learning with the help of student teachers and primary school children.
2. Measure the change in attitude of student teachers and primary school learners before and after the training.

The method of statistical analysis conducted was t-test. Statistically significant differences were found between the pre-test and post-test attitudes scores. The 't' values of 7.71, 4.74, 2.18 and 5.14 of pre-test and post-test TATS scores of student teachers in principles of learning (i.e. Active Learning, Demonstration, Practice and Feedback, Continuous Evaluation and Support) were significant at 0.01 and 0.05 level respectively. This implies that the gain in scores in post-test was due to the effect of training. The 't' values of 7.77, 4.47, 6.12, 4.13 were significant at 0.01 level respectively. This implies that the gain in scores in post-test was due to the effect of training.

Rashid (2000) conducted a study on "Teacher Training Through Distance Education in Pakistan" and he found that at present, there are 215 courses of different levels being offered by the Allama Iqbal Open University in order to cater to the needs of thousands of students of the country. English and national language Urdu are usually the language of instruction. There are two semesters in a year starting from April to September and October to March. After enrolling students, study materials along with assignments, students guide, schedule for Radio/T.V. programme and tutorials are mailed to them. There are four home assignments in each full credit course. A student can take two full credits in one semester. It is compulsory to complete all the assignments on specified dates failing which the student has to repeat the course. The A.I.O.U. started teacher training programme in 1975. The first programme launched was for in-service teacher training. Later on, PTC, CT, and B.Ed. programmes were launched. The year-wise enrolment from 1988 to 1995 are 4164, 7423, 2902, 10747, 21258, 17160, 10778, 21810, 24487, 118729 in B.Ed. Programme

Sharma (2000) studied responses collected from 39 students of first batch of IGNOU B.Ed. Programme from the Jammu and Kashmir region, when the student were in the second year of their study. On the findings about students-teacher's perceptions of assignments, Sharma observed that the students were dissatisfied with the absence of discussion on assignment questions and with the absence of comments. 69 per cent of the students did not receive feedback on their assignments. The students' views concerning assignments are summarized in the table below:

IGNOU B.Ed. students views on assignment holding

Sl. No.	*Assignments*	*Responses in %*	
		Yes	No
1.	Clarity of assignments practical work	92	8
2.	Difficulty of assignments	54	46
3.	Submission of assignments as per schedule	79	21
4.	Discussion of assignment questions by resource person	21	79
5.	Consultation of books for writing assignments	72	28
6.	Feedback on assignments by resource person	31	69

Mishra, S. (2002) studied the process-issues for organizing Research and Training in Distance Teacher education. Major findings of his study were:

Majority of the responding experts viewed to generate the resources (cost of the programme) from teacher trainees as they are salaried people and they will be benefited in terms of career advancement or salary enhancement. Almost a half of the responding experts held the view that the place of personal contact programme should be a teacher training institution where necessary infrastructure and human facilities are available. However, a sizeable proportion of responding experts advocated to a place nearest to the place of work of trainees. Most of the responding experts viewed that practice teaching should be compulsory like formal system so as to modify their teaching skills by updating their practicing skills. Around half of the responding experts were of the opinion that practice teaching should be organized in reputed, recognized local schools nearer to the trainees work place.

All the responding experts agreed upon the process of continuous and comprehensive evaluation of the trainees. Most of the responding experts advocated for evaluating the training programme in terms of its process and output. The evaluation should be carried out by taking the views of teacher trainees, experts of teacher education as well as distance education, mentors and counsellors.

Most of the responding experts thought that the selection of proper media depends upon the nature of the content. About the process of developing course materials, majority of the responding experts emphasized learners to be put at the centre-stage while developing materials. The whole process of adults learning principles should be adequately and scientifically applied in the production of materials. Majority of the responding experts favoured provision of in-text questions to bring interactivity by relating the personal experiences of the learners with the learning processes through self-check exercises. Majority of the responding experts opined that quality and cost are not contradictory to each other and advocated to collect feedback from multiple functionaries and user-students for continuous updating of the material. Majority of the responding experts argued that there should be multiple channels for wide and rapid delivery. Most of the responding experts pleaded for developing proper feedback system for evaluating materials. Both qualitative and quantitative methods of evaluation should be employed to get feedback.

Pradhan (2002) conducted a comparative study of the Effectiveness of Traditional Versus Correspondence B.Ed. Programmes of the Universities of Orissa.

Major findings include there was provision of giving preference to in service teachers for admission in to B.Ed. course both Universities. There was no difference regarding the duration of the course. The application cost and admission fee were higher in correspondence mode than that of traditional one. Merit was the main criterion for admission in to B.Ed course in traditional mode whereas it was experience in correspondence mode. There was no provision of entrance test for selection of candidates in to B.Ed courses in both modes. The minimum and maximum age limit for general candidate were 21 and30 years in traditional mode giving relaxation of five years for SC, ST, and women candidates but there was no such rigid policy regarding age limit in correspondence mode. In traditional mode there was provision of career weightage giving more weightage to graduation and P.G. holder candidates but no such weightage was given in correspondence mode.

There was no systematized reservation quota in correspondence mode but there was specific reservation quota in traditional mode. There existed a significant difference between the course, objectives, student learning activities, instructional materials, instructional methods, support service and evaluation of traditional and correspondence mode. There was significant difference between achievement of Art stream and science stream students of the traditional Vs correspondence mode of the B.Ed. programme.

Ronnie Carr, Fung and Shui Kin (2002) stated that the Open University of Hong Kong (OUHK) is one of an increasing number of institutions offering teacher education programmes through distance education. This article focuses largely on one of the programmes from the OUHK's School of Education and Language, the in-service Bachelor of Education (Honours) in Primary Education (BEDHPE). Some examples of teacher education programmes at a distance are discussed, followed by a brief of the nature of in-service teacher education, and the feature of high-quality distance education materials and learner support systems. The articles then present the result of an evaluation of the above programme. On the basis of survey findings, it is argued that distance education programmes that are well designed and efficiently implemented can provide an effective, flexible alternative to the traditional approach to in-service teacher education.

Ansari and Dash (2003) conducted a study in pursuance of the objectives of universalization of elementary education. There has been considerable expansion in institutional infrastructure of the school system, which has profound impact on teacher demand. As the outcome of schooling technologies are being used for the distribution of materials, to a limited extent for two-way communication, and for making web-based resources available to teachers.

The cost of distance education behave differently from the cost of conventional education and are likely to have relatively high fixed and low variable allowing economies of scale. Where distance education makes it possible to reduce the cost of residence, or allow trainees to work in the classroom as they study, this reduces the comparative cost of approach. Distance education has tended to be funded by governments; through there are examples of some of the cost being met from student fees and more rarely, from the private sector. Models have been developed for the analysis of the costs of distance and conventional education. The record provides only limited data on the cost to be expected for each of the available technologies but does establish that student support, including the supervision of classroom practices, has often demanded between a quarter and a half of the total budget. Global comparisons between distance and conventional approaches suggest that these distance approaches are likely to be at an economic advantage.

Qining (2004) conducted a study on the topic of "Training English Teachers Abroad — The Necessity and Feasibility Research." The purpose of the study is to evaluate the undergoing summer programme of training for Chinese teachers of English within the system of China Radio and Television University (CRTVU). Furthermore, the study tries to ascertain the impact on teacher training and teaching quality improvement. This study also introduces 4 methods on how to operate this short training programme successfully. They are (1) to communicate with the foreign universities in order better to serve the purpose of looking for qualified foreign partners and the suitable training bases abroad; (2) to operate well with the home partners to clear the ways for obtaining visas and to exchange foreign currency etc.; (3) to design a convenient timetable in order to adjust it according as our English teachers' needs; (4) the last and the most important, to design the content and process of what is to be learned during its programme. The results of the study shows that the teachers benefit from the training and surely, it will make contribution to RTVU Open and Distance Education System in China.

Sahoo and Tripathi (2004) carried out a research on Study of Networking of Institutions in Promoting Quality of Students Support Services in Open Universities. Responses of students towards networking on its different components of operation and its effectiveness was independent of students professional and general course background since the observed Chi-square values were not found to be higher than the table value to be significant at 0.05 level of significance. It was also observed that a large chunk of student (40 to 77%) from general as well as professional categories found the networking was poor in terms of sharing of course. The students also did not perceive positive picture of networking of Open University with different kinds of facilities in SSS such availability of radio broadcast/Gyan Vani Programme, telecast/Gyan Darshan programme, computer network and institution providing e-learning facilities. The students also expressed adverse opinion on networking of open universities and study centres in terms of provision of broadcast and telecast, audio-video cassettes, radio and television sets, VCR/VCD players, telephone networking computer, teleconferencing and radio-counselling at study centre level.

The perception of teachers towards networking facility in SSS and its effectiveness was found to be independent of their background since observed Chi-square values were found to be lesser than the table values to be significant at 0.5 level of significance. Unlike the perception of students' a sizable number of teachers (44 to 59%) perceived average level of collaboration between the host institutions of study centres and open universities as well as community resources in terms of provision of academic facilities in organization of various kinds of activities like library support, computer-lab activities, laboratory based experiments, experts, community member supports, involvement of professional and school teachers of communities, non-government organization's cooperation, community-based projects and organization of experiments. It was also observed that as it was in the case of student's perceptions a large chunk of teachers (48 to 58%) perceived poor networking of open universities with other kinds of institutions in terms of provision of radio broadcast/gyanvani at local level, local level telecast/Gyan Darshan, cable networking, computer network and e-learning facilities. Moreover, the teachers perceived poor provision of resource support from open universities to study centres in terms of broadcast and telecast facilities, audio-video based lessons, television sets, radio sets, VCD/VCR, radio counselling and teleconferencing.

The background variables of respondents were not independent of their response pattern since the observed Chi-square values were found to be significant at 0.05 level of significance and 0.01 level of significance. It was observed that the B.Ed. students' responses differed from that of teachers of B.Ed. programme. A large chunk of B.Ed. students (47 to 77%) gave poor rating on provision of facilities by host institutions in getting community support and provision of different facilities of open universities to the study institutions regarding SSS. On the other hand a large size of teachers of B.Ed. (48 to 62%) programme expressed average opinion on these heads of networking. It was observed a large chunk of teachers as well as students expressed poor views on the networking of open universities with other kinds of agencies for organization of SSS. Unlike the response pattern of general course teachers, a large number of B.Ed. programme counsellors (50%) expressed average opinion on the utility of SSS whereas a large number of B.Ed. students (47%) expressed positive response on the utility of SSS.

Srinivasan (2004) carried out a research on developing and validity a training package to permute distance teaching activity through tutor comments on the learners' assignment reprocesses of IGNOU B.Ed. programme in Tamil Nadu. The significant findings of the study were:

1. The incidence of global comments has increased from 62.5 per cent of assignment responses handled by the subject to 100 per cent of assignment responses after training.
2. The use of connected piece of writing for giving global comments is observed in 86.88 per cent of assignments responses handled by the subject after training *vis-à-vis* 2.5 per cent in the pre-training situation, the practices of using 'hints' has been totally given up after training, whereas it was observed in 31.9 per cent of assignment responses handled before training; drastic reduction, though not total elimination has been noticed in the incidence of sentence-level global comments—from 22.5 per cent to 9.8 per cent.

3. The letter format is adopted in preference to report format 87.5 per cent of assignments responses evaluated by the subjects after training; in the pre-training context there was no incidence of letter format. All the subjects trained except one have change over to the use of letter format after training and thus more instances of adoption of letter format have been evidenced.
4. The instances of personal/friendly approach have noticed in 72.5 per cent of assignment responses evaluated after training; the corresponding figure in pre-training situation was 11.25 per cent.
5. Observations on learner strengthen within Global comments were found in 50.60 per cent of assignment responses assessed after training comments on learner weaknesses are found in Global comments concerning 70 per cent of assignment responses. The corresponding figures in pre-training situation were 8.75 per cent and 53.75 per cent respectively.
6. 25.63 per cent of assignment responses evaluated after training contain Global comments offering suggestions for learner improvement marked whereas this feature was offered in 3.75 per cent of assignment responses before training was given.
7. Covering multiple functions under Global comments is found to have improved to the tune of 25.12 per cent in the post-training assessment of assignment responses compared to the pre-training assessment.
8. The assignment responses handled by the subjects after training record on incidence of 978 in-text teacher inventions as specific comments; This was 2.7 times larger than the corresponding incidence of 362 in-text intervention in the pre-training situation. The average intervention per assignment response work out to 6.1 in the post-training case as against 2.26 in the pre-training situation.
9. The distribution of specific comments across word-level, phrase-level and connected utterance-level is also marked by desirable trend change in the post-training situation, with larger number of comments offered in connected pieces of writing and an almost equal distribution between word and phrase level comments.
10. The ratio of specific comments dealing with teachers-Strengths compared with comments on learners-weaknesses; in the post-training situation is 18 : 82; the corresponding pre-training ratio 4 : 96. the imbalance in the pre-training ratio is remedied to so extant in the post-training situation. As error-identifications need

desirably to be sandwiched between strength-appreciations recognition of strengths has to be more frequents. The training has brought about a chance to the tune of 12 times more incidence of strength identification (an average of 1.1 incidence of strength recognition per assignment response after training, against 0.09 incidences before training).

11. In 41.25 per cent of 160 instances, after training learners find the tutor comments clear and self-training.
12. In 26.25 per cent of assignment responses received after evaluation in the post-training context, learners see a tone of encouragement and friendliness in the language of comments.
13. Learners find increased features of personal talk after the teachers went through training in the comments offered in 38.75 per cent assignment reprocesses.
14. The pedagogic value of tutor comments offered in all 160 instances after training taken together stands at 53.9 per cent of the maximum fixed. The pedagogic value corresponding to the per training handing of assignments response stands at 8.7 per cent of the maximum. Thus the overall pedagogic value of tutor comments offered is found to have improved by more than six times.

Nagar and Mahapatra (2005) conducted a study on "Skills for Development: A case study of special Educational Programme through Distance Mode." The aim of the case study was to examine the growth and development of B.Ed. special education programme across the period of last three years at M.P. Bhoj (Open) University, Bhopal. The data collection was done by scanning relevant information of the last three years from the official records of the University. The data were analyzed utilizing descriptive statistics. The major results of the study revealed that the delivery mechanism particularly instructional materials have improved both in terms of quality and quantity across the period of three years. Furthermore, the progressive trend of growth in terms of number of registered students and study centres is evident with maximum registration and study centres in the year 2004 followed by 2003 and 2002. The results further revealed that in the last three years the teachers trained in the area of mental retardation are maximum (53%) followed by hearing impairment (31%), visual impairment (11%) and locomotive impairment (5%). Interestingly, in the year 2004 the performance of the students has shown marked deterioration with only 34 per cent students passing the exam and 41 per cent students failing the examination. The best performance of students was found in the year 2003.

Pandey and Singh (2008) conducted a Study on Qualitative Teaching of Science Subjects through Distance Mode. The Objectives of the study were:

1. acquiring knowledge of attitude of teachers in relation to teaching of Physical Sciences through distance mode.
2. to know the attitude of teachers about appropriateness of contemporary distance education system for the teaching of Physical Sciences.
3. to know the challenges of teaching of Physical Sciences through distance education mode.
4. to know the necessary strategies adopted for qualitative teaching of Physical Science *via* distance mode.

Findings of the study were:

1. According to 50 per cent teachers of higher secondary, 40 per cent teachers of higher level and 20 per cent teachers of teacher education institution can be taught Physical Sciences through distance mode. According to only 25 per cent teachers, contents in Physical Science can be presented objective-wise.
2. According to 75 per cent teachers' only theoretical knowledge of Physical Sciences can be provided.
3. According to 50 per cent teachers for the system of teaching Physical Sciences *via* distance mode necessity-wise changes must be incorporated. According to 25 per cent teacher's practical improvement can also bring a lot of possibilities whereas 25 per cent teacher opines that improvement in system is impossible.

Sahoo, Yadav and Kumar (2009) conducted a study of problems and expectations of distance mode B.Ed. trainees regarding student support services. Descriptive survey method was employed in the study by them. The sample of the study included 240 second year B.Ed. trainees, i.e. 120 each from IGNOU and UPRTOU programme study centres. The sample centres and the trainees enrolled therein covered all the three zones of U.P. Questionnaire consisting of open ended and close type items was developed on three dimensions, viz. Background information; Problem statements and expectation statements. Data were collected from the sample respondents available in the programme study centres towards the completion of second year programme. Descriptive technique was used for analysis of data. Chi-square test was used to test the hypothesis that the response pattern of B.Ed. trainees was not significantly independent from institutional affiliation. The findings of the study were:

A large majority of UPRTOU students (71%) agreed that lectures on theory papers were just repetition of self-study materials. It was difficult to prepare micro-teaching lesson plans as well as general teaching lesson plans. In the case of rest of problem items homogeneous pattern of response was witnessed by IGNOU and UPRTOU B.Ed. trainees. The prominent problems highlighted by a significant number of IGNOU and UPRTOU B.Ed. trainees read as follows:

During counselling sessions lectures were delivered in place of trainee-oriented activities (51-61%). It was problematic to comprehend the demonstrations concerning skill components in micro teaching. (44-56%). Feedback given by counsellors during micro-teaching lessons were inadequate for mastery of skills (42-56%).

They found significant differences between views of IGNOU and UPRTOU students since Chi-square test values were found significant with regard to:

- Facilities for video lesson based demonstrations on teaching skills must be available in programme study centres.
- Lesson plan demonstration must cover different components of teaching competencies.
- In these cases a large majority of IGNOU students (88-99%) expressed more favourable opinion than their UPRTOU counter parts (68-70%).

Yadav (2010) conducted a study of problems related to practice teaching of B.Ed. students of distance mode. Objectives of the study were: Study of problems of B.Ed. students of IGNOU and UPRTOU related to lesson plans, PCP, microteaching, practice teaching, teaching aids, feedback, guidance and counselling, library, discipline of their students, time limitation of curriculum, limitation for admission and related to teachers.

She used survey method and select 120 students as sample. She used Chi-square test for the analysis of data. The findings of the study were:

1. The problems related to practice teaching of B.Ed. students of both the universities are same on the basis of number of students.

2. The problems related to practice teaching of B.Ed. students of both the universities are same on the basis of sex.
3. 68.33 per cent B.Ed. students of IGNOU and 53.33 per cent students of UPRTOU consider that they do not get appropriate knowledge regarding model lesson plans.

Harichandan (2010) had conduced study on teacher education programmes offered through distance education mode in Indian universities. The study attempts to analyse and evaluate the details of programme delivery of Teacher Education Programmes at the all India level. The specific objectives of the study were:

To examine printed course materials, coverage and the media combined packaged used. To study the organization of personal contact programmes for the conduct of lectures and practice teaching lessons. To find out the process evaluation of response sheets. To suggest measures for improving the programme delivery of Teacher Education courses.

The study was a census survey of the descriptive, qualitative type, describing and interpreting what is. Being a census study all the NCTE approved OUs and DEIs in India, conducting teacher education programmes were considered as sample. The following are the major findings of the present research study.

The teacher education programme through the distance mode are offered in 11 NCTE approved distance education institutes and open universities in the entire country. These programmes are offered only for in service teachers.

Institutes like SDLCE, Vishakhapatnam in A.P., H.P. University, Shimla; KSOU, Karnataka; Punjabi University, Patiala and YCMOU, Nashik offer both B.Ed. and M.Ed. programmes whereas the rest of the institutions offer only B.Ed. programme. The enrolment in B.Ed. course varies from 250 to 2000 and in the M.Ed. course from 100 to 475. The higher enrolment figures is in respect of open university only, whose jurisdiction covers the entire country in case of IGNOU and the entire state in case of state open universities like Karnataka and Rajasthan. Enrolment is on the basis of written tests and interviews for B.Ed. and merit alone for M.Ed. In some cases weightage is given to those teachers who are having longer teaching experience in school systems.

The faculty strength varies from a minimum of 4 in Kakatiya University, to a maximum of 23 in Himachal Pradesh University. Most of the faculty members have a doctorate degree to their credit and are generally highly experienced. The course materials are prepared in the

SIM form in case of OU and printed booklets or distance education institutes supply topic-wise notes. They are supplemented by Films, Audio Visual Aids, Audio Cassettes and Computer Assisted Lessons. The size of SIM is usually around 200 pages, written in simple language with adequate topic coverage and bibliography.

Such is quality of study materials of IGNOU and YCMOU that they have bagged international awards and recognition from organisation such as COL Canada for its quality of material production. The course materials are prepared in general by a course team, are evaluated by experts in the field of teacher education and distance education in relation to the relevance of content, style of presentation and language difficulty.

As far as practice teaching goes, all the institutions insist on giving 40 lessons during the course (20 in each method). Lesson guidance is given both individually and in groups. The lessons are evaluated by teacher educators, school teachers, principals of schools and core staff of DEIs. The students are given feedback both individually and in groups.

The Personal Contact Programme lectures are held in varying times depending on the institutions either at the beginning or at the end or in the middle of the course. The duration of PCP is usually a given time slot, which range from 6 days to a maximum of 15 days. The attendance is compulsory. These programmes are conducted at the contact centres or DEIs. The faculty members involved are the staff of the DEIs, visiting faculty or both.

The counselling is given as per the student's demand regarding choice of papers, practice teaching, use of library, examination, confidence building etc.

Evaluation is an ongoing process with 25 to 30 per cent weightage being given to internal. It is usually done through assignments, oral and written tests, seminars and external examination. Remaining 70-75 per cent weightage is being given to term end examination/final examination. Evaluation is continuous in both distance education institute and OUs.

Assignments are compulsory for all students. Staff of DEI or part time tutors evaluates the assignment. The comments given are usually individualistic in nature. The time given for submission ranges from 15 days to 6 months.

2.3 Conclusion

From the above references it is observed that improvement on quality and competency is related with in-service and pre-service training which in turn related with process dynamics of such training programme. Therefore, there exists a strong need to understand and analyse the processes involved in teacher training programme. For this purpose, following questions are relevant. What are the activities carried out for development of teachers competencies? What is its relevance for training activities? And what is the level effectiveness of nature and organisation of various kinds of activities for teacher's competency development? The studies conducted so far have not focused specifically in the above context.

In order to find answers of the raised questions the investigator intends to analyse the process dynamics of B.Ed. programme offered by Distance Education Mode and its relevance. Keeping these points in mind the investigator perceived that there exists a strong need to study the process of B.Ed. programme offered through Distance Education Mode by the open universities.

3

Design of the Study

3.0 Introduction

This chapter deals with the methods and procedures adopted to conduct the study. The chapter covers the research design consisting of population and sample, sampling technique, development of tools, procedure of data collection and plan of data analysis.

Research design is an overall plan for obtaining answer to the research question or for testing the research hypothesis (Polit and Hungler, 1995). It spells out the basic strategies that the researcher adopt to develop information, which is accurate and interpretable. The purpose of research design is to answer research questions in a valid manner and to control sources of variance (Brink and Wood, 1989). Research design includes a plan, structure and strategy for conducting research (Wood, 1994).

The present study has been designed to explore variety of processes related to distance teacher education programmes, therefore, a survey method was chosen to obtain realistic and useful answer to the research questions.

Wood and Haber (1994) highlighted that the descriptive studies are designed to obtain detailed information to know variables so that current conditions and practice can be assessed. In this research designed one can obtain information on the characteristics of particular groups, subjects, institutions or occurrence of particular phenomena.

"A descriptive study is concerned with conditions and relationship that exist, opinions that are held, processes that are going on, effects that are evident or trends that are developing. It is primarily concerned with the present, although it considers past events and influences as they may relate to the current conditions. In fact the events that are observed and described would have happened ever though there had been no observation or analysis" (Best and Kahn, 2001).

3.1 Population and Sample

A population is the entire aggregation of the cases that meet designated criteria (Polit and Hungler, 1995) for the study. Population means all elements (individuals, objects and events) that meet the samplé criteria for inclusion in a study (Crookes and Davies, 1998). The population may be all the individuals of the particular type, or a more restricted part of that group (Best & Kahn, 2001).

Population for the present study includes all the open universities offering B.Ed. programme through distance education mode. It also include all the B.Ed. teacher trainees, counsellors and mentors of the sample university, viz. IGNOU and UPRTOU.

Sample is a small portion or a subset of a population selected for observation and analysis. By observing the characteristics of the sample one can make certain inferences about the characteristics of the population from which it is drawn (West & Kahn, 2001). The sample units of the study are stated in the following:

Open University / *Data*	*IGNOU*	*UPRTOU*	*TOTAL*
Study Centres	6	6	12
Trainees	6 × 50 =300	6 × 50 =300	600
Counsellors	6 × 5 =30	6 × 5 =30	60
Mentors	50	50	100

An Overview of Research Design of the Study

Objective	*Sample*	*Tool*	*Procedure of Data Collection*	*Analysis of Data*
To explore various processes adopted for development of teacher competencies among B.Ed. Students of open Universities	Study Centre = 12 Counsellors = 60 Trainees = 600 Mentors = 100	• Questionnaire for Trainees • Questionnaire for Counsellors • Interview Schedule • Observation Schedule	• Personal visit • Interview after rapports formation • Observation	Content & Percentage Analysis

(Contd.)

Objective	*Sample*	*Tool*	*Procedure of Data Collection*	*Analysis of Data*
To study the relevance of such processes in relation to development of teacher competencies among B.Ed. Students of open Universities	Study Centre = 12 Counsellors = 60 Trainees = 600 Mentors = 100	• Questionnaire for Trainees • Questionnaire for Counsellors • Interview Schedule • Observation Schedule	• Personal visit • Interview after rapports formation • Observation	Content & Percentage Analysis
To study the effectiveness of the nature and organization of various kinds of activities involved in development of teacher competencies among B.Ed. Students of open Universities	Study Centre = 12 Counsellors = 60 Trainees = 600 Mentors = 100	• Questionnaire for Trainees • Questionnaire for Counsellors • Interview Schedule • Observation Schedule	• Personal visit • Interview after rapports formation • Observation	Content & Percentage Analysis

3.2 Tools

Tool is a formal document used to collect and record information, such as questionnaire or interview schedule. In order to collect data the researcher used questionnaire, interview schedule and observation schedule constructed by himself.

1. Questionnaire for trainees
2. Questionnaire for counsellors
3. Interview schedule for counsellors
4. Interview schedule for mentors
5. Study Centre information-cum-observation schedule

Table shows the details about the variables, tools and the target groups of the study area.

Variables	*Tools*	*Target group*
Process exploration	• Questionnaire • Interview schedule	Trainees, Counsellors Counsellors, Mentors

(Contd.)

Variables	*Tools*	*Target group*
	• Study centre information-*cum*-observation schedule	
Process effectiveness	• Questionnaire • Interview schedule • Study centre information-*cum*-observation schedule	Trainees, Counsellors Counsellors, Mentors
Process relevance	• Questionnaire • Interview schedule • Study centre information-*cum*-observation schedule	Trainees, Counsellors Counsellors, Mentors

3.3 Procedure of Construction of Tools

The major steps in developing the tools were:

(i) Identifying the content areas related to various areas to the B.Ed. programmes.
(ii) Enumerating the various aspects of the content.
(iii) Construction of items and statements.
(iv) Establishing content validity.
(v) Preparation of the tools.

3.4 Content Analysis

Content analysis for tools development was done following the phases like:

(i) Field experience.
(ii) Consultation of literature.
(iii) Organization of specific focus group discussion.
(iv) Consultation with expert.

The focus group discussion resulted in identification of following major components and unit components:

I. Preparation of Teaching

(i) Preparing unit-plan.
(ii) Developing micro lesson plan.
(iii) Delivering micro lesson plan.
(iv) Preparing blue-print of lesson plan.

(v) Preparing macro lesson plan.
(vi) Delivering pratice teaching.
(vii) Utilizing feedback in pratice and remodification of lesson plan.
(viii) Doing content analysis experience.
(ix) Presenting model lesson plan.

II. Preparation and Utilization of Instructional Materials

(i) Preparing teaching aids.
(ii) Selecting and using different resources (Library, Laboratory, Media and Local Materials).
(iii) Developing and teaching through power-point presentation.

III. Motivation of Learners

(i) Managing class-room discipline.
(ii) Improving student-teacher interaction.
(iii) Using reinforcement at appropriate time.
(iv) Refreshing students interest through stimulus-variation.

IV. Class-room Communication

(i) Providing effective feedback.
(ii) Demonstrating core teaching skills.
(iii) Organizing activity based class-room.
(iv) Providing minimum level of learning.

V. Methods of Instruction

(i) Conducting practical based project work.
(ii) Leading group discussion.

VI. Evaluation

(i) Completing assignment successfully.
(ii) Providing feedback related to assignment.
(iii) Preparing question paper.
(iv) Evaluating answer copy.
(v) Preparing result/progress report of students.
(vi) Administrating psychological tests.

(vii) Conducting sociometric test in class-room.
(viii) Developing and administrating achievement test.
(ix) Conducting action research.

VII. School Management and Planning

(i) Maintaining school records/register.
(ii) Preparing school time table.
(iii) Preparing school budget.
(iv) Addressing the school assembly.

VIII. Community Participation

(i) Organizing of health educational activities.
(ii) Organizing social (innovative) work/activities.
(iii) Organizing community survey.

IX. Co-curricular Activities

(i) Arranging and organizing field trip/tour.
(ii) Conducting sports and game/cultural programmes.
(iii) Organizing debate competition.
(iv) Organizing seminars on different challenges and innovations.
(v) Planning and organizing annual celebration at school level.

This was followed by expert validity of appropriating the components.

3.5 Description of Tools

The structured questionnaire are divided into there parts, the details of questionnaire are given below and are also presented in Table.

3.5.1 Questionnaire for Trainees and Counsellors

Questionnaires were developed separately for the trainees and counsellors with a view to know their experiences about B.Ed. processes.

3.5.1.1 Questionnaire for Trainees

The tool was developed in order to know the following nine aspects of processes of B.Ed. programme through open universities. This tool has been divided into two sections: **Section I** covers trainees profile like university, teaching status etc.

Section II contains 9 components of distance B.Ed. processes, like—

1. Preparation for teaching—
   (a) Micro-teaching,
   (b) Practice Teaching,
   (c) Unit Plan.
2. Preparation of teaching aids and its use.
3. Classroom teaching motivation.
4. Classroom teaching communication.
5. Students' evaluation.
6. School Management and Planning.
7. Community participation.
8. Co-curricular activities.
9. Self-Learning Materials.

The questionnaire has 114 items related to nine components. The first component has 30 (11+13+6) items, second component has 10 items, third component has 3 items, fourth component has 2 items, fifth component has 12 items, sixth component has 22 items, seventh component has 8 items, eighth component has 30 items and ninth component has 7 items. Every item has four (i-iv) options for response.

3.5.1.2 Questionnaire for Counsellors

The tool was developed in order to know the following eight aspects of processes of B.Ed. programme through open universities. This tool has been divided into two sections: Section I covers counsellors profile like qualification, experience etc. Section II contains 8 similar components, like

1. Preparation for teaching—
   (a) Micro teaching,
   (b) Practice Teaching, and
   (c) Unit Plan.
2. Preparation of teaching aids and its use.
3. Classroom teaching motivation.
4. Classroom teaching communication.
5. Students' evaluation.

6. School Management and Planning.
7. Community Participation.
8. Co-curricular activities.

The questionnaire has 40 items related 8 components. The first component of questionnaire has 17 (4+8+5) items, second component has 2 items, third component has one items, fourth component has one item, fifth component has 5 items, sixth component has 8 items, seventh component has 3 items and eighth component has 7 items. Every item has four (i-iv) options for response.

3.5.2 Interview Schedule for Counsellors and Mentors

Interview schedule developed separately for the counsellors and mentors with a view to know their experiences about B.Ed. processes of open universities. Topics to be covered were specified in advance, in outline forms to make the interview systematic to some extent. These outline forms of issues were again pre-specified in question forms leading to make it more comprehensive. The interview were made fairly conversational and situational.

3.5.2.1 Interview Schedule for Counsellors

The tool was developed in order to know the following eight aspects of processes of B.Ed. programme through open universities. It contains 35 questions covering the required components like:

1. Preparation for teaching.
2. Preparation of teaching aids and its use.
3. Classroom-teaching motivation.
4. Classroom communication.
5. Students' evaluation.
6. School Management and Planning.
7. Community Participation.
8. Co-curricular activities.

The First component of interview schedule has 8 questions, second component has 3 questions, third component has 3 questions, four components has 6 questions, fifth component has 6 questions, sixth component has 2 questions, seventh component has 3 questions and eighth component has 4 questions.

3.5.2.2 Interview Schedule for Mentors

The tool was developed in order to know the following eight aspects of processes of B.Ed. programme through open universities. It contains 31 questions covering the required components, like

1. Preparation for teaching.
2. Preparation of teaching aids and its use.
3. Classroom-teaching motivation.
4. Classroom communication.
5. Students' Evaluation.
6. School Management and Planning.
7. Community participation.
8. Co-curricular activities.

The first component of interview schedule has 9 questions, second component has 5 questions, third component has 3 questions, fourth component has 2 questions, fifth component has 3 questions, sixth component has 3 questions, seventh component has 3 questions and eighth component has 3 questions.

3.5.3 Study Centre Information-cum-Observation Schedule

This tool has been divided into three sections: Section I covers availability and utilization of infrastructure facilities. Section II deals with the resource person. Section III deals with the trainees covering their participation, presentation etc.

3.6 Validity of Tools

The validation procedure of the tools was done systematically. In order to finalize the tools researcher follows the following steps:

(a) As a first step, tools were shown to a few selected Research scholars from education field.
(b) In the second step, the tools were circulated among experts from IGNOU School of Education, Maidan Garhi, New Delhi, Jamia Millia Islamia University, New Delhi, CASE (M.S.University), Baroda, Jammu University, Jammu, Kota Open University, Kota, Banasthali Vidyapeeth, Vanasthali, Rajasthan, Yaswant Narayan

Open University, Maharastra, Bombay University, Bombay, Kumudwati Teachers' Training College, Sikaripur, Simoga (Karnatka), Digamber Jain P.G. College, Baraut, Meerut, Lucknow University, Lucknow (U.P.), Banaras Hindu University, Kamaksha, Varanasi (U.P.), U.P. College, Varansi (U.P.), UPRTOU, Allahabad (U.P.), R.B.S. College, Agra, and University of Allahabad for their comments and suggestions. The researcher personally discussed with some of those experts and got immediate feedback to modify the tools.

The suggestions given by them about the vagueness, difficulties, grammar of the items, were incorporated in the tools. On the basis of the feedback obtained from experts it was relevant to make the following changes:

1. Some questions were rephrased and some questions were repositioned.
2. Some questions were removed or minimized.
3. Some components were merged in required variables.

After development of tools the researcher took a first try out in the field. While trying out these tools on B.Ed. trainees' and counsellors in the field the researcher found the following:

1. Language difficulties.
2. Clarification of terminology.
3. Overlapping dimensions.
4. Exploration of new dimensions.

An Overview of Tools

Sl. No.	*Tool*	*Question no. & Competency Com-ponents ⇨* / *Section of Tools ⇩*	*I*			*II*	*III*	*IV*	*V*	*VI*	*VII*	*VIII*	*IX*
			a	b	c								
1.	Questionnaire for Trainees	(A) Process Explore	5	6	2	4	2	1	6	6	2	2	4
		(B) Process Relevance	3	2	1	2			5	4	1	2	2
		(C) Process Effectiveness	2	2	1	1			2	3	1	1	2

(Contd.)

2.	Questionnaire for Counsellors	(A) Process Explore	2	5	2	2	1	1	4	5	2	2	3
		(B) Process Relevance	1	2	1	2			4	4	1	3	2
		(C) Process Effectiveness	2	2	1	1			2	3	1	1	2
3.	Interview schedule for Counsellors	Process Explore, Process Relevance, Process Effectiveness	10			4	3		5	3	3	2	–
4.	Interview schedule for Mentors	Process Explore, Process Relevance, Process Effectiveness	4			5	5		3	3	4	3	–
5.	Observation Schedule	(A) Resource related	20										
		(B) Counsellors/ Experts related	20										
		(C) Trainees related	16										

Component Details: I Preparation for Teaching (A—Micro Teaching, B—Practice Teaching, C—Unit Plan), II. Preparation of Teaching aids and its use, III. Class room teaching motivation, IV. Classroom communication, V. Student's Evaluation, VI. School Management and Planning, VII. Community Participation, VIII. Co-curricular Activities, IX. Self-learning materials.

3.7 Scoring Procedure

Scoring procedure of the tools is given below tools, viz. separately:

3.7.1 Scoring Procedure of Questionnaire for Trainees

Section 'A' has 40 items are related to different components. The first component is further divided into three parts: (1) Micro teaching, (2) Practice teaching, and (3) Unit Plan. Question No. 1-4 of Micro Teaching are based on percentage analysis and question No. 5 is based on content analysis. Question no. 1-5 of micro-teaching are based on percentage analysis and question no. 6 is based on content analysis. Question no. 1 of unit plan-based on percentage analysis and question no. 2 is based on content analysis.

Question no. 1 and 2 of component II has percentage analysis and questions no. 3 and 4 has content analysis. Question no. 1 of component III has content analysis and question no. 2 is based on percentage analysis Component IV has one question and is based on content analysis. All the questions of component V are based on percentage analysis but the fourth option of the question No. 3-5 and fourth option of question no. 1 of sub-section are based on content analysis.

All the questions of component VI are based on both percentage analysis and content analysis. All questions of components VII and VIII are based on percentage analysis except question no. 2 of component VIII is based on both percentage and content analysis. Question Nos. 1-3 of component IX based on percentage analysis but question no. 4 is based on content analysis.

Sections B and C of this tool are based on percentage analysis.

3.7.2 Scoring Procedure of Questionnaire for Counsellor

This tool has three parts—Section 'A' contains 9 component with 29 items. First component divided into three parts—(1) Micro teaching, (2) Practice teaching, and (3) Unit plan. Question No. 1 of Micro Teaching based on percentage analysis but the fourth option of this question and question no. 2 based on content analysis, question nos. 1, 3, 5 of practice teaching based on percentage analysis but question nos. 2, 4 based on both percentage and content analysis. Question no. 1 of Unit Plan based on both percentage and content analysis but question no. 2 based on content analysis, all questions of component II based on content analysis but all questions of components III and IV are based on content analysis.

All questions of components V and VI are based on both percentage and content analysis. Question no. 1 of component VIII is based on percentage analysis but question no. 2 is based on both percentage and content analysis. All questions of component IX are based on percentage analysis. Sections B and C of this tool are based one percentage analysis.

3.7.3 Scoring Procedure of Interview Schedules

Interview schedule of counsellor and mentor are based on content analysis. Scoring procedure of Study Centre Information-cum-Observation Schedule is based on percentage analysis.

3.8 Procedure of Data Collection

Interview schedule, Questionnaire and Observation Schedule was used for the collection of Data. Questionnaire and Interview Schedule were used to collect the data from counsellors and B.Ed. trainees. Interview schedule was used to collected data from the counsellors and mentors. The researcher had used Observation Schedule to observe various activities in relation to improvement of teacher's competencies and workshop facilities.

3.9 Analysis Procedures

The Chi-square (χ^2) test as well as percentages have been used for analysis of quantitative data. The open responses as well as observation data were analysed qualitatively. The equation for Chi-square (χ^2) is stated as follows:

$$\chi^2 = \Sigma \frac{(fo - fe)^2}{fe}$$

In which fo = frequency of occurrence of observed or experimentally determined facts;

fe = expected frequency of occurrence on some hypothesis.

The number of $df = (r - 1)(c - 1)$
In which r is the number of rows and c the number of columns.

4

Analysis and Interpretation of Data

4.0 Introduction

Analysis is a method of organizing data in such a way that research questions can be answered. Analysis involves description but it may also involve, looking for an association between different characteristics or phenomena or interesting difference between individuals, groups, organizations or changes over the period of time.

In this chapter results are based on the data obtaining through structured questionnaire as well as open-ended questionnaire and interview scale under three sub-sections, viz. Explore of process, Relevance of processes and Effectiveness of processes in nine components (I. Preparation of teaching-oriented processes in distance B.Ed. Programme: Micro teaching, Practice teaching and Unit planning, II. Development of teaching aids by distance mode B.Ed. trainees and their uses, III. Classroom teaching motivation-oriented processes, IV. Classroom communication practices, V. Students evaluation practices, VI. School management and planning related processes, VII. Community participation activities, VIII. Co-curricular activities-oriented practices, and IX. Use of self-learning materials by distance B.Ed. trainees) and as per objectives of the study.

The main objectives of the study were:

1. To explore various processes adopted for development of teacher competencies among B.Ed. students of Open Universities.
2. To study the relevance of such processes in relation to development of teacher competencies among B.Ed. students of Open Universities.

3. To study the effectiveness of the nature and organisation of various kinds of activities involved in development of teacher competencies among B.Ed. students of Open Universities.

I. Preparation of Teaching Oriented Processes in Distance B.Ed. Programme

In this section analysis has been done under three sub-section, viz. Micro teaching practices, Practice teaching processes and Unit planning.

IA. Micro Teaching Practices of Distance Mode B.Ed. Programme

In this sub-section analysis has been done regarding present status, relevance and effectiveness on skills demonstration, preparation of micro lesson plans and practices of micro teaching skills.

4.1 Trainees Response about Number of Micro Teaching Lesson Plans Prepared and Micro Lessons Delivered: University-wise

It can be noticed from Table 4.1 that the calculated χ^2 values of independence with regard to response of B.Ed. trainees and university background on micro teaching lesson plans prepared and taught by them in introduction skill, questioning skill, reinforcement skill, and explanation skill are found to be 6.24, 2.12, 5.11, and 8.00 respectively. The obtained χ^2 values are less than the table value (9.48) at .05 level of significance with df: 4. The observed values are not found significant. Hence the response pattern of B.Ed. trainees and the university background are found independent from each other.

It can be observed that in these skills only 13 to 20 per cent B.Ed. trainees of IGNOU and UPRTOU had prepared 5 micro teaching lesson plans and taught them to fulfil the prescribed norm:

(i) Introduction skill (20.00%)
(ii) Questioning skill (15.33%)
(iii) Explanation skill (15.00%)
(iv) Reinforcement skill (13.33%).

Majority of trainees (51 to 58%) of both the universities have prepared 1 to 4 micro teaching lesson plans and taught them. It is a

Table 4.1: χ^2 test of Independence of trainees' response about micro teaching lesson planning and delivery and university background, skills-wise

Skills	UNIV.	Lesson plans as prepared and delivered by Trainees						Total	χ^2 Value
		Plan 1	Plan 2	Plan 3	Plan 4	Plan 5	No Response		
i. Introduction skill	IGNOU	67 (22.33)	45 (15.00)	32 (10.67)	26 (8.67)	57 (19.00)	73 (24.33)	300 (100.00)	6.24 N.S.
	UPRTOU	48 (16.00)	52 (17.33)	25 (8.33)	35 (11.67)	63 (21.00)	77 (25.67)	300 (100.00)	
	Total	115 (19.17)	97 (16.17)	57 (9.5)	61 (10.17)	120 (20.00)	150 (25.00)	600 (100.00)	
ii. Objective writing skill	IGNOU	62 (20.67)	42 (14.00)	26 (8.67)	43 (14.33)	30 (10.00)	97 (32.33)	300 (100.00)	13.55*
	UPRTOU	56 (18.67)	37 (12.33)	36 (12.00)	24 (8.00)	52 (17.33)	95 (31.67)	300 (100.00)	
	Total	118 (19.67)	79 (13.17)	62 (10.33)	67 (11.17)	82 (13.67)	192 (32.00)	600 (100.00)	
iii. Questioning skill	IGNOU	64 (21.33)	47 (15.67)	38 (12.67)	29 (9.67)	48 (16.00)	74 (24.67)	300 (100.00)	2.12 N.S.
	UPRTOU	62 (20.67)	39 (13.00)	42 (14.00)	27 (9.00)	44 (14.67)	86 (28.67)	300 (100.00)	
	Total	126 (21.00)	86 (14.33)	80 (13.33)	56 (09.33)	92 (15.33)	160 (26.67)	600 (100.00)	
iv. Stimulus variation skill	IGNOU	53 (17.67)	46 (15.33)	24 (8.00)	35 (11.67)	31 (10.33)	111 (37.00)	300 (100.00)	16.64**
	UPRTOU	43 (14.33)	36 (12.00)	31 (10.33)	18 (6.00)	21 (7.00)	151 (50.33)	300 (100.00)	
	Total	96 (16.00)	82 (13.67)	55 (9.17)	53 (8.83)	52 (8.67)	262 (43.67)	600 (100.00)	
v. Reinforcement skill	IGNOU	61 (20.33)	45 (15.00)	33 (11.00)	32 (10.67)	41 (13.67)	88 (29.33)	300 (100.00)	5.11 N.S.
	UPRTOU	52 (17.33)	45 (15.00)	27 (9.00)	25 (8.33)	39 (13.00)	112 (37.33)	300 (100.00)	
	Total	113 (18.83)	90 (15.00)	60 (10.00)	57 (9.5)	80 (13.33)	200 (33.33)	600 (100.00)	
vi. Illustration with example skill	IGNOU	50 (16.67)	59 (19.67)	33 (11.00)	30 (10.00)	40 (13.33)	88 (29.33)	300 (100.00)	22.91**
	UPRTOU	41 (13.67)	30 (10.00)	24 (8.00)	33 (11.00)	35 (11.67)	137 (45.67)	300 (100.00)	

(Contd.)

	Total	91 (15.17)	89 (14.83)	57 (9.5)	63 (10.5)	75 (12.5)	225 (37.5)	600 (100.00)	
vii. Explanation skill	IGNOU	62 (20.67)	51 (17.00)	27 (9.00)	27 (9.00)	48 (16.00)	85 (28.33)	300 (100.00)	8.00 N.S.
	UPRTOU	52 (17.33)	49 (16.33)	19 (6.33)	22 (7.33)	42 (14.00)	116 (38.67)	300 (100.00)	
	Total	114 (19.00)	100 (16.67)	46 (7.67)	49 (8.17)	90 (15.00)	201 (33.5)	600 (100.00)	
viii. Blackboard writing skill	IGNOU	48 (16.00)	38 (12.67)	39 (13.00)	25 (8.33)	59 (19.67)	91 (30.33)	300 (100.00)	17.36**
	UPRTOU	39 (13.00)	35 (11.67)	18 (6.00)	20 (6.67)	55 (18.33)	133 (44.33)	300 (100.00)	
	Total	87 (14.5)	73 (12.17)	57 (9.5)	45 (7.5)	114 (19.00)	224 (37.33)	600 (100.00)	
ix. Demonstration skill	IGNOU	58 (19.33)	30 (10.00)	24 (8.00)	23 (7.67)	44 (14.67)	121 (40.33)	300 (100.00)	17.33**
	UPRTOU	34 (11.33)	24 (8.00)	10 (3.33)	28 (9.33)	56 (18.67)	148 (49.33)	300 (100.00)	
	Total	92 (15.33)	54 (9.00)	34 (5.67)	51 (8.5)	100 (16.67)	269 (44.83)	600 (100.00)	
x. Lesson closer skill	IGNOU	69 (23.00)	39 (13.00)	22 (7.33)	22 (7.33)	54 (18.00)	94 (31.33)	300 (100.00)	14.35*
	UPRTOU	46 (15.33)	34 (11.33)	13 (4.33)	31 (10.33)	48 (16.00)	128 (42.67)	300 (100.00)	
	Total	115 (19.17)	73 (12.17)	35 (5.83)	53 (8.83)	102 (17.00)	222 (37.00)	600 (100.00)	

Note: Figures in parentheses indicate percentages.
N.S.: Not significant
* Indicates significant at .05 level. ** Indicates significant at .01 level.

matter of serious concern that a considerable number of (25 to 33%) B.Ed. trainees of IGNOU and UPRTOU had not prepared any lesson plan and did not deliver any micro lesson.

While these B.Ed. trainees have been considered eligible for completion of B.Ed. course without participating in micro teaching practice a few number of trainees (13 to 20%) adhered to the prescribed norm for delivery of micro teaching lesson scheme. A large majority of trainees (51 to 58%) maintained average status with regard to the above. It reveals a moderate picture of microteaching practices adopted in the B.Ed. programmes offered by the national open university as well as by the state open university.

It can be noticed from Table 4.1 that the calculated χ^2 values of independence between response patterns of B.Ed. trainees and university background on micro teaching lesson plan prepared and taught by them in objective writing skill, stimulus variation skill, explanatory skill along with example, Blackboard writing skill, demonstration skill and lesson closure skill are found to be 13.55, 16.64, 22.91, 17.36, 17.33 and 14.35 respectively, which are greater than the table value (9.48) at .05 level of significance with df: 4. The observed values are found significant. Hence B.Ed. trainees's response pattern and university background are not found independent from each other in the context of micro teaching lesson plans prepared and delivery of lessons on above said skills.

It can be observed that 10 to 20 per cent B.Ed. trainees of IGNOU prepared 5 micro teaching lessons and taught them as per prescribed norm in the following skills:

(i) Blackboard writing skill (19.67%)
(ii) Lesson closure skill (18.00%)
(iii) Explanation skill along with example (13.33%)
(iv) Stimulus variation skill (10.33%).

In the case of above skills 39 to 58 per cent IGNOU trainees prepared 1 to 4 micro teaching lesson plans and delivered the same. Around 29 to 37 per cent B.Ed. trainees neither prepared any micro lesson plan nor taught any micro teaching lesson. Only 17 to 19 per cent B.Ed. trainees of UPRTOU prepared five lesson plans and taught fi,e micro teaching lessons according to the norms of the syllabus in the following teaching skills.

(i) Demonstration skill (18.67%)
(ii) Objective writing skill (17.33%).

In the case of objective writing and demonstration skills 32 to 51 per cent trainees of UPRTOU prepared 1 to 4 micro teaching lesson plans and taught the same. A large number of (32 to 45%) trainees neither prepared any lesson plan nor taught any micro teaching lesson. Thus, it can be concluded that the IGNOU B.Ed. trainees prepared and taught 5 micro teaching lessons each in 8 skills out of 10 teaching skills. While the UPRTOU B.Ed. trainees prepared and taught 5 micro teaching lessons each in 6 teaching skills out of 10 teaching skills. On the basis of such facts it can be concluded that the IGNOU B.Ed. trainees are comparatively more sincere than their UPRTOU counterparts with regard to preparation of lesson plans and delivery of prescribed number of micro teaching lessons.

4.2A Statements of the Trainees in the Context of Micro Teaching Lessons demonstrated by the Counsellors: University-wise

It can be noticed from Table 4.2A that the calculated χ^2 value of independence of the response pattern of B.Ed. trainees and the university background in the context of demonstration lessons by counsellors is found to be 7.69. It is less than the table value (7.81) at the 0.05 level of significance with df: 3. It is not found significant. Hence the response pattern of B.Ed. trainees and the university background in context of micro teaching skills demonstration by counsellors is found to be independent from each other.

According to majority of B.Ed. trainees (51%) of IGNOU and UPRTOU, only 2 to 5 teaching lessons have been demonstrated by the counsellors. According to 38 per cent IGNOU and UPRTOU B.Ed. trainees, 6 to 10 micro teaching lessons have been demonstrated by the counsellors.

On the basis of above analysis, it can be concluded that around 62 per cent trainees of both the category of universities have not been fully benefited by the demonstration of the counsellors on all the required micro teaching skills.

4.2B Statements of the Trainees with Reference to the Means adopted in Micro Teaching Skills Demonstration by the Counsellors: University-wise

It can be noticed from Table 4.2B that the calculated χ^2value of independence of the response pattern of B.Ed. trainees and the university background in reference to the means adopted for micro teaching skills demonstration is 0.60. It is less than the table value (5.99) at the .05 level of significance with df: 2. The observed value is not found significant. Hence the response pattern of the B.Ed. trainees and the university background about means adopted for the micro teaching skills demonstration by the counsellors are found to be independent from each other.

Table 4.2: χ^2 test of Independence of trainees' response about demonstration of skills and feedback on micro teaching practices and university background

A.

Response of trainees on number of skills demonstrated by counsellors						
UNIV.	*i (One)*	*ii (2-5)*	*iii (6-10)*	*iv (Note done)*	*Total*	*χ^2 Value*
IGNOU	31 (10.33)	149 (49.67)	107 (35.67)	13 (4.33)	300 (100.00)	7.69 N.S.
UPRTOU	16 (5.33)	155 (51.67)	122 (40.67)	7 (2.33)	300 (100.00)	
Total	47 (7.83)	304 (50.67)	229 (38.17)	20 (3.33)	600 (100.00)	

B.

Response of trainees on means adopted for demonstration micro teaching lessons by counsellors					
UNIV.	*i (Teaching by person)*	*ii (By Video Cassettes)*	*iii (Not done)*	*Total*	*χ^2 Value*
IGNOU	263 (87.67)	11 (3.67)	26 (8.67)	300 (100.00)	0.6 N.S.
UPRTOU	269 (89.67)	9 (3.00)	22 (7.33)	300 (100.00)	
Total	532 (88.67)	20 (3.33)	48 (8.00)	600 (100.00)	

C.

Response of trainees on providers of feedback in micro teaching lessons						
UNIV.	*i (Only by counsellor)*	*ii (Only by peer trainees)*	*iii (By counsellors and peer trainees)*	*iv None*	*Total*	*χ^2 Value*
IGNOU	50 (16.67)	29 (9.67)	212 (70.67)	9 (3.00)	300 (100.00)	21.44**
UPRTOU	98 (32.67)	20 (6.67)	172 (57.33)	10 (3.33)	300 (100.00)	
Total	148 (24.67)	49 (8.17)	384 (64.00)	19 (3.17)	600 (100.00)	

Note: Figures in parentheses indicate percentages.
N.S.: Not significant.
** Indicates significant at .01 level.

According to a large majority of (89%) B.Ed. trainees of both the universities, the counsellors demonstrated the micro teaching lessons by person and only in the case of 3 per cent cases the lesson demonstration was done with the help of video cassettes.

4.2C Statement of B.Ed. Trainees in Reference to the Feedback Provision in Micro-Teaching Practice: University-wise

It can be noticed from Table 4.2C that the calculated χ^2 value of independence between the response pattern of B.Ed. trainees and the university background on feedback provision in micro teaching practice done by themselves is 21.44, which is greater than the table value (7.81) at the .05 level of significance with df: 3. The observed values is found significant. Hence the response pattern of B.Ed. trainees's and university background in the context of feedback provision in micro teaching done practiced by the trainees are not found independent from each other.

It can be observed that according to majority of B.Ed. trainees (71%) of IGNOU, the provision of feedback in micro teaching practice have been adhered to by the counsellors as well as the peer trainees. On the contrary according to 57 per cent trainees of UPRTOU, the feedback in micro teaching practice had been provided by the counsellors as well the peer trainees.

Problems Faced by B.Ed. Trainees during Micro Teaching Practices

The response to the open ended questions on the problems concerning micro teaching revealed that following problems were faced by B.Ed. trainees during micro teaching practices:

General Problems

- Lack of appropriate feedback given by the counsellors.
- Shortage of time.
- Micro lesson plan not in accordance with the mental capacity of fellow trainees.
- Problem of distinction between specific and general adjectives.
- Lack of confidence among trainees.
- Problem of hesitation among trainees.

- Lack of arrangements to sit in small groups for practice of micro teaching lessons.
- Problem of indiscipline among fellow trainees.
- Problem of repetition of useless words.

Problems Related to Skills

- In framing/making introductory questions.
- In preparing and delivery of questioning skill lesson.
- Problem of not getting the topic through introductory questions.
- Problem of not getting response due to heterogeneous background of fellow trainees.
- In delivery of stimulus variation lesson.
- Problem in preparing and using teaching aids during micro teaching practices.

4.3 Statement of the Counsellors with Reference to the Means Adopted in Micro Teaching Skills Demonstration by Themselves: University-wise

It can be noticed from Table 4.3 that the calculated χ^2 value of independence between the response pattern of B.Ed. trainees and the university background about means adopted for micro teaching skills demonstration by themselves is 2.03, which is less than the table value (7.81) at the .05 level of significance with df: 3. It is not found

Table 4.3: χ^2 test of independence of counsellors response about technique of demonstration on teaching skills and university background

Response of counsellors about techniques of demonstration on teaching skills						
UNIV.	*i (Teaching by person)*	*ii (By video cassettes)*	*iii (i and ii)*	*iv (L.C.D. Computer)*	*Total*	χ^2 *Value*
IGNOU	21 (70.00)	1 (3.33)	7 (23.33)	1 (3.33)	30 (100.00)	2.03 N.S.
UPRTOU	18 (60.00)	1 (3.33)	7 (23.33)	4 (13.33)	30 (100.00)	
Total	39 (65.00)	2 (3.33)	14 (23.33)	5 (8.33)	60 (100.00)	

Note: Figures in parentheses indicate percentages. N.S.: Not significant

significant. It reveals the response pattern of B.Ed. trainees and the university background in the context of means adopted by the counsellors are found to be independent from each other.

It can be observed that near about 65 per cent counsellors of IGNOU and UPRTOU demonstrated the micro teaching skills by person and in case of 23 per cent cases the skills demonstration was done with help of video cassettes. The counsellors response regarding the means of demonstration of micro teaching lessons is very much different from that of B.Ed. trainees, since a large majority of the trainees indicated demonstration of lessons by person. As per trainees, the video lesson based demonstration was very much negligible, i.e. only 3 per cent.

Problems Faced by Counsellors during Micro Teaching Practices

The response to open ended question revealed that following problems were faced by counsellors during micro teaching practices:

General Problems

- Trainees not participating with interest.
- Trainees' not preparing micro teaching lesson plans properly.
- While practicing skills the trainees do not focus on the specific skill components.
- Shortage of time.
- Limited time for feedbacks and re-teach the micro lessons.

Problems Related to Resources and Skills

- Lack of appropriate devices for giving feedbacks (like-language laboratory, audio tape, VCR etc.)
- Lack of availability of teaching aids in study centres.
- Evaluation sheet could not be prepared by trainees.
- Lesson plans prepared by trainees were not up to the mark.
- Micro lesson plans are not prepared by trainees as per skill components.
- Lack of arrangement for small group activities.

It was also clear from the observations done by researcher that in most of the study centres there was disproportion between the availability of counsellors and number of students in various subjects and the room arrangement was not up to the mark. Due to this the students and counsellors have to face number for micro teaching practices.

Interview with Counsellors about Process Adopted for making B.Ed. Trainees Competent in Preparing Micro Lesson Plan

The selected counsellors of IGNOU and UPRTOU informed that the theoretical knowledge regarding preparation of micro teaching lesson plans was provided to B.Ed. trainees. Demonstrations of lessons were given during workshops. Only a handful of counsellors of IGNOU informed that apart from the above mentioned activities, trainees prepared micro lesson plans during the workshop and feedback was provided by the counsellors, whereas counsellors of UPRTOU mentioned that homework was given for the preparation of micro teaching lesson plans. Feedback was provided on the next consecutive day.

Interview with Counsellors about Process Adopted for Micro Teaching Practices during Workshops

Most of the counsellors of IGNOU and UPRTOU interviewed informed that practice of various skills was conducted in small peer groups subject-wise during workshops. Some of the counsellors of UPRTOU informed that practice of any one single skill was conducted during workshops due to limited time. It was not feasible to practice all the prescribed skills. As per the curriculum guideline all the skills must be practiced by trainees to attain mastery in them. It was not feasible to achieve the norm due to limitation of time and resources in correspondence to student strength and availability of counsellors in the study centres.

Interview with Counsellors about Provisions of Feedback in Micro Teaching Practices

The selected counsellors of IGNOU as well as UPRTOU informed that after observing the micro teaching practice, verbal and written feedback is provided to the B.Ed. trainees in group as well as individually. Due to lack of time only a few B.Ed. trainees are made to re-prepare the micro lesson plans and practice the same. Very few counsellors of UPRTOU mentioned that only a few B.Ed. trainees are informed about their specific faults and practiced them till the error was rectified.

4.4 Response of B.Ed. Trainees on Relevance of Micro Teaching: University-wise

It can be noticed from Table 4.4 that the calculated χ^2 values of independence between the response pattern of B.Ed. trainees and the university background in reference to the relevance of preparation and delivery of micro lesson plans by themselves and demonstration of micro lesson plans by the counsellors are found 27.25 and 15.55 respectively. The obtained χ^2 values are greater than the table value

Table 4.4: χ^2 test of Independence of trainees' response about relevance of training process related micro teaching and university background

Response of trainees on level of relevance of micro teaching						
Statements	*UNIV.*	*Highly Agree*	*Agree*	*Disagree*	*Total*	χ^2 *Values*
1. Preparing and delivery micro lesson plans is related to the development of teaching competency.	IGNOU	233 (77.67)	56 (18.67)	11 (3.67)	300 (100.00)	27.25**
	UPRTOU	278 (92.67)	20 (6.67)	2 (0.67)	300 (100.00)	
	Total	511 (85.17)	76 (12.67)	13 (2.17)	600 (100.00)	
2. Demonstration of micro lesson plan by counsellors is related to your subject-teaching.	IGNOU	219 (73.00)	63 (21.00)	18 (6.0)	300 (100.00)	15.55**
	UPRTOU0	257 (85.66)	30 (10.00)	13 (4.33)	300 (100.00)	
	Total	476 (79.33)	93 (15.50)	31 (5.17)	600 (100.00)	
3. Feedback provided during micro teaching is in accordance to your competency.	IGNOU	208 (69.33)	74 (24.67)	18 (6.00)	300 (100.00)	3.01 N.S.
	UPRTOU	226 (75.33)	62 (20.67)	12 (4.00)	300 (100.00)	
	Total	434 (72.33)	136 (22.67)	30 (5.00)	600 (100.00)	

Note: Figures in parentheses indicate percentages. N.S.: Not significant.
** Indicates significant at .01 level.

(5.99) at the .05 level of significance with df: 2. The observed values are found significant. Hence, response pattern of B.Ed. trainees and the university background are not found independent from each other in the context of relevance of preparation and delivery of micro lesson plans by B.Ed. trainees and demonstration of micro lesson plans by the counsellors.

It can be observed that majority of B.Ed. trainees (93%) of UPRTOU and 78 per cent B.Ed. trainees of IGNOU considered preparation of micro lesson plans relevant. 86 per cent B.Ed. trainees of UPRTOU and 73 per cent B.Ed. trainees of IGNOU considered demonstration of micro lessons by counsellors relevant.

It can be noticed from Table 4.4 that the calculated χ^2 value of independence between the response pattern of B.Ed. trainees and the university background in reference to the relevance of feedback provided during micro teaching is found 3.01. It is less than the table value (5.99) at .05 level of significance with df: 2. It is not found significant. Hence the response pattern of B.Ed. trainees and the university background about relevance of feedback provided during micro teaching is found to be independent from each other.

It can be observed that approximately 72 per cent B.Ed. trainees of both the universities IGNOU and UPRTOU considered feedback provided during micro teaching relevant.

4.5 Response of Counsellors on Relevance of Micro Teaching: University-wise

It can be noticed from Table 4.4 that the calculated χ^2 values of independence between the response pattern of counsellors and the university background in reference to the relevance of demonstration of micro lessons by themselves is 2.00. It is less than the table value (5.99) at the .05 level of significance with df: 2. The observed value is not found significant. Hence response pattern of counsellors and the university background are found independent from each other in the context of relevance of demonstration of micro lessons by the counsellors.

It can be observed that according to majority of counsellors (97.00%) of both the universities IGNOU and UPRTOU, demonstration of micro lessons was considered relevant.

Table 4.5: χ^2 test of independence of counsellors response in relation to relevance of micro teaching process of distance B.Ed. training programme and university background

Response of counsellors on level of relevance of micro teaching						
Statement	*UNIV.*	*Highly Agree*	*Agree*	*Disagree*	*Total*	χ^2 *Value*
Demonstration on micro lesson plan by you is related to competency development of B.Ed. trainees.	IGNOU	29 (96.67)	0 (0.00)	1 (3.33)	30 (100.00)	2.00 N.S.
	UPRTOU	29 (96.67)	1 (3.33)	0 (0.00)	30 (100.00)	
	Total	58 (96.67)	1 (1.67)	1 (1.67)	60 (100.00)	

Note: Figures in parentheses indicate percentages.
N.S.: Not significant.

Interview with Counsellors about Relevance of Micro Teaching Practices

The selected counsellors of both the universities IGNOU as well as UPRTOU informed that they consider practice of micro teaching relevant as it enhances the teaching skills, it helps in the effective demonstration of lessons, prepares B.Ed. trainees for the real classroom teaching and delivery of macro lesson plans. Few counsellors of UPRTOU also mentioned that practice in micro teaching assist B.Ed. trainees' help in the construction of good questions and enhances their explanatory skills too.

4.6A Response of B.Ed. Trainees about Effectiveness of Training Process of Micro Teaching Practice: University-wise

It can be noticed from Table 4.6A that the calculated χ^2 values of independence between response pattern of B.Ed. trainees and university background on effectiveness of micro teaching lesson plans prepared and taught by them in introduction skill, objective writing skill, stimulus variation skill, illustration with example skill, lesson closure skill and homework assignment skill are found to be 5.96, 2.69, 3.69, 1.65, 5.91 and 5.70 respectively. The obtained χ^2 values are less than the table value (5.99) at .05 level of significance with df: 2. The obtained χ^2 values are not found significant. Hence the response pattern

Table 4.6: χ^2 test of Independence of trainees' response about effectiveness of training process of micro teaching practices and university background, skill-wise

A.

		Benefits of micro teaching practices				
Development of skills	*UNIV.*	*More extent*	*Some extent*	*Least*	*Total*	χ^2 *Values*
1-i. Introduction skill	IGNOU	246 (82.00)	48 (16.00)	6 (2.00)	300 (100.00)	5.96 N.S.
	UPRTOU	259 (86.33)	30 (10.00)	11 (3.67)	300 (100.00)	
	Total	505 (84.17)	78 (13.00)	17 (2.83)	600 (100.00)	
ii. Objective writing skill	IGNOU	237 (79.00)	52 (17.33)	11 (3.67)	300 (100.00)	2.69 N.S.
	UPRTOU	252 (84.00)	38 (12.67)	10 (3.33)	300 (100.00)	
	Total	489 (81.50)	90 (15.00)	21 (3.50)	600 (100.00)	
iii. Questioning skill	IGNOU	230 (76.67)	61 (20.33)	9 (3.00)	300 (100.00)	12.09**
	UPRTOU	249 (83.00)	33 (11.00)	18 (6.00)	300 (100.00)	
	Total	479 (79.83)	94 (15.67)	27 (4.50)	600 (100.00)	
iv. Stimulus variation skill	IGNOU	218 (72.67)	67 (22.33)	15 (5.00)	300 (100.00)	3.69 N.S.
	UPRTOU	225 (75.00)	52 (17.33)	23 (7.67)	300 (100.00)	
	Total	443 (73.83)	119 (19.83)	38 (6.33)	600 (100.00)	
v. Reinforcement skill	IGNOU	224 (74.67)	67 (22.33)	9 (3.00)	300 (100.00)	20.23**
	UPRTOU	249 (83.00)	30 (10.00)	21 (7.00)	300 (100.00)	
	Total	473 (78.83)	97 (16.17)	30 (5.00)	600 (100.00)	

(Contd.)

vi.	Illustration skill	IGNOU	204 (68.00)	83 (27.67)	13 (4.33)	300 (100.00)	1.65 N.S.
		UPRTOU	214 (71.33)	70 (23.33)	16 (5.33)	300 (100.00)	
		Total	418 (69.67)	153 (25.50)	29 (4.83)	600 (100.00)	
vii.	Explanation skill	IGNOU	229 (76.33)	62 (20.67)	9 (3.00)	300 (100.00)	9.49**
		UPRTOU	258 (86.00)	35 (11.67)	7 (2.33)	300 (100.00)	
		Total	487 (81.17)	97 (16.17)	16 (2.67)	600 (100.00)	
viii.	Blackboard writing skill	IGNOU	239 (79.67)	57 (19.00)	4 (1.33)	300 (100.00)	10.23**
		UPRTOU	244 (81.33)	40 (13.33)	16 (5.33)	300 (100.00)	
		Total	483 (80.50)	97 (16.17)	20 (3.33)	600 (100.00)	
ix.	Demonstration skill	IGNOU	233 (77.67)	56 (18.67)	11 (3.67)	300 (100.00)	7.21*
		UPRTOU	244 (81.33)	36 (12.00)	20 (6.67)	300 (100.00)	
		Total	477 (79.50)	92 (15.33)	31 (5.17)	600 (100.00)	
x.	Lesson closure skill	IGNOU	224 (74.67)	60 (20.00)	16 (5.33)	300 (100.00)	5.91 N.S.
		UPRTOU	236 (78.67)	40 (13.33)	24 (8.00)	300 (100.00)	
		Total	460 (76.67)	100 (16.67)	40 (6.67)	600 (100.00)	
xi.	To decide homework skill	IGNOU	233 (77.67)	47 (15.67)	20 (6.67)	300 (100.00)	5.70 N.S.
		UPRTOU	255 (85.00)	29 (9.67)	16 (5.33)	300 (100.00)	
		Total	488 (81.33)	76 (12.67)	36 (6.00)	600 (100.00)	

(Contd.)

B.

Benefits of feedback in micro teaching practices						
Development of skills	*UNIV.*	*More extent*	*Some extent*	*Least*	*Total*	*χ^2 Values*
2-i. Introductory Lesson Skill	IGNOU	238 (79.33)	50 (16.67)	12 (4.00)	300 (100.00)	14.97**
	UPRTOU	263 (87.67)	20 (6.67)	17 (5.67)	300 (100.00)	
	Total	501 (83.50)	70 (11.67)	29 (4.83)	600 (100.00)	
ii. Objective writing skill	IGNOU	227 (75.67)	60 (20.00)	13 (4.33)	300 (100.00)	3.42 N.S.
	UPRTOU	244 (81.33)	43 (14.33)	13 (4.33)	300 (100.00)	
	Total	471 (78.50)	103 (17.17)	26 (4.33)	600 (100.00)	
iii. Questioning skill	IGNOU	243 (81.00)	45 (15.00)	12 (4.00)	300 (100.00)	11.32**
	UPRTOU	253 (84.33)	23 (7.67)	24 (8.00)	300 (100.00)	
	Total	496 (82.67)	68 (11.33)	36 (6.00)	600 (100.00)	
iv. Stimulus variation skill	IGNOU	226 (75.33)	66 (22.00)	8 (2.67)	300 (100.00)	6.67*
	UPRTOU	223 (74.33)	56 (18.67)	21 (7.00)	300 (100.00)	
	Total	449 (74.83)	122 (20.33)	29 (4.83)	600 (100.00)	
v. Reinforcement skill	IGNOU	220 (73.33)	61 (20.33)	19 (6.33)	300 (100.00)	0.89 N.S.
	UPRTOU	230 (76.67)	53 (17.67)	17 (5.67)	300 (100.00)	
	Total	450 (75.00)	114 (19.00)	36 (6.00)	600 (100.00)	
vi. Illustration with example skill	IGNOU	217 (72.33)	64 (21.33)	19 (6.33)	300 (100.00)	9.54**
	UPRTOU	245 (81.67)	36 (12.00)	19 (6.33)	300 (100.00)	
	Total	462 (77.00)	100 (16.67)	38 (6.33)	600 (100.00)	
vii. Explanation skill	IGNOU	225 (75.00)	58 (19.33)	17 (5.67)	300 (100.00)	7.13*
	UPRTOU	250 (83.33)	35 (11.67)	15 (5.00)	300 (100.00)	

(Contd.)

	Total	475 (79.17)	93 (15.50)	32 (5.33)	600 (100.00)	
viii. Blackboard writing skill	IGNOU	228 (76.00)	57 (19.00)	15 (5.00)	300 (100.00)	18.15**
	UPRTOU	252 (84.00)	23 (7.67)	25 (8.33)	300 (100.00)	
	Total	480 (80.00)	80 (13.33)	40 (6.67)	600 (100.00)	
ix. Demonstration skill	IGNOU	215 (71.67)	58 (19.33)	27 (9.00)	300 (100.00)	17.21**
	UPRTOU	252 (84.00)	24 (8.00)	24 (8.00)	300 (100.00)	
	Total	467 (77.83)	82 (13.67)	51 (8.50)	600 (100.00)	
x. Lesson closure skill	IGNOU	230 (76.67)	51 (17.00)	19 (6.33)	300 (100.00)	3.51 N.S.
	UPRTOU	246 (82.00)	35 (11.67)	19 (6.33)	300 (100.00)	
	Total	476 (79.33)	86 (14.33)	38 (6.33)	600 (100.00)	

Note: Figures in parentheses indicate percentages.
N.S.: Not significant
* Indicates significant at .05 level.
** Indicates significant at .01 level.

of B.Ed. trainees and the university background are found independent from each other.

It can be observed that in these skills majority of B.Ed. trainees (70 to 84%) of IGNOU and UPRTOU considered preparation of micro lesson plans effective:

(i) Introduction skill (84.17%)
(ii) Objective writing skill (81.50%)
(iii) Assignment/homework skill (81.33%)
(iv) Lesson closure skill (76.67%)
(v) Stimulus variation skill (73.83%)
(vi) Illustration with example skill (69.67%).

From the above analysis it is clear that according to 69.67 to 84.17 per cent B.Ed. trainees of IGNOU and UPRTOU, preparation of micro lessons is effective in the development of some of the teaching skills.

It can be noticed from Table 4.6A that the calculated χ^2 values of independence between response pattern of B.Ed. trainees and university background on effectiveness of micro teaching lesson plans prepared and taught by them in questioning skill, reinforcement skill, explanation skill, blackboard writing skill and demonstration skill are found to be 12.09, 20.23, 9.49, 10.23 and 7.21 respectively. The obtained χ^2 values are greater than the table value (5.99) at .05 level of significance with df: 2. The obtained χ^2 values are found significant. Hence the response pattern of B.Ed. trainees and the university background are not found independent from each other.

It can be observed that 81 to 86 per cent B.Ed. trainees of UPRTOU considered preparation of micro lessons effective in the development of following skills:

(i) Explanation skill (86.00%)
(ii) Questioning skill (83.00%)
(iii) Reinforcement skill (83.00%)
(iv) Blackboard writing skill (81.33%)
(v) Demonstration skill (81.33%).

It can also be observed that 75 to 80 per cent B.Ed. trainees of IGNOU considered preparation of micro lessons effective in the development of following skills:

(i) Blackboard writing skill (79.67%)
(ii) Demonstration skill (77.67%)
(iii) Questioning skill (76.67%)
(iv) Explanation skill (76.33%)
(v) Reinforcement skill (74.67%).

It is clear from the above analysis that as compared to IGNOU, B.Ed. trainees of UPRTOU considered preparation of micro lesson plans more effective in the development of teaching skills.

4.6B Response of B.Ed. Trainees about Effectiveness of Feedback in Micro Teaching Practices: University-wise

It can be noticed from Table 4.6B that the calculated χ^2 values of independence between response pattern of B.Ed. trainees and university background in relation to effectiveness of feedback provided during micro teaching practice for the development of introduction skill, questioning skill, stimulus variation skill, illustration with example skill, explanation skill, blackboard writing skill, and demonstration skill are found to be 14.97, 11.32, 6.67, 9.54, 7.13, 18.15, and 17.21 respectively. The obtained χ^2 values are greater than the table value (5.99) at .05 level of significance with df: 2. The obtained χ^2 values are found significant. Hence the response pattern of B.Ed. trainees and the university background in reference to effectiveness of feedback provided for the development of teaching skills are not found independent from each other.

It can be observed that 74 to 88 per cent B.Ed. trainees of UPRTOU considered that feedback provided during micro-teaching is effective in the development of following teaching skills:

(i) Introduction skill (87.67%)
(ii) Questioning skill (84.33%)
(iii) Demonstration skill (84.00%)
(iv) Blackboard writing skill (84.00%)
(v) Explanation skill (83.33%)
(vi) Illustration with example skill (81.67%)
(vii) Stimulus variation skill (74.33%).

It can also be observed that 72 to 81 per cent B.Ed. trainees of IGNOU considered that feedback provided during micro teaching is effective in the development of following teaching skills:

(i) Questioning skill (81.00%)
(ii) Introduction skill (79.33%)
(iii) Blackboard writing skill (76.00%)
(iv) Stimulus variation skill (75.33%)
(v) Explanation skill (75.00%)
(vi) Illustration with example skill (72.33%)
(vii) Demonstration skill (71.67%).

From the above analysis it is clear that as compared to IGNOU B.Ed. trainees, UPRTOU B.Ed. trainees considered feedback provided during micro teaching more effective in the development of teaching skills.

It can be noticed from Table 4.6B that the calculated χ^2 values of independence between response pattern of B.Ed. trainees and university background in relation to effectiveness of feedback provided during micro teaching practice for the development of objective writing skill, stimulus variation skill, and lesson closure skill are found to be 3.42, 0.89, and 3.51 respectively. The obtained χ^2 values are less than the table value (5.99) at .05 level of significance with df: 2. The obtained χ^2 values are not found significant. Hence the response pattern of B.Ed. trainees and the university background in reference to effectiveness of feedback provided for the developments of teaching skills are found independent from each other.

It can be observed that 75 to 79 per cent B.Ed. trainees of IGNOU and UPRTOU considered that feedback provided during micro teaching effective in the development of the following teaching skills:

(i) Lesson closure skill (79.33%)
(ii) Objective writing skill (78.50%)
(iii) Reinforcement skill (75.00%).

From the above analysis it is clear that according to large majority B.Ed. trainees (75 to 79.33%) of IGNOU and UPRTOU feedback provided during micro teaching are found effective in the development of most of the teaching skills.

Interview with Counsellors about Effectiveness of Micro Teaching Practices

The selected counsellors of both the universities IGNOU as well as UPRTOU informed that they consider practice in micro teaching effective for making trainees skilful in teaching to a large extent, their thinking pattern becomes planned, they get knowledge regarding teaching skills and, they gain confidence. In addition they also informed that practice in micro teaching integration of various teaching skills made their teaching effective.

4.7A Response of Counsellors about Effectiveness of Training Process of Micro Teaching Practice: University-wise

It can be noticed from Table 4.7A that the calculated χ^2 values of independence between response pattern of counsellors and university background in relation to effectiveness of feedback provided during micro teaching practice for the development of introduction skill,

Table 4.7: χ^2 test of independence of counsellors response about effectiveness of micro teaching of distance B.Ed. programme and university background, skills-wise

A.

		Benefits of micro teaching practices				
Development of teaching skills	*UNIV.*	*More extent*	*Some extent*	*Least*	*Total*	χ^2 *Values*
1-i. Introduction skill	IGNOU	25 (83.33)	5 (16.67)	0 (0.00)	30 (100.00)	1.11 N.S.
	UPRTOU	25 (83.33)	4 (13.33)	1 (3.33)	30 (100.00)	
	Total	50 (83.33)	9 (15.00)	1 (1.67)	60 (100.00)	
ii. Objective writing skill	IGNOU	23 (76.67)	7 (23.33)	0 (0.00)	30 (100.00)	1.02 N.S.
	UPRTOU	22 (73.33)	7 (23.33)	1 (3.33)	30 (100.00)	
	Total	45 (75.00)	14 (23.33)	1 (1.67)	60 (100.00)	
iii. Questioning skill	IGNOU	26 (86.67)	4 (13.33)	0 (0.00)	30 (100.00)	1.69 N.S.
	UPRTOU	27 (90.00)	2 (6.67)	1 (3.33)	30 (100.00)	
	Total	53 (88.33)	6 (10.00)	1 (1.67)	60 (100.00)	
iv. Stimulus variation skill	IGNOU	21 (70.00)	8 (26.67)	1 (3.33)	30 (100.00)	3.47 N.S.
	UPRTOU	24 (80.00)	3 (10.00)	3 (10.00)	30 (100.00)	
	Total	45 (75.00)	11 (18.33)	4 (6.67)	60 (100.00)	
v. Reinforcement skill	IGNOU	22 (73.33)	7 (23.33)	1 (3.33)	30 (100.00)	9.23**
	UPRTOU	30 (100.00)	0 (0.00)	0 (0.00)	30 (100.00)	
	Total	52 (86.67)	7 (11.67)	1 (1.67)	60 (100.00)	
vi. Illustration with example skill	IGNOU	23 (76.67)	6 (20.00)	1 (3.33)	30 (100.00)	1.02 N.S.
	UPRTOU	24 (80.00)	6 (20.00)	0 (0.00)	30 (100.00)	

(Contd.)

	Total	47 (78.33)	12 (20.00)	1 (1.67)	60 (100.00)	
vii. Explanation skill	IGNOU	23 (76.67)	6 (20.00)	1 (3.33)	30 (100.00)	1.58 N.S.
	UPRTOU	26 (86.67)	4 (13.33)	0 (0.00)	30 (100.00)	
	Total	49 (81.67)	10 (16.67)	1 (1.67)	60 (100.00)	
viii. Blackboard writing skill	IGNOU	23 (76.67)	6 (20.00)	1 (3.33)	30 (100.00)	1.58 N.S.
	UPRTOU	26 (86.67)	4 (13.33)	0 (0.00)	30 (100.00)	
	Total	49 (81.67)	10 (16.67)	1 (1.67)	60 (100.00)	
ix: Demonstration skill	IGNOU	26 (86.67)	3 (10.00)	1 (3.33)	30 (100.00)	3.61 N.S.
	UPRTOU	22 (73.33)	8 (26.67)	0 (0.00)	30 (100.00)	
	Total	48 (80.00)	11 (18.33)	1 (1.67)	60 (100.00)	
x. Lesson closer skill	IGNOU	23 (76.67)	6 (20.00)	1 (3.33)	30 (100.00)	1.02 N.S.
	UPRTOU	24 (80.00)	6 (20.00)	0 (0.00)	30 (100.00)	
	Total	47 (78.33)	12 (20.00)	1 (1.67)	60 (100.00)	
xi. Decide homework	IGNOU	23 (76.67)	6 (20.00)	1 (3.33)	30 (100.00)	3.49 N.S.
	UPRTOU	28 (93.33)	2 (6.67)	0 (0.00)	30 (100.00)	
	Total	51 (85.00)	8 (13.33)	1 (1.67)	60 (100.00)	

B.

Benefits of feedback during micro teaching practices

Development of teaching skills	*UNIV.*	*More extent*	*Some extent*	*Least*	*Total*	χ^2 *Values*
2-i. Introduction skill	IGNOU	28 (93.33)	2 (6.67)	0 (0.00)	30 (100.00)	3.02 N.S.
	UPRTOU	29 (96.67)	0 (0.00)	1 (3.33)	30 (100.00)	

(Contd.)

		Total	57 (95.00)	2 (3.33)	1 (1.67)	60 (100.00)	
ii.	Objective writing skill	IGNOU	25 (83.33)	5 (16.67)	0 (0.00)	30 (100.00)	1.11 N.S.
		UPRTOU	25 (83.33)	4 (13.33)	1 (3.33)	30 (100.00)	
		Total	50 (83.33)	9 (15.00)	1 (1.67)	60 (100.00)	
iii.	Questioning skill	IGNOU	26 (86.67)	4 (13.33)	0 (0.00)	30 (100.00)	1.69 N.S.
		UPRTOU	27 (90.00)	2 (6.67)	1 (3.33)	30 (100.00)	
		Total	53 (88.33)	6 (10.00)	1 (1.67)	60 (100.00)	
iv.	Stimulus variation skill	IGNOU	24 (80.00)	6 (20.00)	0 (0.00)	30 (100.00)	1.42 N.S.
		UPRTOU	25 (83.33)	4 (13.33)	1 (3.33)	30 (100.00)	
		Total	49 (81.67)	10 (16.67)	1 (1.67)	60 (100.00)	
v.	Reinforcement skill	IGNOU	26 (86.67)	3 (10.00)	1 (3.33)	30 (100.00)	3.41 N.S.
		UPRTOU	28 (93.33)	0 (0.00)	2 (6.67)	30 (100.00)	
		Total	54 (90.00)	3 (5.00)	3 (5.00)	60 (100.00)	
vi.	Illustration with example skill	IGNOU	23 (76.67)	6 (20.00)	1 (3.33)	30 (100.00)	0.36 N.S.
		UPRTOU	22 (73.33)	6 (20.00)	2 (6.67)	30 (100.00)	
		Total	45 (75.00)	12 (20.00)	3 (5.00)	60 (100.00)	
vii.	Explanation skill	IGNOU	21 (70.00)	7 (23.33)	2 (6.67)	30 (100.00)	2.09 N.S.
		UPRTOU	22 (73.33)	8 (26.67)	0 (0.00)	30 (100.00)	
		Total	43 (71.67)	15 (25.00)	2 (3.33)	60 (100.00)	
viii.	Blackboard writing skill	IGNOU	21 (70.00)	8 (26.67)	1 (3.33)	30 (100.00)	10.5**
		UPRTOU	30 (100.00)	0 (0.00)	0 (0.00)	30 (100.00)	

(Contd.)

	Total	51 (85.00)	8 (13.33)	1 (1.67)	60 (100.00)	
ix. Demonstration skill	IGNOU	23 (76.67)	5 (16.67)	2 (6.67)	30 (100.00)	3.88 N.S.
	UPRTOU	20 (66.67)	10 (33.33)	0 (0.00)	30 (100.00)	
	Total	43 (71.67)	15 (25.00)	2 (3.33)	60 (100.00)	
x. Lesson closer skill	IGNOU	24 (80.00)	4 (13.33)	2 (6.67)	30 (100.00)	6.67*
	UPRTOU	30 (100.00)	0 (0.00)	0 (0.00)	30 (100.00)	
	Total	54 (90.00)	4 (6.67)	2 (3.33)	60 (100.00)	

Note: Figures in parentheses indicate percentages.
N.S.: Not significant
* Indicates significant at .05 level.
** Indicates significant at .01 level.

objective writing skill, questioning skill, stimulus variation skill, illustration with example skill, explanation skill, blackboard writing skill, demonstration skill and homework giving skill are found to be 1.11, 1.02, 1.69, 3.47, 1.02, 1.58, 1.58, 3.61, 1.02 and 3.49 respectively. The obtained χ^2 values are less than the table value (5.99) at .05 level of significance with df: 2. The obtained χ^2 values are not found significant. Hence the response pattern of counsellors and the university background in reference to effectiveness of feedback provided for the development of teaching skills are found independent from each other.

It can be observed that 75 to 88 per cent counsellors of IGNOU and UPRTOU considered micro teaching effective in the development of following teaching skills:

(i) Questioning skill (88.33%)
(ii) Homework giving skill (85.00%)
(iii) Introduction skill (83.33%)
(iv) Blackboard writing skill (81.67%)
(v) Explanation skill (81.67%)
(vi) Demonstration skill (80.00%)
(vii) Lesson closure skill (78.33%)
(viii) Illustration with example skill (78.33%)

(ix) Stimulus variation skill (75.00%)
(x) Objective writing skill (75.00%).

It can be noticed from Table 4.7A that the calculated χ^2 values of independence between response pattern of counsellors and university background in relation to the enhancement of reinforcement skill due to practice of micro teaching and preparation of micro lesson plans is 9.23. Which is greater than the table value (5.99) at .05 level of significance with df: 2. The obtained χ^2 value is found significant. Hence the response pattern of counsellors and the university background in relation to enhancement of reinforcement skill due to practice of micro teaching and preparation of micro lesson plans are not found independent from each other.

It can be observed that cent-per-cent counsellors of UPRTOU and 73 per cent counsellors of IGNOU considered that reinforcement skill is enhanced due to micro teaching practice and preparation of micro lesson plans.

4.7B Response of Counsellors about Effectiveness of Feedback on Micro Teaching Practice: University-wise

It can be noticed from Table 4.7B that the calculated χ^2 values of independence between response pattern of counsellors and university background in relation to effectiveness of feedback provided during micro teaching practice for the development of introduction skill, objective writing skill, questioning skill, stimulus variation skill, reinforcement skill, illustration with example skill, explanation skill and demonstration skill are found to be 3.02, 1.11, 1.69, 1.42, 3.41, 0.36, 2.09 and 3.88 respectively. The obtained χ^2 values are less than the table value (5.99) at .05 level of significance with df: 2. The obtained χ^2 values are not found significant. Hence the response pattern of counsellors and the university background in reference to effectiveness of feedback provided for the developments of teaching skills are found independent from each other.

It can be observed that majority of the counsellors (72 to 95%) of IGNOU and UPRTOU considered feedback provided during micro teaching effective for the development of following teaching skills:

(i) Introduction skill (95.00%)
(ii) Reinforcement skill (90.00%)

(iii) Questioning skill (88.33%)
(iv) Stimulus variation skill (81.67%)
(v) Objective writing skill (80.33%)
(vi) Illustration with example skill (75.00%)
(vii) Demonstration skill (71.67%)
(viii) Explanation skill (71.67%).

It can be noticed from Table 4.7B that the calculated χ^2 values of independence between response pattern of counsellors and university background in relation to effectiveness of feedback provided during micro teaching practice for the development of black-board writing skill and lesson closure skill are found to be 10.50 and 6.67 respectively. The obtained χ^2 values are greater than the table value (5.99) at .05 level of significance with df: 2. The obtained χ^2 values are found significant. Hence the response pattern of counsellors and the university background in reference to effectiveness of feedback provided for the developments of teaching skills are not found independent from each other.

It can be observed that cent per cent counsellors of UPRTOU considered that feedback provided during micro teaching is helpful in the development of following teaching skills:

(i) Blackboard writing skill
(ii) Lesson closure skill.

It can also be observed that 70 to 80 per cent counsellors of IGNOU considered that feedback provided during micro teaching is helpful in the development of following teaching skills:

(i) Lesson closure skill (80.00%)
(ii) Blackboard writing skill (70.00%).

From the above analysis it is clear that as compared to IGNOU, counsellors of UPRTOU consider feedback provided during micro teaching practice more effective in the development of above mentioned teaching skills.

On the basis of above mentioned data it is clear that only 13 to 20 per cent B.Ed. trainees of IGNOU and UPRTOU considered that micro teaching practice had been done by B.Ed. trainees near to the standard of B.Ed. course in the following skills:

(i) Introduction skill (20.00%)
(ii) Questioning skill (15.33%)
(iii) Explanation skill (15.00%)
(iv) Reinforcement skill (13.33%).

According to 10 to 20 per cent B.Ed. trainees of IGNOU, practice have been done by themselves by preparing lesson plans in the following four teaching skills:

(i) Blackboard writing skill (19.67%)
(ii) Lesson closure skill (18.00%)
(iii) Illustration with example skill (13.33%)
(iv) Stimulus variation skill (10.33%).

According to 17 to 19 per cent B.Ed. trainees of UPRTOU, practice have been done by themselves by preparing micro lesson plans in the following two teaching skills.

(i) Demonstration skill (18.67%)
(ii) Objective writing skill (17.33%).

From the above analysis it is clear that as compared to UPRTOU, IGNOU B.Ed. trainees practiced more *via* preparing micro lesson plans.

Majority of B.Ed. trainees (93.00%) of UPRTOU and 78 per cent B.Ed. trainees of IGNOU considered that micro teaching practice was relevant. Majority of B.Ed. trainees (86%) of UPRTOU and 78 per cent B.Ed. trainees of IGNOU considered that demonstration by counsellors on micro teaching skills relevant. 72 per cent B.Ed. trainees of both the open universities IGNOU and UPRTOU considered feedback provided during micro teaching relevant.

Majority of counsellors (97.00%) of both the universities, IGNOU and UPRTOU, considered feedback provided by them during micro teaching relevant.

Majority of B.Ed. trainees (70 to 84%) of IGNOU and UPRTOU considered practice of micro teaching by preparing micro lesson plans were effective in the following five teaching skills:

(i) Introduction skill (84.17%)
(ii) Objective writing skill (81.33%)

(iii) Homework assignment skill (81.33)
(iv) Lesson closure skill (76.67%)
(v) Stimulus variation skill (73.83%)
(vi) Illustration with example skill (69.67%).

Majority of B.Ed. trainees (81 to 86%) of UPRTOU considered practice of micro teaching after preparing micro lesson plans effective in the following five teaching skills:

(i) Explanation skill (86.00%)
(ii) Reinforcement skill (83.00%)
(iii) Questioning skill (83.00%)
(iv) Demonstration skill (81.33%)
(v) Blackboard writing skill (81.33%).

Majority of B.Ed. trainees 75 to 80 per cent of IGNOU considered practice of micro teaching after preparing micro lesson plans effective in the following five teaching skills:

(i) Blackboard writing skill (79.67%)
(ii) Demonstration skill (77.67%)
(iii) Questioning skill (76.67%)
(iv) Explanation skill (76.33%)
(v) Reinforcement skill (74.67%).

Majority of B.Ed. trainees (74 to 88%) of UPRTOU considered feedback provided during micro teaching effective in the development of following seven teaching skills:

(i) Introduction skill (87.67%)
(ii) Questioning skill (84.33%)
(iii) Demonstration skill (84.00%)
(iv) Blackboard writing skill (84.00%)
(v) Explanation skill (83.33%)
(vi) Illustration with example skill (81.67%)
(vii) Stimulus variation skill (74.33%).

Majority of B.Ed. trainees 72 to 81 per cent of IGNOU considered feedback provided during micro teaching effective in the development of following seven teaching skills:

(i) Questioning skill (81.00%)
(ii) Introduction skill (79.33%)
(iii) Blackboard writing skill (76.00%)
(iv) Stimulus variation skill (75.33%)
(v) Explanation skill (75.00%)
(vi) Illustration with example skill (72.33%)
(vii) Demonstration skill (71.67%).

Seventy five to 79 per cent B.Ed. trainees of both the open universities IGNOU and UPRTOU considered feedback provided during micro teaching effective in the development of following three teaching skills:

(i) Lesson closure skill (79.33%)
(ii) Objective writing skill (78.50%)
(iii) Reinforcement skill (75.00%).

Cent-per-cent counsellors of UPRTOU and 73 per cent counsellors of IGNOU considered practising micro teaching after preparing micro lesson plans effective in the development of reinforcement skill.

Majority of counsellors (72 to 95%) of UPRTOU and IGNOU considered feedback provided during micro teaching effective in the development of following seven teaching skills:

(i) Introduction skill (95.00%)
(ii) Reinforcement skill (90.00%)
(iii) Questioning skill (88.33%)
(iv) Objective writing skill (83.33%)
(v) Illustration with example skill (75.00%)
(vi) Demonstration skill (71.67%)
(vii) Explanation skill (71.67%).

Cent per cent counsellors of UPRTOU considered feedback provided during micro teaching effective in the development of two teaching skills:

(i) Blackboard writing skill
(ii) Lesson closure skill.

Seventy to 80 per cent counsellors of IGNOU considered feedback provided during micro teaching effective in the development of following two teaching skills:

(i) Lesson closure skill (80.00%)
(ii) Blackboard writing skill (70.00%).

Conclusion

Micro teaching is an important activity of B.Ed. programme. It is compulsory to all trainees that every teaching skill must be practiced after preparing micro lesson plans during the workshops. It is clear from the analysis that all the trainees did not give importance to the practice of all the teaching skills. All the trainees did not prepare micro lesson plans. They did not practice it according to the norms of course. It is mandatory that demonstration of all the prescribed micro teaching skills by the counsellors during workshops. However, more than average number of trainees of both the open universities stated that every teaching skill was not demonstrated by the cousellors during workshops. Average trainees of both the open universities stated that their counsellors demonstrated the micro lessons of only 2 to 5 teaching skills out of 10 skills. Majority of trainees stated that their counsellors demonstration the lessons without teaching aids. They also stated that teaching aids were not used by themselves wherever necessary in practice of teaching skills. Majority of trainees of both the open universities stated that feedback was given by their peer trainees as well as counsellors during micro teaching practices. Majority of trainees of both the open universities considered feedback during micro teaching practice as relevant for development of skills. Micro teaching practices had also been considered relevant by counsellors for development of teaching skills among B.Ed. trainees. Various problems were faced by B.Ed. trainees and counsellors during micro teaching practices. Maximum problems of trainees were resolved during workshops by the counsellors. Some of the problems of trainees were resolved with the help of peer trainees. The trainees and counsellors stated that time stipulated by open universities were very much limited for micro teaching practices. The space available in the study centres were not enough for small group simulation practices of micro teaching. As a whole the trainees and the counsellors expressed positive response about the relevance and effectiveness of microteaching practices.

IB. Practice Teaching Processes of Distance Mode B.Ed. Programme

In this sub-section analysis has been done regarding present status, relevance and effectiveness of preparing lesson plans and delivered them by trainees, evaluation of lesson plans and observation of practice teaching classes.

4.8A Response of B.Ed. Trainees about Number of Lesson Plans Prepared by Themselves: University-wise

It can be noticed from Table 4.8A that the calculated χ^2 values of independence between response pattern of B.Ed. trainees and university background in relation to number of lesson plans prepared by them in both the teaching subjects are found to be 22.30 and 18.34 respectively. The obtained χ^2 values are greater than the table value (7.81) at .05 level of significance with df: 3. The observed values are found significant. Hence, the response pattern of B.Ed. trainees and the university background in relation to preparation of lesson plans are not found independent from each other.

It can be observed that majority of B.Ed. trainees (73 to 77%) of IGNOU, prepared 16 to 20 lesson plans in each of the teaching subjects, which is close to the standard set for B.Ed. programme. Whereas lesser number of (59 to 63%) B.Ed. trainees of UPRTOU did the same in comparison to IGNOU. Further it has been observed that 10 to 15 per cent B.Ed. trainees of IGNOU prepared 11 to 15 practice teaching lesson plans, while 21 to 25 per cent B.Ed. trainees of UPRTOU prepare 11 to 15 practice teaching lesson plans in each of the both the teaching subjects.

4.8B Response of B.Ed. Trainees about Number of Lesson Plans Checked by Mentors and Counsellors Already Prepared by Trainees: University-wise

It can be noticed from Table 4.8B that the calculated χ^2 values of independence between response pattern of B.Ed. trainees and university background in relation to number of lesson plans checked by mentors and counsellors already prepared by trainees in both the teaching subjects are found to be 19.58 and 19.58 respectively. The obtained χ^2 values are greater than the table value (7.81) at .05 level of significance with df: 3. The observed values are found significant. Hence, the

Table 4.8: χ^2 test of independence of trainees' response about lesson planning and delivery and university background, subject-wise

A.

Response of trainees on number of lesson plans prepared by themselves

	UNIV.	*i (1-5)*	*ii (6-10)*	*iii (11-15)*	*iv (16-20)*	*Total*	*χ^2 Values*
First Subject	IGNOU	17 (5.67)	31 (10.33)	32 (10.67)	220 (73.33)	300 (100.00)	22.30**
	UPRTOU	19 (6.33)	30 (10.00)	75 (25.00)	176 (58.67)	300 (100.00)	
	Total	36 (6.00)	61 (10.17)	107 (17.83)	396 (66.00)	600 (100.00)	
Second Subject	IGNOU	21 (7.00)	19 (6.33)	29 (9.67)	231 (77.00)	300 (100.00)	18.34**
	UPRTOU	26 (8.67)	22 (7.33)	64 (21.33)	188 (62.67)	300 (100.00)	
	Total	47 (7.83)	41 (6.83)	93 (15.5)	419 (69.83)	600 (100.00)	

B.

	UNIV.	*i (1-5)*	*ii (6-10)*	*iii (11-15)*	*iv (16-20)*	*Total*	*χ^2 Values*
Second Subject	IGNOU	80 (26.67)	65 (21.67)	121 (40.33)	34 (11.33)	30 (100.00)	19.58**
	UPRTOU	96 (32.00)	45 (15.00)	95 (31.67)	64 (21.33)	300 (100.00)	
	Total	176 (29.33)	100 (16.67)	216 (36.00)	98 (16.33)	600 (100.00)	

C.

Response of trainees about lesson plans evaluators

UNIV.	*i (Mentor)*	*ii (Peer Trainees)*	*iii (Counse-llors)*	*iv (None)*	*Other teacher*	*Total*	*χ^2 Value*
IGNOU	280 (93.33)	18 (6.00)	2 (0.67)	0 (0.00)	0 (0.00)	300 (100.00)	
UPRTOU	246 82.00)	24 8.00)	13 4.33)	9 3.00)	8 2.67)	300 100.0)	20.12**
Total	526 (87.67)	42 (7.00)	15 (2.5)	9 (1.5)	8 (1.33)	600 (100.00)	

(Contd.)

D.

Response of trainees on number of lesson plans as delivered by them								
First Subject	*UNIV.*	*i (1-5)*	*ii (6-10)*	*iii (11-15)*	*iv (16-20)*	*Total*	*χ^2 Values*
	IGNOU	34 (11.33)	19 (6.33)	60 (20.00)	187 (62.33)	300 (100.00)	10.08*
	UPRTOU	55 (18.33)	30 (10.00)	58 (19.33)	157 (52.33)	300 (100.00)	
	Total	89 (14.83)	49 (8.17)	118 (19.67)	344 (57.33)	600 (100.00)	
Second Subject	IGNOU	32 (10.67)	21 (7.00)	63 (21.00)	184 (61.33)	300 (100.00)	7.18 N.S.
	UPRTOU	47 (15.67)	33 (11.00)	59 (19.67)	161 (53.67)	300 (100.00)	
	Total	79 (13.17)	54 (9.00)	122 (20.33)	345 (57.5)	600 (100.00)	

E.

Response of trainees about class observer during practice teaching							
UNIV.	*i (Mentor)*	*ii (Peer Trainees)*	*iii (Coun-sellor)*	*iv (Princi-pal)*	*Other teacher*	*Total*	*χ^2 Value*
IGNOU	256 (85.33)	11 (3.67)	31 (10.33)	2 (0.67)	0 (0.00)	300 (100.00)	
UPRTOU	175 (58.33)	14 (4.67)	102 (34.00)	7 (2.33)	2 (0.67)	300 (100.00)	56.26*
Total	431 (71.83)	25 (4.17)	133 (22.17)	9 (1.5)	2 (0.33)	600 (100.00)	

Note: Figures in parentheses indicate percentages. N.S.: Not significant

* Indicates significant at .05 level. ** Indicates significant at .01 level.

response pattern of B.Ed. trainees and the university background in relation to number of lesson plans checked by mentors and counsellors already prepared by trainees are not found independent from each other.

It was observed that 40 to 41 per cent B.Ed. trainees of IGNOU get 11 to 15 lesson plans checked while only 31 to 32 per cent B.Ed. trainees of UPRTOU get 11 to 15 lesson plans checked by counsellors. 21 to 22 per cent B.Ed. trainees of UPRTOU and 11 to 12 per cent B.Ed. trainees of IGNOU get 16 to 20 lesson plans checked by counsellors close to the norms set for the B.Ed. programme.

A large number of B.Ed. trainees (89%) of IGNOU and 78 to 79 per cent of UPRTOU do not get lesson plans checked prepared by themselves as per the norms of course.

It is observed from Tables 4.8A and 4.8B that 73 to 77 per cent B.Ed. trainees of IGNOU prepared 16 to 20 lesson plans which are close to the norms. In which only B.Ed. trainees of IGNOU get their lesson plans (16 to 20) checked as per the norms and teach them. 59 to 63 per cent B.Ed. trainees of UPRTOU prepared lesson plans which are close to the norms, in which only 21 to 22 per cent trainees get it checked before teaching, rest teach without getting the plans checked.

On the basis of above analysis it can be concluded that in comparison to IGNOU, B.Ed. trainees of UPRTOU are more close to the norms of B.Ed. programme in reference to getting their lesson plans checked.

4.8C Response of B.Ed. Trainees about Evaluators of Practice Teaching Lesson Plans Prepared by Themselves: University-wise

It can be noticed from Table 4.8C that the calculated χ^2 value of independence between the response pattern of B.Ed. trainees and the university background in relation to evaluation of practice teaching lesson plans of B.Ed. trainees before practicing is 20.12. Which is greater than the table value (9.48) at .05 level of significance with df: 4. The obtained χ^2 value is found significant. Hence the response pattern of B.Ed trainees and the university background in relation to checkers of practice teaching lesson plans already prepared by trainees before practiced them are not found independent from each other.

It can be observed from Table 4.8C that majority of B.Ed. trainees (93%) of IGNOU and 82 per cent of UPRTOU get their lesson plans checked only by the mentors which is against the norms set for B.Ed. programme where lesson plans must be checked by mentors as well as by the counsellors.

From Tables 4.8B and 4.8C it can observed that approximately all the B.Ed. trainees prepare lesson plans but only 21 to 22 per cent trainees of IGNOU and 11 to 12 per cent trainees of UPRTOU get their lesson plans checked close to the norm. None of the trainees of these universities get their lesson plans checked as per the norms of B.Ed. programme.

It can be concluded that with reference to the provision of lesson plans checked by evaluators, B.Ed. trainees of UPRTOU are more close to the norms set for B.Ed. programmes than their IGNOU counterparts.

4.8D Response of B.Ed. Trainees about Number of Lessons Delivered by Themselves in Practice Teaching: University-wise

It can be noticed from Table 4.8D that the calculated χ^2 value of independence between response pattern of B.Ed. trainees and university background in relation to number of lessons delivered by themselves during practice teaching in the first teaching subject is found as 10.08. This is greater than the table value (7.81) at .05 level of significance with df: 3. The obtained χ^2 value is found significant. Hence the response pattern of B.Ed trainees and the university background in relation to number of lessons delivered by them during practice teaching in the first teaching subject are not found independent from each other.

It can be observed from Table 4.8D that 62 per cent B.Ed. trainees of IGNOU practiced approximately 16 to 20 lesson plans which is close to the norms set for B.Ed. programme, whereas only 52 per cent B.Ed. trainees of UPRTOU practiced the same. Rest 38 per cent B.Ed. trainees of IGNOU and 42 per cent B.Ed. trainees of UPRTOU do not practice in the first teaching subject close to the norms set.

It can be noticed from Table 4.8D that the calculated χ^2 value of independence between response pattern of B.Ed. trainees and university background in relation to number of lesson plans delivered by themselves during practice teaching in the second teaching subject is 7.18, which is greater than the table value (7.81) at .05 level of significance with df: 3. The obtained value is found significant. Hence the response pattern of B.Ed. trainees and the university background in relation to number of lesson plans delivered by them during practice teaching in the second teaching subject are not found independent from each other.

It can be observed from Table 4.8D that approximately 58 per cent B.Ed. trainees of both the open universities IGNOU and UPRTOU practiced approximately 16 to 20 lesson plans which is close to the norms set for B.Ed. programme.

From the above analysis it can be concluded that the B.Ed. trainees of IGNOU (62.33%) are more close to the norms as compared to UPRTOU (52.33) B.Ed. trainees regarding delivery of the first teaching subject lessons.

4.8E Response of Trainees about the Observers of Practice Teaching Lessons: University-wise

It can be noticed from Table 4.8E that the calculated χ^2 value of independence between response pattern of B.Ed. trainees and university background in relation to the observers of practice teaching is 56.26, which is greater than the table value (9.48) at 0.05 level of significance with df: 4. The obtained χ^2 value is found significant. Hence the response pattern of B.Ed. trainees and the university background in reference to the observers of practice teaching lessons are not found independent from each other.

It can be observed that 85 per cent B.Ed. trainees of IGNOU and only 58 per cent B.Ed. trainees of UPRTOU consider that their practice teaching lessons was observed by their respective mentors.

According to the norms of B.Ed. programme, the practice teaching lessons must be observed by both mentors and counsellors or subject experts. It can thereby be concluded from the above analysis that observation of practice teaching is done partially, only by the mentors in both the universities. Such practice is more prominent in IGNOU than UPRTOU.

After observing Table 4.8 A, B, C, D and E it is noticed that nearly 73 to 77 per cent B.Ed. trainees of IGNOU and 59 to 63 per cent B.Ed. trainees of UPRTOU prepare 16 to 20 lesson plans in both the teaching subjects, which is close to the norms of B.Ed. programme. Out of all the B.Ed. trainees who prepared lesson plans only 40 to 41 per cent B.Ed. trainees of IGNOU and 20 to 21 per cent B.Ed. trainees of UPRTOU get 16 to 20 lesson plans checked which is close to the norms set for B.Ed. programme. Out of the total B.Ed. trainees who prepared their lesson plans 93 per cent of B.Ed. trainees of IGNOU and only 58 per cent B.Ed. trainees on UPRTOU get their plans checked by mentors only. It implies that they are not serious about getting plans checked by the counsellors or subject teachers. According to norms at least 5 lesson plans in each of the teaching subjects must be checked by the counsellors.

Out of the total B.Ed. trainees 62 per cent of IGNOU and 52 per cent B.Ed. trainees of UPRTOU delivered 16 to 20 lessons and rest 38 per cent B.Ed. trainees of IGNOU and 48 per cent B.Ed. trainees of UPRTOU do not delivered lessons as per the norms.

In total 85 per cent B.Ed. trainees of IGNOU and 58 per cent of UPRTOU were observed by their mentors only. Hence it is clear that B.Ed.

trainees of both the universities do not get their lesson plans checked and observed by their counsellors as per the norms of B.Ed. Programme.

Interview with Mentors about Limitations of B.Ed. Trainees during Teaching Practices

The selected mentors of both the universities stated that during classroom teaching B.Ed. trainees were lacking following skills:

- Introduction.
- Questioning.
- Stimulus variation.
- Time management.
- Lesson plan preparation.

Interview with Counsellors about their Assistance for Resolving Problems faced by B.Ed. Trainees during Classroom Teaching

The selected counsellors of both the universities stated that for resolving the problems of B.Ed. trainees they made the trainees discipline.

4.9A Response of Counsellors about Number of Lesson Plans Prepared by Trainees: University-wise

It can be noticed from Table 4.9A that the calculated χ^2 values of independence between response pattern of counsellors and university background in relation to number of lesson plans prepared by B.Ed. trainees in both the teaching subjects are found to be 5.92 and 3.46 respectively. The obtained χ^2 values are less than the table value (7.81) at 0.05 level of significance with df: 3. The observed values are not found significant. Hence the response pattern of counsellors and the university background in reference to number of lesson plans prepared by trainees in both the teaching subjects are found independent from each other.

It can be observed that as per 83 per cent counsellors of IGNOU and UPRTOU the number of practice teaching plans prepared by B.Ed. trainees in both the teaching subjects is close to the norms of B.Ed. programme.

Only 17 per cent counsellors of both the universities stated that B.Ed. trainees prepared 1 to 15 lesson plans in each of the teaching subjects.

Table 4.9: χ^2 test of independence of counsellors response about delivery of lessons by trainees and university background, subject-wise

A.

Response of counsellors on number of lesson plans as prepared by trainees							
First Subject	UNIV.	i (1-5)	ii (6-10)	iii (11-15)	iv (16-20)	Total	χ^2 Values
	IGNOU	4 (13.33)	1 (3.33)	3 (10.00)	22 (73.33)	30 (100.00)	5.92 N.S.
	UPRTOU	0 (0.00)	0 (0.00)	2 (6.67)	28 (93.33)	30 (100.00)	
	Total	4 (6.67)	1 (1.67)	5 (8.33)	50 (83.33)	60 (100.00)	
Second Subject	IGNOU	2 (6.67)	1 (3.33)	4 (13.33)	23 (76.67)	30 (100.00)	3.46 N.S.
	UPRTOU	0 (0.00)	0 (0.00)	3 (10.00)	27 (90.00)	30 (100.00)	
	Total	2 (3.33)	1 (1.67)	7 (11.67)	50 (83.33)	60 (100.00)	

B.

Response of counsellors about class observer during practice teaching									
UNIV.	i (Mentor)	ii (Peer Trainees)	Iii (Subject Teacher)	iv (i&iii)	v (ii&iii)	vi (Nominee of centre)	vii (None)	Total	χ^2 Value
IGNOU	12 (40.00)	4 (13.33)	8 (26.67)	3 (10.00)	0 (0.00)	1 (3.33)	2 (6.67)	30 (10.00)	19.80**
UPRTOU	7 (23.33)	0 (0.00)	19 (63.33)	0 (0.00)	4 (13.33)	0 (0.00)	0 (0.00)	30 (100.00)	
Total	99 (31.67)	4 (6.67)	27 (45.00)	3 (5.00)	4 (6.67)	1 (1.67)	2 (3.33)	60 (100.00)	

C.

Response of counsellors about number of lesson plans observed of trainees by mentors during practice teaching							
Subjects	UNIV.	i (1-5)	ii (6-10)	iii (11-15)	iv (16-20)	Total	χ^2 Values
First Subject	IGNOU	11 (36.67)	1 (3.33)	9 (30.00)	9 (30.00)	30 (100.00)	7.39 N.S.
	UPRTOU	10 (33.33)	4 (13.33)	2 (6.67)	14 (46.67)	30 (100.00)	

(Contd.)

	Total	21 (35.00)	5 (8.33)	11 (18.33)	23 (38.33)	60 (100.00)	
Second Subject	IGNOU	11 (36.67)	1 (3.33)	8 (13.33)	10 (33.33)	30 (100.00)	4.51 N.S.
	UPRTOU	10 (33.33)	4 (13.33)	3 (10.00)	13 (21.67)	30 (100.00)	
	Total	21 (35.00)	5 (8.33)	11 (18.33)	23 (38.33)	60 (100.00)	

D.

Response of counsellors about lesson plans evaluators prepared by trainees

UNIV.	*i (Mentor)*	*ii (Peer Trainees)*	*iii (Subject Teacher)*	*iv (i&ii)*	*v (i&iii)*	*vi (None)*	*Total*	χ^2 *Value*
IGNOU	7 (23.33)	1 (3.33)	17 (56.67)	1 (3.33)	1 (3.33)	3 (10.00)	30 (100.00)	3.44 N.S.
UPRTOU	6 (20.00)	2 (6.67)	16 (53.33)	0 (0.00)	0 (0.00)	6 (20.00)	30 (100.00)	
Total	13 (21.67)	3 (5.00)	33 (55.00)	1 (1.67)	1 (1.67)	9 (15.00)	60 (100.00)	

E.

Response of counsellors about number of lesson plans observed by themselves during practice teaching.

Subjects	*UNIV.*	*i (1-5)*	*ii (6-10)*	*iii (11-15)*	*iv (16-20)*	*Total*	χ^2 *Values*
First Subject	IGNOU	11 (36.67)	6 (20.00)	2 (6.67)	11 (36.67)	30 (100.00)	13.88**
	UPRTOU	4 (13.33)	0 (0.00)	6 (20.00)	20 (66.67)	30 (100.00)	
	Total	15 (25.00)	6 (10.00)	8 (13.33)	31 (51.67)	60 (100.00)	
Second Subject	IGNOU	11 (36.67)	6 (20.00)	3 (10.00)	10 (33.33)	30 (100.00)	10.63*
	UPRTOU	4 (13.33)	1 (3.33)	6 (20.00)	19 (63.33)	30 (100.00)	
	Total	15 (25.00)	7 (11.67)	9 (15.00)	29 (48.33)	60 (100.00)	

Note: Figures in parentheses indicate percentages.
N.S.: Not significant
* Indicates significant at .05 level.
** Indicates significant at .01 level.

4.9B Response of Counsellors about Observation of Practice Teaching Lessons: University-wise

It can be noticed from Table 4.9B that the calculated χ^2 value of independence between response pattern of counsellors and university background in relation to class observation during practice teaching practiced by trainees is 19.80, which is greater than the table value (12.59) at .05 level of significance with df: 6. The obtained χ^2 value is found significant. Hence the response pattern of counsellors and the university background in reference to observation of practice teaching lessons are not found independent from each other.

It can be observed that according to 40 per cent counsellors of IGNOU and 23 per cent counsellors of UPRTOU the lessons were observed by mentors only. According to 63 per cent counsellors of IGNOU and 27 per cent counsellors of UPRTOU the practice lessons were observed by subject teachers.

According to 10 per cent counsellors of IGNOU the classes taught by B.Ed. trainees were observed by both mentors and subject teachers. None of the counsellors of UPRTOU mentioned that classes taught by B.Ed. trainees were observed by both mentors as well as subject teachers. Thus it can be concluded that although the number is less but IGNOU follow norms more seriously as compared to UPRTOU in relation to observation of lessons taught by B.Ed. trainees.

4.9C Response of Counsellors about Norms of Number of Lessons Observed by Mentors: University-wise

It can be noticed from Table 4.9C that the calculated χ^2 values of independence between response pattern of counsellors and university background in relation to norms of number of lessons observed by mentors in both the subjects are found to be 7.39 and 4.51 respectively. The obtained χ^2values are less than the table value (7.81) at .05 level of significance with df: 3. The observed values are not found significant. Hence the response pattern of counsellors and the university background in reference to the norms of number of class observed by mentors during practice teaching practiced by trainees are found independent from each other.

It can be observed that according to only 38 per cent counsellors of IGNOU and UPRTOU, approximately 15 to 20 lessons were observed by mentors.

According to merely 18 per cent counsellors of IGNOU and UPRTOU approximately 11 to 15 lessons were observed by mentors, which is close to the norms of B.Ed. programme.

4.9D Response of Counsellors about Evaluators of Lesson Plans: University-wise

It can be noticed from Table 4.9D that the calculated χ^2 value of independence between response pattern of counsellors and university background in relation to evaluators of lesson plans is 3.44, which is less than the table value (11.07) at .05 level of significance with df: 5. The obtained χ^2 values are not found significant. Hence the response pattern of counsellors and the university background in reference to evaluators of lesson plans are found independent from each other.

It can be observed that according to approximately 55 per cent counsellors of IGNOU and UPRTOU the lesson plans of B.Ed. trainees were assessed by subject experts prior to teaching. According to approximately 22 per cent counsellors of IGNOU and UPRTOU lesson plans of B.Ed. trainees were assessed by mentors alone before teaching.

According to majority number of (2%) counsellors of IGNOU and UPRTOU the lesson plans of B.Ed. trainees of both the universities were assessed by both subject experts and mentors prior to teaching as per the norms of B.Ed. programme.

4.9E Response of Counsellors about Number of Classes Observed by Themselves during Practice Teaching: University-wise

It can be noticed from Table 4.9E that the calculated χ^2 values of independence between response pattern of counsellors and university background in relation to number of classes observed by themselves during practice teaching in both the teaching subjects are 13.88 and 10.63 respectively. The obtained χ^2 values are greater than the table value (7.81) at .05 level of significance with df: 3. The observed values are found significant. Hence the response pattern of counsellors and the university background in reference to above said are not found independent from each other.

It can be observed that according to 63 to 67 per cent counsellors of UPRTOU and 33 to 57 per cent counsellors of IGNOU approximately 16 to 20 lesson plans of both the teaching subjects of B.Ed. trainees of both the universities were observed by counsellors.

According to 37 per cent counsellors of IGNOU and 13 per cent counsellors of UPRTOU approximately 1 to 5 lesson plans were observed by counsellors in both the teaching subjects as per the norms of B.Ed. programme.

4.10 Response of B.Ed. Trainees in Reference to Level of Relevance of Preparing Lesson Plans: University-wise

It can be noticed from Table 4.10 that the calculated χ^2 value of independence between the response pattern of B.Ed. trainees and university background in reference to the relevance of preparation of lesson plans by themselves is 0.23. It is less than the table value (5.99) at the .05 level of significance with df: 2. The observed value is not found significant. Hence response pattern of B.Ed. trainees and the University background are found independent from each other in the context of relevance of preparation lesson plans by B.Ed. trainees.

It can be observed that according to approximately 82 per cent B.Ed. trainees of both the universities—IGNOU and UPRTOU the preparation of practice teaching lesson plans was relevant.

Table 4.10: χ^2 test of Independence of trainees' response towards relevance of training process related practice teaching and university background

Response of trainees about level of relevance of practice teaching						
Statements	*UNIV.*	*Highly Agree*	*Agree*	*Disagree*	*Total*	*χ^2 Values*
1. Preparing lesson plans for practice teaching is related to your school teaching.	IGNOU	243 (81.00)	46 (15.33)	11 (3.67)	300 (100.00)	0.23 N.S.
	UPRTOU	246 (82.00)	45 (15.00)	9 (3.00)	300 (100.00)	
	Total	489 (81.50)	91 (15.17)	20 (3.33)	600 (100.00)	
2. Practice teaching vitalizes you in your school teaching.	IGNOU	236 (78.67)	43 (14.33)	21 (7.00)	300 (100.00)	11.74**
	UPRTOU	263 (87.67)	31 (10.33)	6 (2.00)	300 (100.00)	
	Total	499 (83.17)	74 (12.33)	27 (4.50)	600 (100.00)	

Note: Figures in parentheses indicate percentages.
N.S.: Not significant.
** Indicates significant at .01 level.

In Table 4.10 the calculated χ^2 value of independence between the response pattern of B.Ed. trainees and the university background in reference to the relevance of practice teaching lesson plans is 11.74. It is greater than the table value (5.99) at the .05 level of significance with df: 2. The observed value is found significant. Hence, response pattern of B.Ed. trainees and the university background are not found independent from each other in the context of relevance of practice teaching lesson plans.

It can be observed that according to 88 per cent B.Ed. trainees of UPRTOU and 79 per cent B.Ed. trainees of IGNOU practice teaching lesson plans tends to strengthen their teaching. It can be observed from the above analysis that as compared to IGNOU, B.Ed. trainees of UPRTOU (87.67%) considered practice teaching more relevant.

4.11 Response of Counsellors Level of Relevance of Practice Teaching: University-wise

It can be noticed from Table 4.11 that the calculated χ^2 values of independence between the response pattern of counsellors and the

Table 4.11: χ^2 test of independence of counsellors response in relation to relevance of practice teaching of distance B.Ed. programme and university background

Response of cousellors about level of relevance of practice teaching						
Statements	*UNIV.*	*Highly Agree*	*Agree*	*Disagree*	*Total*	χ^2 *Values*
1. Preparared lesson plan by trainees is related to their school teaching	IGNOU	23 (76.67)	7 (23.33)	0 (0.00)	30 (100.00)	2.78 N.S.
	UPRTOU	26 (86.67)	3 (10.00)	1 (3.33)	30 (100.00)	
	Total	49 (81.67)	10 (16.67)	1 (1.67)	60 (100.00)	
2. Feedback provided to B.Ed. trainees during practice teaching is accordance to their competency development.	IGNOU	26 (86.67)	3 (10.00)	1 (3.33)	30 (100.00)	1.35 N.S.
	UPRTOU	27 (90.00)	1 (3.33)	2 (6.67)	30 (100.00)	
	Total	53 (88.33)	4 (6.67)	3 (5.00)	60 (100.00)	

Note: Figures in parentheses indicate percentages.
N.S.: Not significant

university background in reference to the relevance of preparation of lesson plans by B.Ed. trainees and feedback provided during practice teaching are found 2.78 and 1.35 respectively. The obtained χ^2 values are less than the table value (5.99) at the .05 level of significance with df: 2. The observed values are not found significant. Hence response pattern of B.Ed. trainees and the university background are found independent from each other in the context of relevance of preparation of lesson plans by B.Ed. trainees and feedback provided during practice teaching.

It can be observed that according to 88 per cent counsellors of IGNOU and UPRTOU the feedback provided by counsellors during delivery of lessons by B.Ed. trainees was relevant. According to 82 per cent counsellors of IGNOU and UPRTOU the lesson plans prepared by B.Ed. trainees were relevant.

4.12 (A and B) Response of B.Ed. Trainees about Level of Effectiveness of Practice Teaching: University-wise

It can be noticed from Table 4.12A that the calculated χ^2 values of independence between the response pattern of B.Ed. trainees and the university background in reference to the enhancement of writing instructional objectives and writing questions appropriately due to preparation of lesson plans for practice teaching are found to be 0.60 and 5.27 respectively. The obtained χ^2 values are less than the table value (5.99) at the .05 level of significance with df: 2. The observed values are not found significant. Hence response pattern of B.Ed trainees and the university background are found independent from each other in the context of enhancement of writing instructional objectives and writing questions appropriately due to preparation of lesson plans for practice teaching.

It can be observed that 80-81 per cent B.Ed. trainees of IGNOU and UPRTOU considered preparation of lesson plans for practice teaching effective in the enhancement of following teaching skills:

(i) Writing instructional objectives (81.00%)
(ii) Writing questions appropriately (80.33%).

It can be noticed from Table 4.12A that the calculated χ^2 value of independence between the response pattern of B.Ed. trainees and the university background in reference to the enhancing writing content

Table 4.12: χ^2 test of Independence of trainees' response about effectiveness of training process of practice teaching and university background

A.

Benefits of preparation of lesson plans for practice teaching						
Development of skills	*UNIV.*	*More extent*	*Some extent*	*Least*	*Total*	χ^2 *Values*
1-i. Writing instructional objectives	IGNOU	246 (82.00)	45 (15.00)	9 (3.00)	300 (100.00)	0.60 N.S.
	UPRTOU	240 (80.00)	48 (16.00)	12 (4.00)	300 (100.00)	
	Total	486 (81.00)	93 (15.50)	21 (3.50)	600 (100.00)	
ii. Writing subject-matter correctly	IGNOU	235 (78.33)	55 (18.33)	10 (3.33)	300 (100.00)	9.51**
	UPRTOU	251 (83.67)	31 (10.33)	18 (6.00)	300 (100.00)	
	Total	486 (81.00)	86 (14.33)	28 (4.67)	600 (100.00)	
iii. Writing questions appropriately	IGNOU	231 (77.00)	55 (18.33)	14 (4.67)	300 (100.00)	5.27 N.S.
	UPRTOU	251 (83.67)	35 (11.67)	14 (4.67)	300 (100.00)	
	Total	482 (80.33)	90 (15.00)	28 (4.67)	600 (100.00)	

B.

Benefits of practice teaching						
Development of skills	*UNIV.*	*More extent*	*Some extent*	*Least*	*Total*	χ^2 *Values*
2-i. Competence in creating appropriate situation for introducing the lesson in class-room.	IGNOU	238 (79.33)	49 (16.33)	13 (4.33)	300 (100.00)	0.18 N.S.
	UPRTOU	240 (80.00)	49 (16.33)	11 (3.67)	300 (100.00)	
	Total	478 (79.67)	98 (16.33)	24 (4.00)	600 (100.00)	
ii. Competence in state introduction of the lesson effectively.	IGNOU	242 (80.67)	48 (16.00)	10 (3.33)	300 (100.00)	11.97**
	UPRTOU	267 (89.00)	21 (7.00)	12 (4.00)	300 (100.00)	
	Total	509 (84.83)	69 (11.50)	22 (3.67)	600 (100.00)	

(Contd.)

iii. Competence in acceptance of student response appropriately.	IGNOU	235 (78.33)	50 (16.67)	15 (5.00)	300 (100.00)	1.52 N.S.
	UPRTOU	247 (82.33)	41 (13.67)	12 (4.00)	300 (100.00)	
	Total	482 (80.33)	91 (15.17)	27 (4.50)	600 (100.00)	
iv. Competence in explanation of facts appropriately.	IGNOU	223 (74.33)	62 (20.67)	15 (5.00)	300 (100.00)	9.82**
	UPRTOU	251 (83.67)	34 (11.33)	15 (5.00)	300 (100.00)	
	Total	474 (79.00)	96 (16.00)	30 (5.00)	600 (100.00)	
v. Competence in presentation of appropriate example.	IGNOU	234 (78.00)	57 (19.00)	9 (3.00)	300 (100.00)	5.05 N.S.
	UPRTOU	253 (84.33)	37 (12.33)	10 (3.33)	300 (100.00)	
	Total	487 (81.17)	94 (15.67)	19 (3.17)	600 (100.00)	
vi. Competence in selection of appropriate teaching aids.	IGNOU	226 (75.33)	60 (20.00)	14 (4.67)	300 (100.00)	10.38**
	UPRTOU	245 (81.67)	33 (11.00)	22 (7.33)	300 (100.00)	
	Total	471 (78.50)	93 (15.50)	36 (6.00)	600 (100.00)	
vii. Competence in provide reinforcement to student.	IGNOU	246 (82.00)	44 (14.67)	10 (3.33)	300 (100.00)	5.14 N.S.
	UPRTOU	256 (85.33)	28 (9.33)	16 (5.33)	300 (100.00)	
	Total	502 (83.67)	72 (12.00)	26 (4.33)	600 (100.00)	
viii. Competence in make class-room communication effective.	IGNOU	239 (79.67)	41 (13.67)	20 (6.67)	300 (100.00)	3.11 N.S.
	UPRTOU	255 (85.00)	32 (10.67)	13 (4.33)	300 (100.00)	
	Total	494 (82.33)	73 (12.17)	33 (5.50)	600 (100.00)	
ix. Competence in appropriate lesson closuring.	IGNOU	239 (79.67)	46 (15.33)	15 (5.00)	300 (100.00)	5.74 N.S.
	UPRTOU	255 (85.00)	27 (9.00)	18 (6.00)	300 (100.00)	
	Total	494 (82.33)	73 (12.17)	33 (5.50)	600 (100.00)	

Note: Figures in parentheses indicate percentages. N.S.: Not significant.

** Indicates significant at .01 level.

properly due to preparation of lesson plans for practice teaching is 9.51. The obtained χ^2 values are greater than the table value (5.99) at the .05 level of significance with df: 2. It is found significant. Hence response pattern of B.Ed. trainees and the university background are not found independent from each other in the context of enhancing writing content properly due to preparation of lesson plans for practice teaching.

It can be observed that according to 84 per cent B.Ed. trainees of UPRTOU and 78 per cent B.Ed. trainees of IGNOU preparation of lesson plans for practice teaching in regard to enhancing teaching skills was found effective.

It can be noticed from Table 4.12B that the calculated χ^2 values of independence between response pattern of counsellors and the university background in relation to enhancement in the following six skills like creating appropriate situation for introducing the lesson, accepting response of students appropriately, presenting appropriate examples, providing reinforcement to the students, making classroom environment effective and closing the lesson appropriately due to practice teaching are found to be 0.18, 1.52, 5.05, 5.14, 3.11 and 5.74 respectively. The obtained χ^2 values are found to be lesser than the table value (5.99) at .05 level of significance with df: 2. The observed values are not found significant. Hence, the response pattern of counsellors and the university background in reference to the enhancement in the above mentioned skills due to practice teaching are found independent from each other.

It can be observed that according 80 to 84 per cent B.Ed. trainees of IGNOU and UPRTOU, practice teaching programme was found to be effective in the enhancement of following teaching skills:

(i) Reinforcing the students (83.67%)
(ii) Making classroom teaching effective (82.33%)
(iii) Closing the lesson appropriately (82.33%)
(iv) Presenting appropriate examples (81.17%)
(v) Accepting the responses of students appropriately (80.33%)
(vi) Creating appropriate situation for introducing the lesson (79.67%)

Table 4.12B reveals that the calculated χ^2 values of independence between the response pattern of B.Ed. trainees and the university background in reference to the enhancement in the following skills, viz.

presenting introduction to the lesson effectively, illustrating the facts appropriately and selecting appropriate teaching aids due to practice teaching are found to be 11.97, 9.82 and 10.38 respectively. The obtained χ^2 values are greater than the table value (5.99) at the .05 level of significance with df: 2. The observed values are found significant. Hence response pattern of B.Ed. trainees and the university background are not found independent from each other in the context of enhancement in above mentioned skills due to practice teaching.

It can be observed that according 82 to 89 per cent B.Ed. trainees of UPRTOU practice teaching helped in the enhancement of following teaching skills:

(i) Presenting introduction to the lesson effectively (89.00%)
(ii) Illustrating the facts in appropriate manner (83.67%)
(iii) Selecting appropriate teaching aids (81.67%)

According 74 to 81 per cent B.Ed. trainees of IGNOU practice teaching helped in the enhancement of following teaching skills:

(i) Presenting introduction to the lesson effectively (80.67%)
(ii) Selecting appropriate teaching aids (75.33)
(iii) Illustrating the facts in appropriate manner (74.33%)

4.13 (A and B) Response of Counsellors about Effectiveness of Practice Teaching Programme: University-wise

It can be noticed from Table 4.13A that the calculated χ^2 values of independence between response pattern of counsellors and university background in relation to effectiveness of preparing lesson plans to enhancement of following three skills of practice teaching, viz. writing instructional objectives, writing content appropriately and writing questions appropriately are found to be 2.15 and 3.49 respectively. The obtained χ^2 values are less than the table value (5.99) at 0.05 level of significance with df: 2. The observed values are not found significant. Hence the response pattern of counsellors and the university background in reference to effectiveness of preparing lesson plans for practice teaching to enhancement in above mentioned skills are found independent from each other.

Table 4.13: χ^2 test of independence of counsellors response background about effectiveness of practice teaching of distance B.Ed. programme and university

A.

Response of counsellors on level of effectiveness of preparing lesson plans by B.Ed. trainees for practice teaching

Benefits of skills	*UNIV.*	*More extent*	*Some extent*	*Least*	*Total*	χ^2 *Values*
1-i. Writing of instructional objectives	IGNOU	22 (73.33)	7 (23.33)	1 (3.33)	30 (100.00)	2.15 N.S.
	UPRTOU	26 (86.67)	4 (13.33)	0 (0.00)	30 (100.00)	
	Total	48 (80.00)	11 (18.33)	1 (1.67)	60 (100.00)	
ii. Writing subject-matter correctly	IGNOU	23 (76.67)	6 (20.00)	1 (3.33)	30 (100.00)	3.49 N.S.
	UPRTOU	28 (93.33)	2 (6.67)	0 (0.00)	30 (100.00)	
	Total	51 (85.00)	8 (13.33)	1 (1.67)	60 (100.00)	
iii. Writing questions appropriately	IGNOU	21 (70.00)	8 (26.67)	1 (3.33)	30 (100.00)	5.60 N.S.
	UPRTOU	28 (93.33)	2 (6.67)	0 (0.00)	30 (100.00)	
	Total	49 (81.67)	10 (16.67)	1 (1.67)	60 (100.00)	

B.

Response of counsellors on level of effectiveness of practice teaching

Benefits of skills/competency	*UNIV.*	*More extent*	*Some extent*	*Least*	*Total*	χ^2 *Values*
2-i. Creating appropriate situation for introducing the lesson in class-room	IGNOU	24 (80.00)	5 (16.67)	1 (3.33)	30 (100.00)	2.59 N.S.
	UPRTOU	28 (93.33)	2 (6.67)	0 (0.00)	30 (100.00)	
	Total	52 (86.67)	7 (11.67)	1 (1.67)	60 (100.00)	

(Contd.)

ii. Stetting introduction of the lesson effectively	IGNOU	24 (80.00)	6 (20.00)	0 (0.00)	30 (100.00)	3.18 N.S.
	UPRTOU	27 (90.00)	2 (6.67)	1 (3.33)	30 (100.00)	
	Total	51 (85.00)	8 (13.33)	1 (1.67)	60 (100.00)	
iii. Accepting of student response appropriately	IGNOU	24 (80.00)	5 (16.67)	1 (3.33)	30 (100.00)	1.19 N.S.
	UPRTOU	26 (86.67)	4 (13.33)	0 (0.00)	30 (100.00)	
	Total	50 (83.33)	9 (15.00)	1 (1.67)	60 (100.00)	
iv. Explaining of facts appropriately	IGNOU	22 (73.33)	7 (23.33)	1 (3.33)	30 (100.00)	1.24 N.S.
	UPRTOU	24 (80.00)	4 (13.33)	2 (6.67)	30 (100.00)	
	Total	46 (76.67)	11 (18.33)	3 (5.00)	60 (100.00)	
v. Presenting of appropriate example	IGNOU	24 (80.00)	6 (20.00)	0 (0.00)	30 (100.00)	1.42 N.S.
	UPRTOU	25 (83.33)	4 (13.33)	1 (3.33)	30 (100.00)	
	Total	49 (81.67)	10 (16.67)	1 (1.67)	60 (100.00)	
vi. Selection of appropriate teaching aids	IGNOU	25 (83.33)	5 (16.67)	0 (0.00)	30 (100.00)	3.48 N.S.
	UPRTOU	19 (63.33)	10 (33.33)	1 (3.33)	30 (100.00)	
	Total	44 (73.33)	15 (25.00)	1 (1.67)	60 (100.00)	
vii. Providing reinforcement to student	IGNOU	24 (80.00)	6 (20.00)	0 (0.00)	30 (100.00)	3.18 N.S.
	UPRTOU	27 (90.00)	2 (6.67)	1 (3.33)	30 (100.00)	
	Total	51 (85.00)	8 (13.33)	1 (1.67)	60 (100.00)	
viii. Making class-room communication effective	IGNOU	25 (83.33)	5 (16.67)	0 (0.00)	30 (100.00)	6.30*
	UPRTOU	29 (96.67)	0 (0.00)	1 (3.33)	30 (100.00)	
	Total	54 (90.00)	5 (8.33)	1 (1.67)	60 (100.00)	

(Contd.)

ix. Appropriate lesson closuring	IGNOU	23 (76.67)	6 (20.00)	1 (3.33)	30 (100.00)	1.02 N.S.
	UPRTOU	24 (80.00)	6 (20.00)	0 (0.00)	30 (100.00)	
	Total	47 (78.33)	12 (20.00)	1 (1.67)	60 (100.00)	

Note: Figures in parentheses indicate percentages. N.S.: Not significant.
* Indicates significant at .05 level.

It can be observed that according 80 to 85 per cent counsellor of IGNOU and UPRTOU preparing lesson plans for practice teaching helped in the enhancement of following teaching skills:

(i) Writing teaching content appropriately (85.00%)
(ii) Writing questions appropriately (81.67%)
(iii) Writing instructional objectives (80.00%)

It can be noticed from Table 4.13B that the calculated χ^2 values of independence between response pattern of counsellors and university background in relation to enhancement of following eight teaching skills due to practice teaching, viz. creating appropriate situation during introducing the lesson, presenting introduction to the lesson effectively, illustration of facts appropriately, presenting appropriate examples, selecting appropriate teaching aids, reinforcing the students and closing the lesson appropriately are found to be 2.59, 3.18, 1.19, 1.24, 1.42, 3.48, 3.18 and 1.02 respectively. The obtained χ^2 values are less than the table value (5.99) at .05 level of significance with df:2. The observed values are not found significant. Hence the response pattern of counsellors and the university background in reference to enhancement in above mentioned teaching skills are found independent from each other.

It can be observed that according to 73 to 78 per cent counsellors of IGNOU and UPRTOU practice teaching activities helped students in the enhancement of following teaching skills:

(i) Creating appropriate situation during introducing the lesson (86.67%).
(ii) Presenting introduction to the lesson effectively (85.00%)
(iii) Reinforcing the students (85.00%)
(iv) Accepting the responses of students (83.33%)
(v) Presenting appropriate examples (81.67%)

(vi) Closing the lesson appropriately (78.33%)
(vii) Illustrating the facts appropriately (76.67%)
(viii) Selecting appropriate teaching aids (73.33%).

It can be noticed from Table 4.13B that the calculated χ^2 value of independence between response pattern of counsellors and the university background in reference to the enhancement in classroom teaching skill due to practice teaching is 6.30, which is greater than the table value (5.99) at the .05 level of significance with df: 2. The observed value is found significant. Hence, response pattern of counsellors and the university background are not found independent from each other in the context of enhancement in classroom teaching skill due to practice teaching.

It can be observed that according to 97 per cent counsellors of UPRTOU and 83 per cent counsellors of IGNOU practice teaching was found effective for enhancement of classroom teaching skills.

Conclusion

Practice teaching is a component of B.Ed. programme, which makes trainees competent in teaching competency. It is clear from the analysis that according more than average trainees they prepared practice lesson plans according to norm of B.Ed. course. A very less number of trainees had reported that they had done practice teaching *via* getting their lesson plans cheeked according to the norms. Rest of trainees either did not getting their lesson plans checked or they had done practice teaching without getting checked lesson plans. Maximum trainees stated that only mentors had cheeked their lesson plans and observed the classes delivered by trainees, while it is mandatory that checking of lesson plans of trainees and observation of classes delivered by trainees should be by mentors as well as counsellors. Average number of counsellors stated on the basis of norms that checking of lesson plans of trainees and observation of classes delivered by trainees had done by subject teachers, also.

Average counsellors of both the open universities stated that the classes observed by them delivered by trainees according to the norms. It is also clear from the analysis that majority of trainees and counsellors consider preparing lesson plans for practice teaching, delivery of practice teaching, feedback of counsellors and mentors as relevant and effective. Mentors told that various problems faced by

B.Ed. trainees during practice teaching, i.e. in introduction skills, in question skills, in stimulus variation skills, management of time and in making lesson plans. The problems faced by trainees were resolved by mentors. As a whole the trainees and the counsellors expressed positive response about the relevance and effectiveness of practice teaching.

IC. Unit Planning Processes of Distance mode B.Ed. Programme

In this sub-section analysis has been done regarding present status, relevance and effectiveness of processes adopted for development of competency of unit planning among B.Ed. trainees.

4.14 Response of B.Ed. Trainees about Guidance Provided for Preparation of Unit Plan: University-wise

It can be noticed from Table 4.14 that the calculated χ^2 value of independence between response pattern of B.Ed. trainees and university background in relation to guidance provided for preparation of unit plan is 8.95. Which is greater than the table value (5.99) at .05 level of significance with df: 2. The obtained χ^2 value is found significant. Hence the response pattern of B.Ed trainees and the university background in relation to guidance provided for preparation of unit plan are not found independent from each other.

Table 4.14: χ^2 test of independence of trainees' response about training provided for preparing unit plan and university background

Response of trainees about training provided for preparing unit plan					
UNIV.	*i (Regularly)*	*ii (Sometimes)*	*iii (Never)*	*Total*	χ^2 *Value*
IGNOU	138 (46.00)	155 (51.67)	7 (2.33)	300 (100.00)	8.95*
UPRTOU	150 (50.00)	130 (43.33)	20 (6.67)	300 (100.00)	
Total	288 (48.00)	285 (47.5)	27 (4.5)	600 (100.00)	

Note: Figures in parentheses indicate percentages.
* Indicates significant at .05 level.

It can be observed from Table 4.14 that 50 per cent B.Ed. trainees of UPRTOU and 46 per cent B.Ed. trainees of IGNOU considered that regular guidance for the preparation of unit plan is given.

From the above analysis it is clear that B.Ed. trainees of UPRTOU as compared to IGNOU are at more profitable position in regard to the availability of guidance for the preparation of unit plan.

4.15 Response of Counsellors about Guidance Provided for Preparation of Unit Plan: University-wise

It can be noticed from Table 4.15 that the calculated χ^2 value of independence between response pattern of counsellors and university background in relation to guidance provided for preparation of unit plan is 4.75, which is less than the table value (5.99) at .05 level of significance with df: 2. The obtained χ^2 value is not found significant. Hence the response pattern of counsellors and the university background in relation to guidance provided for preparation of unit plan are found independent from each other.

Table 4.15: χ^2 test of independence of counsellors response about training provided for preparing unit plan and university background

Response of counselors about training provided by themselves					
UNIV.	*i (Regularly)*	*ii (Some Times)*	*iii (Never)*	*Total*	χ^2 *Value*
IGNOU	22 (73.33)	4 (13.33)	4 (13.33)	30 (100.00)	4.75 N.S.
UPRTOU	14 (46.67)	6 (20.00)	10 (33.33)	30 (100.00)	
Total	36 (60.00)	10 (16.67)	14 (46.67)	60 (100.00)	

Note: Figures in parentheses indicate percentages. N.S.: Not significant

It can be observed from Table 4.15 that 60 per cent counsellors of IGNOU and UPRTOU considered that regular guidance for the preparation of unit plan was provided and according to 47 per cent counsellors guidance for the preparation of unit plan was never provided.

4.16 Response of B.Ed. Trainees about Relevance of Guidance Provided for Preparation of Unit Plan: University-wise

It can be noticed from Table 4.16 that the calculated χ^2 value of independence between response pattern of B.Ed. trainees and university background in relation to relevance of guidance provided for preparation of unit plan is 2.30. The obtained χ^2 is less than the table value (5.99) at .05 level of significance with df: 2. The observed value is not found significant. Hence the response pattern of B.Ed trainees and the university background in relation to relevance of guidance provided for preparation of unit plan are found independent from each other.

Table 4.16: χ^2 test of Independence of trainees' response about relevance of training process related preparation of unit plan and university background, statement-wise

Response of trainees about lever of relevance of training process for preparing unit plan						
Statement	*UNIV.*	*Highly Agree*	*Agree*	*Disagree*	*Total*	χ^2 *Value*
1. Guidance provided during workshop for preparing Unit Plan is must for completing durinal syllabus timely.	IGNOU	199 (66.33)	64 (28.00)	17 (5.67)	300 (100.00)	2.30 N.S.
	UPRTOU	215 (71.67)	68 (22.67)	17 (5.67)	300 (100.00)	
	Total	414 (69.00)	152 (25.33)	34 (5.67)	600 (100.00)	

Note: Figures in parentheses indicate percentages.
N.S.: Not significant

It can be observed from Table 4.16 that 69 per cent B.Ed. trainees of IGNOU and UPRTOU considered that guidance provided for the preparation of unit plans relevant.

4.17 Response of Counsellors about Relevance of Guidance provided for Preparation of Unit Plan: University-wise

It can be noticed from Table 4.17 that the calculated χ^2 value of independence between response pattern of counsellors and university background in relation to relevance of guidance provided for preparation of unit plan is 2.56. The obtained χ^2 is less than the table value (5.99) at .05 level of significance with df: 2. The observed value is not found significant. Hence, the response pattern of counsellors and the university background in relation to relevance of guidance provided for preparation of unit plan are found independent from each other.

Table 4.17: χ^2 test of independence of counsellors response in relation to relevance of unit planning process and university background

Response of counsellors about level of relevance of guidance provided by them for preparing unit plan						
Statement	*UNIV.*	*Highly Agree*	*Agree*	*Disagree*	*Total*	χ^2 *Value*
1. Guidance provided by you for preparing unit plan is assisting for completing daily syllabus timely.	IGNOU	18 (60.00)	10 (33.33)	2 (6.67)	30 (100.00)	2.56 N.S.
	UPRTOU	17 (56.67)	7 (23.33)	6 (20.00)	30 (100.00)	
	Total	35 (58.33)	17 (28.33)	8 (13.33)	60 (100.00)	

Note: Figures in parentheses indicate percentages. N.S.: Not significant

It can be observed from Table 4.17 that 58 per cent counsellors of IGNOU and UPRTOU considered that guidance provided for the preparation of unit plans relevant.

4.18 Response of B.Ed. Trainees about Effectiveness of Guidance Provided for Preparation of Unit Plan: University-wise

It can be noticed from Table 4.18 that the calculated χ^2 value of independence between response pattern of B.Ed. trainees and university background in relation to effectiveness of guidance provided for preparation of unit plan is 1.78. The obtained χ^2 is less than the table value (5.99) at .05 level of significance with df: 2. The observed value is not found significant. Hence, the response pattern of B.Ed. trainees and the university background in relation to effectiveness of guidance provided for preparation of unit plan are found independent from each other.

It can be observed from Table 4.18 that 72 per cent B.Ed. trainees of IGNOU and UPRTOU considered that the guidance provided for the preparations of unit plan were found effective.

Table 4.18: χ^2 test of independence of trainees' response about effectiveness of training process of preparation of unit plan and university background

Response of trainees on level of effectiveness of training process of preparation of unit plan						
Benefits of skill	*UNIV.*	*More extent*	*Some extent*	*Least*	*Total*	χ^2 *Value*
1. Preparation of unit plan	IGNOU	223 (74.33)	53 (17.67)	24 (8.00)	300 (100.00)	1.78 N.S.
	UPRTOU	209 (69.67)	60 (20.00)	31 (10.33)	300 (100.00)	
	Total	432 (72.00)	113 (18.83)	55 (9.17)	600 (100.00)	

Note: Figures in parentheses indicate percentages. N.S.: Not significant

4.19 Response of Counsellors about Effectiveness of Guidance Provided for Preparation of Unit Plan: University-wise

It can be noticed from Table 4.19 that the calculated χ^2 value of independence between response pattern of counsellors and university background in relation to effectiveness of guidance provided for preparation of unit plan is 2.71. The obtained χ^2 is less than the table value (5.99) at .05 level of significance with df: 2. The observed value is not found significant. Hence the response pattern of counsellors and

Table 4.19: χ^2 test of Independence of trainees' response about effectiveness of training process of preparation of unit plan and university background

Response of counsellors on level of effectiveness of training process of preparation of unit plan						
Benefits of skill	*UNIV.*	*More extent*	*Some extent*	*Least*	*Total*	χ^2 *Value*
1. Preparation of unit plan	IGNOU	23 (76.67)	5 (16.67)	2 (6.67)	30 (100.00)	2.71 N.S.
	UPRTOU	22 (73.33)	8 (26.67)	0 (0.00)	30 (100.00)	
	Total	45 (75.00)	13 (21.67)	2 (3.33)	60 (100.00)	

Note: Figures in parentheses indicate percentages.
N.S.: Not significant

the university background in relation to effectiveness of guidance provided for preparation of unit plan are found independent from each other.

It can be observed from the Table 4.19 that 75 per cent counsellors of IGNOU and UPRTOU considered that the guidance provided for the preparation of unit plan were found effective.

Conclusion: Unit plan is compulsory in preparing lesson plans. Maximum trainees and counsellors of both the open universities stated that help was provided during workshops for preparing unit plan. As a whole the trainees and the counsellors expressed positive response about the process adopted for making competent B.Ed. trainees in preparation of unit plan.

II. Preparation of Teaching Aids by B.Ed. Trainees and their Uses

In this section analysis has been done regarding present status, relevance and effectiveness of teaching aids as well as their preparation by trainees and help rendered by counsellors in preparation of teaching aids.

4.20A Response of Trainees about Use of Teaching Aids by Themselves: University-wise

It can be noticed from Table 4.20A that the calculated χ^2 values of independence between the response pattern of B.Ed. trainees and the university background in relation to the use of teaching aids like charts, readymade model, natural objects and ICT based equipments used during teaching are found as 22.95, 17.57, 20.07 and 37.22 respectively, which are greater than the table value (5.99) at .05 level of significance with df: 2. Thus the observed values are significant. Hence, it is clear that the response pattern of B.Ed. trainees and the university background are not found independent from each other in the context of use of teaching aids like charts, model, natural objects and ICT based equipments during teaching.

It can be observed that 20 to 73 per cent B.Ed. trainees of IGNOU, utilized following teaching aids to the maximum extent.

(i) Chart (72.67%)
(ii) Natural object (69.00%)
(iii) Artificial/Readymade models (35.33%)
(iv) ICT based material (20.33%).

In the case of UPRTOU 7 to 68 per cent B.Ed. trainees utilized following teaching aids to the maximum extent.

(i) Chart (67.67%)
(ii) Natural object (49.00%)
(iii) Artificial/Readymade models (32.00%)
(iv) ICT based material (6.67%).

Table 4.20: χ^2 test of independence of trainees' response about use of teaching aids during teaching and preparation of teaching aids and university background

A.

Response of trainees about level of using aids by themselves							
	Teaching Aids	*UNIV.*	*Max. Lim.*	*Low. Lim.*	*Not. at all*	*Total*	χ^2 *Values*
i.	Chart	IGNOU	218 (72.67)	71 (23.67)	11 (3.67)	300 (100.00)	22.95**
		UPRTOU	203 (67.67)	53 (17.67)	44 (14.67)	300 (100.00)	
		Total	421 (70.17)	124 (20.67)	55 (9.17)	600 (100.00)	
ii.	Artificial/Readymade Model	IGNOU	106 (35.33)	163 (54.33)	31 (10.33)	300 (100.00)	17.57**
		UPRTOU	96 (32.00)	135 (45.00)	69 (23.00)	300 (100.00)	
		Total	202 (33.67)	298 (49.67)	100 (16.67)	600 (100.00)	
iii.	Natural Objects (Flowers leaf etc.)	IGNOU	207 (69.00)	61 (20.33)	32 (10.67)	300 (100.00)	27.07**
		UPRTOU	147 (49.00)	85 (28.33)	68 (22.67)	300 (100.00)	
		Total	354 (59.00)	146 (24.33)	100 (16.67)	600 (100.00)	
iv.	ICT based (Computer, Television, and Radio etc.)	IGNOU	61 (20.33)	106 (35.33)	133 (44.33)	300 (100.00)	37.22**
		UPRTOU	20 (6.67)	81 (27.00)	199 (66.33)	300 (100.00)	
		Total	81 (13.5)	187 (31.17)	332 (55.33)	600 (100.00)	

(Contd,)

B.

	Response of trainees about help provider for preparation of teaching aids								
UNIV.	i (Mentor)	ii (Peer Trainees)	iii (Counsellors)	iv (Other Teacher)	v (Student)	vi (i, ii, iii, iv&v)	vii (None)	Total	χ^2 Value
IGNOU	113 (37.67)	95 (31.67)	68 (22.67)	15 (5.00)	5 (1.67)	2 (0.67)	2 (0.67)	300 (100.00)	105.78**
UPRTOU	45 (15.00)	71 (23.67)	156 (52.00)	0 (0.00)	0 (0.00)	7 (2.33)	21 (7.00)	300 (100.00)	
Total	158 (26.33)	166 (27.67)	224 (37.33)	15 (2.5)	5 (0.83)	9 (1.5)	23 (3.83)	600 (100)	

Note: Figures in parentheses indicate percentages.
** Indicates significant at .01 level.

From the above analysis it is clear that B.Ed. trainees of IGNOU in comparison to B.Ed. trainees of UPRTOU utilized teaching aids during practice teaching to a larger extent.

4.20B. Response of Trainees about Facilitator for Preparing Teaching Aids: University-wise

It can be noticed from Table 4.20B that the calculated χ^2 value of independence between the response pattern of B.Ed. trainees and the university background in relation to facilitator for preparing teaching aids is 105.78. The observed value is greater than the table value (12.59) at .05 level of significance with df: 6. Thus, the observed value is found significant. Hence, it is clear that the response patterns of B.Ed. trainees and university background in the context of facilitator for preparing teaching aids are not found independent from each other.

It can be observed that according to 38 present B.Ed. trainees of IGNOU and 15 per cent B.Ed. trainees of UPRTOU, mentors provided assistance in the preparation of teaching aids. According to 32 per cent B.Ed. trainees of IGNOU and 24 per cent B.Ed. trainees of UPRTOU, peer trainees provided assistance in the preparation of teaching aids. According to 52 per cent B.Ed. trainees of UPRTOU and 23 per cent B.Ed. trainees of IGNOU, counsellors provided assistance in the preparation of teaching aids.

Response of B.Ed. Trainees about Problems Faced in using of Teaching Aids during Delivery Lesson in Real Classroom Setting

Problems faced by B.Ed. trainees during practice teaching in relation to the use of teaching aids were as follows:

General Problems

- Lesson not completed within time due to the usage of teaching aids.
- Teaching aid was not visible to back benchers in the class.
- Lack of appropriate facilities to demonstrate teaching aids in the classrooms.
- Lack of appropriate space in class for exhibiting teaching aids.
- Non-availability of electricity on time.
- Attention of students was directed upon teaching aids only.
- Students are diverted from the content and more interested in telling the merits and demerits of teaching aids.
- Lack of fund to buy readymade teaching aids.
- Problem of maintaining available teaching aids.
- Non-availability of materials to prepare teaching aids.
- Indiscipline among students in classroom setting.
- Problem of carrying teaching aids to the practice teaching schools.
- Lack of cooperation from mentors.

Problem Related to Skill

- Could not prepare charts properly.
- Problem pertaining to presentation of teaching aids.
- Could not prepare appropriate models.
- Non-availability of computers for delivery of lessons.
- Material not, in accordance with the lesson.
- Teaching aids not being interesting.

Response of B.Ed. Trainees about Process Adopted by Themselves to Rectify Errors in using Teaching aids During Classroom Teaching

Efforts to resolve problems faced during teaching in the utilization of teaching aids by the trainees are as follows:

- By taking guidance from counsellors and mentors.
- Resolving problems of students by themselves.
- By using appropriate teaching aids.
- By presenting teaching content interestingly.
- By using appropriate charts.
- By taking help from students in showing teaching aids.
- By using generator at the time of power cut.
- Using appropriate model.
- By making pictures, diagrams, writing word-meaning etc. on roller board.
- By taking help from colleagues.
- By taking help from other employees of school.
- By reinforcing students appropriately.

Interview with Mentors about their Guidance on Teaching Aids

The selected mentors mentioned that they helped in resolving the problems faced by B.Ed. trainees through help in selection of appropriate teaching aids, by giving the knowledge of time management, when and how teaching aids would be displayed etc.

Interview with Counsellors about Help given to B.Ed. Trainees for Preparation of TLM

The selected counsellors of both the universities mentioned that they provided theoretical knowledge regarding teaching aids, demonstrated already prepared teaching aids, make the trainees prepare teaching aids during workshops in groups and made them learn to use readymade teaching aids. Proper guidance was given to prepare subject-wise appropriate teaching aids and make the trainees prepare teaching aids in a small group during workshops.

Interview with Mentors about Solving Problems Faced by B.Ed. Trainees during Preparing Teaching Aids

The selected mentors of both the universities mentioned that they helped trainees in framing questions, in framing introductory questions, by checking prepared lesson plans and providing feedback, making them understand the steps of lesson plan, making them prepare lesson plans, making them selecting the teaching aids, and rectified errors of lesson plan. Some of the mentors mentioned that they do not provide any help of the above mentioned sort to the B.Ed. trainees.

Interview with Mentors about Guidance on Preparation of Teaching Aids

Selected mentors of both the universities mentioned that they helped B.Ed. trainees by helping them in selection of appropriate teaching aids related to topic. The mentors mentioned that they help in preparing charts, they practiced to remove the shortcoming in models prepared by B.Ed. trainees, they helped in making teaching aids sitting with each other in free periods and they help in selecting the teaching aids on the basis of present resources of schools.

Interview with Mentors about Problems of B.Ed. Trainees in Use of Teaching Aids

The selected mentors of both the universities stated about shortage of time of B.Ed. trainees. They did not prepare teaching aids according to lessons, they did not demonstrate teaching aids appropriately, students make indiscipline due to non-attractive aids, lack of facility for electronic resources, i.e. computer, L.C.D., O.H.P. etc.

Interview with Mentors about Problems of B.Ed. Trainees about Classroom Interaction

The selected mentors stated that the problems faced by B.Ed. trainees in classroom interaction were indiscipline of students. They had no understanding of students problems. The B.Ed. trainees did not know local language. They have no command on the subject matter.

Interview with Counsellors about Help Given to B.Ed. Trainees For Appropriate use of Library/Laboratory/Media and other Facilities

The selected counsellors of both the universities stated that proper guidance was given for the utilization of library, laboratory, media and other useful material was provided to B.Ed. trainees during counselling sessions. Importance of aforementioned utilities was dealt in detail with them. They were sent to the study centre, library and books were made available to them. During micro teaching and practice teaching sessions equipment like beaker, pendulum, prism etc. were made available to them from the laboratory.

Some counsellors mentioned that facilities of library and laboratory could not be provided due to paucity of resources and time. Arrangements and utilization of media was also neglected. Although IGNOU had provided T.V. disconnection computer etc. to the study centres they are limited to office use only.

Through the observation of the researcher it was also found that the counsellors ordinarily use maps, charts and model etc. during providing training. Training in the use of television and computer etc. was neither provided nor used during micro teaching. Only theoretical knowledge regarding teaching aids was provided during workshop. Computer and other electronic gadgets were used for office works. The VCR/DVD player could be used for training of B.Ed. students for demonstration lessons.

Interview with Counsellors about Reinforcement to B.Ed. Trainees for using ICT Based Teaching Aids

The selected counsellors of both the universities mentioned that they motivated and encouraged students to use computer, OHP, multimedia, power point presentation, audio-visual aids, internet etc. to make their teaching effective. Some counsellors of UPRTOU mentioned encouragement for trainees to use T.V. and video lessons.

Interview with Counsellors about Relevance of Help Given to B.Ed. Trainees for Preparation and Use of TLM

The selected counsellors of both the universities considered that their helps were relevant since it enhances participation of students in teaching, prepare and utilize teaching aids to make their subject and content lucid, learn to make interesting teaching aids using cheap and affordable material, due to all these they tend to solve problems incurred during teaching.

4.21A Response of Counsellors about Place where Teaching Aids are Prepared by B.Ed. Trainees: University-wise

It can be noticed from Table 4.21A that the calculated χ^2 value of independence between response pattern of the counsellors and

Table 4.21: χ^2 test of independence of counsellors response background about place of preparation of teaching aids and number of teaching aids prepared by trainees and university

A.

UNIV.	Response of counsellors about place of preparing teaching aids by trainees					
	i (Their own school)	*ii (During workshops)*	*iii (i&ii)*	*iv (Not prepared)*	*Total*	χ^2 *Value*
IGNOU	3 (10.00)	10 (33.33)	16 (53.33)	1 (3.33)	30 (100.00)	8.95*
UPRTOU	0 (0.00)	4 (13.33)	26 (86.67)	0 (0.00)	30 (100.00)	
Total	3 (5.00)	14 (23.33)	42 (70.00)	1 (1.67)	60 (100.00)	

B.

UNIV.	Response of counsellors about number of teaching aids prepared during workshops by B.Ed. trainees					
	i (1-5)	*ii (6-10)*	*iii (11-15)*	*iv (None)*	*Total*	χ^2 *Value*
IGNOU	17 (56.67)	7 (23.33)	3 (10.00)	3 (10.00)	30 (100.00)	3.92 N.S.
UPRTOU	22 (73.33)	6 (20.00)	2 (6.67)	0 (0.00)	30 (100.00)	
Total	39 (65.00)	13 (21.67)	5 (8.33)	3 (5.00)	60 (100.00)	

Note: Figures in parentheses indicate percentages.
N.S.: Not significant.
* Indicates significant at .05 level.

the university background in relation to the place where B.Ed. trainees prepare their teaching aids is 8.95. The observed value is greater than the table value (7.81) at .05 level of significance with df: 3. Thus the calculated χ^2 value is found significant. Hence, it is clear that the response pattern of counsellors and the university background is not found independent from each other in the context of the place of preparation of teaching aids.

It can be observed that according to 87 per cent counsellors of UPRTOU and 53 per cent counsellors of IGNOU, B.Ed. trainees prepared their teaching aids both at workshops and in their own school. According to 33 per cent counsellors of IGNOU and only 12 per cent counsellors of UPRTOU, teaching aids were prepared at the workshops, as per the norms.

From the above analysis it is clear the B.Ed. trainees of IGNOU perform more close to the norms in comparison to UPRTOU B.Ed. trainees for preparation of teaching aids.

4.21B Response of Counsellors about Number of Teaching Aids Prepared by B.Ed. Trainees during Workshops: University-wise

It can be noticed from Table 4.21B that the calculated χ^2 value of independence between response pattern of the counsellors and the university background in relation to the number of teaching aids prepared by B.Ed. trainees during workshops is 3.92. The observed value is less than the table value (7.81) at .05 level of significance with df: 3. Thus the calculated χ^2 value is not found significant. Hence, it is clear that the response pattern of counsellors and the university background are found to be independent from each other in relation to the number of teaching aids prepared by B.Ed. trainees during workshops.

It can be observed that 65% per cent counsellors of both the universities considered that B.Ed. trainees prepared 1 to 5 teaching aids during workshops as per the norms.

4.22 Response of Trainees about Relevance of Training Process for Development of Teaching Aids and their Uses: University-wise

It can be noticed from Table 4.22 that the calculated χ^2 value of independence between the response pattern of B.Ed. trainees and the university background in relation to the relevance of training process for preparation of teaching aids is 6.74, which is greater than the table value (5.99) at .05 level of significance with df: 2. Hence, the observed value is found significant. Thus, it is clear that the response pattern of B.Ed. trainees and the university background are not found to be independent from each other in relation to the relevance of training process for preparation of teaching aids.

It can be observed that almost 76 per cent B.Ed. trainees of IGNOU and 74 per cent B.Ed. trainees of UPRTOU considered that guidance for the preparation of teaching aids was in accordance with the availability of resources in their own schools.

Table 4.22: χ^2 test of Independence of trainees' response about relevance of training process of development of teaching aids and their uses and university background

Response of trainees towards relevance of teaching aids and their use						
Statements	*UNIV.*	*Highly Agree*	*Agree*	*Disagree*	*Total*	χ^2 *Values*
1. Training given for preparing teaching aids is related to the available resources at your schools	IGNOU	229 (76.33)	64 (21.33)	7 (2.33)	300 (100.00)	6.74*
	UPRTOU	223 (74.33)	57 (19.00)	20 (6.67)	300 (100.00)	
	Total	452 (75.33)	121 (20.17)	27 (4.50)	600 (100.00)	
2. Training for the use of teaching aids is in accordance to the B.Ed. syllabus	IGNOU	230 (76.67)	58 (19.33)	12 (4.00)	300 (100.00)	0.57 N.S.
	UPRTOU	232 (77.33)	53 (17.67)	15 (5.00)	300 (100.00)	
	Total	462 (77.00)	111 (18.50)	27 (4.50)	600 (100.00)	

Note: Figures in parentheses indicate percentages. N.S.: Not significant.
* Indicates significant at .05 level.

From the above analysis it is clear that in comparison to 74 per cent B.Ed. trainees of UPRTOU, 76 per cent B.Ed. trainees of IGNOU considered training for the preparation of teaching aids more relevant.

It can be noticed from Table 4.22 that the calculated χ^2 value of independence between the response pattern of B.Ed. trainees and the university background in relation to the relevance of training for the utilization of teaching aids in classroom is 0.57. The observed value is less than the table value (5.99) at .05 level of significance with df: 2. Hence the calculated χ^2 value is not found significant. Thus, it is clear that the response pattern of B.Ed. trainees and the university background are found to be independent from each other in relation to the relevance of training for utilization of teaching aids in classroom.

It can be observed that 77 per cent B.Ed. trainees of IGNOU and UPRTOU considered that the training provided for the utilization of teaching aids in classroom is relevant.

4.23 Response of Counsellors about Relevance of Training Process for the Development of Teaching Aids and their Use by Trainees: University-wise

It can be noticed from Table 4.23 that the calculated χ^2 values of independence with the response pattern of counsellors and the university background in relation to the relevance of training for the preparation and utilization of teaching aids are found as 2.40 and 2.37 respectively. The observed values are less than the table value (5.99) at .05 level of significance with df: 2. Thus the calculated χ^2 values are not significant. Hence, it is clear that the response pattern of counsellors and the university background are found to be independent from each other in relation to the relevance of training for the preparation and utilization of teaching aids.

Table 4.23: χ^2 test of independence of counsellors response in relation to relevance of training process of development of teaching aids and their use and university background

Response of counsellors about level of relevance of development of teaching aids and their use						
Statements	*UNIV.*	*Highly Agree*	*Agree*	*Disagree*	*Total*	χ^2 *Values*
1. Training given to B.Ed. trainees by you for preparation of teaching aids is in accordance to their B.Ed. syllabus	IGNOU	21 (70.00)	9 (30.00)	0 (0.00)	30 (100.00)	2.40 N.S.
	UPRTOU	16 (53.33)	13 (43.33)	1 (3.33)	30 (100.00)	
	Total	37 (61.67)	22 (36.67)	1 (1.67)	60 (100.00)	
2. Training given to B.Ed. trainees by you for the use of teaching aids is accordance to their school resources	IGNOU	14 (46.67)	15 (50.00)	1 (3.33)	30 (100.00)	2.37 N.S.
	UPRTOU	19 (63.33)	11 (36.67)	0 (0.00)	30 (100.00)	
	Total	33 (55.00)	26 (43.33)	1 (1.67)	60 (100.00)	

Note: Figures in parentheses indicate percentages. N.S.: Not significant

It can be observed that 55 to 62 per cent counsellors of IGNOU and UPRTOU considered training provided to B.Ed. trainees for the preparation and utilization of teaching aids as relevant.

4.24 Response of B.Ed. Trainees about Effectiveness of Training Process for Preparation of Teaching Aids and their use by Themselves: University-wise

It can be noticed from Table 2.24 that the calculated χ^2 value of independence between the response pattern of B.Ed. trainees and the university background in relation to the effectiveness of training provided for the preparation of teaching aids is 2.50 which is less than the table value (5.99) at .05 level of significance with df: 2. Thus the calculated χ^2 value is not found significant. Hence, the response pattern of B.Ed. trainees and the university background are found to be independent from each other in relation to the effectiveness of training provided for the preparation of teaching aids.

Table 4.24: χ^2 test of Independence on trainees' response about effectiveness of training process of preparation of teaching aids and their use and university background, skill-wise

Benefits of training process of preparation of teaching aids and their use						
Development of skills	*UNIV.*	*More extent*	*Some extent*	*Least*	*Total*	χ^2 *Values*
1-i. Prepare teaching aid by waste materials	IGNOU	211 (70.33)	75 (25.00)	14 (4.67)	300 (100.00)	2.50 N.S.
	UPRTOU	213 (71.00)	65 (21.67)	22 (7.33)	300 (100.00)	
	Total	424 (70.67)	140 (23.33)	36 (6.00)	600 (100.00)	
ii. Successfully utilization of teaching aids	IGNOU	250 (83.33)	36 (12.00)	14 (4.67)	300 (100.00)	9.71**
	UPRTOU	267 (89.00)	15 (5.00)	18 (6.00)	300 (100.00)	
	Total	517 (86.17)	51 (8.50)	32 (5.33)	600 (100.00)	
iii. Making classroom teaching interesting	IGNOU	239 (79.67)	45 (15.00)	16 (5.33)	300 (100.00)	10.94**
	UPRTOU	260 (86.67)	20 (6.67)	20 (6.67)	300 (100.00)	
	Total	499 (83.17)	65 (10.83)	36 (6.00)	600 (100.00)	

Note: Figures in parentheses indicate percentages. N.S.: Not significant.

** Indicates significant at .01 level.

It can be observed that around 71 per cent B.Ed. trainees of IGNOU as well as UPTROU considered training provided for the preparation of teaching aids as effective.

It can be noticed from Table 4.24 that the calculated χ^2 values of independence between the response pattern of B.Ed. trainees and the university background in relation to the training provided for the development of skills in successful utilization of teaching aids for making teaching interesting are 9.71 and 10.94 respectively, which are greater than the table value (5.99) at .05 level of significance with df: 2. Thus the observed values are not found significant. Hence, it is clear that the response pattern of B.Ed. trainees and the university background are found to be independent from each other in relation to the training provided for the development of skills in successful utilization of teaching aids and making teaching more interesting.

It can be observed that 87 to 89 per cent B.Ed. trainees of UPRTOU considered training provided for the development of skills for making teaching interesting via utilization of teaching aids as effective and the extent was as follows:

(i) Successful utilization of teaching aids (89.00%).
(ii) Making classroom teaching interesting (86.67%).

Majority of B.Ed. trainees (80 to 83%) of IGNOU considered training provided for the development of skills for making teaching interesting via utilization of teaching aids as effective and the extent was as follows:

(i) Successful utilization of teaching aids (83.33%).
(ii) Making classroom teaching interesting (79.67%).

4.25 Response of Counsellors about Effectiveness of Process Adopted for Development of Teaching Aids and its use by Trainees: University-wise

It can be noticed from Table 4.25 that the calculated χ^2 values of independence between the response pattern of counsellors and the university background in relation to the effectiveness of process adopted for the development of skills in successful utilization of teaching aids and making teaching interesting are 1.44, 1.15 and 1.08 respectively, which are less than the table value (5.99) at 0.05 level of significance with df: 2. Thus, the observed values are not found

Table 4.25: χ^2 test of Independence of counsellors response about effectiveness of training process of development of teaching aids and their use and university background, skill-wise

Benefits of training process of development of teaching aids and their use						
Development of skills	*UNIV.*	*More extent*	*Some extent*	*Least*	*Total*	χ^2 *Values*
1i. Preparing teaching aid by waste materials	IGNOU	19 (63.33)	10 (33.33)	1 (3.33)	30 (100.00)	1.44 N.S.
	UPRTOU	22 (73.33)	8 (26.67)	0 (0.00)	30 (100.00)	
	Total	41 (68.33)	18 (30.00)	1 (1.67)	60 (100.00)	
ii. Successfully utilization of teaching aids	IGNOU	20 (66.67)	9 (30.00)	1 (3.33)	30 (100.00)	1.15 N.S.
	UPRTOU	22 (73.33)	8 (26.67)	0 (0.00)	30 (100.00)	
	Total	42 (70.00)	17 (28.33)	1 (1.67)	60 (100.00)	
iii. Making classroom teaching interesting	IGNOU	23 (76.67)	6 (20.00)	1 (3.33)	30 (100.00)	1.08 N.S.
	UPRTOU	23 (76.67)	7 (23.33)	0 (0.00)	30 (100.00)	
	Total	46 (76.67)	13 (21.67)	1 (1.67)	60 (100.00)	

Note: Figures in parentheses indicate percentages. N.S.: Not significant

significant. Hence it is clear that the response pattern of counsellors and their university background are found to be independent from each other in relation to the effectiveness of training provided for the development of skills in successful utilization of teaching aids and making teaching interesting.

It can be observed that 68 to 77 per cent counsellors of IGNOU and UPRTOU considered training provided for the development of teaching aids and its uses as follows:

(i) Making classroom teaching interesting (76.67%).
(ii) Successful utilization of teaching aids (70.00%).
(iii) Preparing teaching aids from waste material (68.33%).

Conclusion

In this component study had been conducted about process adopted for development of skills of preparation of teaching aids and their use among B.Ed. trainees. It is clear from the analysis that B.Ed. trainees used chart and natural objects as teaching aids during teaching in the classroom. B.Ed. trainees told that help had been provided by mentors, peer trainees and counsellors for preparing teaching aids. Majority of counsellors of UPRTOU and average number of IGNOU stated that teaching aids prepared by trainees at their own working school as well as during workshops. Counsellors also stated that more trainees prepared teaching aids during workshops. Maximum trainees informed that they faced various problems during use of teaching aids. Most of the trainees resolved their problems with the help of their colleagues, mentors and counsellers. As a whole the trainees and the counsellors consider process adopted for development of competency related to preparation of teaching aids their use among B.Ed. trainees as relevant and effective.

III. Classroom Teaching Motivation-oriented Practices in Distance B.Ed. Programme

In this section analysis has been done regarding present status, relevance and effectiveness of processes adopted for making B.Ed. trainees competent in classroom teaching motivation skill.

4.26 Response of B.Ed. Trainees about Guidance for Motivating the Students: University-wise

It can be noticed from Table 4.26 that the calculated χ^2 value of independence between the response pattern of B.Ed. trainees and the university background in relation to guidance provider to B.Ed. trainees for motivating the students is 60.04. The obtained χ^2 value is greater than the table value (11.07) at .05 level of significance with df: 5. The observed value is found significant. Hence, the response pattern of B.Ed. trainees and the university background in reference to guidance provider to B.Ed. trainees for motivating the students are not found independent from each other.

It can be observed that 70 per cent B.Ed. trainees of UPRTOU considered that counsellors provided guidance to them to motivate their

Table 4.26: χ^2 test of independence of trainees' response about guidance provider to motivate to the students and university background

UNIV.	*Response of B.Ed. trainees about guidance provider*							
	i Mentor	*ii Peer Trainees*	*iii Counseller*	*iv (i&iii)*	*v (i, ii & iii)*	*vi (None)*	*Total*	χ^2 *Value*
IGNOU	139 (46.33)	23 (7.67)	127 (42.33)	4 (1.33)	3 (1.00)	4 (1.33)	300 (100.00)	60.043**
UPRTOU	60 (20.00)	17 (5.67)	209 (69.67)	4 (1.33)	10 (3.33)	0 (0.00)	300 (100.00)	
Total	199 (33.17)	40 (6.67)	336 (56.00)	8 (1.33)	13 (2.17)	4 (0.67)	600 (100.00)	

Note: Figures in parentheses indicate percentages.
** Indicates significant at .01 level.

students, while only 42 per cent B.Ed. trainees of IGNOU considered that counsellors provided guidance to them for the same.

It can be also observed that only 46 per cent B.Ed. trainees of IGNOU mentioned that mentors provided guidance to them to motivate their students, while only 20 per cent B.Ed. trainees of UPRTOU considered that mentors provided guidance to them for the same.

Response of B.Ed. Trainees about Guidance for Motivating Students

On the basis of response of B.Ed. trainees of both the universities it is clear that following guidance was given to them for motivating their students:

- Use of appropriate teaching aids during classroom teaching.
- Use of appropriate charts, models and other equipments with skilfulness.
- Use of proper reinforcement during classroom teaching.
- Preparation of lesson plan and using it appropriately during teaching.
- To make interaction with their students during teaching.
- To be friendly with students.
- Drawing figures and diagrams on blackboard.
- To give correct answer of their students questions.
- Enhancing interest of students in the subjects.
- To organise co-curricular activities in the school.

- To give reward to their students.
- To provide freedom of presentation to their students in classroom.
- To conduct activities related to practicals.
- To conduct action research in their schools.

Response of Counsellors about Process Adopted during Workshops for making B.Ed. Trainees Competent in Motivation Skill

It is clear from the responses of counsellors of both the universities that they make B.Ed. trainees to learn following for providing motivation to their students:

- Teaching with the help of teaching aids in the classroom.
- Making appropriate arrangement of class.
- Adopting various process of evaluation of their students.
- Using appropriate techniques of questioning in the claşsroom.
- Providing appropriate reinforcement to their students.
- Being sympathetic to students.
- Making good preparation of content to teach in the class.
- Giving reward to their students for their better performance.
- Paying attention towards interest of students.
- To develop interest of students towards teaching.
- To motivate students for learning.
- To take care of individual differences of their students.
- Maintain discipline in the classroom.

Conclusion

In this component study was conducted regarding development of competency related classroom teaching motivation among B.Ed. trainees. It is clear from the analysis that mentors, peer trainees and counsellors helped B.Ed. trainees in classroom teaching motivation. Majority of trainees and counsellors make clear that for making B.Ed. trainees competent in classroom motivation various activities make learn them during workshop, i.e. use of appropriate teaching aids, use of proper reinforcement during classroom teaching, to be friendly with students, to give correct and appropriate answer of their students questions, organizing co-curricular activities, to give reward to their students and enhancing interest of student in the subjects etc. As a whole majority of trainees as well as counsellors expressed positive response regarding the relevance and effectiveness of process adopted for developing competency related classroom motivation among trainees.

IV. Classroom Communication Practices in Distance B.Ed. Programme

In this section analysis has been done regarding process adopted for making B.Ed. trainees competent in classroom communication skill.

Response of B.Ed. Trainees about Counsellors Guidance for Making Effective Classroom Communication

On the basis of response of B.Ed. trainees of both the universities it is clear that the counsellors guided them for making effective classroom communication:

- To have complete knowledge regarding subject matter.
- To make classroom presentation effective.
- To make appropriate environment of class for teaching.
- Understanding of student's behaviour during teaching.
- To develop feeling of discipline among their students.
- Teaching through lesson plan in the classroom.
- To organise group discussion in the classroom for their students.
- To deliver appropriate lecture in the classroom.
- To pronounce correctly during teaching and while communicating with others.
- To teach students with the help of their previous knowledge.
- To speak loudly in the classroom.
- To give reinforcement for motivating the students.
- To use simple language in the classroom.
- To make interaction with every students in the classroom.
- To motivate students by asking questions in the classroom.
- To examine previous knowledge of students in the classroom.
- To make voice modulation during teaching in the classroom.
- To teach students by using TLM.
- Teaching through making chart, model.
- To use local materials in the form of teaching aids.
- To teach by using various teaching skills.

Response of Counsellors about Process Adopted during Workshops for Making Classroom Communication Effective

The counsellors expressed following means to be adopted by trainees for classroom communications.

- To use of effective teaching methods during classroom teaching.
- To teach the class with the help of using effective teaching aids.
- To adopt appropriate language and correct pronunciation during teaching in the classroom.
- To make appropriate classroom management.
- To use various evaluation processes.
- To administer psychological tests.
- Teaching through preparation of appropriate lesson plans.
- Appropriate use of different teaching skills in the classroom during teaching.
- To conduct competitions in their school.
- To make voice modulation during classroom teaching.
- To organise group discussion in the class.
- To have proper command on content.
- To give attention on whole class during teaching.
- To motivate the students for asking questions in the classroom.
- To provide appropriate reinforcement to students in the classroom.

Interview with Counsellors about Process Adopted for Making Competent B.Ed. Trainees Competent Regarding Maintaining Discipline in the Classroom

The selected counsellors of both the universities mentioned that they emphasised on knowing and rectifying the personal and educational problems of their students, establishing good relation between student and teacher and maintaining discipline in the classroom. It was also told by counsellors to B.Ed. trainees during workshops to making analytical study of problems of their students through action research, to give exercise work to their students in order to discipline them, make self-discipline in the classroom, to be punctual, to keeping command over the subject and provide proper guidance to their students.

It is also clear from the observation done by researcher during workshops that some of the counsellors provided theoretical knowledge regarding various activities by giving specific example.

Interview with Counsellors about their Help to B.Ed. Trainees for Improving Interaction with their Own Students

The selected counsellors of both the universities stated that for improving interaction with their own students they ask B.Ed. trainees to concentrate on students. They ask more questions related to the topic and motivating students to do same. In addition they also informed that knowledge was provided to them regarding different techniques and methods to increase the interaction with their students.

Interview with Mentors about their Guidance to B.Ed. Trainees on Classroom Interaction

The following kinds of guidance are provided:

- To use local language.
- To use charts and models.

Conclusion

In this component study had been conducted about process adopted for development of skill of classroom communication among B.Ed. trainees. It is clear from the analysis that according to trainees and counsellors of both the open universities, counsellors guided to adopt various activities for making effective classroom communication, i.e. to make classroom presentation effective, to develop feeling of discipline among their students, to make pronunciation correctly during teaching and communicating with others, to give reinforcement for motivating the students, to use simple language in the classroom, to make interaction with every students in classroom and to motivate students for asking questions in the classroom etc. In addition they also informed that they make trainees to understand appropriate classroom management, use of effective teaching methods during classroom teaching. Majority of trainees and counsellors of both the universities expressed positive response about the effectiveness and relevance of guidance about classroom communication.

V. Students' Evaluation Practices by Distance B.Ed. Trainees

In this section analysis has been made regarding present status, relevance and effectiveness of processes adopted for development of competency of students' evaluation among B.Ed. trainees.

4.27A Response of B.Ed. Trainees about Helps Provided by Mentors for Developing Abilities Related to Students' Evaluation in B.Ed. Trainees: University-wise

It can be noticed from Table 4.27A that the calculated χ^2 value of independence between the response pattern of B.Ed. trainees and the university background in relation to helps provided by mentors for development of abilities related to student's evaluation in B.Ed. trainees is found 27.57. The obtained χ^2 value is greater than the table value (7.81) at .05 level of significance with df: 3. The observed value is found significant. Hence, the response pattern of B.Ed. trainees and the university background are not found independent from each other in relation to help provided by mentors for development of abilities related to student's evaluation.

Table 4.27: χ^2 test of independence of trainees' response about help of mentors, counsellors and peer trainees in developing competency related to students' evaluation and presenting assignment and university background

A.

Response of B.Ed. trainees about types of help by mentors for development of competency related to students evaluation

UNIV.	*i (By blue Print)*	*ii (By copy Evaluation)*	*iii (By report Prepared)*	*iv (i, ii & iii)*	*Total*	χ^2 *Value*
IGNOU	52 (17.33)	21 (7.00)	41 (13.67)	186 (62.00)	300 (100.00)	27.57**
UPRTOU	27 (9.00)	41 (13.67)	16 (5.33)	216 (72.00)	300 (100.00)	
Total	79 (13.17)	62 (10.33)	57 (9.5)	402 (67.00)	600 (100.00)	

(Contd.)

B.

Response of B.Ed. trainees about types of help by counsellors for development of competency related to students' evaluation

UNIV.	i (By Assignment)	ii (By psychological test)	iii (By group Discussion)	iv (i, ii & iii)	Total	χ^2 Value
IGNOU	42 (14.00)	13 (4.33)	69 (23.00)	176 (58.67)	300 (100.00)	23.49**
UPRTOU	51 (17.00)	5 (1.67)	30 (10.00)	214 (71.33)	300 (100.00)	
Total	93 (15.5)	18 (3.00)	99 (16.5)	390 (65.00)	600 (100.00)	

C.

Response of B.Ed. trainees about activities of counsellors to make competent trainees for making examination question papers

UNIV.	i (Demonstration Method)	ii (Feedback)	iii (i & ii)	iv (Nothing)	Total	χ^2 Value
IGNOU	36 (12.00)	44 (14.67)	208 (69.33)	12 (4.00)	300 (100.00)	9.23*
UPRTOU	49 (16.33)	25 (8.33)	206 (68.67)	20 (6.67)	300 (100.00)	
Total	85 (14.17)	69 (11.5)	414 (69.00)	32 (5.33)	600 (100.00)	

D.

Response of B.Ed. trainees about activities of counsellors to make competent trainees in psychological test administration

UNIV.	i (Demonstration Method)	ii (Feedback)	iii (i & ii)	iv (Nothing)	Total	χ^2 Value
IGNOU	48 (16.00)	47 (15.67)	173 (57.67)	32 (10.67)	300 (100.00)	13.99**
UPRTOU	51 (17.00)	20 (6.67)	203 (67.67)	26 (8.67)	300 (100.00)	
Total	99 (16.5)	67 (11.17)	376 (62.67)	58 (9.67)	600 (100.00)	

(Contd.)

E.

Response of B.Ed. trainees about types of help provided by mentors for solving their problems faced during evaluation of students in classroom

UNIV.	*i (Help in evaluation)*	*ii (Giving Knowledge)*	*iii (i & ii)*	*iv (Nothing)*	*Total*	χ^2 *Value*
IGNOU	16 (5.33)	127 (42.33)	156 (52.00)	1 (0.33)	300 (100.00)	3.87 N.S.
UPRTOU	8 (2.67)	128 (42.67)	164 (54.67)	0 (0.00)	300 (100.00)	
Total	24 (4.00)	255 (42.5)	320 (53.33)	1 (0.17)	600 (100.00)	

F.

Response of B.Ed. trainees about types of help provided by peer trainees for solving their problems faced during evaluation of students in classroom

UNIV.	*i (By discussion)*	*ii (Help in evaluation)*	*iii (i & ii)*	*iv (No help)*	*Total*	χ^2 *Value*
IGNOU	143 (47.67)	23 (7.67)	120 (40.00)	14 (4.67)	300 (100.00)	7.14 N.S.
UPRTOU	141 (47.00)	9 (3.00)	136 (45.33)	14 (4.67)	300 (100.00)	
Total	284 (47.33)	32 (5.33)	256 (42.67)	28 (4.67)	600 (100.00)	

G.

Response of B.Ed. trainees about the help taken from resources for presenting assignments

UNIV.	*i (Help by Counsellor)*	*ii (By reading book)*	*iii (By help of library)*	*iv (By reading old assignments*	*v (i, ii, iii & iv)*	*total*	χ^2 *Value*
IGNOU	47 (15.67)	59 (19.67)	21 (7.00)	32 (10.67)	141 (47.00)	300 (100.00)	1.11 N.S.
UPRTOU	50 (16.67)	50 (16.67)	24 (8.00)	31 (10.33)	145 (48.33)	300 (100.00)	
Total	97 (16.17)	109 (18.17)	45 (7.5)	63 (10.5)	286 (47.67)	600 (100.00)	

Note: Figures in parentheses indicate percentages. N.S.: Not significant

* Indicates significant at .05 level. ** Indicates significant at .01 level.

It can be observed that according to majority of B.Ed. trainees (72%) of UPRTOU, mentors helped them in preparing blue print, evaluating answer books and preparing report. While according to 62 per cent B.Ed. trainees of IGNOU, mentors helped B.Ed. trainees in preparing blue print, evaluating answer books and preparing report.

Interview with Mentors about Process Adopted by B.Ed. Trainees for Evaluation of their Students

The selected mentors of both the universities told that B.Ed. trainees make question paper, organize weekly test, make co-operation in organization of half yearly and yearly examination for evaluation of their students. For above said activities the B.Ed. trainees give and evaluate home work of their students, they evaluate exercise work in the classroom of their students, they prepare progress report and result card of their students, they evaluate calligraph written by students and they provide reinforcement to their students also.

Interview with Mentors about Problems Faced by B.Ed. Trainees during Evaluation of their Students

The selected mentors stated that during evaluation of their students various problems are faced by B.Ed. trainees, i.e. not able to prepare correct question papers, not able to evaluate answer booklet within stipulated time.

Interview with Mentors about their Help for Solving Problems faced by B.Ed. Trainees in Evaluation Work

The selected mentors of both the universities expressed that they helped B.Ed. trainees in proper evaluation of answer booklet and setting accurate question papers.

4.27B Response of B.Ed. Trainees about Help Provided by Counsellors for Developing Abilities Related to Students' Evaluation: University-wise

It can be noticed from Table 4.27B that the calculated χ^2 value of independence between the response pattern of B.Ed. trainees and the university background in relation to helps provided by counsellors for development of abilities related to student's evaluation among B.Ed. trainees is found 23.49. The obtained χ^2 value is found greater than the table value (7.81) at .05 level of significance with df: 3. The observed value is found significant. Hence the response pattern of B.Ed. trainees and the university background are not found independent from each other in relation to helps provided by counsellors for development of abilities related to students' evaluation among B.Ed. trainees.

It can be observed that 71 per cent B.Ed. trainees of UPRTOU stated that counsellers helped to them in preparing assignments, administration of psychological tests and organization of group discussion for developing competency of students' evaluation among the trainees. While, 62 per cent B.Ed. trainees of IGNOU stated that counsellors helped them by preparing assignments, administration of psychological tests and organization of group discussion for development of competency of students' evaluation.

4.27C Response of B.Ed. Trainees about Counsellors Assistance in Constructing Examination Question Papers: University-wise

It can be noticed from Table 4.27C that the calculated χ^2 value of independence between the response pattern of B.Ed. trainees and the university background in relation to assistance in constructing examination question papers is found 9.23. The obtained χ^2 value is found greater than the table value (7.81) at .05 level of significance with df: 3. The observed value is found significant. Hence the response pattern of B.Ed. trainees and the university background are not found independent from each other in relation to counsellors assistance in constructing examination question papers.

It can be observed that 69 per cent B.Ed. trainees of IGNOU as well as UPRTOU considered that counsellors adopted demonstration method and feedback sessions. So it can be stated that majority of counsellors of both the universities perform same kind of activities to make B.Ed. trainees competent in constructing question papers.

4.27D Response of B.Ed. Trainees of Counsellors Assistance in Administration of Psychological Tests: University-wise

It can be noticed from Table 4.27D that the calculated χ^2 value of independence between the response pattern of B.Ed. trainees and the university background in relation to counsellors assistance in administration of psychological test is found 13.99. The obtained χ^2 value is greater than the table value (7.81) at .05 level of significance with df: 3. The observed value is found significant. Hence, the response pattern of B.Ed. trainees and the university background are not found independent from each other in relation to activities of counsellors enabling the trainees in administration of psychological tests.

It can be observed that 68 per cent B.Ed. trainees of UPRTOU and 58 per cent B.Ed. trainees of IGNOU stated that counsellors demonstrated the method of test administration and provided feedback regarding administration of psychological test to the trainees.

Interview with Counsellors about Process Adopted during Workshop for making B.Ed. Trainees Capable in Administration of Psychological Test, Preparation and Administration of Achievement Test

The selected counsellors of IGNOU as well as UPRTOU stated that they provided knowledge of administration of psychological test by demonstrating psychological tests, report writing after administration of psychological test on their peer trainees. The counsellors also informed that they also taught the steps of construction of achievement tests. The trainees prepared blue prints and constructed the test items.

It was also clear from the observation done by researcher during workshops that B.Ed. trainees became familiar with standardized tests with the help of counsellors.

4.27E. Response of B.Ed. Trainees about Help Provided by Mentors for Solving their Problems Faced during Evaluation of Students: University-wise

It can be noticed from Table 4.27E that the calculated χ^2 value of independence between the response pattern of B.Ed. trainees and the university background in reference to helps provided by mentors for solving their problems faced during evaluation of their students in classroom is found 3.87. The obtained χ^2 value is less than the table value (7.81) at .05 level of significance with df: 3. The observed value is not found significant. Hence, the response pattern of B.Ed. trainees and the university background are found independent from each other in relation to helps provided by mentors for solving their problems faced during evaluation of their students in classroom.

It can be observed that only 53 per cent B.Ed. trainees of IGNOU and UPRTOU stated that their mentors helped them in solving problem at the time of evaluation in the classroom by participating in the evaluation work and provided relevant knowledge for problem-solving. While, 47 per cent helped them in problem solving by providing relevant knowledge.

4.27F Response of B.Ed. Trainees about Help Provided by Peer Trainees for Solving Problems Faced during Evaluation of their Students: University-wise

It can be noticed from Table 4.27F that the calculated χ^2 value of independence between the response pattern of B.Ed. trainees and the university background in relation to help provided by peer trainees for solving their problems faced during evaluation of their students in classroom is found 7.14. The obtained χ^2 value is less than the table value (7.81) at .05 level of significance with df: 3. The observed value is not found significant. Hence, the response pattern of B.Ed. trainees and the university background are found to be independent from each other in reference to help provided by peer trainees for solving problems of B.Ed. trainees faced during evaluation of their students in classroom.

It can be observed that only 47 per cent B.Ed. trainees of IGNOU and UPRTOU mentioned that peer trainees discussed how to solve the problems which occurred at the time of evaluation work in the classroom. This was also observed that only 45 per cent trainees of both the universities stated that peer trainees helped them in solving the problems in evaluation through discussion and by participating in evaluation work.

4.27G Response of B.Ed. Trainees about the Help taken from Different Resources for Preparing Assignments: University-wise

It can be noticed from Table 4.27G that the calculated χ^2 value of independence between the response pattern of B.Ed. trainees and the university background in reference to the help taken from different resources for preparing assignments is found 1.11. The obtained χ^2 value is less than the table value (9.48) at .05 level of significance with df: 4. The observed value is not found significant. Hence, the response pattern of B.Ed. trainees and the university background are found to be independent from each other in relation to the helps taken from different resources for presenting assignments.

It can be observed that according only 48 per cent B.Ed. trainees of IGNOU and UPRTOU took helped from their counsellors, library and from assignments of ex-trainees. Only 18 per cent trainees of IGNOU and UPRTOU stated that they prepared their assignments only through reading the books.

4.28A Response of Counsellors about their Help to B.Ed. Trainees: University-wise

It can be noticed from Table 4.28A that the calculated χ^2 value of independence between the response pattern of counsellors and university background in relation to their help to B.Ed. trainees is found 26.67. The obtained χ^2 value is greater than the table value (11.07) at .05 level of significance with df: 5. The observed value is found to be significant. Hence the response pattern of counsellors and the university background are not found independent from each other in relation to their help provided to B.Ed. trainees.

It can be observed that only 47 per cent counsellors of IGNOU considered that they provided following help for the development of competency of evaluation in B.Ed. trainees.

(i) Helping in preparing blue print.
(ii) Helping in administration of psychological tests.
(iii) Providing theoretical knowledge.

While only 7 per cent counsellors of UPRTOU stated that they provided above mentioned help for the development of competence related to evaluation in B.Ed. trainees. It can be also observed that 53 per cent counsellors of UPRTOU considered that they provided help by providing theoretical knowledge, while 10 per cent counsellors of IGNOU considered that they provided help only by theoretical knowledge for the development of competency related to evaluation in B.Ed. trainees.

4.28B Response of Counsellors about their Assistance to B.Ed. Trainees in Preparing Examination Question Papers: University-wise

It can be noticed from Table 4.28B that the calculated χ^2 value of independence between the response pattern of counsellors and the university background in relation to their assistance in preparing examination question paper is found 7.20. The obtained χ^2 value is less than the table value (7.81) at .05 level of significance with df: 3. The observed value is not found significant. Hence, the response pattern of counsellors and the university background are not found to be independent from each other in reference to the counsellors assistance in preparing examination question papers.

It can be observed that 53 per cent counsellors of IGNOU and UPRTOU considered that they presented examples of question papers and provided feedback in already prepared question papers to the trainees during workshops. Whereas, 17 per cent counsellors of both the universities considered that they provided feedback for making B.Ed. trainees competent.

Table 4.28: χ^2 test of independence of counsellors response about help provided by themselves to trainees in development of competency related to evaluation and assignments presentation and university background

A.

Response of counsellors about help provided by themselves to B.Ed. trainees								
UNIV.	*i (By preparing blue-print/ question paper)*	*ii (By administration of psychological test)*	*iii (By providing theory knowledge)*	*iv (i & iii)*	*v (ii & By achievement test)*	*vi (i, ii, iii & v)*	*Total*	χ^2 *Value*
IGNOU	4 (13.33)	3 (10.00)	3 (10.00)	4 (13.33)	2 (6.67)	14 (46.67)	30 (100.00)	26.67**
UPRTOU	10 (33.33)	2 (6.67)	16 (53.33)	0 (0.00)	0 (0.00)	2 (6.67)	30 (100.00)	
Total	14 (23.33)	5 (8.33)	19 (31.67)	4 (6.67)	2 (3.33)	16 (26.67)	60 (100.00)	

B.

Response of counsellors about their activities for making competent B.Ed. trainees in preparing examination question papers						
UNIV.	*i (By giving example)*	*ii (By feed-back)*	*iii (i&ii)*	*iv (Nothing)*	*Total*	χ^2 *Value*
IGNOU	4 (13.33)	8 (26.67)	16 (53.33)	2 (6.67)	30 (100.00)	7.20 N.S.
UPRTOU	4 (13.33)	2 (6.67)	16 (53.33)	8 (26.67)	30 (100.00)	
Total	8 (13.33)	10 (16.67)	32 (53.33)	10 (16.67)	60 (100.00)	

(Contd.)

C.

Response of counsellors about their activities for making competent B.Ed. trainees in administration of psychological test

UNIV.	*i (By telling preparation procedure & administration method)*	*ii (By providing feedback)*	*iii (i&ii)*	*iv (Nothing)*	*v (*)*	*Total*	χ^2 *Value*
IGNOU	7 (23.33)	6 (20.00)	15 (50.00)	1 (3.33)	1 (3.33)	30 (100.00)	8.84 N.S.
UPRTOU	8 (26.67)	2 (6.67)	12 (40.00)	8 (26.67)	0 (0.00)	30 (100.00)	
Total	15 (25.00)	8 (13.33)	27 (45.00)	9 (15.00)	1 (1.67)	60 (100.00)	

*Preparation of report after administration of standard psychological test.

D.

Response of counsellors about help provided to B.Ed. trainees in assignment work

UNIV.	*i (By giving theoretical knowledge)*	*ii (By feedback)*	*iii (i&ii)*	*Total*	χ^2 *Value*
IGNOU	7 (23.33)	3 (10.00)	20 (66.67)	30 (100.00)	3.89 N.S.
UPRTOU	5 (16.67)	0 (0.00)	25 (83.33)	30 (100.00)	
Total	12 (20.00)	3 (5.00)	45 (75.00)	60 (100.00)	

Note: Figures in parentheses indicate percentages. N.S.: Not significant.
** Indicates significant at .01 level.

4.28C Response of Counsellors about their Assistance in Administration of Psychological Test: University-wise

It can be noticed from Table 4.28C that the calculated χ^2 value of independence between the response pattern of counsellors and the university background in relation to counsellors activities for making competent to B.Ed. trainees competent in administration of psychological test is found to be 8.84. The obtained χ^2 value is less than the table value (9.48) at .05 level of significance with df: 4. The observed value is not found significant. Hence, the response pattern of counsellors and the university background is found to be independent from each other in relation to counsellors assistance in administration of psychological test.

It can be observed that only 45 per cent counsellors of IGNOU and UPRTOU considered that they provided instruction for construction and administration of psychological tests and gave feedback regarding construction of psychological tests during the workshops.

4.28D Response of Counsellors about their Help for Assignment Work: University-wise

It can be noticed from Table 4.28D that the calculated χ^2 value of independence between the response pattern of counsellors and the university background in relation to their help to B.Ed. trainees in assignment work is found 3.89. The obtained χ^2 value is less than the table value (5.99) at .05 level of significance with df: 2. The observed value is not found significant. Hence, the response pattern of counsellors and the university background are found to be independent from each other in relation to the above.

It can be observed that majority of counsellors (75%) of IGNOU and UPRTOU considered that they helped B.Ed. trainees in their assignment work by giving them theoretical knowledge and feedback in assignment prepared by B.Ed. trainees.

Interview with Counsellors about Activities Organized during Workshop for Development of Competency of Students' Evaluation among B.Ed. Trainees

The selected counsellors of both the universities mentioned that theoretical knowledge was provided during workshops regarding evaluation of students, blue print was prepared for construction of question paper by trainees, question paper were prepared by trainees in concerning subjects and achievement test was also prepared by them.

4.29 Response of B.Ed. Trainees about Relevance of the Process Adopted for Development of Students Evaluation Competency: University-wise

It can be noticed from Table 4.29 that the calculated χ^2 value of independence between the response pattern of B.Ed. trainees and the university background in relation to relevance of home-work given by counsellors for preparing question papers, administration of psychological test, curriculum base assignments and experience base assignment are found as 2.62, 4.76, 0.59 and 0.08 respectively. The obtained χ^2 value is less than the table value (5.99) at .05 level of significance with df: 2. The observed value is not found significant. Hence, the response pattern of B.Ed. trainees and the university background are found to be independent from each other in relation to relevance of above mentioned activities.

It can be observed that according to 72 to 80 per cent B.Ed. trainees of IGNOU and UPRTOU, the training process of development of student evaluation were relevant in relation to the following activities:

(i) Assignment work given by counsellors to B.Ed. trainees was related to their curriculum (80.17%).
(ii) Psychological test administration (78.83%).
(iii) Home work for construction of question papers (75.50%).
(iv) Assignment given to B.Ed. trainees are experience based (72.17%).

It can be noticed from Table 4.29 that the calculated χ^2 value of independence between the response pattern of B.Ed. trainees and the university background in relation to relevance of assignments given to B.Ed. trainees is found 20.78. The obtained χ^2 value is found greater than the table value (5.99) at .05 level of significance with df: 2. Hence, the response pattern of B.Ed. trainees and the university background are not found independent from each other in relation to relevance of assignments given to B.Ed. trainees.

It can be observed that according to 76 per cent B.Ed. trainees of UPRTOU, assignments given to B.Ed. trainees were activity oriented. While according to 72 per cent B.Ed. trainees of IGNOU assignment given to B.Ed. trainees were activity oriented, so it was relevant.

Table 4.29: χ^2 test of Independence of trainees' response about relevance of training process of development of students' evaluations in them and university background, statement-wise

Response of B.Ed. trainees about relevance of training process adopted for development of competency in students' evaluation						
Statements	*UNIV.*	*Highly Agree*	*Agree*	*Disagree*	*Total*	χ^2 *Values*
1. Home work given by counsellors for preparing question paper is related to your teaching competence	IGNOU	218 (72.67)	65 (21.67)	17 (5.67)	300 (100.00)	2.62 N.S.
	UPRTOU	235 (78.33)	52 (17.33)	13 (4.33)	300 (100.00)	
	Total	453 (75.50)	117 (19.50)	30 (5.00)	600 (100.00)	
2. Activities related to psychological test are helpful in understanding the students	IGNOU	232 (77.33)	60 (20.00)	8 (2.67)	300 (100.00)	4.76 N.S.
	UPRTOU	241 (80.33)	44 (14.67)	15 (5.00)	300 (100.00)	
	Total	473 (78.83)	104 (17.33)	23 (3.83)	600 (100.00)	
3. Assignment given to you is according to your syllabus	IGNOU	237 (79.00)	54 (18.00)	9 (3.00)	300 (100.00)	0.59 N.S.
	UPRTOU	244 (81.33)	47 (15.67)	9 (3.00)	300 (100.00)	
	Total	481 (80.17)	101 (16.83)	18 (3.00)	600 (100.00)	
4. Assignment given to you is activity oriented	IGNOU	215 (71.67)	76 (25.33)	9 (3.00)	300 (100.00)	20.78**
	UPRTOU	227 (75.67)	43 (14.33)	30 (10.00)	300 (100.00)	
	Total	442 (73.67)	119 (19.83)	39 (6.50)	600 (100.00)	
5. Assignment given to you is related to your experience	IGNOU	215 (71.67)	66 (22.00)	19 (6.33)	300 (100.00)	0.08 N.S.
	UPRTOU	218 (72.67)	64 (21.33)	18 (6.00)	300 (100.00)	
	Total	433 (72.17)	130 (21.67)	37 (6.17)	600 (100.00)	

Note: Figures in parentheses indicate percentages. N.S.: Not significant.
** Indicates significant at .01 level.

4.30 Response of Counsellors about Relevance of the Process Adopted for Development of Students Evaluation Competency: Universitywise

It can be noticed from Table 4.30 that the calculated χ^2 value of independence between the response pattern of counsellors and the university background in relation to relevance of homework given to

Table 4.30: χ^2 test of independence of counsellors response in relation to relevance of training process adopted for development of skills of students' evaluation and university background, statement-wise

		Response of counsellors about level of relevance of training process adopted for development of skills of students' evaluation				
Statements	*UNIV.*	*Highly Agree*	*Agree*	*Disagree*	*Total*	χ^2 *Values*
Home work given to B.Ed. trainees by you for preparing question paper construction is related to their teaching competency	IGNOU	14 (46.67)	11 (36.67)	5 (16.67)	30 (100.00)	1.09 N.S.
	UPRTOU	11 (36.67)	15 (50.00)	4 (13.33)	30 (100.00)	
	Total	25 (41.67)	26 (43.33)	9 (15.00)	60 (100.00)	
1. Assignment given to B.Ed. trainees by you is in accordance to their syllabus	IGNOU	23 (76.67)	5 (16.67)	2 (6.67)	30 (100.00)	1.97 N.S.
	UPRTOU	18 (60.00)	8 (26.67)	4 (13.33)	30 (100.00)	
	Total	41 (68.33)	13 (21.67)	6 (10.00)	60 (100.00)	
2. Assignment given to B.Ed. trainees by you is oriented to activity	IGNOU	23 (76.67)	5 (16.67)	2 (6.67)	30 (100.00)	4.14 N.S.
	UPRTOU	16 (53.33)	12 (40.00)	2 (6.67)	30 (100.00)	
	Total	39 (65.00)	17 (28.33)	4 (6.67)	60 (100.00)	
3. Assignment given to B.Ed. trainees by you is related to their experience	IGNOU	21 (70.00)	8 (26.67)	1 (3.33)	30 (100.00)	5.19 N.S.
	UPRTOU	14 (46.67)	10 (33.33)	6 (20.00)	30 (100.00)	
	Total	35 (58.33)	18 (30.00)	7 (11.67)	60 (100.00)	

Note: Figures in parentheses indicate percentages. N.S.: Not significant

B.Ed. trainees for construction of question papers, curriculum based assignments, activity based assignments and experience based assignments are found to be 1.09, 1.97, 4.14 and 5.19 respectively. The obtained χ^2 values are less than the table value (5.99) at .05 level of significance with df: 2. The observed values are not found significant. Hence, the response pattern of counsellors and the university background are found to be independent from each other in relation to relevance of above mentioned processes.

It can be observed that 42 to 68 per cent counsellors of IGNOU and UPRTOU considered that on the basis of following process training given to B.Ed. trainees were relevant for development of competency of students' evaluation in B.Ed. trainees:

(i) Assignment given to B.Ed. trainees is in accordance to their syllabus (68.33%).
(ii) Assignments given to B.Ed. trainees is activity-oriented (65.00%).
(iii) Assignments given to B.Ed. trainees were related to their experience (58.33%).
(iv) Homework given to B.Ed. trainees for construction of question papers is related to their teaching competency (41.67%).

4.31A Response of B.Ed. Trainees about Effectiveness of the Process Adopted for Development of Students' Evaluation Competency: University-wise

It can be noticed from Table 4.31A that the calculated χ^2 values of independence between the response pattern of B.Ed. trainees and the university background in relation to effectiveness of training given to B.Ed. trainees for constructing good question papers and preparation of progress report of students are found as 8.25 and 14.16. The obtained χ^2 values are greater than the table value (5.99) at .05 level of significance with df: 2. The observed values are found significant. Hence, the response pattern of B.Ed. trainees and the university background are not found independent from each other in relation to effectiveness of training given to B.Ed. trainees for constructing good question papers and preparation of progress report of the students.

Table 4.31: χ^2test of Independence of trainees response towards effectiveness of training process adopted for development of competency of students' evaluation and university background, skill-wise

A.

Benefits of training process

Development of skills	*UNIV.*	*More extent*	*Some extent*	*Least*	*Total*	$\chi 2$ *Values*
1i. Construction of good question paper	IGNOU	251 (83.67)	38 (12.67)	11 (3.67)	300 (100.00)	8.25*
	UPRTOU	267 (89.00)	18 (6.00)	15 (5.00)	300 (100.00)	
	Total	518 (86.33)	56 (9.33)	26 (4.33)	600 (100.00)	
ii. Preparation of progress report of students	IGNOU	233 (77.67)	56 (18.67)	11 (3.67)	300 (100.00)	14.16**
	UPRTOU	259 (86.33)	25 (8.33)	16 (5.33)	300 (100.00)	
	Total	492 (82.00)	81 (13.50)	27 (4.50)	600 (100.00)	
iii. Administration of psychological test	IGNOU	218 (72.67)	62 (20.67)	20 (6.67)	300 (100.00)	0.43 N.S.
	UPRTOU	220 (73.33)	57 (19.00)	23 (7.67)	300 (100.00)	
	Total	438 (73.00)	119 (19.83)	43 (7.17)	600 (100.00)	

B.

Benefits of assignments

Development of skills	*UNIV.*	*More extent*	*Some extent*	*Least*	*Total*	$\chi 2$ *Values*
1i To know self-progress	IGNOU	255 (85.00)	32 (10.67)	13 (4.33)	300 (100.00)	5.92 N.S.
	UPRTOU	272 (90.67)	16 (5.33)	12 (4.00)	300 (100.00)	
	Total	527 (87.83)	48 (8.00)	25 (4.17)	600 (100.00)	

(Contd.)

ii. To rectify their mistakes	IGNOU	230	55	15	300	7.80*
		(76.67)	(18.33)	(5.00)	(100.00)	
	UPRTOU	256	32	12	300	
		(85.33)	(10.67)	(4.00)	(100.00)	
	Total	486	87	27	600	
		(81.00)	(14.50)	(4.50)	(100.00)	
iii. Preparation of examination	IGNOU	219	65	16	300	13.71**
		(73.00)	(21.67)	(5.33)	(100.00)	
	UPRTOU	253	32	15	300	
		(84.33)	(10.67)	(5.00)	(100.00)	
	Total	472	97	31	600	
		(78.67)	(16.17)	(5.17)	(100.00)	
iv. Readiness for teaching related activities	IGNOU	228	57	15	300	10.54**
		(76.00)	(19.00)	(5.00)	(100.00)	
	UPRTOU	248	30	22	300	
		(82.67)	(10.00)	(7.33)	(100.00)	
	Total	476	87	37	600	
		(79.33)	(14.50)	(6.17)	(100.00)	

Note: Figures in parentheses indicate percentages. N.S.: Not significant
* Indicates significant at .05 level. ** Indicates significant at .01 level.

It can be observed that majority of B.Ed. trainees (86 to 89%) of UPRTOU considered that training given to them for development of competency of students evaluation were effective in relation to development of the following skills:

(i) Construction of good question papers (89.00%).
(ii) Preparation of progress report of students (86.33%).

While 78 to 84 per cent B.Ed. trainees of IGNOU considered that training given to those for development of competency of students evaluation were effective in relation to the development of the following skills:

(i) Construction of good question papers (89.00%).
(ii) Preparation of progress report of students (77.67%).

It can be noticed from Table 4.31A that the calculated χ^2 value of independence between the response pattern of B.Ed. trainees and the university background in relation to effectiveness of training given to B.Ed. trainees for development of competency of administration of psychological test is found 0.43. The obtained χ^2 value is lesser than the table value (5.99) at .05 level of significance with df: 2. The observed value is not found significant. Hence the response pattern of B.Ed. trainees and the university background are found to be independent from each other in relation to effectiveness of training given to B.Ed. trainees for development of competency of administration of psychological test in B.Ed. trainees.

It can be observed that 43 per cent B.Ed. trainees of IGNOU and UPRTOU considered that training given to them for development of competency of administration of psychological test as effective.

4.31B Response of B.Ed. Trainees about Effectiveness of Assignments: University-wise

It can be noticed from Table 4.31B that the calculated χ^2 value of independence between the response pattern of B.Ed. trainees and the university background in relation to effectiveness of assignments given to B.Ed. trainees for knowing about self-development is found 5.92. The obtained χ^2 value is less than the table value (5.99) at .05 level of significance with df: 2. The observed value is not found significant. Hence the response pattern of B.Ed. trainees and the university background are found to be independent from each other in relation to effectiveness of assignments given to B.Ed. trainees for knowing about self-development.

It can be observed that majority of B.Ed. trainees (88%) of IGNOU and UPRTOU considered assignments given to them as effective because assignments were helpful for their development.

It can be noticed from Table 4.31B that the calculated χ^2 values of independence between the response pattern of B.Ed. trainees and the university background in relation to effectiveness of assignments given to B.Ed. trainees for improving their own demerits, preparation of examination and readiness for teaching related activities are found as 7.80, 13.71 and 10.54. The obtained χ^2 values are greater than the table value (5.99) at .05 level of significance with df: 2. The observed values are found to be significant. Hence the response pattern of B.Ed. trainees and the university background are not found to be independent from each other in relation to effectiveness of assignments given to B.Ed. trainees for development of above said skills.

It can be observed that majority of B.Ed. trainees (83 to 85%) of UPRTOU considered assignments given to B.Ed. trainees as effective for following developments:

(i) Rectify their demerits (85.33%).

(ii) Preparation of examination (84.33%).
(iii) Ready to perform teaching related activities (82.67%).

While 73 to 77 per cent B.Ed. trainees of IGNOU considered assignment given to B.Ed. trainees as effective for following developments:

(i) Remove their demerits (76.67%).
(ii) Ready to perform teaching related activities (76.00%).
(iii) Preparation of examination (73.00%).

4.32A Response of Counsellors about Effectiveness of Process Adopted for Development of Evaluation Competency: University-wise

It can be noticed from Table 4.32A that the calculated χ^2 values of independence between the response pattern of counsellors and the university background in relation to effectiveness of training process for development of competency in B.Ed. trainees related with constructing good question papers, preparation of progress report of students and administration of psychological test are found as 4.14, 1.02 and 2.03 respectively. The obtained χ^2 values are lesser than the table value (5.99) at .05 level of significance with df: 2. The observed values are not found significant. Hence, the response pattern of counsellors and the university background are not found to be independent from each other in relation to effectiveness of training process on above mentioned areas.

It can be observed that 65 to 68 per cent counsellors considered process adopted as effective for development of competency of evaluation in B.Ed. trainees in enhancement of the following:

(i) Construction of good question papers (88.33%);
(ii) Preparation of progress report of students (78.33%); and
(iii) Administration of psychological test (65.00%).

4.32B Response of Counsellors about Effectiveness of Assignment provided to B.Ed. Trainees for Development of Students Evaluation Competency: University-wise

It can be noticed from Table 4.32B that the calculated χ^2 value of independence between the response pattern of counsellors and the

Table 4.32: χ^2 test of independence of counsellors response about effectiveness of training process of development of students' evaluation among B.Ed. trainees and university background, skill-wise

A.

Benefits of training process of development of students' evaluation						
Development of skills	*UNIV.*	*More extent*	*Some extent*	*Least*	*Total*	χ^2 *Values*
1i. Constructing good question paper	IGNOU	29 (96.67)	1 (3.33)	0 (0.00)	30 (100.00)	4.14 N.S.
	UPRTOU	24 (80.00)	5 (16.67)	1 (3.33)	30 (100.00)	
	Total	53 (88.33)	6 (10.00)	1 (1.67)	60 (100.00)	
ii. Preparation of progress report of students	IGNOU	24 (80.00)	6 (20.00)	0 (0.00)	30 (100.00)	1.02 N.S.
	UPRTOU	23 (76.67)	6 (20.00)	1 (3.33)	30 (100.00)	
	Total	47 (78.33)	12 (20.00)	1 (1.67)	60 (100.00)	
iii. Administration of psychological test	IGNOU	21 (70.00)	8 (26.67)	1 (3.33)	30 (100.00)	2.03 N.S.
	UPRTOU	18 (60.00)	12 (40.00)	0 (0.00)	30 (100.00)	
	Total	39 (65.00)	20 (33.33)	1 (1.67)	60 (100.00)	

B.

Benefits of assignments						
Development of skills	*UNIV.*	*More extent*	*Some extent*	*Least*	*Total*	χ^2 *Values*
1i. To knowing self-progress	IGNOU	25 (83.33)	4 (13.33)	1 (3.33)	30 (100.00)	6.14*
	UPRTOU	18 (60.00)	12 (40.00)	0 (0.00)	30 (100.00)	
	Total	43 (71.67)	16 (26.67)	1 (1.67)	60 (100.00)	

(Contd.)

ii. To rectify their mistakes	IGNOU	23 (76.67)	7 (23.33)	0 (0.00)	30 (100.00)	3.86 N.S.
	UPRTOU	18 (60.00)	9 (30.00)	3 (10.00)	30 (100.00)	
	Total	41 (68.33)	16 (26.67)	3 (5.00)	60 (100.00)	
iii. To the preparation of examination	IGNOU	26 (86.67)	3 (10.00)	1 (3.33)	30 (100.00)	2.28 N.S.
	UPRTOU	22 (73.33)	4 (13.33)	4 (13.33)	30 (100.00)	
	Total	48 (80.00)	7 (11.67)	5 (8.33)	60 (100.00)	
iv. To readiness in teaching related activities	IGNOU	21 (70.00)	8 (26.67)	1 (3.33)	30 (100.00)	2.04 N.S.
	UPRTOU	25 (83.33)	5 (16.67)	0 (0.00)	30 (100.00)	
	Total	46 (76.67)	13 (21.67)	1 (1.67)	60 (100.00)	

Note: Figures in parentheses indicate percentages. N.S.: Not significant.
* Indicates significant at .05 level.

university background in relation to effectiveness of assignments given to B.Ed. trainees is found 6.14. The observed value is greater than the table value (5.99) at .05 level of significance with df: 2. The obtained χ^2 value is found significant. Hence, the response pattern of counsellors and the university background are not found independent from each other in relation to effectiveness of assignments given to B.Ed. trainees.

It can be observed that a large majority of counsellors (83%) of IGNOU considered assignments provided to B.Ed. trainees for knowing about self-development as effective. While, 60 per cent counsellors of UPRTOU considered, assignments provided to B.Ed. trainees for knowing about self-development as effective.

It can be noticed from Table 4.32B that the calculated χ^2 value of independence between the response pattern of counsellors and the university background in relation to effectiveness of assignments given to B.Ed. trainees for rectifing their mistakes, preparation of examination and readiness in teaching related activities are found as 3.86, 2.28 and 2.04 respectively. The obtained χ^2 values are less than the table value (5.99) at .05 level of significance with df: 2. The observed values are not found to be significant. Hence, the response pattern of counsellors and the university background are found to be independent from each other in relation to effectiveness of assignment given to B.Ed. trainees for improvement in above mentioned skills.

It can be observed that 68 to 80 per cent counsellors of IGNOU and UPRTOU considered assignments provided to B.Ed. trainees as effective for development in the following skills:

(i) Preparation of examination (80.00%)
(ii) Readiness to perform teaching related activities (76.67%)
(iii) Rectify their mistakes (68.33%).

Conclusion

In this component study had been conducted about process adopted for development of competency of students' evaluation among B.Ed. trainees. It is clear from the analysis that trainees stated that mentors helped them in preparing blue print and in evaluation of answer copy. Majority of B.Ed. trainees of UPRTOU and more than average number of IGNOU stated that group discussion organized by the counsellors, help provided in assignments and administered psychological test by counsellors during workshops for development of competency of students' evaluation among them. The selected counsellors of both the open universities mentioned that theoretical knowledge was provided during workshops regarding evaluation of students, blueprint was prepared for construction of question papers by trainees, question paper prepared by trainees in concerned subjects and achievement test was prepared. Average number of trainees informed that knowledge provided by counsellors for resolving the problems faced by them during evaluating of their students. Mentors informed that B.Ed. trainees faced problems of time limitation in evaluation their students. Mentors helped B.Ed. trainees in resolving their problems. Trainees also considered that their peer trainees discuss on the problems faced by trainees and help them in resolving their problems. Majority of trainees stated that by taking help from counsellors, by reading books, by taking help from library and by reading all assignment of ex-trainees they completed their assignments. Counsellors of IGNOU as well as UPRTOU stated that they provided knowledge of administration of psychological test by demonstrating psychological tests, report writing after administration of psychological test on their peer trainees. The counsellors also informed that knowledge was provided to them regarding construction of achievement test. The trainees prepared blueprint and constructed the test items during workshops. As a whole the trainees and the counsellors expressed positive response about the relevance and effectiveness of process adopted for development of skill of students' evaluation among B.Ed. trainees.

VI. School Management and Planning Related Processes in Distance B.Ed. Programme

In this section analysis has been done regarding help of mentors, counsellors and peer trainees for preparation of time table, school records/register, school budget and conducting action research by trainees and present status of other processes adopted for development of competency of school management and planning among B.Ed. trainees. Relevance and effectiveness of above mentioned activities also analyzed under this section.

4.33A Response of B.Ed. Trainees about Help Provided by Mentors for Preparation of Time-table: University-wise

It can be noticed from Table 4.33A that the calculated χ^2 value of independence between the response pattern of B.Ed. trainees and the university background in relation to the assistance provided by mentors in the preparation of time-table is 3.76. The obtained χ^2 value is less than the table value (7.81) at .05 level of significance with df: 3. Thus the observed value is not found significant. Hence, the response pattern of B.Ed. trainees and the university background in relation to the assistance provided by the mentors for the preparation of time-table are found to be independent from each other.

It can be observed that 70 per cent B.Ed. trainees of IGNOU and UPRTOU considered that mentors provided important information related to periods and also rectified errors in time-table preparation.

4.33B Response of B.Ed. Trainees about Help Provided by the Counsellors for Preparation of Time-table: University-wise

It can be noticed from Table 4.33B that the calculated χ^2 value of independence between the response pattern of B.Ed. trainees and university background in relation to the assistance provided by counsellors for the preparation of time-table is found as 7.04.

Table 4.33: χ^2 test of independence of trainees response about help of mentors, counsellors and peer trainees for preparation of time-table, school record/register, school budget and conducting action research and university background

A.

Response of B.Ed. trainees about help provided by mentors for preparation of time-table

UNIV.	*i (By giving important knowledge about period)*	*ii (By correcting time-table)*	*iii (i & ii)*	*Iv (No help provided)*	*Total*	χ^2 *Value*
IGNOU	37 (12.33)	36 (12.00)	204 (68.00)	23 (7.67)	300 (100.00)	3.76 N.S.
UPRTOU	36 (12.00)	38 (12.67)	214 (71.33)	12 (4.00)	300 (100.00)	
Total	73 (12.17)	74 (12.33)	418 (69.67)	35 (5.83)	600 (100.00)	

B.

Response of B.Ed. trainees about help provided by counsellors for preparation of time-table

UNIV.	*i (By presenting example)*	*Ii (By provide feedback)*	*iii (i & ii)*	*iv (No help provided)*	*Total*	χ^2 *Value*
IGNOU	48 (16.00)	57 (19.00)	184 (61.33)	11 (3.67)	300 (100.00)	7.04 N.S.
UPRTOU	47 (15.67)	35 (11.67)	202 (67.33)	16 (5.33)	300 (100.00)	
Total	95 (15.83)	92 (15.33)	386 (64.33)	27 (4.5)	600 (100.00)	

C.

Response of B.Ed. trainees about help provided by peer trainees for preparation of time-table

UNIV.	*i (By telling experience)*	*ii (Help in making)*	*iii (Assist in making it together)*	*iv (i, ii & iii)*	*Total*	χ^2 *Value*
IGNOU	173 (57.67)	49 (16.33)	68 (22.67)	10 (3.33)	300 (100.00)	4.96 N.S.
UPRTOU	164 (54.67)	70 (23.33)	58 (19.33)	8 (2.67)	300 (100.00)	

(Contd.)

Total	337 (56.17)	119 (19.83)	126 (21.00)	18 (3.00)	600 (100.00)	

D.

Response of B.Ed. trainees about help of mentor for preparation of school records

UNIV.	*i (By providing right information)*	*ii (By amending correction)*	*iii (i & ii)*	*iv (Do not take any initiative)*	*Total*	χ^2 *Value*
IGNOU	53 (17.67)	32 (10.67)	205 (68.33)	10 (3.33)	300 (100.00)	5.85 N.S.
UPRTOU	35 (11.67)	31 (10.33)	217 (72.33)	17 (5.67)	300 (100.00)	
Total	88 (14.67)	63 (10.5)	422 (70.33)	27 (4.5)	600 (100.00)	

E.

Response of B.Ed. trainees about help provided by counsellors for preparation of school records

UNIV.	*i (By providing example)*	*ii (By providing feed-back)*	*iii (i & ii)*	*iv (Do not take any initiative)*	*Total*	χ^2 *Value*
IGNOU	46 (15.33)	55 (18.33)	180 (60.00)	19 (6.33)	300 (100.00)	14.49**
UPRTOU	19 (6.33)	53 (17.67)	213 (71.00)	15 (5.00)	300 (100.00)	
Total	65 (10.83)	108 (18.00)	393 (65.5)	34 (5.67)	600 (100.00)	

F.

Response of B.Ed. trainees about help provided by peer trainees for preparation of school records

UNIV.	*i (By discussing self-experiences)*	*ii (Assist in making the register)*	*iii (By Providing feedback)*	*iv (i, ii & iii)*	*V (No help provided)*	*Total*	χ^2 *Value*
IGNOU	202 (67.33)	46 (15.33)	40 (13.33)	9 (3.00)	3 (1.00)	300 (100.00)	11.60*
UPRTOU	165 (55.00)	76 (25.33)	45 (15.00)	11 (3.67)	3 (1.00)	300 (100.00)	

(Contd.)

Total	367 (61.17)	122 (20.33)	85 (14.17)	20 (3.33)	6 (1.00)	600 (100.00)

G.

Response of B.Ed. trainees about help provided by mentors for preparation of school budget

UNIV.	*i* *(By providing right information)*	*ii* *(By amending)*	*iii* *(i & ii)*	*iv* *(Do not take any initiative)*	*Total*	χ^2 *Value*
IGNOU	113 (37.67)	23 (7.67)	138 (46.00)	26 (8.67)	300 (100.00)	3.02 N.S.
UPRTOU	100 (33.33)	20 (6.67)	159 (53.00)	21 (7.00)	300 (100.00)	
Total	213 (35.5)	43 (7.17)	297 (49.5)	47 (7.83)	600 (100.00)	

H.

Response of B.Ed. trainees about help provided by counsellors for preparation of school budget

UNIV.	*i* *(By providing examples)*	*ii* *(By preparing and providing feedback)*	*iii* *(Both i & ii)*	*iv* *(Do not take any initiative)*	*Total*	χ^2 *Value*
IGNOU	60 (20.00)	47 (15.67)	169 (56.33)	24 (8.00)	300 (100.00)	3.13 N.S.
UPRTOU	50 (16.67)	59 (19.67)	161 (53.67)	30 (10.00)	300 (100.00)	
Total	110 (18.33)	106 (17.67)	330 (55.00)	54 (9.00)	600 (100.00)	

I.

Response of B.Ed. trainees about help provided by peer trainees for preparation of school budget

UNIV.	*i* *(By discussing self-experiences)*	*ii* *(Assist in making it)*	*iii* *(By amending school budget)*	*iv* *(No help provided)*	*Total*	χ^2 *Value*
IGNOU	140 (46.67)	43 (14.33)	101 (33.67)	16 (5.33)	300 (100.00)	8.12*

(Contd.)

UPRTOU	116 (38.67)	65 (21.67)	96 (32.00)	23 (7.67)	300 (100.00)
Total	256 (28.44)	108 (18.00)	197 (32.83)	39 (6.5)	600 (100.00)

J.

Response of B.Ed. trainees about conducting action research by themselves

UNIV.	*Yes*	*No*	*Total*
IGNOU	264 (88.00)	36 (12.00)	300 (100.00)
UPRTOU	106 (35.33)	194 (64.67)	300 (100.00)
Total	370 (61.67)	230 (38.33)	600 (100.00)

K.

Response of B.Ed. trainees about help provided by mentors for organisation of action research

UNIV.	*i (By selecting the problem)*	*ii (By resolving the problem)*	*iii (Both selecting and resolving problem)*	*iv (Do not take any initiative)*	*Total*	χ^2 *Value*
IGNOU	22 (7.33)	65 (21.67)	177 (59.00)	36 (12.00)	300 (100.00)	206.94**
UPRTOU	10 (3.33)	21 (7.00)	60 (20.00)	209 (69.67)	300 (100.00)	
Total	32 (5.33)	86 (14.33)	237 (39.50)	245 (40.83)	600 (100.00)	

L.

Response of B.Ed. trainees about help provided by counsellors for organisation of action research

UNIV.	*i (By theoretical knowledge)*	*ii (By feedback)*	*iii (By help from library)*	*iv (Do not take any initiative)*	*v (i, ii & iii)*	*vi (No response)*	*Total*	χ^2 *Value*
IGNOU	108 (36.00)	124 (41.33)	27 (9.00)	2 (0.67)	3 (1.00)	36 (12.00)	300 (100.00)	193.74**

(Contd.)

UPRTOU	32 (10.67)	50 (16.67)	14 (4.67)	10 (3.33)	0 (0.00)	194 (64.67)	300 (100.00)
Total	140 (23.33)	174 (29.00)	41 (6.83)	12 (2.00)	3 (0.5)	230 (38.33)	600 (100.00)

M.

Response of B.Ed. trainees about help provided by peer trainees for organisation of action research

UNIV.	*i (By discus-sing self-experi-ences)*	*ii (In selection problem)*	*iii (By showing their report)*	*iv (Do not take any initiative)*	*v (No response)*	*Total*	χ^2 *Value*
IGNOU	169 (56.33)	47 (15.67)	40 (13.33)	8 (2.67)	36 (12.00)	300 (100.00)	187.56**
UPRTOU	54 (18.00)	19 (6.33)	20 (6.67)	13 (4.33)	194 (64.67)	300 (100.00)	
Total	223 (37.17)	66 (11.00)	60 (10.00)	21 (3.5)	230 (38.33)	600 (100.00)	

N.

χ^2 test of independence of trainees' response and university background about process adopted for making assembly meaningful and attractive

Response of B.Ed. trainees about training given to them for making assembly meaningful and attractive

UNIV.	*i (By presentation of students)*	*ii (Daily news presentation by students)*	*iii (Honour intellectual students in assembly)*	*iv (i, ii & iii)*	*v (Nothing)*	*Total*	χ^2 *Value*
IGNOU	31 (10.33)	29 (9.67)	41 (13.67)	182 (60.67)	17 (5.67)	300 (100.00)	18.01**
UPRTOU	14 (4.67)	12 (4.00)	34 (11.33)	221 (73.67)	19 (6.33)	300 (100.00)	
Total	45 (7.5)	41 (6.83)	75 (12.5)	403 (67.17)	36 (6.0)	600 (100.00)	

Note: Figures in parentheses indicate percentages. N.S.: Not significant

* Indicates significant at .05 level.

** Indicates significant at .01 level.

The obtained χ^2 value is less than the table value (7.81) at .05 level of significance with df: 3. Thus the observed value is not found significant. Hence, the response pattern of B.Ed. trainees and the university background in relation to the assistance provided by counsellors for the preparation of time table are found to be independent from each other.

It can be observed that 64 per cent B.Ed. trainees of IGNOU and UPRTOU mentioned that counsellors presented examples and provided feedback during workshops.

4.33C Response of B.Ed. Trainees about Help Provided by Peer Trainees for Preparation of Time-table: University-wise

It can be noticed from Table 4.33C that the calculated χ^2 value of independence between the response pattern of B.Ed. trainees and the university background in relation to the help provided by peer trainees in the preparation of time-table is found to be 4.96. The obtained χ^2 value is less than the table value (7.81) at .05 level of significance with df: 3. Thus the observed value is not found significant. Hence, it is clear that the response pattern of B.Ed. trainees and the university background in relation to the help provided by peer trainees in the preparation to time-table are found to be independent from each other.

According to around 20 per cent B.Ed. trainees of IGNOU and UPRTOU, peer trainees provided feedback for the successful preparation of time-table and the peer trainees sat together to assist each other in the preparation of time-table.

4.33D Response of B.Ed. Trainees about Help Provided by Mentors for Preparation of School Records: University-wise

It can be noticed from Table 4.33D that the calculated χ^2 value of independence between the response pattern of B.Ed. trainees and the university background in relation to the help provided by their mentors for the preparation of school records is found 5.85. The obtained χ^2 value is less than the table value (7.81) at .05 level of significance with df: 3. Thus the observed value is not found to be significant. Hence, it is clear that the response pattern of B.Ed. trainees and the university background in relation to the help provided by mentors for the preparation of school records are found to be dependent from each other.

It can be observed that 70 per cent B.Ed. trainees of IGNOU and UPRTOU mentioned that their mentors assisted them for the preparation of school records by providing them correct information regarding school activities and also by rectifying errors in the prepared records.

4.33E Response of B.Ed. Trainees about Help Provided by Counsellors for Preparation of School Records: University-wise

It can be noticed from Table 4.33E that the calculated χ^2 value of independence between the response pattern of B.Ed. trainees and the university background in relation to the help provided by counsellors in the preparation of school records is found 14.49. The obtained χ^2 value is less than the table value (7.81) at .05 level of significance with df: 3. Thus the observed value is not found significant. Hence, it is clear that the response pattern of B.Ed. trainees and the university background in relation to the help provided by counsellors in the preparation of school records are found to be independent from each other.

It can be observed that 71 per cent B.Ed. trainees of UPRTOU and 60 per cent B.Ed. trainees of IGNOU mentioned that counsellors helped them in the preparation of school records by giving examples and rectifying errors in the prepared school records.

4.33F Response of B.Ed. Trainees about Help Provided by Peer Trainees for Preparation of School Records: University-wise

It can be noticed from Table 4.33F that the calculated χ^2 value of independence between the response pattern of B.Ed. trainees and the university background in relation to the help provided by peer trainees in the preparation of school records is found 14.60. The calculated χ^2 value is than the table value (7.81) at .05 level of significance with df: 3. Thus the observed value is found significant. Hence it is clear that the response pattern of B.Ed. trainees and the university background in relation to the help provided by peers in preparation of school records are not found independent from each other.

It can be observed that 67 per cent B.Ed. trainees of IGNOU and 55 per cent B.Ed. trainees of UPRTOU mentioned that the peer trainees provide help on the basis of their experience for the preparation of school records. 25 per cent B.Ed. trainees of UPRTOU and 15 per cent B.Ed. trainees of IGNOU mentioned that they sat together and get school records prepared.

4.33G Response of B.Ed. Trainees about Help Provided by Mentors for Preparation of School Budget: University-wise

It can be noticed from Table 4.33G that the calculated χ^2 value of independence between the response pattern of B.Ed. trainees and the university background in relation to the help provided by mentors in the preparation of school budget is found 3.02. The calculated χ^2 value is less than the table value (7.81) at .05 level of significance with df: 3. Thus the observed value is not found significant. Hence, it is clear that the response pattern of B.Ed. trainees and the university background in relation to the help provided by mentors for the preparation of school budget are found to be independent from each other.

It can be observed that 50 per cent B.Ed. trainees of IGNOU and UPRTOU mentioned that the mentors provided information regarding income expenditure for the preparation of the school budget they also rectified the errors committed in preparation of school budget.

4.33H Response of B.Ed. Trainees about Help Provided by Counsellors for Preparation of School Budget: University-wise

It can be noticed from Table 4.33H that the calculated χ^2 value of independence between the response pattern of B.Ed. trainees and the university background in relation to the help provided by counsellors in the preparation of school budget is found 3.13. The obtained χ^2 value is less than the table value (7.81) at .05 level of significance with df: 3. Thus, the observed value is not found significant. Hence it is clear that the response pattern of B.Ed. trainees and the university background in relation to the help provided by counsellors in the preparation of school budget are found to be independent from each other.

It can be observed that 55 per cent B.Ed. trainees of IGNOU and UPRTOU mentioned that counsellors provided assistance in the preparation of school budget by presenting examples, by getting it prepared during workshops and also by providing feedback.

4.33I Response of B.Ed. Trainees about Help Provided by the Peers for Preparation of School Budget: University-wise

It can be noticed from Table 4.33I that the calculated χ^2 value of independence between the response pattern of B.Ed. trainees and the university background in relation to the helps provided by peer trainees in the preparation of school budget is found 8.12. The calculated χ^2 value is greater than the table value (7.81) at .05 level of significance with df: 3. Thus the observed value is found to be significant. Hence, it is clear that the response pattern of B.Ed. trainees and the university background in relation to the helps provided by peers in preparation of school budget are not independent from each other.

It can be observed that 47 per cent B.Ed. trainees of IGNOU and 39 per cent B.Ed. trainees of UPRTOU stated that the peers provided help to each other on the basis of only their experiences for preparation of school budget. While 34 per cent of IGNOU and 32 per cent of UPRTOU stated that the peers provided help to each other by only amending school budget.

Interview with Mentors about their Help to B.Ed. Trainees in Preparing of School Records, Register, School Budget and Time-table

The selected mentors of both the universities stated that they helped B.Ed. trainees in preparing school records, register, school budget and time-table. They corrected the limitations of register, school budget and time-table prepared by B.Ed. trainees.

Response of B.Ed. Trainees about the Topics on which they have Conducted Action Research

On the basis of response of B.Ed. trainees of IGNOU it was clear that the following were the topics on which they had done action research:

- Pronunciation errors among students.
- Students absence in the assembly.
- Indifferent behaviour of students in the classroom.
- Problem of low presentation of female students in the classroom.
- Problem of indiscipline among students.
- Problem of late coming of students.
- Problem of students taking no interest in science.
- Problem of students taking no interest in social science.
- Problem of students taking no interest in mathematics.
- Problem of students taking no interest in English.
- Problem of non-completion of homework by students.

- Copying of homework by students.
- Problem of making late enrollment/admission of students by their guardians.
- Problem of rough handwriting of students.
- Problem of students taking no interest regarding use of Map in Geography.
- Low presentation of students after lunch break.
- Problem of slow learners.

Interview with Counsellors about Provision of Action Research in B.Ed. Progrmame

The selected counsellors of IGNOU stated that action research was related to school based activity conducted by B.Ed. trainees at their own schools. The basic steps of action research were explained during workshops. Report was prepared through selecting a problem of their own school by trainees and submitted in second workshops. Feedback was provided by counsellors on submitted report. The selected counsellors of UPRTOU stated that there was no provision of action research in B.Ed. programme.

It is also clear from the observation done by researcher that report of action research had been submitted by almost all B.Ed. trainees and feedback was provided by counsellors during workshops. There were instances of copying of action research report with their own peer trainees. Less number of B.Ed. trainees had taken action research seriously.

Interview with Counsellors about their Guidance to B.Ed. Trainees Regarding Action Research

The selected counsellors of both the universities stated that they helped B.Ed. trainees conducting action research in selection of problem, making action hypothesis and writing summary of action research. They demonstrated model action research report for the trainees.

Interview with Counsellors about Relevance of Action Research

The selected counsellors of both the universities mentioned the action research as relevant because it was directly related to problems of schools. By conducting action research, trainees developed understanding of problems of schools and they developed skills to select the problems and solved selected problems. It had made them capable for resolving problems related to schools. Correct instruction had provided regarding action research.

Interview with Mentors about Problems Faced by B.Ed. Trainees in Action Research

Selected mentors of IGNOU as well as UPRTOU made clear that the most of the problem of B.Ed. trainees is that they do not understand action research problems. They were not able to frame action research topic. They were not able to frame appropriate format of reporting action research. The B.Ed. trainees did not complete action research within stipulated time. They were not able to write action research report on prescribed format.

Interview with Mentors about their Guidance on Action Research

The selected mentors stated that they helped the B.Ed. trainees in selecting problems, and adopting different techniques of conducting action research. They helped the trainees by providing list of problems for action research. The trainees select the specific problem from the given list. Mentors helped them in writing of report.

4.33J Response of B.Ed. Trainees about Conducting Action Research: University-wise

It can be observed from Table 4.33J that 88 per cent B.Ed. trainees of IGNOU and only 35 per cent B.Ed. trainees of UPRTOU considered that action research had been conducted by them.

4.33K Response of B.Ed. Trainees about Help Provided by Mentors for Conducting Action Research: University-wise

It can be noticed from Table 4.33K that the calculated χ^2 value of independence between the response pattern of B.Ed. trainees and the university background in relation to the help provided by their mentors for doing action research is found 206.94. The obtained χ^2 value is greater than the table value (7.81) at .05 level of significance with df: 3. Thus the observed value is found to be significant. Hence, it is clear that the response pattern of B.Ed. trainees and the university background in relation to the help provided by their mentors for doing action research are not found to be independent from each other.

It can be observed that 59 per cent B.Ed. trainees of IGNOU and 20 per cent B.Ed. trainees of UPRTOU mentioned that their mentors provided help in the selection of problems for action research and provided remedy for resolving the problems encountered during action research.

It is also observed that 70 per cent B.Ed. trainees of UPRTOU and merely 12 per cent B.Ed. trainees of IGNOU mentioned that their mentors did not provide any help in conducting action research.

4.33L Response of B.Ed. Trainees about Help Provided by Counsellors for Conducting of Action Research: University-wise

It can be noticed from Table 4.33L that the calculated χ^2 value of independence between the response pattern of B.Ed. trainees and the university background in relation to help provided by counsellors for performing action research is found 193.74. The obtained χ^2 value is greater than the table value (11.07) at .05 level of significance with df: 5. Thus the observed value is found to be significant. Hence it is clear that the response pattern of B.Ed. trainees and the university background in relation to the help provided by councellors for performing action research are not found to be independent from each other.

It can be observed that 41 per cent B.Ed. trainees of IGNOU and only 17 per cent B.Ed. trainees of IGNOU mentioned that only feedback is provided for conducting action research during workshop.

It can be observed that 36 per cent B.Ed. trainees of IGNOU and 11 per cent B.Ed. trainees of UPRTOU mentioned that the counsellors provided only theoretical knowledge regarding action research. 65 per cent of UPRTOU and 12 per cent trainees of IGNOU did not give response regarding help of counsellors in conducting action research.

4.33M Response of B.Ed. Trainees about Help Provided by Peer-trainees for Conducting Action Research: University-wise

It can be noticed from Table 4.33M that the calculated χ^2 value of independence between the response pattern of B.Ed. trainees and the university background in relation to the help provided by peer trainees for conducting action research is found 187.56. The obtained χ^2 value is greater than the table value (9.48) at .05 level of significance with df: 4. Thus the observed value is significant. Hence it is clear that the response pattern of B.Ed. trainees and the university background in relation to the help provided by peer trainees for conducting action research are not found to be independent from each other.

It can be observed that 56 per cent B.Ed. trainees of IGNOU and 18 per cent B.Ed. trainees of UPRTOU mentioned that the peer trainees shared their experiences for assisting in action research. While 38 per cent trainees of UPRTOU and 12 per cent of IGNOU gave no response regarding help of peer trainees.

4.33N Response of B.Ed. Trainees about Training Provided to them for Making Assembly Meaningful and Attractive: University-wise

It can be noticed from Table 4.33N that the calculated χ^2 value of independence between the response pattern of B.Ed. trainees and the university background in relation to the training provided to them for making school prayer assembly more interesting and meaningful is found 18.01. The obtained χ^2 value is greater than the table value (9.48) at .05 level of significance with df: 4. Thus the observed value is found to be significant. Hence, it is clear that the response pattern of B.Ed. trainees and the university background in relation to the training provided for making school prayer assembly more interesting and meaningful are not found to be independent from each other.

It can be observed that 74 per cent B.Ed. trainees of UPRTOU and 61 per cent B.Ed. trainees of IGNOU mentioned that for making school prayer assembly more interesting and meaningful, they made the students present noble thoughts, present news of current events and honour brilliant students.

4.34A Response of Counsellors about Help Provided by Themselves to B.Ed. Trainees for Making Time-table: University-wise

It can be noticed from Table 4.34A that the calculated χ^2 value of independence between the response pattern of counsellors and the university background in relation to the helps provided by counsellors for the preparation of time table is found 8.05. The obtained χ^2 value is greater than the table value (7.81) at .05 level of significant with df: 3. Thus the observed value is found to be significant. Hence, it is clear that

Table 4.34: χ^2 test of independence of counsellors response about their help to B.Ed. trainees in making time-table, preparation of school record/register, school budget and conducting action research and university background

A.

Response of counsellors about help provided by themselves to B.Ed. trainees for making time-table

UNIV.	*i (By Giving theoretical knowledge)*	*ii (By preparing during workshops & giving feedback)*	*iii (i&ii)*	*iv (They make their own)*	*Total*	χ^2 *Value*
IGNOU	7 (23.33)	8 (26.67)	14 (46.67)	1 (3.33)	30 (100.00)	8.05*
UPRTOU	4 (13.33)	2 (6.67)	24 (80.00)	0 (0.00)	30 (100.00)	
Total	11 (18.33)	10 (16.67)	38 (63.33)	1 (1.67)	60 (100.00)	

B.

Response of counsellors about preparation of school records/register by B.Ed. trainees

UNIV.	*i (Yes)*	*Ii (No)*	*iii (Not required)*	*Total*	χ^2 *Value*
IGNOU	24 (80.00)	5 (16.67)	1 (3.33)	30 (100.00)	2.72 N.S.
UPRTOU	15 (50.00)	6 (20.00)	9 (30.00)	30 (100.00)	
Total	39 (65.00)	11 (18.33)	10 (16.67)	60 (100.00)	

C.

Response of counsellors about their activities for preparation of school record/register

UNIV.	*i (By giving Assignment)*	*ii (By feedback)*	*iii (i & ii)*	*iv (None)*	*Total*	χ^2 *Value*
IGNOU	12 (40.00)	7 (23.33)	10 (33.33)	1 (3.33)	30 (100.00)	

(Contd.)

UPRTOU	10 (33.33)	6 (20.00)	14 (46.67)	0 (0.00)	30 (100.00)	1.93 N.S.
Total	22 (36.67)	13 (21.67)	24 (40.00)	1 (1.67)	60 (100.00)	

D.

Response of counsellors about their activities in preparation of school budget

UNIV.	*i (Telling by example)*	*ii (By feedback)*	*iii (i&ii)*	*iv (By discussion)*	*v (None)*	*Total*	$\chi 2$ *Value*
IGNOU	11 (36.67)	2 (6.67)	15 (50.00)	1 (3.33)	1 (3.33)	30 (100.00)	4.76 N.S.
UPRTOU	10 (33.33)	0 (0.00)	20 (66.67)	0 (0.00)	0 (0.00)	30 (100.00)	
Total	21 (35.00)	2 (3.33)	35 (58.33)	1 (1.67)	1 (1.67)	60 (100.00)	

E.

Response of counsellors about guidance provided to B.Ed. trainees by themselves for conducting action research successfully

UNIV.	*i (By theoretical knowledge)*	*ii (By feedback)*	*iii (i&ii)*	*iv (None)*	*Total*	$\chi 2$ *Value*
IGNOU	5 (16.67)	2 (6.67)	23 (76.67)	0 (0.00)	30 (100.00)	41.00**
UPRTOU	7 (23.33)	22 (73.33)	0 (0.00)	1 (3.33)	30 (100.00)	
Total	12 (20.00)	24 (40.00)	23 (38.33)	1 (1.67)	60 (100.00)	

Note: Figures in parentheses indicate percentages. N.S.: Not significant
* Indicates significant at .05 level.
** Indicates significant at .01 level.

the response pattern of counsellors and university background in relation to the help provided by counsellors in preparation of time-table are not found to be independent from each other.

It can be observed that 80 per cent counsellors of UPRTOU and merely 47 per cent counsellors of IGNOU mentioned that they provided theoretical knowledge, helped trainees in preparing time-table during workshops and provided feedback.

4.34B Response of Counsellors about Preparation of School Records/Registers by B.Ed. Trainees: University-wise

It can be noticed from Table 4.34B that the calculated χ^2 value of independence between the response pattern of counsellors and university background in relation to the preparation of school records is found 2.72. The obtained χ^2 value is lesser than the table value (5.99) at .05 level of significant with df: 2. Thus the observed value is not found significant. Hence, it is clear that the response pattern of counsellors and the university background in relation to help provided by counsellors in preparation of school records are found to be independent from each other.

It can be observed that 65 per cent counsellors of IGNOU and UPRTOU mentioned that they got the school records prepared by B.Ed. trainees. Only 18 per cent counsellors of IGNOU and UPRTOU mentioned that they did not get the school records prepared by B.Ed. trainees, whereas approximately 17 per cent counsellors considered that preparation of school records by B.Ed. trainees was not at all important.

4.34C Response of Counsellors about their Assistance in Preparation of School Records/Register: University-wise

It can be noticed from Table 4.34C that the calculated χ^2 value of independence between the response pattern of counsellors and the university background in relation to making B.Ed. trainees competent in the preparation of school records is found 1.93. The obtained χ^2 value is lesser than the table value (7.81) at 0.05 level of significance with df: 3. Thus the observed value is not found to be significant. Hence, it is clear that the response pattern of counsellors and the university background in relation to making B.Ed. trainees competent in the preparation of school records are found to be independent from each other.

It can be observed that 40 per cent counsellors of IGNOU and UPRTOU mentioned that assignments and feedback were provided during workshops to make B.Ed. trainees competent in the preparation of school records. Whereas 37 per cent counsellors of both the open universities stated that only assignment were given to B.Ed. trainees during workshops for development of competency in same activity.

Interview with Counsellors about Relevance of Process Adopted for Preparation of School Records and School Time-table

The selected counsellors of both the universities considered process adopted for preparation of school records and school time-table as relevant.

4.34D Response of Counsellors about their Assistance in Preparation of School Budget: University-wise

It can be noticed from Table 4.34D that the calculated χ^2 value of independence between the response pattern of counsellors and the university background in relation to the activities of counsellors to make B.Ed. trainees competent in preparation of school budget is found 4.76. The obtained χ^2 value is lesser than the table value (9.48) at 0.05 level of significance with df: 4. Thus, the observed value is not found significant. Hence, it is clear that the response pattern of counsellors and the university background are found to be independent from each other in relation to the activities of counsellors for make B.Ed. trainees competent in preparation of school budget.

It can be observed that 58 per cent counsellors of IGNOU and UPRTOU mentioned that they gave examples and feedback in prepared school budget by B.Ed. trainees during workshop to make B.Ed. trainees competent in the preparation of school budget. 35 per cent counsellors of IGNOU and UPRTOU mentioned that they gave only examples to making competent B.Ed. trainees in preparation of school budget.

Interview with Counsellors about their Helps to B.Ed. Trainees for Preparation of School Records and Register

The selected counsellors of both the universities mentioned that theoretical knowledge had provided to B.Ed. trainees about the records and registers by telling importance of maintenance of register. The trainees prepared school records related to their own school.

Interview with Counsellors about their Help to B.Ed. Trainees for Construction of School Time-table and School Budget

The selected counsellors of both the universities mentioned that theoretical knowledge had provided regarding preparation of time-table and school budget during workshops. The counsellors demonstrated by making the model one of each time-table and school budget. The counsellors helped B.Ed. trainees by making them competent to prepare the budget and time-table during workshops. Problems of B.Ed. trainees were reformed by counsellors during workshops.

It was observed by the researcher that after demonstration by the counsellors B.Ed. trainees prepared school budgets and time-tables in groups. They submited the prepared records during workshops.

4.34E Response of Counsellors about Guidance Provided in Action Research: University-wise

It can be noticed from Table 4.34E that the calculated χ^2 value of independence between the response pattern of counsellors and the university background in relation to the guidance provided in action research is found 41.00. The obtained χ^2 value is greater than the table value (7.81) at .05 level of significance with df: 3. Thus the observed value is found to be significant. Hence, it is clear that the response pattern of counsellors and the university background in relation to the guidance provided in action research are not found to be independent from each other.

It can be observed that 77 per cent counsellors of IGNOU mentioned that theoretical knowledge had been provided regarding action research and feedback in respect to the shortcomings of action research had provided during workshops.

It can also be observed that 73 per cent counsellors of UPRTOU and only 7 per cent counsellors of IGNOU mentioned that only feedback had been provided in respect to the shortcoming of action research during workshops.

4.35 Response of B.Ed. Trainees about Relevance of Process Adopted for Development of Competency of School Management and Planning: University-wise

It can be noticed from Table 4.35 that the calculated χ^2 values of independence between the response pattern of B.Ed. trainees and the university background in relation to the relevance of process adopted for the preparation of time-table and school records are found as 4.08 and 2.62 respectively. The obtained χ^2 value is lesser than the table

Table 4.35: χ^2 test of Independence of B.Ed. trainees response about relevance for training process of development of competency of school management and planning and university background

Response of B.Ed. trainees about relevance of training process for development of competency on school management and planning

Statements	*UNIV.*	*Highly Agree*	*Agree*	*Disagree*	*No response*	*Total*	χ^2 *Values*
1. Training given for the preparation of school time-table is in accordance with the time-table prepared at your school	IGNOU	213 (71.00)	67 (22.33)	20 (6.67)	0 (0.00)	300 (100.00)	4.08 N.S.
	UPRTOU	233 (77.67)	55 (18.33)	12 (4.00)	0 (0.00)	300 (100.00)	
	Total	446 (74.33)	122 (20.33)	32 (5.33)	0 (0.00)	600 (100.00)	
2. Training given for the maintenance of register work is related to the work given by principal in your school	IGNOU	196 (65.33)	84 (28.00)	20 (6.67)	0 (0.00)	300 (100.00)	2.62 N.S.
	UPRTOU	213 (71.00)	67 (22.33)	20 (6.67)	0 (0.00)	300 (100.00)	
	Total	409 (68.17)	151 (25.17)	40 (6.67)	0 (0.00)	600 (100.00)	
3. Guidance provided for conducting action research is in accordance to problem resolution at your school	IGNOU	193 (64.33)	60 (20.00)	11 (3.67)	36 (12.00)	300 (100.00)	232.30**
	UPRTOU	40 (13.33)	30 (10.00)	36 (12.00)	194 (64.67)	300 (100.00)	
	Total	233 (38.83)	90 (15.00)	47 (7.83)	230 (38.33)	600 (100.00)	
4. Training given to make school assembly interesting and knowledgeable is	IGNOU	235 (78.33)	55 (18.33)	10 (3.33)	0 (0.00)	300 (100.00)	13.28**
	UPRTOU	261 (87.00)	25 (8.33)	14 (4.67)	0 (0.00)	300 (100.00)	

(Contd.)

according to your school's environment.	Total	496 (82.67)	80 (13.33)	24 (4.00)	0 (0.00)	600 (100.00)

Note: Figures in parentheses indicate percentages. N.S.: Not significant.
** Indicates significant at .01 level.

value (7.81) at .05 level of significant with df: 3. Thus the observed values are not found significant. Hence it is clear that the response pattern of B.Ed. trainees and the university background in relation to the relevance of practices adopted for the preparation of time-table and school records are found to be independent from each other.

It can be observed that 68 to 74 per cent B.Ed. trainees of IGNOU and UPRTOU considered practices adopted for development of skills related to school administration and planning as relevant.

(i) Training for the preparation of school time table was in accordance with the time table of their school (68.17%).
(ii) Training for the preparation of school records was in accordance with their school activities (74.33%).

It can be noticed from Table 4.35 that the calculated χ^2 values of independence between the response patterns of B.Ed. trainees and the university background in relation to the relevance of guidance given for conducting action research and making school assembly more interesting and meaningful are found as 232.30 and 13.28 respectively. The obtained χ^2 value is greater than the table value (7.81) at .05 level of significance with df: 3. Thus the observed values are found to be significant. Hence, it is clear that the response patterns of B.Ed. trainees and the university background in relation to the relevance of guidance provided for conducting action research and making school prayer assembly more interesting and meaningful are not found to be independent from each other.

It can be observed that 13 to 87 per cent B.Ed. trainees of UPRTOU consider training adopted for the development of skills related to school administration and planning as relevant according to the following statements:

(i) Training provided for making school assembly more

interesting and meaningful was in accordance with the school environment (87.00%).

(ii) Guidance provided for conducting action research was in accordance with the problems of school (13.35%).

According to 64 to 78 per cent B.Ed. trainees of IGNOU training adopted for the development of skills related to school administration and planning as relevant according to the following statements:

(i) Training provided for making school assembly more interesting and meaningful was in accordance with the school environment (78.33%).

(ii) Guidance provided for conducting action research was in accordance with the problems of school (64.33%).

4.36 Response of Counsellors about Relevance of Practice Adopted for Development of Competency Regarding School Management and Planning: University-wise

It can be noticed from Table 4.36 that the calculated χ^2 values of independence between the response pattern of counsellors and the university background in relation to the relevance of training provided to B.Ed. trainees for the preparation of time table and school records are found as 0.39 and 0.95 respectively. The obtained χ^2 value are less than the table value (5.99) at .05 level of significance with df: 3. Thus the observed values are not found to be significant. Hence, it is clear that the response pattern of counsellors and the university background in relation to the relevance of training provided to B.Ed. trainees for the preparation of time table and school records are found to be independent from each other.

It can be observed that 67 per cent counsellors of IGNOU and UPRTOU consider training provided to B.Ed. trainees for the development of skills related to school administration and planning as relevant according to the following statements:

(i) Training provided for the preparation of time-table was in accordance with their school time-table (66.67%).

(ii) Training provided for the preparation of school record was in accordance with the school (66.67%).

Table 4.36: χ^2 test of independence of counsellors response about relevance of training process for development of competency of school management and planning among B.Ed. trainees and university background, statements-wise

Response of counsellors about relevance of training process for development of competency of school management and planning						
Statements	*UNIV.*	*Highly Agree*	*Agree*	*Disagree*	*Total*	χ^2 *Values*
Training given to B.Ed. trainees by you for preparation of school time-table is related to their school's time table	IGNOU	20 (66.67)	9 (30.00)	1 (3.33)	30 (100.00)	0.39 N.S.
	UPRTOU	20 (66.67)	8 (26.67)	2 (6.67)	30 (100.00)	
	Total	40 (66.67)	17 (28.33)	3 (5.00)	60 (100.00)	
Training given to B.Ed. trainees by you for preparation of school record is related to their own school work given by their principal	IGNOU	20 (66.67)	8 (26.67)	2 (6.67)	30 (100.00)	0.95 N.S.
	UPRTOU	20 (66.67)	6 (20.00)	4 (13.33)	30 (100.00)	
	Total	40 (66.67)	14 (23.33)	6 (10.00)	60 (100.00)	
Guidance provided to B.Ed. trainees by you for conducting action research is in accordance to their school problems	IGNOU	19 (63.33)	10 (33.33)	1 (3.33)	30 (100.00)	7.71*
	UPRTOU	24 (80.00)	2 (6.67)	4 (13.33)	30 (100.00)	
	Total	43 (71.67)	12 (20.00)	5 (8.33)	60 (100.00)	
Training given to B.Ed. trainees by you to make school assembly interesting and knowledgeable is according to their own school environment	IGNOU	21 (70.00)	8 (26.67)	1 (3.33)	30 (100.00)	7.30*
	UPRTOU	12 (40.00)	18 (60.00)	0 (0.00)	30 (100.00)	
	Total	33 (55.00)	26 (43.33)	1 (1.67)	60 (100.00)	

Note: Figures in parentheses indicate percentages. N.S.: Not significant.
* Indicates significant at .05 level.

It can be noticed from Table 4.36 that the calculated χ^2 values of independence between the response pattern of counsellors and the university background in relation to the relevance of guidance provided for conducting action research and training provided for making prayer assembly more interesting and knowledgeable are found as 7.71 and

7.30 respectively. The obtained χ^2 value is greater than the table value (5.99) at .05 level of significance with df: 2. Thus the observed values are found to be significant. Hence, it is clear that the response pattern of counsellors and the university background in relation to the relevance of training provided for making prayer assembly more interesting and knowledgeable and guidance provided for conducting action research are not found to be independent from each other.

It can be observed that 40 to 80 per cent counsellors of UPRTOU considered training provided for the development of skills related to school administration and planning as relevant according to the following statements:

(i) Guidance provided for the conduction of action research was in accordance with the problems of their school (80%).
(ii) Training provided for making school prayer assembly more interesting and knowledgeable was in accordance with their school (40%).

It can also be observed that 63 to 70 per cent counsellors of IGNOU consider training provided for the development of skills related to school administration and planning as relevant according to the following statements:

(i) Guidance provided for the conduction of action research was in accordance with the problems of their school (70%).
(ii) Training provided for making school prayer assembly more interesting and knowledgeable was in accordance with their school (63.33%).

4.37 Response of B.Ed. Trainees about Effectiveness of Process Adopted for Development of Competency of School Management and Planning: University-wise

It can be noticed from Table 4.37 that the calculated χ^2 values of independence between the response pattern of B.Ed. trainees and the university background in relation to the effectiveness of training provided for the preparing of time-table, conducting action research, presenting time table, conducting action research, presenting research report and assimilating various activities during school prayer assembly are found as 10.70, 210.28, 167.39 and 7.30 respectively. The obtained

Table 4.37: χ^2 test of Independence of trainees' response about effectiveness of training process adopted for development of competency of school management and planning and university background, skills-wise

		Benefits of training process for school management and planning					
Developments of skills	*UNIV.*	*More extent*	*Some extent*	*Least*	*No Response*	*Total*	χ^2 *Values*
1i. Preparation of school time-table	IGNOU	252 (84.00)	41 (13.67)	7 (2.33)	0 (0.00)	300 (100.00)	10.70**
	UPRTOU	260 (86.67)	22 (7.33)	18 (6.00)	0 (0.00)	300 (100.00)	
	Total	512 (85.33)	63 (10.50)	25 (4.17)	0 (0.00)	600 (100.00)	
ii. Preparation of school records	IGNOU	224 (74.67)	66 (22.00)	10 (3.33)	0 (0.00)	300 (100.00)	3.86 N.S.
	UPRTOU	222 (74.00)	58 (19.33)	20 (6.67)	0 (0.00)	300 (100.00)	
	Total	446 (74.33)	124 (20.67)	30 (5.00)	0 (0.00)	600 (100.00)	
iii. Making school budget directed by principal	IGNOU	217 (72.33)	65 (21.67)	18 (6.00)	0 (0.00)	300 (100.00)	1.30 N.S.
	UPRTOU	211 (70.33)	75 (25.00)	14 (4.67)	0 (0.00)	300 (100.00)	
	Total	428 (71.33)	140 (23.33)	32 (5.33)	0 (0.00)	600 (100.00)	
2i. Conduction of action research	IGNOU	246 (82.00)	39 (13.00)	15 (5.00)	0 (0.00)	300 (100.00)	210.28**
	UPRTOU	18 (6.00)	46 (15.33)	42 (14.00)	194 (64.67)	300 (100.00)	
	Total	264 (44.00)	85 (14.17)	57 (9.50)	194 (32.33)	600 (100.00)	
ii. Presentation of research report	IGNOU	224 (74.67)	68 (22.67)	8 (2.67)	0 (0.00)	0 (0.00)	167.39**
	UPRTOU	33 (11.00)	38 (12.67)	35 (11.67)	0 (0.00)	194 (64.67)	
	Total	257 (42.83)	106 (17.67)	43 (7.17)	0 (0.00)	194 (32.33)	
3i. Organization of appropriate assembly	IGNOU	242 (80.67)	40 (13.33)	18 (6.00)	0 (0.00)	300 (100.00)	0.44 N.S.
	UPRTOU	248 (82.67)	35 (11.67)	17 (5.67)	0 (0.00)	300 (100.00)	

(Contd.)

	Total	490 (81.67)	75 (12.50)	35 (5.83)	0 (0.00)	600 (100.00)	
ii. Inclusion of various activities in assembly	IGNOU	224 (74.67)	62 (20.67)	14 (4.67)	0 (0.00)	300 (100.00)	7.30*
	UPRTOU	237 (79.00)	40 (13.33)	23 (7.67)	0 (0.00)	300 (100.00)	
	Total	461 (76.83)	102 (17.00)	37 (6.17)	0 (0.00)	600 (100.00)	

Note: Figures in parentheses indicate percentages. N.S.: Not significant
* Indicates significant at .05 level.
** Indicates significant at .01 level.

χ^2 value is greater than the table value (5.99) at .05 level of significance with df: 2. Thus the observed values are found to be significant. Hence, it is clear that the response pattern of B.Ed. trainees and the university background in relation to the effectiveness of training provided for preparation of time-table, conducting action research, presenting research report and assimilating various activities during school prayer assembly are not found to be independent from each other.

It can be observed that 87 to 79 per cent B.Ed. trainees of UPRTOU considered training provided for the development of skills related to school administration and planning as effective on following items:

(i) Preparing school time table (86.67%)
(ii) Assimilating various types of activities in school prayer assembly (79.00%).

It can also be observed that 75 to 84 per cent B.Ed. trainees of IGNOU considered training provided for the development of skills related to school administration and planning as effective on following items:

(i) Preparing school time table (84.00%);
(ii) Conducting action research (82.00%);
(iii) Assimilating various types of activities in school assembly (74.67%); and
(iv) Presenting action research report (74.67%).

It can be noticed from Table 4.37 that the calculated χ^2 values of independence between the response pattern of B.Ed. trainees and the university background in relation to the effectiveness of training provided for the preparation of school records, preparation of school budget, conducting school prayer assembly appropriately are found as 3.86, 1.30 and 0.44 respectively. The obtained χ^2 value are less than the table value (5.99) at 0.05 level of significance with df: 2. Thus the observed values are not found significant. Hence, it is clear that the response patterns of B.Ed. trainees and the university background in relation to the effectiveness of training provided for the preparation of school records, preparation of school budget and conducting school prayer assembly are found to be independent from each other.

It can be observed that 71 to 82 per cent B.Ed. trainees of IGNOU and UPRTOU considered training provided for the development of skills related to school administration and planning as effective on following items:

(i) Conducting school assembly appropriately (81.67%);
(ii) Preparing school record (74.33%); and
(iii) Preparing school budget (71.33%).

4.38 Response of Counsellors about Effectiveness of Training Process for Development of Competency of School Management and Planning: University-wise

It can be noticed from Table 4.38 that the calculated χ^2 values of independence between the response pattern of counsellors and the university background in relation to the effectiveness of training adopted for preparing school time-table, preparing school records, preparing school budget, conducting action research, presenting action research report, organizing school prayer assembly appropriately and assimilating various activities in school prayer assembly are found as 1.27, 1.08, 0.76, 5.02, 2.84, 2.08 and 2.65 respectively. The obtained χ^2 value are lesser than the table value (5.99) at .05 level of significance with df: 2. Thus the observed values are not found significant. Hence, it is clear that the response patterns of counsellors and the university background in relation to the effectiveness of training for preparing school time-table, preparing school records, preparing school budget, conducting action research, presenting action research report, organizing school prayer assembly appropriately and assimilating various activities in school prayer assembly are found to be independent from each other.

Table 4.38: χ^2 test of Independence of counsellors response about effectiveness of training process adopted for development of competency of school management and planning and university background, skills-wise

Benefits of training process for development of school management and planning						
Developments of skills	*UNIV.*	*More extent*	*Some extent*	*Least*	*Total*	χ^2 *Values*
1i. Preparation of school time-table	IGNOU	26 (86.67)	3 (10.00)	1 (3.33)	30 (100.00)	1.27 N.S.
	UPRTOU	28 (93.33)	2 (6.67)	0 (0.00)	30 (100.00)	
	Total	54 (90.00)	5 (8.33)	1 (1.67)	60 (100.00)	
ii. Preparation of school records	IGNOU	23 (76.67)	7 (23.33)	0 (0.00)	30 (100.00)	1.08 N.S.
	UPRTOU	23 (76.67)	6 (20.00)	1 (3.33)	30 (100.00)	
	Total	46 (76.67)	13 (21.67)	1 (1.67)	60 (100.00)	
iii. Making school budget directed by principal	IGNOU	21 (70.00)	7 (23.33)	2 (6.67)	30 (100.00)	0.76 N.S.
	UPRTOU	18 (60.00)	10 (33.33)	2 (6.67)	30 (100.00)	
	Total	39 (65.00)	17 (28.33)	4 (6.67)	60 (100.00)	
2i. Conduction of action research	IGNOU	25 (83.33)	2 (6.67)	3 (10.00)	30 (100.00)	5.02 N.S.
	UPRTOU	24 (80.00)	6 (20.00)	0 (0.00)	30 (100.00)	
	Total	49 (81.67)	8 (13.33)	3 (5.00)	60 (100.00)	
ii. Presentation of research report	IGNOU	24 (80.00)	3 (10.00)	3 (10.00)	30 (100.00)	2.84 N.S.
	UPRTOU	20 (66.67)	8 (26.67)	2 (6.67)	30 (100.00)	
	Total	44 (73.33)	11 (18.33)	5 (8.33)	60 (100.00)	
3i. Organization of appropriate assembly	IGNOU	24 (80.00)	4 (13.33)	2 (6.67)	30 (100.00)	2.08 N.S.
	UPRTOU	26 (86.67)	4 (13.33)	0 (0.00)	30 (100.00)	

(Contd.)

	Total	50 (83.33)	8 (13.33)	2 (3.33)	60 (100.00)	
ii. Includusion of various activities in assembly?	IGNOU	20 (66.67)	8 (26.67)	2 (6.67)	30 (100.00)	2.65 N.S.
	UPRTOU	24 (80.00)	6 (20.00)	0 (0.00)	30 (100.00)	
	Total	44 (73.33)	14 (23.33)	2 (3.33)	60 (100.00)	

Note: Figures in parentheses indicate percentages.
N.S.: Not significant

It can be observed that 65 to 90 per cent counsellors of IGNOU and UPRTOU considered training provided for the development of skills related to school administration and planning as effective on following items:

(i) Preparing school time-table (90.00%)
(ii) Appropriately organizing assembly (83.33%)
(iii) Conducting action research (81.67%)
(iv) Preparing school record (76.67%)
(v) Presenting action research report (73.33%)
(vi) Assimilating various activities in school assembly (73.33%)
(vii) Preparing school budget (65.00%).

Conclusion

In this component B.Ed. trainees as well as mentors stated that mentors helped B.Ed. trainees in preparing school records, register, school budget and time-table. They corrected the limitation of register, school budget and time-table prepared by B.Ed. trainees of both the open universities stated that peer trainees helped them in preparing time-table and by discussing their experiences. Trainees told that appropriate knowledge is provided by mentors for preparing school records and school budget. They corrected records and budget prepared by trainees. Demonstration had been done by counsellors *via* preparing school records and school budget during workshops. Feedback was also provided in prepared records by trainees. Peer trainees also discussed their experiences and help by correcting of prepared records by trainees.

Majority of the trainees also informed that action research on various problems of school were conducted by themselves. Counsellors of IGNOU stated that action research is related to school based activity conducted by B.Ed. trainees at their own schools. The basic steps of action research were explained during workshop by themselves. Feedback provided by counsellors on submitted report of trainees. Counsellors of both the open universities stated that they helped B.Ed. trainees in conducting action research, trainees as well as counsellors of both the universities mentioned action research as relevant. Trainees considered that by conducting action research they make themselves capable for resolving problems related to schools.

As a whole the trainees and the counsellors expressed positive response about relevance and effectiveness of process adopted for making B.Ed. trainees competent in school management and planning.

VII. Community Participation Activities-oriented Process in Distance B.Ed. Programme

In this section analysis has been done regarding present status, relevance and effectiveness of processes adopted for development of competency related community participation activities among B.Ed. trainees.

4.39A Response of B.Ed. Trainees about Organisation of Activities Related to Community Participation: University-wise

It can be observed from Table 4.39A that 85 per cent trainees of UPRTOU and 82 per cent trainees of IGNOU stated that activities related to community participation had been organised during workshops.

4.39B Response of Trainees about Organised Activities Related to Community Participation during Workshop: University-wise

It can be noticed from Table 4.39 that the calculated χ^2 value of independence between the response pattern of B.Ed. trainees and the university background in relation to the conduction of varied activities to community participation workshop is found 4.39. The obtained χ^2 value is less than the table value (7.81) at 0.05 level of significance with df: 3. The observed value is not found significant. Hence it is clear that the response pattern of B.Ed. trainees and the university background are found to be independent from each other in relation to the conduction of varied activities related to community participation.

Table 4.39: χ^2 test of Independence of trainees' response about activities and help for resolving problems related community participation organised during the workshops and university background

A.

Response of B.Ed. trainees about organised of activities related to community participation during workshops

UNIV.	Yes	No	Total
IGNOU	245 (81.67)	55 (18.33)	300 (100.00)
UPRTOU	256 (85.33)	44 (14.67)	300 (100.00)
Total	501 (83.5)	99 (16.5)	600 (100.00)

B.

Response of B.Ed. trainees about organisation of activities related to community participation during workshops

UNIV.	i (Health education)	ii (Community work)	iii (i & ii)	iv (Nothing)	Total	χ^2 Value
IGNOU	25 (8.33)	34 (11.33)	186 (62.00)	55 (18.33)	300 (100.00)	4.39 N.S.
UPRTOU	35 (11.67)	44 (14.67)	177 (59.00)	44 (14.67)	300 (100.00)	
Total	60 (10.00)	78 (13.00)	363 (60.5)	99 (16.5)	600 (100.00)	

C.

Response of B.Ed. trainees about assistance providers for solving problems faced during organisation of community participation related work during workshops

UNIV.	i (Only mentor)	ii (Only peer trainees)	iii (i & ii)	iv (None)	Total	χ^2 Value
IGNOU	62 (20.67)	46 (15.33)	177 (59.00)	15 (5.00)	300 (100.00)	12.17**
UPRTOU	45 (15.00)	41 (13.67)	210 (70.00)	4 (1.33)	300 (100.00)	
Total	107 (17.83)	87 (14.5)	387 (64.5)	19 (3.17)	600 (100.00)	

Note: Figures in parentheses indicate percentages. N.S.: Not significant.
** Indicates significant at .01 level.

It can be observed that according to 61 per cent B.Ed. trainees of IGNOU and UPRTOU, community work related to health education and survey was conducted. Further 13 per cent B.Ed. trainees of IGNOU and UPRTOU considered that only community work and survey were conducted.

4.39C Response of B.Ed. Trainees about Assistance Provided for Solving Problems Faced Related to Community Participation: University-wise

It can be noticed from Table 4.39C that the calculated χ^2 value of independence between the response of B.Ed. trainees and the university background in relation to the person who solve problems during community work is found 12.17, which is greater than the table value (7.81) at 0.05 level of significance with df: 3. Thus the calculated χ^2 value is found to be significant. Hence, it is clear that the response pattern of B.Ed. trainees and the university background are not found independent from each other in relation to the person who solved problems during community work.

It can be observed that according to 70 per cent B.Ed. trainees of UPRTOU, the problems encountered during community work were resolved with the help of mentors and peer trainees, whereas only 59 per cent B.Ed. trainees of IGNOU considered the same.

Interview with Mentors about Activities Organised by B.Ed. Trainees related to Health Education, Social and Community Work at their own School Level

The selected mentors of IGNOU as well as UPRTOU stated that the B.Ed. trainees organised rallies for public awareness, cleaning the school and making plantation. They organized sports and cultural programmes and educational tours.

Interview with Mentors about Process of Organisation of Activities by B.Ed. Trainees Related to Health Education, Social and Community Work

The selected mentors of both the universities stated that B.Ed. trainees organised health education, social and community works with the help of students and teachers of their school. The B.Ed. trainees prepared poster by students on the topic "For good health". They organised educational tour, community works, plantation programmes and cultural programmes.

Interview with Mentors about Problems faced by B.Ed. Trainees during Organisation of Activities Related to Health Education, Social and Community Works in their own School

The selected mentors of both the universities informed that various problems were faced by B.Ed. trainees during organisation of activities related to health education, social and community work, i.e. indiscipline among students, non-cooperation of students and problem of controlling of students during the tour etc.

Interview with Mentors about their Help to B.Ed. Trainees in Organisation of Activities Related to Health Education, Social and Community Work

The selected mentors stated that they helped B.Ed. trainees in organisation of health education, social and community activities. They helped them in maintaining discipline among students.

4.40A Response of Counsellors about Organisation of Activities Related to Community Participation during Workshop: University-wise

It can be noticed from Table 4.40A that the calculated χ^2 value of independence between response patterns of counsellors and the university background in relation to the activities performed related to community participation is found 15.77, which is greater than the table value (11.07) at 0.05 level of significance with df: 5. Thus the obtained χ^2 value is found to be significant. Hence, it is clear that the response pattern of counsellors and the university background are not found to be independent from each other in relation to the activities performed related to community participation.

It can be observed that 77 per cent counsellors of UPRTOU mentioned that activities related to health education, community work and survey was conducted during workshops, whereas only 33 per cent counsellors of IGNOU mentioned the same.

Table 4.40: χ^2 test of independence of counsellors response about organisation of activities related to community participation during the workshops and university background

A.

UNIV.	*Response of counsellors about organisation of activities related to community participation*							χ^2 Value
	i (Health education related)	*ii (Community work and survey)*	*iii (i&ii)*	*iv (Group project)*	*v (Group discussion)*	*vi (None)*	*Total*	
IGNOU	7 (23.33)	6 (20.00)	10 (33.33)	1 (3.33)	1 (3.33)	5 (16.67)	30 (100.00)	15.77**
UPRTOU	6 (20.00)	1 (3.33)	23 (76.67)	0 (0.00)	0 (0.00)	0 (0.00)	30 (100.00)	
Total	13 (21.67)	7 (11.67)	33 (55.00)	1 (1.67)	1 (1.67)	5 (8.33)	60 (100.00)	

B.

UNIV.	*Response of counsellors about types of training provided for organisation of activities related to community participation*					χ^2 Value
	i (By providing detailed knowledge)	*ii (By organizing Activities)*	*iii (i&ii)*	*iv (None)*	*Total*	
IGNOU	6 (20.00)	9 (30.00)	10 (33.33)	5 (16.67)	30 (100.00)	10.45*
UPRTOU	4 (13.33)	5 (16.67)	21 (70.00)	0 (0.00)	30 (100.00)	
Total	10 (16.67)	14 (23.33)	31 (51.67)	5 (8.33)	60 (100.00)	

Note: Figures in parentheses indicate percentages.

* Indicates significant at .05 level.

** Indicates significant at .01 level.

23 per cent counsellors of IGNOU and 20 per cent counsellors of UPRTOU mentioned that only activities related to health education were conducted during workshops.

4.40B Response of Counsellors about Training Provided by Themselves to B.Ed. Trainees for Organisation of Activities Related to Community Participation: University-wise

It can be noticed from Table 4.40B that the calculated χ^2 value of independence between the response patterns of counsellors and the university background in relation to the training provided for organizing activities related to community participation is found 10.45, which is greater than the table value (7.81) at .05 level of significance with df: 3. Thus the obtained χ^2 value is found to be significant. Hence it is clear that the response pattern of counsellors and the university background in relation to the training provided for organizing activities related to community participation are not found to be independent from each other.

It can be observed that 70 per cent counsellors of UPRTOU and merely 33 per cent counsellors of IGNOU mentioned that they provided theoretical knowledge regarding organization and implementation of activities related to community participation during the workshops.

Interview with Counsellors about Activities Related to Social Work and Community Survey Organised during Workshops

The selected counsellors of both the universities stated only survey work and educational tour were organised during workshops. The trainees submited report of educational tour organised by themselves at their own schools.

Interview with Counsellors about Process Adopted for Making Competent to B.Ed. Trainees in Activities of Health Education

The selected counsellors of both the universities made clear that there was no provision of separate session for conducting activities related to health education, but it was included in school based activities for some credits for the development of above mentioned activities. The B.Ed. trainees were made aware of first aid.

4.41 Response of B.Ed. Trainees about Relevance of Training given to them for Development of Competency of Community Participation: University-wise

It can be noticed from Table 4.41 that the calculated χ^2 value of independence between the response patterns of B.Ed. trainees and the

Table 4.41: χ^2 test of Independence of trainees' response about relevance of training process for development of community participation skill and university background

Response of B.Ed. trainees about relevance of training for development of competency of community participation						
Statements	*UNIV.*	*Max. Agree*	*Least Agree*	*Disagree*	*Total*	χ^2 *Values*
1. Community work conducted during workshops is related to surrounding environment of your school	IGNOU	214 (71.33)	65 (21.67)	21 (7.00)	300 (100.00)	0.80 N.S.
	UPRTOU	215 (71.67)	69 (23.00)	16 (5.33)	300 (100.00)	
	Total	429 (71.50)	134 (22.33)	37 (6.17)	600 (100.00)	

Note: Figures in parentheses indicate percentages. N.S.: Not significant.

university background in relation to the relevance of training provided for the development of competency related to community participation activities is found 0.80, which is less than the table value (5.99) at .05 level of significance with df: 2. Thus the obtained χ^2 value is not found to be significant. Hence, it is clear that the response pattern of B.Ed. trainees and the university background in relation to the relevance of training provided for the development of competency related to community participation activities are found to be independent from each other.

It can be observed that 72 per cent B.Ed. trainees of IGNOU and UPRTOU considered training provided for the development of competency about organisation and implementation activities regarding to community participation related to local environment to their school as more relevant.

4.42 Response of Counsellors about Relevance of Training given to B.Ed. Trainees for Development of Competency of Community Participation: University-wise

It can be noticed from Table 4.42 that the calculated χ^2 value of independence between the response pattern of counsellors and the university background in relation to the relevance of training given to B.Ed. trainees for development of competency in activities related to community participation is found 3.70, which is less than the table

Table 4.42: χ^2 test of Independence of counsellors response about relevance of process adopted for development of competency of community participation and university background

Response of counsellors about relevance of training for development of competency of community participation						
Statement	*UNIV.*	*Highly Agree*	*Agree*	*Disagree*	*Total*	χ^2 *Value*
1. Community work conducted by you related to surrounding environment of B.Ed. trainee's school	IGNOU	17 (56.67)	10 (33.33)	3 (10.00)	30 (100.00)	3.70 N.S.
	UPRTOU	16 (53.33)	14 (46.67)	0 (0.00)	30 (100.00)	
	Total	33 (55.00)	24 (40.00)	3 (5.00)	60 (100.00)	

Note: Figures in parentheses indicate percentages. N.S.: Not significant.

value (5.99) at .05 level of significance with df: 2. Thus the obtained χ^2 value is not found to be significant. Hence it is clear that the response pattern of counsellors and the university background in relation to the relevance of training given to B.Ed. trainees for development of competency in activities related to community participation are found to be in dependent from each other.

It can be observed that 55 per cent counsellors of IGNOU and UPRTOU considered training provided for the development of competency in activities related to community participation related to local environment of their school as more relevant, and 45 per cent counsellors of IGNOU and UPRTOU did not consider such activities relevant.

4.43 Response of B.Ed. Trainees about Effectiveness of Training Provided to them for Development of Competency of Community Participation in B.Ed. Trainees: University-wise

It can be noticed from Table 4.43 that the calculated χ^2 values of independence between the response patterns of B.Ed. trainees and the university background in relation to the effectiveness of training provided for reducing pollution and maintaining hygenic environment in and around school are found 11.34 and 11.70 respectively, which is greater than the table value (5.99) at .05 level of significance with df: 2. Thus the obtained χ^2 values are found to be significant. Hence, it is clear that the response pattern of B.Ed. trainees and the university

Table 4.43: χ^2 test of Independence on trainees' response about effectiveness of process adopted for development of competency of community participation and university background, skill-wise

Benefits of training for development of competency of community participation						
Developments of skills	*UNIV.*	*More extent*	*Some extent*	*Least*	*Total*	χ^2 *Values*
1i. Development of reduce pollution by plantation	IGNOU	233 (77.67)	52 (17.33)	15 (5.00)	300 (100.00)	11.34**
	UPRTOU	250 (83.33)	26 (8.67)	24 (8.00)	300 (100.00)	
	Total	483 (80.50)	78 (13.00)	39 (6.50)	600 (100.00)	
ii. Development to cleanness arrangement near school	IGNOU	221 (73.67)	63 (21.00)	16 (5.33)	300 (100.00)	11.70**
	UPRTOU	230 (76.67)	38 (12.67)	32 (10.67)	300 (100.00)	
	Total	451 (75.17)	101 (16.83)	48 (8.00)	600 (100.00)	
iii. Development to enrich participation of students in Pulse Polio Programme	IGNOU	212 (70.67)	69 (23.00)	19 (6.33)	300 (100.00)	5.66 N.S.
	UPRTOU	218 (72.67)	51 (17.00)	31 (10.33)	300 (100.00)	
	Total	430 (71.67)	120 (20.00)	50 (8.33)	600 (100.00)	
iv. Development to motivate students and guardians for the success of adult education?	IGNOU	236 (78.67)	39 (13.00)	25 (8.33)	300 (100.00)	3.00 N.S.
	UPRTOU	225 (75.00)	37 (12.33)	38 (12.67)	300 (100.00)	
	Total	461 (76.83)	76 (12.67)	63 (10.50)	600 (100.00)	

Note: Figures in parentheses indicate percentages. N.S.: Not significant.
** Indicates significant at .01 level.

background in relation to the effectiveness of training provided for reducing pollution and maintaining hygienic environment in and around school are not found to be independent from each other.

It can be observed that majority of B.Ed. trainees (77 to 83%) of UPRTOU mentioned training provided for the development of skills in community participation as effective on following items:

(i) Reducing pollution *via* tree plantation (83.33%)
(ii) Arranging hygienic conditions in and around school (76.67%).

While 74 to 78 per cent B.Ed. trainees of IGNOU mentioned training provided for the development of skills in community participation as effective on following items:

(i) Reducing pollution via tree plantation (77.67%).
(ii) Arranging hygienic conditions in and around school (73.67%).

It can be noticed from Table 4.43 that the calculated χ^2 values of independence between the response pattern of B.Ed. trainees and the university background in relation to the effectiveness of training provided for increasing participation of students in pulse polio programme and motivating students and guardians for developing skills for adult education programme are found 5.66 and 3.00 respectively, which are less than the table value (5.99) at .05 level of significance with df: 2. Thus the obtained χ^2 values are found not significant. Hence, it is clear that the response pattern of B.Ed. trainees and the university background in relation to the above mentioned community participation programme are found to be independent from each other.

It can be observed that 72 to 77 per cent B.Ed. trainees of IGNOU and UPRTOU considered training provided for the development of skills for community participation effective on following items:

(i) Motivating students and guardians for adult education (76.83%).
(ii) Increasing participation of students in pulse polio programme (71.67%).

4.44 Response of Counsellors about Effectiveness of Training Provided for Development of Competency of Community Participation in B.Ed. Trainees: University-wise

It can be noticed from Table 4.44 that the calculated χ^2 values of independence between the response pattern of counsellors and the university background in relation to the effectiveness of training provided for development of competency for reducing pollution *via* tree plantation, arranging hygienic conditions in and around school, motivating students and guardians for adult education are found 4.36,

Table 4.44: χ^2 test of Independence on counsellors response about effectiveness of process adopted for development of competency of community participation and university background, skill-wise

Benefits of training process for development of competency of community participation among B.Ed. trainees						
Developments of skills	*UNIV.*	*More extent*	*Some extent*	*Least*	*Total*	χ^2 *Values*
1i. Rreducing pollution by plantation	IGNOU	23 (76.67)	4 (13.33)	3 (10.00)	30 (100.00)	4.36 N.S.
	UPRTOU	22 (73.33)	8 (26.67)	0 (0.00)	30 (100.00)	
	Total	45 (75.00)	12 (20.00)	3 (5.00)	60 (100.00)	
ii. Cleanness arrangement near school	IGNOU	23 (76.67)	4 (13.33)	3 (10.00)	30 (100.00)	4.36 N.S.
	UPRTOU	22 (73.33)	8 (26.67)	0 (0.00)	30 (100.00)	
	Total	45 (75.00)	12 (20.00)	3 (5.00)	60 (100.00)	
iii. Enriching participation of students in Pulse Polio Programme	IGNOU	18 (60.00)	10 (33.33)	2 (6.67)	30 (100.00)	9.51**
	UPRTOU	28 (93.33)	2 (6.67)	0 (0.00)	30 (100.00)	
	Total	46 (76.67)	12 (20.00)	2 (3.33)	60 (100.00)	
iv. Motivating students and guardians for the success of adult education	IGNOU	21 (70.00)	6 (20.00)	3 (10.00)	30 (100.00)	4.02 N.S.
	UPRTOU	20 (66.67)	10 (33.33)	0 (0.00)	30 (100.00)	
	Total	41 (68.33)	16 (26.67)	3 (5.00)	60 (100.00)	

Note: Figures in parentheses indicate percentages. N.S.: Not significant.
** Indicates significant at .01 level.

4.36 and 4.02 respectively which is less than the table value (5.99) at .05 level of significance with df: 2. Thus the obtained χ^2 values are not found significant. Hence, it is clear that the response pattern of counsellors and the university background in relation to the above mentioned skills for community participation are found to be independent from each other.

It can be observed that 68 to 75 per cent counsellors of IGNOU and UPRTOU mentioned training provided for the development of skills for enhancing community participation as effective on the following items:

(i) Reducing pollution via tree plantation (75.00%);
(ii) Arranging hygienic conditions in and around school (75.00%);
(iii) Motivating students and guardians for success of adult; and education programme (68.33%).

It can be noticed from Table 4.44 that the calculated χ^2 value of independence between the response pattern of counsellors and the university background in relation to the effectiveness of training given for enhancing student participation in Pulse Polio programme is 9.51, which is greater than the table value (5.99) at 0.05 level of significance with df: 2. Thus the obtained χ^2 value is found significant. Hence, it is clear that the response pattern of counsellors and the university background in relation to the effectiveness of training provided for enhancing student's participation in Pulse Polio programme are not found to be independent from each other.

It can be observed that majority of counsellors (93%) of UPRTOU and 60 per cent counsellors of IGNOU considered training provided for the development of skills in community participation for enhancing participation of trainees for Pulse Polio programme as effective.

Conclusion

In this component study had been conducted about process adopted for development of competency related community participation among B.Ed. trainees. Majority of trainees of both the open universities stated that activities of community participation were organised during workshops. Trainees told that activities related to health education and community survey were organised during workshops. Trainees also stated that for removing problems that occurs during organisation of activities related to community participation mentors and peer trainees helped them.

Mentors stated that B.Ed. trainees organised rallies for public awareness, making plantation, organised sports and cultural programmes and educational tour. Mentors also stated that B.Ed. trainees organised health education, social and community works with the help of students and teachers of their schools. Mentors stated that they helped trainees in organization of activities related to community participation and maintaining discipline among students. The selected counsellors of both the open universities stated only survey and educational tour were organised during workshops. Counsellors told that trainees submitted the report of educational tour organised by themselves at their own schools and they were provided feedback and grades also.

Majority of trainees and counsellors of both the universities considered that process of making trainees competent in community participation as relevant and effective.

VIII. Co-curricular Activities-oriented Practices in Distance B.Ed. Programme

In this section analysis has been done regarding present status, relevance and effectiveness of processes adopted for making trainees competent in organisation of co-curricular activities.

4.45 Response of Trainees about Organisation of Co-curricular Activities, Types of Co-curricular Activities during Workshop and Types of Activities for Development of Competency for Organisation of Co-curricular Activities: University-wise

It can be noticed from Table 4.45A that the calculated χ^2 value of independence between the response pattern of B.Ed. trainees and the university background in relation to co-curricular activities is found 4.50. The obtained χ^2 value is lesser than the table value (5.99) at 0.05 level of significance with df: 2. Thus the observed value is not found significant. Hence, it is clear that the response pattern of B.Ed. trainees and the university background are found to be independent from each other in the context of conducting co-curricular activities during workshop.

It can be noticed from Table 4.45B that the calculated χ^2 value of independence between the response pattern of B.Ed. trainees and the university background in relation to organization of co-curricular activities during workshops is found 35.95. The obtained χ^2 value is greater than the table value (12.59) at .05 level of significance with df: 6. Thus the observed value is found to be significant. Hence it is clear that the response pattern of B.Ed. trainees and the university

Table 4.45: χ^2 test of Independence on trainees' response about organisation of co-curricular activities, types of co-curricular activities organised during the workshops and types of activities for development of competency of organisation of co-curricular activities and university background

A.

Response of B.Ed. trainees about organisation of co-curricular activities during workshops

UNIV.	*i (Regularly)*	*ii (Some times)*	*iii (Never)*	*Total*	χ^2 *Value*
IGNOU	112 (37.33)	167 (55.67)	21 (7.00)	300 (100.00)	4.50 N.S.
UPRTOU	93 (31.00)	192 (64.00)	15 (5.00)	300 (100.00)	
Total	205 (34.17)	359 (59.83)	36 (6.0)	600 (100.00)	

B.

Response of B.Ed. trainees about types of co-curricular activities conducted during workshops

UNIV	*i (Educa-tional tour)*	*ii (Sports and game)*	*iii (Debate compe-tition)*	*iv (Semi-nar)*	*v (ii, iii, iv, v)*	*vi (Func-tions related to school)*	*vii (i, ii, iii, iv & vi)*	*Total*	χ^2 *Value*
IGNOU	28 (9.33)	37 (12.33)	77 (25.67)	113 (37.67)	23 (7.67)	4 (1.33)	18 (6.00)	300 (100.00)	35.95**
UPRTOU	29 (9.67)	40 (13.33)	48 (16.00)	112 (37.33)	44 (14.67)	15 (5.00)	12 (4.00)	300 (100.00)	
Total	57 (9.50)	77 (12.83)	125 (20.83)	225 (37.50)	67 (11.17)	19 (3.17)	30 (5.00)	600 (100.00)	

C.

Response of trainees about organisation of activities during workshops for development of competency related to co-curricular activities

UNIV.	*Group Discussion, Presentation of report, Cultural programme*	*V (nothing)*	*Total*
IGNOU	291 (97.00)	9 (3.00)	300 (100.00)

(Contd.)

UPRTOU	293 (97.67)	7 (2.33)	300 (100.00)
Total	584 97.33)	16 (2.67)	600 (100.00)

Note: Figures in parentheses indicate percentages. N.S.: Not significant.
** Indicates significant at .01 level.

background are not found independent from each other in the context of organisation of co-curricular activities during workshops.

It can be observed from Table 4.45A that 60 per cent B.Ed. trainees of IGNOU and UPRTOU, mentioned that co-curricular activities were conducted some times during workshops, 34 per cent of them mentioned that co-curricular activities were conducted regularly.

It can be further observed from Table 4.45B that out of many co-curricular activities the prominent activities were seminar (37 to 38%) and debates competition (16 to 26%) conducted during workshops.

It can be observed from Table 4.45C that group discussion, presentation of report and cultural programmes (97%) were organised for the development of competencies among trainees in organization of co-curricular activities during the workshops in almost all cases.

Interview with Mentors about Co-curricular Activities in which B.Ed. Trainees make Active Participation

The selected mentors of both the universities mentioned that they helped B.Ed. trainees in organisation of sports, educational tour, plantation, cleaning of their school's field, making poster, in celebration of cultural programmes in their school, in making toys and other social useful work.

Interview with Mentors about Problems Faced by B.Ed. Trainees during Organisation of Educational Tour, Sports and other Cultural Programmes

The selected mentors of both the universities informed that during organisation of educational tour, sports and other cultural programmes the problems of students indifference and indiscipline were faced by B.Ed. trainees.

Interview with Mentors about their Help for Resolving Problems Faced by B.Ed. Trainees during Organisation of Educational Tour, Sports and other Cultural Programmes

The selected mentors informed that they tried to maintain student's discipline, and encouraging students for their active participation and successful completion of educational tour, sports and other cultural programmes.

4.46 χ^2Values of Independence Test on Counsellor's and University Background, Response about Organisation of Co-curricular Activities during Workshops and Activities for Developments of Competency in Co-curricular Activities

It can be observed from Table 4.46A that 96.67 per cent counsellors of IGNOU and almost all cases of UPRTOU stated that educational tour, sports, debate competition, seminar and cultural programme are conducted during the workshops.

It can be observed from Table 4.46B that cent per cent counsellors of IGNOU and 87 per cent counsellors of UPRTOU stated that group discussion, report presentation and cultural programmes were organised during the workshops for development of competencies among B.Ed. trainees in organisation of co-curricular activity.

Interview with Counsellors about Relevance of Group Discussion Organised during Workshops

The selected counsellors of both the universities considered group discussion as relevant because all the trainees got opportunity to listening ideas of each other and discussing upon them. Group discussion provided narrow and wider information regarding the topic. Development of their skills related to communication and interaction were available by group discussion. With the help of group discussion they learn to respect others' ideas and new ideas were created in them. It also increases their power of expression.

Interview with Counsellors about Process Adopted during Workshops for Development of Competency related to Sports and other Cultural programmes among B.Ed. Trainees

The selected counsellors of both the universities mentioned that there was no provision of separate session about sports and other cultural

Table 4.46: χ^2 test of Independence of counsellors response about organisation of co-curricular activities during the workshops and activities for developments of competency of organisation of co-curricular activities and university background

A.

Response of counsellors about co-curricular activities conducted during workshops			
UNIV.	*Tour, Sports, Debate, Seminar, Cultural Programmes*	*None*	*Total*
IGNOU	29 (96.67)	1 (3.33)	30 (100.00)
UPRTOU	30 (100.00)	0 (0.00)	30 (100.00)
Total	59 (98.33)	1 1.67)	60 (100.00)

B.

Response of counsellors about development of competency related to organisation of co-curricular activities among B.Ed. trainees			
UNIV.	Group discussion, Report presentation, Cultural Programmes organized	None	Total
IGNOU	30 (100.00)	0 (0.00)	30 (100.00)
UPRTOU	26 (86.67)	4 (13.33)	30 (100.00)
Total	56 (93.33)	4 (6.67)	60 (100.00)

Note: Figures in parentheses indicate percentages.

programmes. The cultural programme had organised during inaugural and valedictory session by the B.Ed. trainees only.

It is also clear from the observation done by researcher that some cultural programme and speech were organised during inaugural and valedictory session of workshops by the B.Ed. trainees.

Interview with Counsellors about Relevance of Seminar during Workshops

The selected counsellors of both the universities considered that organisation of seminar during workshops as relevant. It develops confidence among B.Ed. trainees. Seminar develops capability of B.Ed. trainees of speech, skill of questioning and expression of their views.

4.47 Response of B.Ed. Trainees about Relevance of Process Adopted for Co-curricular Activities: University-wise

It can be noticed from Table 4.47 that the calculated χ^2 values of independence between the response pattern of B.Ed. trainees and the university background in relation to the relevance of seminar and group discussion conducted during workshops are found as 0.73 and 1.26 respectively. The obtained χ^2 values are lesser than the table value (5.99) at .05 level of significance with df: 2. Thus the observed values are not found to be significant. Hence, the response pattern of B.Ed. trainees and the university background are found to be independent from each other in the context of relevance of above mentioned activities.

Table 4.47: χ^2 test of Independence of trainees' response about relevance of training process adopted for development of competency of organisation of co-curricular activities and university background

Response of B.Ed. trainees about relevance of training process adopted for development of competency related to organisation of co-curricular activities

Statement	*UNIV.*	*Highly Agree*	*Agree*	*Disagree*	*Total*	*χ^2 Values*
1. Seminar conducted during workshop is related to your school activities	IGNOU	218 (72.67)	60 (20.00)	22 (7.33)	300 (100.00)	0.73 N.S.
	UPRTOU	218 (72.67)	55 (18.33)	27 (9.00)	300 (100.00)	
	Total	436 (72.67)	115 (19.17)	49 (8.17)	600 (100.00)	
2. Organization of group discussion during workshop is related to skill development in you	IGNOU	220 (73.33)	66 (22.00)	14 (4.67)	300 (100.00)	1.26 N.S.
	UPRTOU	230 (76.67)	55 (18.33)	15 (5.00)	300 (100.00)	
	Total	450 (75.00)	121 (20.17)	29 (4.83)	600 (100.00)	

Note: Figures in parentheses indicate percentages. N.S.: Not significant

It can be observed that 73 to 75 per cent B.Ed. trainees of IGNOU as well as UPRTOU considered seminar and group discussion as more relevant in relation to the following statements:

(i) Organization of group discussion during workshop was related to skill development among B.Ed. trainees (75.00%).
(ii) Seminar conducted during workshop was related to school activities of B.Ed. trainees (72.67%).

4.48 Response of Counsellors about Relevance of Process Adopted for Co-curricular Activities: University-wise

It can be noticed from Table 4.48 that the calculated χ^2 values of independence between the response pattern of counsellors and the university background in relation to the relevance of seminar, debate and group discussion conducted by counsellor for development of skills of conduction of co-curricular activities among B.Ed. trainees are found as 2.50, 3.18 and 1.06 respectively. The obtained χ^2 values are lesser than the table value (5.99) at .05 level of significance with df: 2. Thus the observed values are not found significant. Hence, the response pattern of counsellors and the university background are found to be independent from each other in the context of relevance of seminar, debate and group discussion conducted by counsellors for development of skills of conducting co-curricular activities.

It can be observed that 70 to 77 per cent counsellors of IGNOU as well as UPRTOU considered seminar, debate and group discussion conducted by themselves for development of skills of conduction of co-curricular activities among B.Ed. trainees as more relevant in the context of following statement:

(i) Conducting of debate is related to skills development among B.Ed. trainees (76.67%).
(ii) Conducting of Seminars during workshop is related to skill development of B.Ed. trainees (70.00%).
(iii) Conducting of group discussion is related to skills development of B.Ed. trainees (70.00%).

Table 4.48: χ^2 test of independence of counsellors response about relevance of training process adopted for development of skill of organisation of co-curricular activities and university background

Response of counsellors about relevance of training process adopted for development of skill of organisation of co-curricular activities among B.Ed. trainees						
Statements	*UNIV.*	*Highly Agree*	*Agree*	*Disagree*	*Total*	χ^2 *Values*
1. Seminar conducted by during workshop is related to school activities of B.Ed. trainees	IGNOU	22 (73.33)	2 (6.67)	6 (20.00)	30 (100.00)	2.50 N.S.
	UPRTOU	20 (66.67)	6 (20.00)	4 (13.33)	30 (100.00)	
	Total	42 (70.00)	8 (13.33)	10 (16.67)	60 (100.00)	
2. Conduction of the debate by you is related to skills development of B.Ed. trainees	IGNOU	22 (73.33)	5 (16.67)	3 (10.00)	30 (100.00)	3.18 N.S.
	UPRTOU	24 (80.00)	6 (20.00)	0 (0.00)	30 (100.00)	
	Total	46 (76.67)	11 (18.33)	3 (5.00)	60 (100.00)	
3. Conduction of the group discussion by you is related to skill development of B.Ed. trainees	IGNOU	21 (70.00)	9 (30.00)	0 (0.00)	30 (100.00)	1.06 N.S.
	UPRTOU	21 (70.00)	8 (26.67)	1 (3.33)	30 (100.00)	
	Total	42 (70.00)	17 (28.33)	1 (1.67)	60 (100.00)	

Note: Figures in parentheses indicate percentages. N.S.: Not significant

4.49 Response of B.Ed. Trainees about Effectiveness of Co-curricular Activities: University-wise

It can be noticed from Table 4.49 that the calculated χ^2 value of independence between the response pattern of B.Ed. trainees and the university background in relation to effectiveness of process adopted for enhancement of implementation of sports and cultural programme in the school, conducting of educational tour successfully and participation of students in sports and cultural programmes are found as 14.58, 7.64 and 17.47 respectively. The obtained χ^2 values are greater than the table value (5.99) at .05 level of significance with df: 2. Thus the observed values are found to be significant. Hence, the response

Table 4.49: χ^2 test of Independence of trainees' response about effectiveness of training process adopted for development of skills of organisation of co-curricular activities and university background, skill-wise

Developments of skills	*UNIV.*	*Benefits of training process of co-curricular activities*				*χ^2 Values*
		More extent	*Some extent*	*Least*	*Total*	
1i. Implementing sports and cultural programme in the school	IGNOU	243 (81.00)	41 (13.67)	16 (5.33)	300 (100.00)	14.58**
	UPRTOU	256 (85.33)	16 (5.33)	28 (9.33)	300 (100.00)	
	Total	499 (83.17)	57 (9.50)	44 (7.33)	600 (100.00)	
ii. Conduction of educational tour successfully	IGNOU	216 (72.00)	66 (22.00)	18 (6.00)	300 (100.00)	7.64*
	UPRTOU	220 (73.33)	47 (15.67)	33 (11.00)	300 (100.00)	
	Total	436 (72.67)	113 (18.83)	51 (8.50)	600 (100.00)	
iii. Enrich participation of students in sports and cultural programme	IGNOU	237 (79.00)	52 (17.33)	11 (3.67)	300 (100.00)	17.47**
	UPRTOU	240 (80.00)	28 (9.33)	32 (10.67)	300 (100.00)	
	Total	477 (79.50)	80 (13.33)	43 (7.17)	600 (100.00)	

Note: Figures in parentheses indicate percentages.

* Indicates significant at .05 level.

** Indicates significant at .01 level.

pattern of B.Ed. trainees and the university background are not found to be independent from each other in the context of effectiveness of process adopted for enhancement of above mentioned areas.

It can be observed that majority of B.Ed. trainees (73 to 85%) of UPRTOU considered process adopted as effective for development of following:

(i) Implementation of sports and cultural programme in own school of B.Ed. trainees (85.33%);

(ii) Enhance participation of students in sports and cultural programme (80.00%);

(iii) Conducting educational tour successfully (73.33%).

While 72 to 81 per cent B.Ed. trainees of IGNOU considered training process adopted as effective for development of following:

(i) Implementation sports and cultural programme in own school of B.Ed. trainees (81.00%).
(ii) Enhance participation of students in sports and cultural programme (79.00%).
(iii) Conducting of educational tour successfully (72.00%).

4.50 Response of Counsellors about Effectiveness of Process Adopted for Co-curricular Activities among B.Ed. Trainees: University-wise

It can be noticed from Table 4.50 that the calculated χ^2 value of independence between the response pattern of counsellors and the university background in relation to effectiveness of training process adopted organisation of sports and cultural programme in school as a co-curricular activities is found as 5.64. The obtained χ^2 value is lesser than the table value (5.99) at 0.05 level of significance with df: 2. Thus the observed value is not found significant. Hence, the response pattern of counsellors and the university background are found to be independent from each other in the context of effectiveness of training process adopted for development of above areas.

It can be observed that majority of counsellors (87%) of IGNOU as well as UPRTOU considered process adopted as effective for organising sports and cultural programme in school as co-curricular activities.

It can be noticed from Table 4.50 that the calculated χ^2 values of independence between the response pattern of counsellors and the university background in relation to effectiveness of training process adopted for development of skills of conduction of co-curricular activities among B.Ed. trainees like conduction of educational tour successfully and enriching participation of students in sports and cultural programme are found as 7.78 and 7.48 respectively. The obtained χ^2 values are greater than the table value (5.99) at .05 level of significance with df: 2. Thus the observed values are found to be significant. Hence, the response pattern of counsellors and the university background are not found to be independent from each other

Table 4.50: χ^2 test of Independence of counsellors response about effectiveness of training process adopted for development of skills of organisation of co-curricular activities and university background, skill-wise

Benefits of training process for development of skill of organisation of co-curricular activities						
Developments of skills	*UNIV.*	*More extent*	*Some extent*	*Least*	*Total*	χ^2 *Values*
1i. Implementing sports and cultural programme in the school	IGNOU	24 (80.00)	1 (3.33)	5 (16.67)	30 (100.00)	5.64 N.S.
	UPRTOU	28 (93.33)	2 (6.67)	0 (0.00)	30 (100.00)	
	Total	52 (86.67)	3 (5.00)	5 (8.33)	60 (100.00)	
ii. Conduction of educational Tour successfully	IGNOU	23 (76.67)	2 (6.67)	5 (16.67)	30 (100.00)	7.78*
	UPRTOU	23 (76.67)	7 (23.33)	0 (0.00)	30 (100.00)	
	Total	46 (76.67)	9 (15.00)	5 (8.33)	60 (100.00)	
iii. Enriching participation of students in sports and cultural programme	IGNOU	22 (73.33)	2 (6.67)	6 (20.00)	30 (100.00)	7.48*
	UPRTOU	25 (83.33)	5 (16.67)	0 (0.00)	30 (100.00)	
	Total	47 (78.33)	7 (11.67)	6 (10.00)	60 (100.00)	

Note: Figures in parentheses indicate percentages. N.S.: Not significant.
* Indicates significant at .05 level.

in the context of effectiveness of process adopted for enhancement in above mentioned skills among B.Ed. trainees.

It can be observed that majority of counsellors (77 to 83%) of IGNOU considered process adopted for development of skills of co-curricular activities among B.Ed. trainees as effective in the context of development in the following skills:

(i) Enhancing participation of students in sports and cultural programme (83.33%).
(ii) Conducting of educational tour successfully (76.67%).

While 73 to 77 per cent counsellors of both the universities considered process adopted for development of following skills of co-curricular activities:

(i) Conduction of educational tour successfully (76.67%).
(ii) Enrich participation of students in sports and cultural programme (73.33%).

Conclusion

In this component study had been conducted about process adopted for making B.Ed. trainees competent in co-curricular activities. It is clear from the analysis that according to average number of B.Ed. trainees of both the open universities co-curricular activities conducted sometimes during workshops. More trainees and counsellors stated that educational tour, sports, seminar, group discussion and cultural programmes were organised during workshops. According to the observation of researcher seminar, group discussion and cultural programmes were organised during workshops. Mentors stated that the problems of students discipline faced by B.Ed. trainees during organisation of co-curricular activities. Mentors stated that they helped trainees in establishing student discipline and encouraging students for their active participation and successful completion of educational tour, sports and other cultural programmes.

B.Ed. trainees as well as counsellors stated that seminar was conducted during workshops. Trainees and counsellors consider that organisation of seminar during workshops as relevant. As a whole trainees as well as counsellors expressed positive response about relevance and effectiveness of process adopted for development of competency related co-curricular activities.

IX. Use of Self-learning Materials by Distance B.Ed. Trainees

In this section analysis has been done regarding help taken by trainees from SLM and student-teachers' hand book. Relevance and effectiveness of SLM and student teachers' hand book provided by open universities are also analyzed in this section.

4.51A Response of B.Ed. Trainees about Kinds of Help Taken from Self-learning Materials: University-wise

It can be noticed from Table 4.51A that the calculated χ^2 value of independence between the response pattern of B.Ed. trainees and the university background about kinds of help taken from self-learning materials is 8.50, which is less than the table value (9.48) at the .05 level of significance with df: 4. The obtained χ^2 value is not found significant. Hence the response pattern of B.Ed. trainees and the university background is found independent from each other in relation to kinds of help taken by B.Ed. trainees from self-learning materials.

Table 4.51: χ^2 test of Independence of trainees' response about types of help taken from self-learning material and student teachers handbook and university background

A.

Response of B.Ed. trainees about help taken from self-learning material							
UNIV.	*i (Selection of appropriate teaching methods)*	*ii (Development of teaching learning skills)*	*iii (In preparing Lesson Plan)*	*iv (To write assignments properly)*	*v (i, ii, iii & iv)*	*Total*	χ^2 *Value*
IGNOU	9 (3.00)	15 (5.00)	18 (6.00)	17 (5.67)	241 (80.33)	300 (100.00)	8.50 N.S.
UPRTOU	16 (5.33)	26 (8.67)	15 (5.00)	8 (2.67)	235 (78.33)	300 (100.00)	
Total	25 (4.17)	41 (6.83)	33 (5.50)	25 (4.17)	476 (79.33)	600 (100.00)	

B.

Response of B.Ed. trainees about help taken from student teachers' handbook							
UNIV.	*i (Information about theoretical paper)*	*ii (Information about practical programmes)*	*iii (Information about workshop based activities)*	*iv (It works like a silent guide)*	*v (i, ii, iii & iv)*	*Total*	χ^2 *Value*
IGNOU	9 (3.00)	22 (7.33)	46 (15.33)	13 (4.33)	210 (70.00)	300 (100.00)	3.19 N.S.
UPRTOU	10 (3.33)	20 (6.67)	32 (10.67)	15 (5.00)	223 (74.33)	300 (100.00)	
Total	19 (3.17)	42 (7.00)	78 (13.00)	28 (4.67)	433 (72.17)	600 (100.00)	

(Contd.)

C.

Response of B.Ed. trainees about correlation between lessons of self-learning materials and training provided them during workshops

UNIV.	*i (Large extent)*	*ii (Average extent)*	*iii (Less extent)*	*iv (Not at all)*	*Total*	χ^2 *Value*
IGNOU	166 (55.33)	95 (31.67)	27 (9.00)	12 (4.00)	300 (100.00)	4.98 N.S.
UPRTOU	141 (47.00)	114 (38.00)	35 (11.67)	10 (3.33)	300 (100.00)	
Total	307 (51.17)	209 (34.83)	62 (10.33)	22 (3.67)	600 (100.00)	

Note: Figures in parentheses indicate percentages. N.S.: Not significant

It can be observed that 79 per cent B.Ed. trainees of IGNOU and UPRTOU stated that self-learning materials help them in the selection of appropriate teaching methods, development of teaching-learning skills, preparing lesson plans and in writing assignment in appropriate manner.

4.51B Response of B.Ed. Trainees about Helps Sought from Student Teachers' Handbook: University-wise

It can be noticed from Table 4.51B that the calculated χ^2 value of independence between the response pattern of B.Ed. trainees and the university background about type of helps taken from student teachers handbook is 3.19. It is less than the table value (9.48) at the .05 level of significance with df: 4. The obtained χ^2 value is not found significant. Hence, the response pattern of B.Ed. trainees and the university background are found independent from each other in relation to help taken by B.Ed. trainees from student teachers' handbook.

It can be observed that majority B.Ed. trainees (72%) of IGNOU and UPRTOU stated that student teachers' hand book provided the knowledge about theoretical papers, experimental programmes, all activities of workshops and it worked as a guide to them.

Response of B.Ed. Trainees about the Utility of Student Teachers' Handbook

It is clear from the responses of B.Ed. trainees that student teachers' handbook was useful on following areas:

- It provides knowledge of theoretical subjects/programmes.
- It provides knowledge of practical programmes/activities.
- It acquaints them with seminar and discussion organized during workshops.
- It acquaints them in advance about various activities organized during workshops.
- It helps in the completion of assignments to be submitted during workshops.
- It is helpful in doing exercises.
- It provides details about programmes of workshops initially.
- It helps in making pre-planning of activities of workshops.
- It helps in preparing lesson plans.

4.51C Response of Trainees about Correlation between Lessons of Self-Learning Materials and Guidance Provided to them during Workshops: University-wise

It can be noticed from Table 4.51C that the calculated χ^2 value of independence between response pattern of B.Ed. trainees and the university background in relation to the correlation between lessons of self-learning materials and guidance provided to B.Ed. trainees during workshop is 4.98. It is less than the table value (7.81) at .05 level of significance with df:3. The obtained χ^2 value is not found significant. Hence the response pattern of B.Ed. trainees and the university background are found independent from each other in relation to the correlation between lessons of SLM and training provided to B.Ed. trainees.

It can be observed that 51 per cent B.Ed. trainees of IGNOU and UPRTOU stated that lessons of self-learning materials and guidance given to them during workshops was rated at large extent. While 35 per cent B.Ed. trainees of IGNOU and UPRTOU stated that lesson of self-learning materials and guidance given to them during workshops was rated at average extent and 10 per cent trainees of both the universities stated that same was rated at less extent.

4.52A Response of Counsellors with Reference to Help taken by B.Ed. Trainees from Self-learning Materials: University-wise

It can be noticed from Table 4.52A that the calculated χ^2 value of independence between response pattern of counsellors and the university background in relation to help taken by B.Ed. trainees from Self-Learning Materials is 13.47. It is greater than the table value (9.48) at .05 level of significance with df: 4. The obtained χ^2 value is found significant. Hence, the response pattern of counsellors and the university background are not found independent from each other in reference to helps taken by B.Ed. trainees from self-learning materials.

It can be observed that according to 63 per cent counsellors of IGNOU, Self-Learning Materials helped B.Ed. trainees in following skills:

(i) Selection of appropriate teaching methods.
(ii) Writing assignment appropriately.
(iii) Development of teaching-learning skills.
(iv) Preparing lessons plans.

While, according to 60 per cent counsellors of UPRTOU, self-learning materials helped B.Ed. trainees in following skills:

(i) Writing assignment appropriately.
(ii) Development of teaching-learning skills.
(iii) Selection of appropriate teaching methods.
(iv) Preparing lessons plans.

4.52B Response of Counsellors in Relation to Assistance taken by B.Ed. Trainees from Student Teachers Handbook: University-wise

It can be noticed from Table 4:52B that the calculated χ^2 value of independence between response pattern of counsellors and the university background in relation to assistance taken by B.Ed. trainees from student teachers handbook is 5.36. It is less than the table value (9.48) at .05 level of significance with df: 4. The obtained χ^2 value is not found significant. Hence, the response pattern of counsellors and the university background are found independent from each other in reference to assistance taken by B.Ed. trainees from student teachers handbook.

Table 4.52: χ^2 test of Independence of counsellors response about help taken by B.Ed. trainees from self-learning materials and student teachers' handbook and university background

A.

Response of counsellors about help taken by B.Ed. trainees from self-learning material

UNIV.	*i (In selection appropriate method)*	*ii (Development of teaching learning skills)*	*iii In (preparing lesson plan)*	*iv (In writing assignment correctly)*	*v (i, ii, iii & iv)*	*Total*	χ^2 *Value*
IGNOU	7 (23.33)	1 (3.33)	1 (3.33)	2 (6.67)	19 (63.33)	30 (100.00)	13.47**
UPRTOU	0 (0.00)	5 (16.67)	0 (0.00)	7 (23.33)	18 (60.00)	30 (100.00)	
Total	7 (11.67)	6 (10.00)	1 (1.67)	9 (15.00)	37 (61.67)	60 (100.00)	

B.

Response of counsellors about help taken by B.Ed. trainees from student teachers' handbook

UNIV.	*i (Provides theoretical knowledge)*	*ii (Provide practical programme)*	*iii (Knowledge about workshop's activities)*	*iv (Like guide)*	*v (i, ii, iii & iv)*	*Total*	χ^2 *Value*
IGNOU	6 (20.00)	1 (3.33)	2 (6.67)	2 (6.67)	19 (63.33)	30 (100.00)	5.36 N.S.
UPRTOU	6 (20.00)	0 (0.00)	2 (6.67)	8 (26.67)	14 (46.67)	30 (100.00)	
Total	12 (20.00)	1 (1.67)	4 (6.67)	10 (16.67)	33 (55.00)	60 (100.00)	

C.

Response of counsellors about similarity between lessons of SLM and training given to B.Ed. trainees

UNIV.	*i (Maximum limit)*	*ii (Average limit)*	*iii (Low limit)*	*iv (Not at all)*	*Total*	χ^2 *Value*
IGNOU	18 (60.00)	12 (40.00)	0 (0.00)	0 (0.00)	30 (100.00)	12.00**

(Contd.)

UPRTOU	8 (26.67)	14 (46.67)	4 (13.33)	4 (13.33)	30 (100.00)
Total	26 (43.33)	26 (43.33)	4 (6.67)	4 (6.67)	60 (100.00)

Note: Figures in parentheses indicate percentages. N.S.: Not significant.
** Indicates significant at .01 level.

It can be observed that almost 55 per cent counsellors of IGNOU and UPTROU considered that student teachers handbook provided the knowledge to B.Ed. trainees about theoretical papers, experimental programmes and about all activities of workshops and also it worked as a guide also.

4.52C Response of Counsellors about Correlation between Lessons of Self-learning Materials and Guidance given to B.Ed. Trainees: University-wise

It can be noticed from Table 4.52C that the calculated χ^2 value of independence between response pattern of counsellors and the university background in relation to correlation between lessons of self-learning materials and training given to B.Ed. trainees is 12.00. It is greater than the table value (7.81) at 0.05 level of significance with df: 3. The obtained χ^2 value is found significant. Hence the response pattern of counsellors and the university background are not found independence in reference to correlation between lessons of self-learning materials and training given to B.Ed. trainees.

It can be observed that almost 60 per cent counsellors of IGNOU told that there was correlation between lessons of self-learning materials and guidance given to B.Ed. trainees at maximum extent. While only 27 per cent counsellors of UPRTOU told that there was correlation between lessons of self-learning materials and guidance given to B.Ed. trainees up to maximum extent.

4.53 Response of B.Ed. Trainees about Relevance of Self-Learning Materials and Student Teachers Handbook: University-wise

It can be noticed from Table 4.53 that the calculated χ^2 value of independence between response pattern of B.Ed. trainees and the university background in relation to relevance of Self-learning Materials is 0.29. It is less than the table value (5.99) at .05 level of

Table 4.53: χ^2 test of Independence of trainees' response about relevance of self-learning materials and student teachers' handbook and university background, statement-wise

Response of B.Ed. trainees about relevance of self-learning materials and student teachers' hand book						
Statements	*UNIV.*	*Highly Agree*	*Agree*	*Disagree*	*Total*	χ^2 *Values*
1. Self learning materials given to you by open University is related to teaching learning syllabus	IGNOU	231 (77.00)	55 (18.33)	14 (4.67)	300 (100.00)	0.29 N.S.
	UPRTOU	236 (78.67)	50 (16.67)	14 (4.67)	300 (100.00)	
	Total	467 (77.83)	105 (17.50)	28 (4.67)	600 (100.00)	
2. Student-teacher hand book is related with the activities being performed by you	IGNOU	222 (74.00)	66 (22.00)	12 (4.00)	300 (100.00)	8.39*
	UPRTOU	211 (70.33)	59 (19.67)	30 (10.00)	300 (100.00)	
	Total	433 (72.17)	125 (20.83)	42 (7.00)	600 (100.00)	

Note: Figures in parentheses indicate percentages. N.S.: Not significant.
* Indicates significant at .05 level.

significance with df: 2. The obtained χ^2 value is not found significant. Hence the response pattern of B.Ed. trainees and the university background are found independent from each other in reference to relevance of self-learning materials.

It can be observed that majority of trainees (78%) of IGNOU and UPRTOU considered that self-learning materials provided by open universities to them as relevant because it was related to their curriculum.

It can be noticed from Table 4.53 that the calculated χ^2 value of independence between response pattern of B.Ed. trainees and the university background in relation to relevance of student teachers handbook provided by open universities is 8.39. It is greater than the table value (5.99) at .05 level of significance with df: 2. The obtained χ^2 value is found significant. Hence, the response pattern of B.Ed. trainees and the university background are not found independent from each other in relation to relevance of student teachers handbook provided by open universities.

It can be observed that 74 per cent B.Ed. trainees of IGNOU considered that the student teachers handbook provided for support to them was according to the activities done by them. While 70 per cent B.Ed. trainees of UPRTOU considered that student teachers handbook as relevant because it was in accordance to the activities done by them.

4.54 Response of Counsellors about Relevance of Self-learning Materials and Student Teachers' Handbook: University-wise

It can be noticed from Table 4.54 that the calculated χ^2 value of independence between response pattern of counsellors and university background in relation to relevance of Self-Learning Materials is 1.68. It is less than the table value (5.99) at .05 level of significance with df: 2. The obtained χ^2 value is not found significant. Hence the response pattern of counsellors and the university background are found independent from each other in relation to relevance of self-learning materials.

Table 4.54: χ^2 test of Independence of counsellors response about relevance of self-learning materials and student teachers' handbook and university background, statement-wise

Response of counsellors abut relevance of self-learning materials and student teachers' handbook						
Statements	*UNIV.*	*Highly Agree*	*Agree*	*Disagree*	*Total*	χ^2 *Values*
1. Self-learning material given by open universities is related to teaching learning syllabus of B.Ed. trainees	IGNOU	21 (70.00)	8 (26.67)	1 (3.33)	30 (100.00)	1.68 N.S.
	UPRTOU	25 (83.33)	4 (13.33)	1 (3.33)	30 (100.00)	
	Total	46 (76.67)	12 (20.00)	2 (3.33)	60 (100.00)	
2. Student-teacher hand book provided to B.Ed. trainees is according to activities performed by them	IGNOU	26 (86.67)	4 (13.33)	0 (0.00)	30 (100.00)	6.03*
	UPRTOU	18 (60.00)	10 (33.33)	2 (6.67)	30 (100.00)	
	Total	44 (73.33)	14 (23.33)	2 (3.33)	60 (100.00)	

Note: Figures in parentheses indicate percentages. N.S.: Not significant.

* Indicates significant at .05 level.

It can be observed that almost 77 per cent counsellors of IGNOU and UPRTOU considered that self-learning materials provided by open universities to them as relevant because it was related to their teaching-learning curriculum.

It can be noticed from Table 4.54 that the calculated χ^2 value of independence between response pattern of counsellors and the university background in relation to relevance of student teachers' handbook is 6.03. It is greater than the table value (5.99) at 0.05 level of significance with df: 2. The obtained χ^2 value is found significant. Hence, the response pattern of counsellors and the university background are not found independent from each other in relation to relevance of student teachers' handbook.

It can be observed that majority of counsellors (87%) of IGNOU considered students teachers' handbook as relevant, while only 60 per cent counsellors of UPRTOU considered student teachers' handbook as relevant because it was in accordance to activities performed by trainees.

4.55 Response of B.Ed. Trainees about Effectiveness of Self-learning Materials and Student Teachers Handbook: University-wise

It can be noticed from Table 4.55 that the calculated χ^2 values of independence between response pattern of B.Ed. trainees and the university background in relation to effectiveness of Self-Learning Materials provided by open universities for the enhancement in selection of appropriate teaching methods, development of teaching learning skills and maintaining correlation between training and theoretical subjects are found to be 3.91, 4.36 and 1.32 respectively. The obtained χ^2 values are less than table value (5.99) at 0.05 level of significance with df: 2. Hence the observed χ^2 values are not found significant. Hence, the response pattern of B.Ed. trainees and the university background are found independent from each other in relation to enhancement of above mentioned skills.

It can be observed that 78 to 84 per cent B.Ed. trainees of IGNOU and UPRTOU considered that for the enhancement in following three skills—self-learning materials provided by open universities were effective in the development of following skills:

Table 4.55: χ^2 test of Independence of trainees' response about effectiveness of self-learning materials and student teachers' handbook and university background, skill-wise

Benefits of self-learning materials and student teachers' hand book						
Developments of skills	*UNIV.*	*More extent*	*Some extent*	*Least*	*Total*	χ^2 *Values*
1i. Selection of appropriate teaching methods	IGNOU	248 (82.67)	43 (14.33)	9 (3.00)	300 (100.00)	3.91 N.S.
	UPRTOU	255 (85.00)	30 (10.00)	15 (5.00)	300 (100.00)	
	Total	503 (83.83)	73 (12.17)	24 (4.00)	600 (100.00)	
ii. Development of teaching learning skills	IGNOU	225 (75.00)	54 (18.00)	21 (7.00)	300 (100.00)	4.36 N.S.
	UPRTOU	246 (82.00)	39 (13.00)	15 (5.00)	300 (100.00)	
	Total	471 (78.50)	93 (15.50)	36 (6.00)	600 (100.00)	
iii. Preparing lesson plan	IGNOU	234 (78.00)	57 (19.00)	9 (3.00)	300 (100.00)	10.29**
	UPRTOU	246 (82.00)	34 (11.33)	20 (6.67)	300 (100.00)	
	Total	480 (80.00)	91 (15.17)	29 (4.83)	600 (100.00)	
iv. Writing assignments correctly	IGNOU	210 (70.00)	79 (26.33)	11 (3.67)	300 (100.00)	17.88**
	UPRTOU	248 (82.67)	38 (12.67)	14 (4.67)	300 (100.00)	
	Total	458 (76.33)	117 (19.50)	25 (4.17)	600 (100.00)	
2-i. Maintaining correlation between training and theoretical subjects	IGNOU	229 (76.33)	51 (17.00)	20 (6.67)	300 (100.00)	1.32 N.S.
	UPRTOU	237 (79.00)	41 (13.67)	22 (7.33)	300 (100.00)	
	Total	466 (77.67)	92 (15.33)	42 (7.00)	600 (100.00)	
ii. Understanding subject matter related to teaching competency	IGNOU	224 (74.67)	62 (20.67)	14 (4.67)	300 (100.00)	8.14*
	UPRTOU	243 (81.00)	37 (12.33)	20 (6.67)	300 (100.00)	
	Total	467 (77.83)	99 (16.50)	34 (5.67)	600 (100.00)	

Note: Figures in parentheses indicate percentages. N.S.: Not significant
* Indicates significant at .05 level. ** Indicates significant at .01 level.

(i) Selection of appropriate teaching methods (83.83%).
(ii) Development of teaching learning skills (78.50%).
(iii) Maintaining the correlation between training and theoretical subject (77.67%).

It can be noticed from Table 4.55 that the calculated χ^2 values of independence between response pattern of B.Ed. trainees and the university background in relation to effectiveness of Self-Learning Materials provided by open universities for the enhancement in following three skills like preparation of lesson plans, writing assignment and understanding subject matter related to teaching competency are 10.29, 17.88 and 8.14 respectively. The obtained χ^2 values are greater than the table value (5.99) at .05 level of significance with df: 2. The observed values are found significant. Hence the response pattern of B.Ed. trainees and the university background are not found independent from each other in relation to effectiveness of self-learning materials provided by open universities for the enhancement in above maintained skills.

It can be observed that majority of B.Ed. trainees (81 to 83%) of UPRTOU considered that self-learning materials provided by open universities as effective for the enhancement of following three skills:

(i) Writing assignment appropriately (82.67%).
(ii) Preparing lessons plans (82.00%).
(iii) Understanding the subject matter related to teaching competency (81.00%).

While majority of B.Ed. trainees (70 to 90%) of IGNOU considered that Self-Learning Materials provided by open universities as effective for the enhancement of following three skills:

(i) Preparing lesson plans (78.00%).
(ii) Understanding subject matter related to teaching competency (74.67%).
(iii) Writing assignment appropriately (70.00%).

4.56 Response of Counsellors about Effectiveness of Self-Learning Materials and Student Teachers' Handbook: University-wise

It can be noticed from Table 4.56 that the calculated χ^2 values of independence between response pattern of counsellors and the

Table 4.56: χ^2 test of Independence of counsellors response about effectiveness of self-learning materials and student teachers' handbook and university background, skill-wise

Benefits of self-learning materials and student teachers' handbook						
Developments of skills	*UNIV.*	*More extent*	*Some extent*	*Least*	*Total*	χ^2 *Values*
1.i. Selection of appropriate teaching methods	IGNOU	26 (86.67)	4 (13.33)	0 (0.00)	30 (100.00)	1.14 N.S.
	UPRTOU	26 (86.67)	3 (10.00)	1 (3.33)	30 (100.00)	
	Total	52 (86.67)	7 (11.67)	1 (1.67)	60 (100.00)	
ii. Development of teaching learning skills	IGNOU	24 (80.00)	6 (20.00)	0 (0.00)	30 (100.00)	4.88 N.S.
	UPRTOU	28 (93.33)	1 (3.33)	1 (3.33)	30 (100.00)	
	Total	52 (86.67)	7 (11.67)	1 (1.67)	60 (100.00)	
iii. Preparing lesson plan	IGNOU	22 (73.33)	8 (26.67)	0 (0.00)	30 (100.00)	5.11 N.S.
	UPRTOU	27 (90.00)	2 (6.67)	1 (3.33)	30 (100.00)	
	Total	49 (81.67)	10 (16.67)	1 (1.67)	60 (100.00)	
iv. Writing assignments correctly	IGNOU	23 (76.67)	6 (20.00)	1 (3.33)	30 (100.00)	1.02 N.S.
	UPRTOU	24 (80.00)	6 (20.00)	0 (0.00)	30 (100.00)	
	Total	47 (78.33)	12 (20.00)	1 (1.67)	60 (100.00)	
2-i. Maintaining correlation between training and theoretical subjects	IGNOU	28 (93.33)	1 (3.33)	1 (3.33)	30 (100.00)	4.88 N.S.
	UPRTOU	24 (80.00)	6 (20.00)	0 (0.00)	30 (100.00)	
	Total	52 (86.67)	7 (11.67)	1 (1.67)	60 (100.00)	
ii. Understanding subject matter related to teaching competency	IGNOU	28 (93.33)	1 (3.33)	1 (3.33)	30 (100.00)	2.87 N.S.
	UPRTOU	26 (86.67)	4 (13.33)	0 (0.00)	30 (100.00)	
	Total	54 (90.00)	5 (8.33)	1 (1.67)	60 (100.00)	

Note: Figures in parentheses indicate percentages. N.S.: Not significant.

university background in relation to effectiveness of Self-learning Materials and student teachers handbook provided by open universities for assistance in selection of appropriate teaching methods, development of teaching learning skills, preparing lesson plans, writing assignment appropriately, maintaining correlation between training and theoretical subjects and understanding subject matter are found as 4.88, 2.87, 1.14, 4.88, 5.11 and 1.02 respectively. The obtained χ^2 values are less than the table value (5.99) at .05 level of significance with df: 2. The observed values are not found significant. Hence, the response pattern of counsellors and the university background are found independent from each other in relation to effective self-learning materials and students teachers hand book provided by open universities for assistance on above mentioned skills.

It can be observed that majority of counsellors (78 to 90%) of IGNOU and UPRTOU considered, self-learning materials and student teachers' hand book as effective for the enhancement of the following skills:

(i) Understanding subject matter related to teaching competency (90.00%).
(ii) Selection of appropriate teaching methods (86.67%).
(iii) Preparing lesson plan (81.670%).
(iv) Writing assignment appropriately (78.33%).

Conclusion

In this component study had conducted about usability, relevance and effectiveness of SLM and student teachers' handbook. It is clear from the analysis that majority trainees and counsellors of both the open universities stated that self-learning materials helped B.Ed. trainees in selection of appropriate methods, in development of different teaching learning skills, in preparing lesson plans and in writing assignments appropriately.

Maximum trainees and counsellors of both the open universities informed that student teachers' handbook provided various knowledge regarding theoretical papers, activities of practical programmes and various activities organised during workshops. They also stated that it worked as a guide. They stated that lessons of self-learning material and training provided during workshops were same.

As whole the trainees and the counsellors expressed positive response about the relevance and effectiveness of self-learning materials as well as students teachers' handbook.

5

Findings and Implications

5.0 Introduction

This chapter entails major findings of the study, discussion and the implications of the study. The suggestions and recommendations for future research have also been discussed at the end.

Distance education has revolutionized the concept of higher education throughout the world and it considered as an attractive mode to democratize higher education. The distance education system has emerged to be a popular non-formal channel to provide answer to the questions of equity, access, flexibility and cost effectiveness. Moreover, globalization, liberalization and market-oriented economy have added new dimensions and as a result the knowledge and skills of learners need to be continuously updated. This is only possible through distance learning because resources by conventional means are inadequate to meet the requirement of life long learning process.

Advent of lifelong learning, geographical mobility and concern for human resource development to empower teachers to function within the context of rapid and continuous change in the characteristics of information society resonates in development of higher education system.

There are still wide shortages of teachers and still large number under-qualified teachers. All our teachers need updated training at various levels of varying steps and at varying stages of their career. Many of our teachers are untrained or underqualified.

In response to the growing emphasis on professional development of untrained teachers continuing professional education, need to enhance practice and skills of teachers Indira Gandhi National Open University developed and launched a two-year B.Ed. degree programme in 2001, through distance mode programme study centres all over the country and UPRTOU launched same in 2003 all over U.P. state.

The present study is not only relevant for teachers but of significance to social needs development, because teachers are the largest groups in human development.

Till date no comprehensive study has been conducted related to distance B.Ed. programme to throw light upon various issues related to distance education system in teacher training such as what are the process adopted for development of teacher? What is the relevance of such process and what is the level of effectiveness of the process?

5.1 Major Findings of the Study

The findings of the study have been categorized on three heads, viz. Exploration of processes, Relevance of processes and effectiveness of processes under nine components of processes of B.Ed. programmes such as:

1. Preparation of teaching-oriented processes in distance mode B.Ed. programme.
   1.1 Micro teaching practices of distance mode B.Ed. programme.
   1.2 Practice teaching processes of distance mode B.Ed. programme.
   1.3 Unit planning processes of distance mode B.Ed. programme.
2. Preparation of teaching aids by distance B.Ed. trainees and their use.
3. Classroom teaching motivation-oriented practices in distance B.Ed. programme.
4. Classroom communication practices in distance B.Ed. programme.
5. Students' evaluation practices by distance B.Ed. trainees.
6. School management and planning related processes in distance B.Ed. programme.
7. Community participation activities in distance B.Ed. programme.
8. Co-curricular activities-oriented practices in distance B.Ed. programme.
9. Use of self-learning materials by distance B.Ed. trainees.

5.1.1 Preparation of Teaching-oriented Processes in Distance Mode B.Ed. Programme

Major findings regarding preparation of teaching are given below in three subsections like micro teaching, practice teaching and unit plan.

5.1.1.1 Micro Teaching Practices of Distance mode B.Ed. Programme

Micro teaching is an important activity of B.Ed. programme. It is compulsory to all trainees that every teaching skill must be practiced after preparing micro lesson plans during the workshops. It is clear from the analysis that all the trainees did not give importance to the practice of all the teaching skills. All the trainees did not prepare micro lesson plans. They did not practice it according to the norms of course. It is mandatory that demonstration of all the prescribed micro teaching skills by the counsellors during workshops. However, more than average number of trainees (62%) of both the open universities stated that every teaching skill was not demonstrated by the cousellors during workshops. Average trainees (51%) of both the open universities stated that their counsellors demonstrated the micro lessons of only 2 to 5 teaching skills out of 10 skills. Majority of trainees (89%) stated that their counsellors demonstration the lessons without teaching aids. They also stated that teaching aids were not used by themselves wherever necessary in practice of teaching skills. Maximum trainees (64%) of both the open universities stated that feedback was given by their peer trainees as well as counsellors during micro teaching practices. Majority of trainees (72%) considered feedback micro teaching practice relevant for development of skills. Feedback during micro teaching practices had also been considered relevant by majority of cousellors (97%) for development of teaching skills among B.Ed. trainees. Majority of B.Ed. trainees (70 to 84%) of both the universities consider micro teaching practice as effective. Majority of counsellors (72 to 95%) of UPRTOU and IGNOU considered feedback provided by them during micro teaching as effective.

Various problems were faced by B.Ed. trainees and counsellors during micro teaching practices, like—

- Lack of appropriate feedback given by the counsellors.
- Shortage of time.
- Micro lesson plan not in accordance with the mental capacity of fellow trainees.
- Problem of distinction between specific and general adjectives.
- Lack of confidence among trainees.
- Lack of arrangements to sit in small groups for practice of micro teaching lessons.

- Problem of repetition of useless words.
- In framing making introductory questions.
- In preparing and delivery of questioning skill lesson.
- Problem of not getting the topic through introductory questions.
- Problem of not getting response due to heterogeneous background of fellow trainees.
- In delivery of stimulus variation lesson.
- Problem in preparing and using teaching aids during micro teaching practices.
- Trainees not participating with interest.
- Trainees not preparing micro teaching lesson plans properly.
- Limited time for feedbacks and re-teach the micro lessons.
- Lack of appropriate devices for giving feedbacks (like language laboratory, audio tape, VCR etc.).
- Lack of availability teaching aids in study centres.
- Lesson plans prepared by trainees were not up to the mark.
- Micro lesson plans are not prepared by trainees as per skill components.
- Lack of arrangement for small group activities.

Maximum problems of trainees were resolved during workshops by the counsellors. Some of the problems of trainees were resolved with the help of peer trainees. The trainees and counsellors stated that time stipulated by open universities were very much limited for micro teaching practices. The space available in the study centres were not enough for small group simulation practices of micro teaching.

As a whole the trainees and the counsellors expressed positive response about the relevance and effectiveness of microteaching practices.

5.1.1.2 Practice Teaching Processes of Distance mode B.Ed. Programme

Practice teaching is a component of B.Ed. programme, which makes trainees competent to in teaching competency. It is clear from the analysis that majority of B.Ed. trainees (73 to 77%) of IGNOU and lesser number of B.Ed. trainees (59 to 63%) of UPRTOU considered that 16 to 20 lesson plans in each of the teaching subjects prepared by them. According to 83 per cent counsellors of both the universities the number of practice teaching plans prepared by B.Ed. trainees in both the teaching subjects was close to the norms of B.Ed. programmes. According to approximately 82 per cent B.Ed. trainees of both the universities preparation of practice teaching lesson plans as relevant. A very less number of trainees (11 to 22%) had reported that they had done practice teaching *via* getting their lesson plans checked according to the norms. Rest of trainees (89%) of IGNOU and near about 79 per cent of UPRTOU either did not getting their lesson plans checked or they had done practice teaching without getting checked lesson plans. In the provision of lesson plan checked by evaluator, according to B.Ed. trainees of UPRTOU they were close to the norms set for B.Ed. programmes than their IGNOU counterparts. Because majority of B.Ed. trainees (93%) of IGNOU and 82 per cent of UPRTOU get their lesson plans checked only by the mentors, which was against the norms set for B.Ed. programmes where lesson plans must be checked by mentors as well as counsellors. While it is mandatory that checking of lesson plans of trainees and observation of classes delivered by trainees should be by mentors as well as counsellors. Average number of counsellors stated on the basis of norms that checking of lesson plans of trainees and observation of classes delivered by trainees had done by subject teachers, also.

According to approximately 55 per cent counsellors of IGNOU as well as UPRTOU the lesson plans of B.Ed. trainees were assessed by subject teacher prior to teaching and according to approximately 22 per cent counsellors of both the universities lesson plans of B.Ed. trainees were assessed by mentors alone before teaching. According to 62 per cent B.Ed. trainees of IGNOU they practiced approximately 16 to 20 lesson plans which was close to the norms set for B.Ed. programmes, whereas only 52 per cent B.Ed. trainees of UPRTOU practiced the same in one teaching subject. According 58 per cent B.Ed. trainees of both the universities they practiced same in the second teaching subject. It can be concluded that the B.Ed. trainees of IGNOU (62.33%) were more close to the norms as compared to UPRTOU (52.33%) B.Ed. trainees regarding delivery of the first teaching subject lessons. It is also clear from the analysis that majority of trainees and counsellors consider preparing lesson plans for practice teaching, delivery of practice teaching, feedback of counsellors and mentors as relevant and effective. Mentors told that various problems faced by B.Ed. trainees during practice teaching, i.e. in introduction skills, in question skills, in stimulus variation skills, management of time and in making lesson plans. The problems faced by trainees were resolved by mentors. As a whole the trainees and the counsellors expressed positive response about the relevance and effectiveness of practice teaching.

5.1.1.3 Unit Planning Processes of Distance mode B.Ed. Programme

Unit plan is compulsory in preparing lesson plans. Average number of trainees (46 to 50%) and approximately 60 per cent counsellors of both the open universities stated that help provided during workshops for preparing unit plan. Average number of B.Ed. trainees 69 per cent of IGNOU and UPRTOU and average number (58%) of counsellors of both the Open Universities considered that guidance provided for the preparation of unit plan as relevant. More than average number B.Ed. trainees 72 per cent of IGNOU and UPRTOU and maximum number of (75%) counsellors of IGNOU as well as UPRTOU considered that the guidance provided for the preparation of unit plan as effective. The selected counsellors of both the open universities stated that various activities were conducted during workshops for the preparation of unit plan, like—

- Theoretical knowledge regarding unit was provided.
- Demonstration of format of unit plan made by the counsellors through preparing unit-plan by themselves.
- Steps of unit plan were described.
- Components of unit plan were elaborated.
- Trainees were made to sit in small groups and prepared unit plans.
- Homework for unit plan was assigned.
- Prepared unit plan was checked and feedback was provided to the trainees.
- Problems related to the preparation of unit plans during workshops were solved.
- Evaluation had done in prepared Unit plan of trainees.

As a whole the trainees and the counsellors expressed positive response about the process adopted for making competent B.Ed. trainees in preparation of unit plan.

5.1.2 Preparation of Teaching Aids by Distance B.Ed. Trainees and their Use

In this component study was conducted about process adopted for development of skills of preparation of teaching aids and their use among B.Ed. trainees. It is clear from the analysis that 20 to 73 per cent trainees of IGNOU and 7 to 68 per cent trainees ɔf UPRTOU used chart and natural objects as teaching aids during teaching in the classroom. B.Ed. trainees told that help provided by mentors (26%), peer trainees (28%) and counsellors (37%) for preparing teaching aids. Majority of counsellors (87%) UPRTOU and 53 per cent of IGNOU of stated that teaching aids prepared by trainees at their own working school as well during workshops. 65 per cent counsellors also stated that more trainees prepared teaching aids during workshops as per the norms. Maximum trainees informed that various problems faced by themselves during use of teaching aids, like—

- Lesson not completed within time due to the usage of teaching aids.
- Teaching aid was not visible to back benchers in the class.
- Lack of appropriate facilities to demonstrate teaching aids in the classrooms.
- Lack of appropriate space in class for exhibiting teaching aids.
- Non-availability of electricity on time.
- Attention of students was directed upon teaching aids only.
- Students were diverted from the content and more interested in telling the merits and demerits of teaching aids.
- Lack of fund to buy readymade teaching aids.
- Problem of maintaining the available teaching aids.
- Non-availability of materials to prepare teaching aids.
- Indiscipline among students in classroom setting.
- Problem of carrying teaching aids to the practice teaching schools.
- Lack of cooperation from mentors.
- Could not prepare charts properly.
- Problem pertaining to presentation of teaching aids.
- Could not prepare appropriate models.
- Non-availability of computers for delivery of lessons.
- Material not in accordance with the lesson.
- Teaching aids not being interesting.

More trainees resolved their problems with the help of their colleagues, mentors and counsellers. The 77 per cent trainees and the counsellor 55 to 62 per cent considered process adopted for development of competency related to preparation of teaching aids and their use among B.Ed. trainees as relevant. Around 71 per cent trainees and 87 to 89 per cent counsellors of both the open universities consider it as effective.

5.1.3 Classroom Teaching Motivation-oriented Practices in Distance B.Ed. Programme

In this component study was conducted regarding development of competency related classroom teaching motivation among B.Ed. trainees. It is clear from the analysis that mentors, peer trainees and counsellors helped B.Ed. trainees in classroom teaching motivation. Around 70 per cent B.Ed. trainees of UPRTOU and only 42 per cent B.Ed. trainees of IGNOU considered that counsellors provided guidance to them for motivating their students. It was also observed that only 46 per cent B.Ed. trainees of IGNOU and only 20 per cent B.Ed. trainees of UPRTOU that mentors provided guidance to them for the same. Majority of trainees and counsellors make clear that for making competent B.Ed. trainees in classroom motivation various activities make learn them during workshop i.e. use of appropriate teaching aids, use of proper reinforcement during classroom teaching, to be friendly with students, to give correct and appropriate answer of their students questions, organizing co-curricular activities, to give reward to their students and enhancing interest of student in the subjects etc. As whole majority of trainees as well as counsellors expressed positive response regarding the relevance and effectiveness of process adopted for developing competency related classroom motivation among trainees.

5.1.4 Classroom Communication Practices in Distance B.Ed. Programme

In this component study was conducted about process adopted for development of skill of classroom communication among B.Ed. trainees. It is clear from the analysis that according trainees and counsellors of both the open universities counsellors guided about following adopted by B.Ed. trainees for making effective classroom communication, i.e. to make classroom presentation effective, to develop feeling of discipline among their students, to make pronunciation correctly during teaching and communicating with others, to give reinforcement for motivating to students, to use simple language in the classroom, to make interaction with every students in classroom and to motivate students for asking questions in the classroom etc. In addition they also informed that make them understand appropriate classroom management, use of effective teaching methods during classroom teaching. Majority of trainees and counsellors of both the universities expressed positive response about the effectiveness and relevant of guidance about classroom communication.

5.1.5 Students' Evaluation Practices by Distance B.Ed. Trainees

In this component study was conducted about process adopted for development of competency of students' evaluation among B.Ed. trainees. It is clear from the analysis that majority of trainees (72%) of UPRTOU and 62 per cent trainees of IGNOU stated that mentors helped them in preparing blueprint and in evaluation of answer copy. Majority of B.Ed. trainees (71%) of UPRTOU and 62 per cent of IGNOU stated that group discussion organized by the counsellors, help provided in assignments and administered psychological test by counsellors during workshops for development of competency of students evaluation among them. The selected counsellors of both the open universities mentioned that theoretical knowledge was provided during workshops regarding evaluation of students, blueprint was prepared for construction of question papers by trainees, question paper prepared by trainees in concerning subjects and achievement test was prepared. Average trainees informed that knowledge provided by counsellors for resolving problems of trainees during evaluation of their students. Mentors informed that B.Ed. trainees faced problems of time limitation in evaluation their students. Mentors helped B.Ed. trainees in resolving their problems. Trainees also considered that their peer trainees discuss on the problems faced by trainees and helping them in resolving their problems. Trainees stated that by taking help from counsellors (16%), by reading books (18%), by taking help from library (8%) and by reading all assignment of ex-trainees (11%) they completed their assignments. Counsellors of IGNOU as well as UPRTOU stated that they provided knowledge of administration of psychological test by demonstrating psychological tests (25%), report writing after administration of psychological test on their peer trainees (8%). Thc counsellors (23%) also informed that knowledge provided them regarding construction of achievement test. The trainees prepared blueprint and constructed the test items during workshops. 72 to 80 per cent trainees and the counsellors (42 to 68%) expressed positive response about the relevance and 73 to 84 per cent trainees and 62 to 97 per cent counsellors of both the Open Universities about effectiveness of process adopted for development of skill of students' evaluation among B.Ed. trainees.

5.1.6 School Management and Planning Related Processes in Distance B.Ed. Programme

In this component B.Ed. trainees as well as mentors stated that mentors helped B.Ed. trainees in preparing school records, register, school budget and time table. They corrected the limitation of register, school budget and time table prepared by B.Ed. trainees of both the open universities stated that peer trainees helped them in preparing time table and by discussing their experiences. Majority of trainees (70%) told that appropriate knowledge was provided by mentors for preparing school records and school budget. They corrected records and budget prepared by trainees. Demonstration had been done by counsellors *via* preparing school records and school budget during workshops. Feedback also provided in preparing records by trainees. Peer trainees also discussed their experiences and helped by correcting of prepared records by trainees.

It was observed that 50 per cent B.Ed. trainees of IGNOU and UPRTOU mentioned that the mentors provided information regarding income expenditure for the preparation of the school budget, also they rectified the errors in preparation of school budget. It was observed that 55 per cent B.Ed. trainees of IGNOU and UPRTOU mentioned that counsellors provided assistance in the preparation of school budget by presenting examples, by getting it prepared during workshops and also by providing feedback. It was observed that 47 per cent B.Ed. trainees of IGNOU and 39 per cent B.Ed. trainees of UPRTOU stated that the peers provided help to each other on the basis of only their experiences for preparation of school budget. While 34 per cent of IGNOU and 32 per cent of UPRTOU stated that the peers provided help to each other by only amending school budget. Only 18 per cent B.Ed. trainees of UPRTOU and 56 per cent B.Ed. trainees of IGNOU mentioned that the peer trainees shared their experiences for assisting in action research. While, 12 per cent of IGNOU and 38 per cent trainees of UPRTOU gave no response regarding help of peer trainees. 65 per cent counsellors of IGNOU and UPRTOU mentioned that they got the school records prepared by B.Ed. trainees. Only 18 per cent counsellors of IGNOU and UPRTOU mentioned that they did not get the school records prepared by B.Ed. trainees, whereas approximately 17 per cent counsellors considered that preparation of school records by B.Ed. trainees was not at all important. It was observed that 58 per cent counsellors of IGNOU and UPRTOU mentioned that they gave examples and feedback in preparing school budget by B.Ed. trainees during workshops to making competent B.Ed. trainees in the preparation of school budget. 35 per cent counsellors of IGNOU and UPRTOU mentioned that they gave only examples for making competent B.Ed. trainees in preparation of school budget.

Majority of trainees (88%) also informed that action research and various problems of school conducted by themselves. Counsellors of IGNOU stated that action research is related to school based activity conducted by B.Ed. trainees at their own schools. The basic steps of action research were explained during workshop by themselves. Feedback was provided by counsellors (40%) on submitted report of trainees. Counsellors of both the open universities stated that they helped B.Ed. trainees in conducting action research; trainees as well as counsellors of both the universities mentioned that the action research as relevant. Trainees considered that by conducting action research they make themselves capable for resolving problems related to schools.

As a whole the trainees and the counsellors expressed positive response about relevance and effectiveness of process adopted for making competent to B.Ed. trainees in school management and planning.

5.1.7 Community Participation Activities in Distance B.Ed. Programme

In this component study was conducted about process adopted for development of competency related community participation among B.Ed. trainees. Majority of trainees (61%) of both the open universities stated that activities of community participation were organised during workshops. Only 13 per cent trainees told that activities related to health education and community survey organised during workshops. Majority of trainees (70%) of UPRTOU and 59 per cent trainees of IGNOU also stated that for removing problems during organisation of activities related to community participation mentors and peer trainees helped them.

Most of counsellors (77%) of UPRTOU mentioned that activities related to health education, community work and survey had conducted during workshops, whereas, only 33 per cent counsellors of IGNOU mentioned the same. 23 per cent counsellors of IGNOU and 20 per cent counsellors of UPRTOU mentioned that only health education related activities had conducted during workshops. Merely 33 per cent counsellors of IGNOU and 70 per cent counsellors of UPRTOU mentioned that they elaborated theoretical knowledge regarding activities related to community participation and organised and implemented same during workshops.

Mentors stated that B.Ed. trainees organised rallies for public awareness, making plantation, organised sports and cultural programmes and educational tour. Mentors also stated that B.Ed. trainees organised health education, social and community works with the help of students and teachers of their schools. Mentors stated that they helped trainees in organization of activities related community participation and maintaining discipline among students. The selected counsellors of both the open universities stated only survey and educational tour were organised during workshops. Counsellors told that trainees submitted the report of educational tour organised by themselves at their own schools and they provided feedback and grades also.

Majority of trainees (77 to 83%) of UPRTOU and 74 to 78 per cent of IGNOU, 60 per cent counsellors of IGNOU and 93 per cent cousellors of UPRTOU considered that process of making trainees competent in community participation as relevant and effective.

5.1.8 Co-curricular Activities Oriented Practices in Distance B.Ed. Programme

In this component study was conducted about process adopted for making B.Ed. trainees competent in co-curricular activities. It is clear from the analysis that according average number of B.Ed. trainees (60%) of both the open universities co-curricular activities conducted sometimes during workshops. More than average trainees (60%) and counsellors (99%) stated that educational tour, sports, seminar, group discussion and cultural programmes were organised during workshops. According to observation of researcher seminar, group discussion and cultural programmes were organised during workshops. Mentors stated that problems of students discipline faced by B.Ed. trainees during organisation of co-curricular activities. Mentors stated that they helped trainees in establishing student discipline and encouraging students for their active participation and successful completion of educational tour, sports and other cultural programmes. Cent-per-cent counsellors of IGNOU and 87 per cent counsellors of UPRTOU stated that group discussion, report presentation and cultural programmes were organised during the workshops for development of competencies among B.Ed. trainees in organisation of co-curricular activities.

B.Ed. trainees as well as counsellors stated that seminar was conducted during workshops. Majority of (73 to 75%) trainees and 70 to 77 per cent counsellors consider that organisation of seminar during workshops as relevant. As a whole trainees as well as counsellors expressed positive response about relevance and effectiveness of process adopted for development of competency related co-curricular activities.

5.1.9 Use of Self-learning Materials by Distance B.Ed. Trainees

In this component study was conducted about usability, relevance and effectiveness of SLM and student teachers' handbook. It is clear from the analysis that majority trainees (72 to 79%) and 60 to 63 per cent counsellors of both the open universities stated that self-learning materials helped B.Ed. trainees in selection of appropriate methods, in development of different teaching learning skills, in preparing lesson plans and in writing assignments appropriately. Almost 55 per cent counsellors of IGNOU and UPTROU considered that student teachers handbook provided the knowledge to B.Ed. trainees about theoretical papers, experimental programmes and about all activities of workshops and also it worked as a guide. Almost 60 per cent counsellors of IGNOU told that there was correlation between lessons of self-learning materials and guidance given to B.Ed. trainees at maximum limit. While, only 27 per cent counsellors of UPRTOU told that there was correlation between lessons of self-learning materials and guidance given to B.Ed. trainees up to maximum limit.

Selected trainees and counsellors of both the open universities informed that student teachers' handbook provided various knowledge regarding theoretical papers, activities of practical programmes and various activities organised during workshops. They also stated that it worked as a guide. They stated that lessons of self-learning material and training provided during workshops were same.

As whole the trainees and the counsellors expressed positive response about the relevance and effectiveness of self-learning materials as well as students teachers' handbook.

5.2 Discussion on Findings of the Study

The present study indicates that according 96 per cent trainees of IGNOU and 98 per cent trainees of UPRTOU, demonstration on micro teaching skills had done by counsellors. Majority of B.Ed. trainees (86%) of UPRTOU as well as trainees (73%) of IGNOU and majority of counsellors (97%) of both the open universities gave positive response about relevance of demonstration. This result is supported by previous studies where seventy two per cent participants of B.Ed. trainees found presentation and demonstration of lessons useful (Phalchandra & Veena, 2000).

It can be concluded that while many trainees gave positive response about micro teaching practices they had stated about different problems as per observation of the researcher and his interviews with mentors and the counsellors on the above matter.

The findings of present study revealed that majority of trainees (72%) gave positive response regarding relevance of feedback during micro teaching. It was also clear from the study according to 64 per cent trainees of both the open universities stated that feedback provided by counsellors and peer trainees. 74 to 83 per cent trainees and 70 to 83 per cent counsellors of both the open universities gave positive response regarding effectiveness of feedback during microteaching practices. However other study indicates that 42 per cent trainees stated that feedback given by counsellors during micro teaching lessons were inadequate for mastery of skills (Sahoo *et al.*, 2010). Sahoo (2010) had found that in case of 44 to 56 per cent trainees it was problematic to comprehend the demonstration of concerning skill components in micro teaching. The findings of present study regarding feedback during micro teaching is related to counsellors and peer trainees but in above reference it was related to the role of counsellors.

The present study indicated that B.Ed. trainees expressed lack of time regarding different activities like, micro teaching practices and other practical activities. This result is supported by Acharya (1995) that duration of contact programme was very short. The findings of study of Sahoo (1999) revealed that most of the students expressed dissatisfaction about lack of timely communication from the KOU regarding different activities (i.e. theory and practical examinations). With regard to duration of the programmes he found in his study that it was quite short according to trainees. They stated that short duration of PCP lectures were concentrated on few topics. With regard to duration of the programmes the students found it quite short. Because of short duration of PCP lectures were concentrated on a few topics. Practical activities were neglected. Students did not get opportunity to interact with tutors.

According to the norms of distance B.Ed. programme the practice teaching lessons must be observed (i.e. 5 lessons) by counsellors and by mentors (i.e. 15 lessons). The findings of the present study revealed only 40 to 41 per cent trainees of IGNOU and 20 to 21 per cent trainees of UPRTOU get 16 to 20 lesson plans checked which is close to the norms set for B.Ed. programme even though majority of the trainees (59 to

77%) prepare 16 to 20 lesson plans. Out of the total B.Ed. trainees who prepared lesson plans 93 per cent trainees of IGNOU and only 58 per cent trainees of UPRTOU get their lesson plans checked by mentors only. It implies that they were not serious about getting plans checked by the counsellors or subject teachers. According to norms at least 5 lesson plans in each of the teaching subjects must be checked by the counsellors. Out of total B.Ed. trainees 62 per cent trainees of IGNOU and 52 per cent trainees of UPRTOU delivered 16 to 20 lessons as per the norms. The present study highlighted that mentors and counsellors evaluated and observed practices teaching lessons. Only 32 per cent counsellors stated that mentors observed lessons during practice teaching.

It can be concluded that observation of practice teaching was done partially only by the mentors of both the open universities. Such practice was more prominent in IGNOU than that of UPRTOU.

This result is supported by previous studies where the trainees felt that sufficient guidance had not been provided to them regarding teaching practice. Majority of the teaching practice classes lacked adequate seating arrangements (Prasad and John, 1992). 37 to 55 per cent trainees stated that it was problematic to find out the mentor teacher on the part of a B.Ed. trainee who can guide them well in lesson plans preparation and its delivery (Sahoo, 2010). He found in his study that the teaching of trainees was practised to be incomplete because of lack of provision for teacher educators for observation of practice teaching lessons (46 to 50%). Yadav (2010) found that the problems related to practice teaching of B.Ed. students of both the universities are same on the basis of number of students and the basis of sex background. 68.33 per cent B.Ed. students of IGNOU and 53.33 per cent students of UPRTOU considered that they did not get appropriate knowledge regarding model lesson plans.

It can be concluded that while many trainees gave positive response about practice teaching they had stated about different problems as per interview of the researcher with mentors and the counsellors on the above matter.

The present study indicates that problems faced by trainees as well as counsellors of both the open universities during micro teaching practices. The problems were faced by trainees in preparing lesson plans according to skills. The selected counsellors stated that lesson plans prepared by trainees were not up to the mark. This result is supported by previous study where according 46 to 50 per cent trainees preparation of micro teaching lesson plans as well as general teaching lesson plans were difficult (Sahoo, 2010).

The present study indicates that help provided by counsellors, mentors and peer trainees for development of evaluation related competency among trainees. Seventy two per cent trainees of UPRTOU and 62 per cent trainees of IGNOU stated that mentors helped them by preparing progress report for development of evaluation related competency. 71 per cent trainees of UPRTOU and 59 per cent trainees of IGNOU stated that the counsellors helped them by group discussion for development of above said skill. This result is supported by Mishra (2002), he stated that evaluation should be carried out by taking the views of teacher trainees, experts of teacher education as well as distance education, mentors and counsellors.

In the present study 48 per cent trainees of IGNOU and UPRTOU stated that they took help from their counsellors, by reading books, by help of library and from reading of assignments of ex-trainees. Only 18 per cent trainees of them presented their assignments only through reading the books. The present study indicates that 67 per cent counsellors of IGNOU helped trainees by providing theoretical knowledge and by feedback in assignment work. 17 per cent counsellors of UPRTOU helped B.Ed. trainees only by providing theoretical knowledge and they did not provide feedback in assignments. The researcher found that 76 per cent trainees of UPRTOU as well as 72 per cent trainees of IGNOU rated assignments as relevance. While 58 to 68 per cent counsellors of both the open universities rated it as relevant. 72 to 88 per cent trainees of both the open universities rated assignments as effective.

This result is supported by previous studies where majority of students (59.67%) found assignments useful to some extent. In the case of teacher educators views that existing system of assignment was very formal. Most of the students took submission of assignment as mere formality. Common pattern of questions were followed in all the assignments. There was no proper provision for giving guidance by counsellors to students on how to prepare assignments. Feedback mechanism of assignments evaluation was almost non-existent. No comment was given on assignments by tutors. The students did not get feedback on assignments (Sahoo, 1999). Sharma (2000) found that student-teachers were dissatisfied with the absence of discussion on assignment questions and with the absence of comments. 69 per cent of the students did not receive feedback on their assignments. 54 per cent B.Ed. students found difficulties in assignments, 79 per cent students found lack of discussion on assignments by resource person and 72 per cent consult the books for writing assignments. Srinivasan (2004) indicated that the incidence of global comments has increased from 62.5

per cent of assignment responses handled by the subject to 100 per cent of assignment responses after training. The use of connected piece of writing for giving global comments is observed in 86.88 per cent of assignments responses handled by the subject after training *vis-à-vis* 2.5 per cent in the pre-training situation. Sahoo (2010) indicated that 45 to 50 per cent trainees faced difficulties to understand assignments and counsellors did not solve the trainees' problems concerning assignments. Harichandan (2010) reported that assignments are compulsory for all students. Staff of DEI or part time tutors evaluates the assignments. The comments given are usually individualistic in nature. The time given for submission ranges 15 days to 6 months.

The present study indicates that various objects used by trainees of IGNOU as teaching aids like: chart (72.67%), natural objects (69%), artificial models (35.33%) and ICT-based materials (20.33%). In the case of UPRTOU 7 to 68 per cent trainees utilized such teaching aids to the maximum extent like: chart (67.67%), natural objects (49%), artificial model (32%) and IC-based materials (6.67%).

These findings supported by previous study where Prasad and John (1992) found that trainees from both conventional and distance institutions could not use sufficient chart and three dimentional aids. Murugan (1996) argued poor utilization of educational technology by student teachers who were resident in remote and distant areas, i.e. audio cassettes (19%), video cassettes (49.50%). In the extremely deprived communities which have access only to postal service, all types of electrical and electronic media are beyond the reach of student teachers in their home or schools like: radio (9.4%), audio cassettes (1.09%), telephone (1.9%) and postal service (61%).

It can be concluded that use of different general and ICT based materials are effective means for teaching and learning. Trainees can use above said means for self-learning and during teaching in the class. There is need to support increased interest of B.Ed. trainees for using ICT based materials.

It is clear from the observation done by researcher that at most of the study centres there was disproportion between the availability of counsellors and the room arrangement was not up to the mark. Due to this the students and counsellors faced a number of problems during micro teaching and discussion in group. There was also lack of library facilities for distance B.Ed. trainees. There was no proper arrangement of furniture and other electronic and media facilities.

This result is supported by previous studies where seventy two per cent of B.Ed. trainees and 83 per cent of M.Ed. students found the functioning of the study centres inadequate and efficient. The physical facilities provided during contact programmes were not found to be satisfactory (Pugazenthi, 1991). Acharya (1995) advocated that infrastructure facilities of distance education cell were inadequate. Students felt the non-availability of library books. There was no library facility and laboratory facilities for instruction during FCP (Sahoo, 1999).

It can be concluded that many studies indicated discouraging picture response regarding physical facilities of workshops or contact programmes. As per observation of the researcher and his interviews with the counsellors on the above matter similar situations were observed. There is urgent need to set up appropriate facility for B.Ed. trainees at every study centre because without physical resources the training could not be run properly. Headquarters and Regional centres must set up adequate resources urgently and make them functional as per norms.

The findings of the present study revealed that out of many co-curricular activities conducted during workshops the prominent activities were seminar (37 to 38%) and debate competition (16 to 26%). Group discussion, presentation of report and cultural programme were organised during the workshops for the development of competency of co-curricular activities among traines in almost all cases of trainees. Trainees had active participation in such co-curricular activities during the workshops. 73 to 75 per cent trainees and 70 to 77 per cent counsellors of both the open universities considered seminar, group discussion, and debate competition organised during the workshops as relevant. 73 to 85 per cent trainees and 77 to 83 per cent counsellors of both the open universities considered above said activities as effective.

These findings are supported by Phalchandra and Veena (2000) where 69 per cent participants of B.Ed. trainees found the panel discussion as useful. The question-answer session and panel-discussion were found to be interesting and effective. The methodology used in the experiments was found to be better than the conventional method. The answer given by the experts were found to be satisfactory, relevant and useful.

The findings of present study revealed that 79 per cent trainees of both the open universities stated that self-learning materials help them in selection of appropriate teaching methods, development of teaching learning skills, preparing lesson plans and in writing assignments in appropriate manner. 72 per cent trainees of both the open universities also stated about student teachers' handbook that it provides them knowledge about theoretical papers, practical programmes, about various activities of workshops and it worked as a guide to them.

Majority of trainees (78%) and almost 77 per cent of counsellors of both the open universities considered self-learning materials provided by open universities as relevant. Self-learning materials was considered as effective by 78 to 84 per cent trainees and majority of counsellors (78 to 90%) of both the open universities.

The findings of this study are supported by previous studies where Bangladesh Open University (Kabir, 2010) has recently conducted a survey to obtain students' feedback on its study materials. It came out that quality of text materials is considered an important factor in distance education. On the average, 52.1 per cent rated the learning contents of the books from very good to excellent Kabir (2000). Phalchandra and Veena (2000), found that reading materials was considered useful by 57 per cent participants of B.Ed. trainees. Sahoo (1999) found in his study that around 47 per cent of total students opined that course materials were sufficient to complete the course. Almost equal number of students opined about its partial contribution to complete the course requirement successfully. A large majority of students (57 to 78%) found the unit contents appropriate to some extent for theory courses well as methods of teaching courses. Specially in case of methods of teaching courses only 17 per cent students found them appropriate to large extent. Whereas 78 per cent students found them appropriate to some extent.

Majority of students (52%) found the methods of teaching course materials useful to a large extent in the completion of practical work. However significant section of students (48%) found them useful to some extent or least in practical work. Majority of students (55%) found course materials appropriate to large extent in getting self-assignment, feedback. While performing learning activities through study of materials B.Ed. course material were found to be most appropriate by 68 per cent of trainees. It can be concluded that many trainees and counsellors expressed positive response about the relevance and effectiveness of self-learning materials as well as student teachers' handbook.

As a whole the findings of the present study revealed that each trainee neither prepared nor practiced micro lessons according to the norms. Maximum problems of trainees were resolved during workshops by the counsellors. All counsellors did not demonstrate on teaching skills. Majority of trainees (70 to 84%) and majority of counsellors (72 to 95%) consider process adopted for micro teaching as effective. A very less number of trainees (11 to 22%) had reported that they had done practice teaching according to the norms but they consider eligible for completion the course. It is also clear from the study that majority of trainees (72 to 79%) and 60 to 63 per cent counsellors of both the open universities stated that self-learning materials helped B.Ed. trainees in selection of appropriate methods in development of different teaching learning skills in preparing lesson plans and writing assignment appropriately.

These findings are supported by previous studies, where according 72 per cent of the B.Ed. and 83 per cent of the M.Ed. students the functioning of the study centres inadequate and inefficient. Methodology adopted during contact programme was not found to be satisfactory Pugazenthi (1991).

In the study of Acharya (1995) it was found that the Distance System of teacher education programme was partly successful as opined by 81.8 per cent of teachers and 18.2 per cent of the teachers rated it was a poor system of learning. Murugan (1996) argued that present system of centralistic training offered to the academic counsellors of IGNOU is inadequate and inappropriate. Findings of study of Sahoo (1999) revealed that a large number of students (44 to 68%) rated PCP least beneficial in the case of rest of items, viz. to understand theoretical subjects, to develop skills and practical work abilities, to develop abilities for solving educational problems. Pradhan (2000) found a significant difference between the course objectives, students learning activities, instructional materials, instructional methods, support service and evaluation of traditional and correspondence B.Ed. course. He found that the instructional programmes of traditional mode are highly effective than correspondence mode. Kabir (2000) found in his study that 477 of rural students and 657 of urban students rated the B.Ed. programmes from very good to excellent. About overall 44 per cent of female and 54 per cent of male students rated the programme from very good to excellent. About the learning objectives of the programme, more than 66 per cent of the rural and 65 per cent of the urban students rated the B.Ed. Programme from very good to excellent in improving their teaching skills. A sample of 45.5 per cent of rural students and 56.7 per cent of urban students rated B.Ed. tutorial services from good to excellent and most of the students considered problem-solving type of tutorial support as the most effective for their learning. It is argued by Ronnie Carr, Fung and Shui Kin (2002) that distance education programmes well designed and efficiently implemented can provide an effective, flexible alternative to the traditional approach to in-service teacher education.

5.3 Major Implications of the Study

The findings of the study have major implications for delivery of B.Ed. programme for teacher trainees already employed in government/private managed educational institutions.

5.3.1 Implications for B.Ed. Programme Incharge at Headquarters Level

The need of the hour is that open universities must reframe the design of operation of training activities, make it realistic and effective. There must be provision for identification of local level mentors, teacher educators, counsellors and experts, their role in B.Ed. training must be curriculum specific, their acquaintance with different kinds of open and distance learning strategies must be highlighted. Their handbooks' self-learning materials and programme guide must be prepared systematically. Appropriate mechanism must be evolved to train and motivate to trainees in their participation in distance mode of teacher education programme.

Although majority trainees of both the open universities considered micro teaching practices as relevant and effective, but lesser number of trainees of both the universities did not practiced according to the norms. It is matter of serious concern that a considerable number of B.Ed. trainees of both the open universities without preparing and without delivering they have also been considered eligible for completion of the B.Ed. course. Adequate demonstration on micro teaching skills had not done by counsellors. There must be urgent need to be careful about counselling programme, workshops, about role of counsellors and role of programme incharge at study centre level also.

Remarkably majority of trainees and cousellors also stated that demonstration on micro teaching skills had done by counsellors without helps of teaching aids and media also. All the programme study centres need to be equipped with study materials, audio-video, teleconferencing facilities to facilitate flexibility in training. There must be arrangement of media and materials like computer, L.C.D. projector, O.H.P. at study centre levels. There must be efforts to promote the use of technology to enhance the quality of training.

The stipulated time of workshops and counselling session are very short regarding to completion of various activities (like micro teaching practices, preparing teaching aids group discussion, administration of psychological tests preparing blue print and achievement test etc.) during workshops and counselling sessions. They will have to revise time schedule for theory and practical activities.

The findings related to practice teaching shows that all the trainees of both the open universities hade not done according to the norms and coursellors also did not provide proper help regarding checking and observing of practiced classes of trainees. The counsellor's role must be highlighted regarding practice teaching also.

Although B.Ed. trainees of UPRTOU as compared to their counterparts IGNOU were more profitable position in regards to the availability of guidance for the preparation of unit plan. But the headquarters must be highlighted the role of regional centres and study centres.

There is a need to support increased funding and development of infrastructure conductive to high quality transmission of B.Ed. programmes with media technology. There is a need for substantial institutional financial investment in equipment infrastructure and faculty development. Therefore, administrators need to commit funds to enable academic staff to pursue their area that helps them to deliver equitable course to promote a two-way communication of trainees.

Other facilities like computer, L.C.D. projector, O.H.P., reference books and psychological tests must also be provided at appropriate time and place. There is provision of proper remuneration for cousellors but it is not timely available which must be checked. Facility for remuneration for mentors must also be worked upon so that the hard work and efforts of mentors is encouraged.

More specifically, the teacher educators' role in counselling sessions highlighting use of appropriate methods and media in theoretical and practical course activities must be highlighted appropriately. Their role in clarifying the nature of assignments, practical activities, co-curricular activities, teaching aids and guiding B.Ed. trainees to complete assignments and other above said activities must be fully focused.

Headquarter, must be set up urgently and made functional as per norms. They should meet two times during workshops for review and facilitate training to support and encourage quality monitoring. They must set up their expertise with various distance methods, quality monitoring. They must set up their expertise with various distance methods, guidance and support should be provided for counsellors and mentors.

Although, there is provision for one counsellor at every study centre at the time of practical examination which is not sufficient. There must be arrangement of at least one counsellors at every study centre appointed by open university on the regular pay basis.

5.3.2 Implications for Programme Developers

There is a need to adopt following strategies for designing and implementing the distance B.Ed. programmes by the programme developers. Designing and creation of proactive and strategic plans for the development of infrastructure, resource allocation and faculty development for implementation of distance B.Ed. programmes.

Update and revise the self-learning course material periodically, develop and provide supplementary materials to include recent developments in the field. There is a need to create their own websites regarding teacher education and put old papers, research studies, video programme for micro and practice teaching. Internet can also be used for communicating with counsellors and trainees. Counselling, as an effective media of two-way communication needs to be strengthened. Therefore, there is a need to plan, design and conduct intensive counselling and practical contact sessions as per need and convenience of the trainees. Orient counsellors' supervisors in the innovative counselling techniques such as problem solving, focus group discussions, brain storming and mastering learning projects in order to achieve excellence.

Develop and design innovative and practical situation specific audio-video programmes, teleconferencing sessions, and interactive radio counselling sessions to attract interest of the trainees and make them available at all programme study centres. Special programmes can be launched for disadvantaged teachers.

Frame creative assignments and activities, which are thought provoking and use alternative models for practical assessment. Pattern of supervised activities has to ensure that the design should address the nature, competency and capability of the trainees the teacher education and the content and fit between content and delivery methods.

Self-activities need to be prepared in the form of assignments and case studies and dispatched to the learners along with the course material. This will help to facilitate the change of pattern and avoid repletion of these activities year after year.

Ensure that the theory counselling, practical contact sessions and term end examination do not overlap with each other. Schedule the counselling sessions and practical contact sessions in phased manner to follow up the trainees and continue learning process through out the year so that trainees may not feel isolated.

Practical examination needs to be rescheduled, as the learners feed over loaded with multiple activities in short duration. There is a felt need for conducting practical sessions after theory counselling and practical examination after the completion of counselling and contact sessions with more gaps.

Develop an alternative strategy of evaluation to provide feedback to the trainees on continuous basis about their grades and results, because assignment grades, final results and grade cards have been the cause of concern to majority of the trainees.

Orient all the counsellors involved in counselling/supervision in distance B.Ed. programme. Organize periodical workshops for counsellors to acquaint them with changing needs and trends of distance learning and needs of distance learners. Conduct review meetings with counsellors, programme incharges, employers and supervisors to get feedback about the various aspects of the programmes to strengthen it.

Make periodic visits to programme study centres to meet the trainees' counsellors and programme incharges to solve their practical problems. Conduct periodical evaluation of programme by obtaining feedback from programme incharges, counsellors, students, employers and supervisors to assess the quality of performance of trainees.

Continuing evaluation of the programme over the time is necessary to identify improvements and responses to change. Programme developer should evaluate the materials from time to time to see its quality and effectiveness.

5.3.3 Implications for Regional Centres

The study centres are located in recognized traditional B.Ed. colleges. Many of such colleges are not reputed institutions. They are of self-financing nature and given temporary conditional recognition by the NCTE and the concerned universities. They need to be equipped with study materials, audio-video, teleconferencing facility. There are also lack of room facility and seating arrangement for group as well as combined classes. There is also lack of facility of micro teaching practices.

The faculty members are mostly newcomers and they have no more experience. Many of them may not be well versed with practical exercises like giving demonstration of model lessons, giving demonstration of microteaching lessons related to skill components, appropriate observation techniques and appropriate feedback mechanism etc. In such context, the regional centres must be extremely careful in identification of programme study centres in reputed and well organized institutions of teacher education in the state. They must be careful about counselling programmes, workshops and about counsellors also. Supply of appropriate materials, compulsory equipment like computer, L.C.D. projectors, O.H.P., reference books, tests, to the study centres and library services must be ensured by the regional centres.

Although majority of trainees of both the open universities were satisfied with demonstration and feedback of counsellors in micro teaching and practice teaching observation also but it should be cent-per-cent. They are satisfied with counsellors and mentors regarding their problems resolved by counsellors and mentors.

Majority of counsellors helped to trainees in preparing unit plan, preparing blue print, they also make understand to B.Ed. trainees prepare and use teaching aids, conducting co-curricular activities, conducting action research, preparing records, in completion assignments also.

Study shows that majority of mentors also help B.Ed. trainees in all above mentioned activities. But the help of cousellors and mentors regarding above mentioned activities should be cent-per-cent. All the findings indicate to making counsellors and mentors trained in all above mentioned activities.

For this purpose the regional centres will have to ensure appropriate training of teacher educators, study centre co-ordinators, counsellors and mentors. They also ensure to regular monitoring and observation of study centres. They must evolve suitable monitoring mechanism for operation of B.Ed. programme of open universities through involvement of local level functionaries. The regional centres must motivate the voluntary resource persons and functionaries in promoting innovative practices in development of competency among trainees. They also motivate the counsellors and functionaries in promoting practices of practicals like micro teaching practice teaching and lesson planning. They must be ensured regular monitoring and observation of study centres also.

5.3.4 Implications for Programme Study Centres

The findings of the study revealed an indifferent picture about organization of course specific theory classes, assignment based counselling, practical based assignments and its evaluation, micro teaching practices, macro teaching practices, real classroom based training practices, guidance for development of teaching learning materials and its use, guidance for development of motivation, classroom communication, evaluation and organisation of co-curricular activities among trainees.

Findings of the study shows that IGNOU is better that UPROU

regarding preparation and practice of micro teaching lesson. There found heterogynous nature regarding skills demonstration by counsellors. IGNOU is better than their counterparts regarding practice teaching lessons delivery but in observation of practice teaching lesson UPRTOU were better than their counterparts. Findings of the study show that IGNOU as well as UPRTOU homogenous nature regarding guidance for unit plan but it was of average level.

In preparation of teaching aids there are more differences among both the open universities but IGNOU was more close to the norms of course. There are more difference among both the open universities regarding guidance to trainees about students evaluation of counsellors and mentors.

Majority of trainees of both the open universities, stated about help of mentors and average number of trainees of both the open universities stated about guidance of counsellors regarding school management and planning. Majority of trainees of UPRTOU and average number of trainees of IGNOU mentioned that their problems regarding community work were resolved by mentors. The findings also indicated that guidance regarding co-curricular activities not provided by every counsellors.

In this context it will be appropriate on the part of programme study centre to be dynamic in planning and implementation of distance mode B.Ed. training as per guidelines of the concerned open universities. Hence, selection of appropriate motivated teacher educators, their orientation in distance education based B.Ed. training, provision of appropriate facilities for operationalisation of counselling sessions, identification of practice teaching schools, identification of mentors and their orientation etc., are very much significant for incharge of programme study centre. The programme study centre must ensure proper arrangement of classroom for organisation of seminar classes, micro teaching practices and discussion in groups as well as for general orientation classes. They also ensure to seating arrangement and general uses like electric, water, toilet etc. The programme study centre must ensure proper orientation of teacher educators, mentors and trainees regarding their role in course specific activities. They ensure proper orientation specially about mentors regarding their better role performance guide and help the trainees. Moreover, appropriate monitoring mechanism must be evolved for smooth conduct of the programme and focusing on solution of problems of every needy trainees.

5.3.5 Implications for Teacher Educators/Counsellors

As revealed in the study the trainees have a lot of expectations from their teacher educators/counsellors and mentors in carrying out different course based learning activities of theoretical as well as of practical nature. Hence, the teacher educators/counsellors and mentors must be sensitive about their own role. They must be accountable to the job assigned to them for specific purpose. The teacher educators must make use of small group based methods of teaching; encourage trainees' participation in the Sunday counselling session as well as workshops.

The findings of the study indicate proper demonstration on skills had not done by counsellors and proper means did not adopted by counsellors for the same. The counsellors must prepared themselves for counselling, use appropriate technology for demonstration.

The findings of the study indicate that lesson plan of trainees was not checked and practice lesson of trainees also not observed by cousellors according to the norms. The counsellors must be sensitive about evaluation of lessons and provide guidance for micro and macro lesson plans; make observation of lesson plans and do proper evaluation.

They can discuss among themselves and have proper communication with study centre co-ordinator, regional centre incharge and the faculty members at headquarters level on issues, problems and innovative practices.

Study shows that proper guidance for unit plan; development to teaching aids, classroom teaching motivation and classroom communication did not provide by counsellors. They prepare themselves to provide proper and appropriate guidance in above mentioned activities. They must prepare themselves to provide proper guidance for assignments preparation give proper feedback on assignments of theoretical and practical nature. They organise practical activities for teaching learning and evaluation materials developments.

The responses of majority trainees and counsellors show that satisfactory guidance did not provide by every counsellors in assignments, preparing school records and school budget, school time table, and action research. They must be accountable to provide satisfactory guidance in above mentioned activities. They must be also accountable to provide help in organisation of community participation and co-curricular activities during workshops.

5.3.6 Implication for Mentors

The trainees have a lot of expectations from their mentors. There are also provisions for mentors to help provide their colleague/B.Ed. trainees in all practical activities like practice teaching, unit planning, lesson planning, in preparing teaching aids, record preparation, assignment completion, conducting co-curricular activities and in evaluation work etc. It is mandatory that lessons practiced by trainees should be assessed and observed by mentors also. The findings of the study indicate that lessons prepared and practiced by trainees were not assessed by all the mentors. The mentors must be serious about evaluation and observation of lessons. The mentors must be serious about their responses regarding help in preparation of unit plan to trainees. Because study indicate none of one mentors help them in preparing unit plan.

The study shows that proper and adequate help for preparing teaching aids, in classroom teaching motivation, classroom communication were not provided by mentors to B.Ed. trainees. They must be prepared themselves to provide proper and adequate help to trainees in all above mentioned activities.

Study shows that mentors of both the open universities did not pay specific attention towards help to trainees in evaluation work. The mentors will help them in preparing blue print, evaluating answer copy and in preparing report card of their students. It is clear from the study that majority of trainees told that mentors assisted them in preparing school records. Average number of trainees also informed that help provided by mentors in preparing school budget and some trainees also informed that they help in correcting the errors committed during preparing of school budget. Average number of trainees indicated that their mentors did not help them in conducting action research. While, it is mandatory according to the norms of course that all mentors provide help in all activities like assignments, preparing school record, preparing time-table, and conducting action research to trainees. They will be helpful in all above mentioned activities.

Large number of trainees of UPRTOU and average number of trainees of IGNOU considered that mentors provided help them in resolving problems encountered during organising community work. They will be more helpful to trainees in organising community work and co-curricular activities.

The mentors need to be sensitive about their role in guidance of trainees of local level, for practical activities and assignments.

5.3.7 Implications for B.Ed. Trainees

For the learners a big challenge is to engage in academic task and strategies as well as critiquing the content, media, audio-video and teleconferencing as a tool for effective learning. There is a read for self-determination, self-discipline and self-motivation of trainees.

The B.Ed. trainees must be serious about their role in open and distance mode based teaching-learning activities. They must be vigilant about their difficulties. They must be proactive and sincere in pursuing various kinds of practical activities (like assignments, action research, co-curricular activities, practice teaching etc.), participating in different activities during workshops (like group discussion, micro teaching practices, micro and macro lesson planning, cultural programmes etc.) and teaching learning experiences as per guidelines stated in their handbooks. They must take initiative in exploring all possible avenues of guidance for completion of the courses as per the guidelines of open universities successfully.

Findings of the study indicate that majority of trainees of both the universities considered microteaching, practice teaching and guidance provided during workshops for unit plan as relevant and effective but they did not participated in that activity with actively. Maximum trainees did not prepare lesson plans nor practiced according to the norms of course. They must be serious about micro and practice teaching.

It is mandatory that every trainee prepare teaching aids and they use them appropriately in the classroom, but study indicate that all the trainees did not prepare teaching aids according to the norms. They will be aware about preparation of teaching aids for better performance in the class.

For evaluation of their students there are provision that every trainee should prepare blue print, evaluate answer copy, prepare progress report. There is also provision of assignment for trainees. It is expected that they prepare assignment and submit it at proper time and receive feedback from their counsellors. But the findings of the study indicate that every trainee had no active participation in above mentioned activities. They must be proactive and sincere about various kinds of activities of students' evaluation and making assignment within time.

Guidance had provided during workshops regarding preparation time table, records, school budget and conducting action research. Demonstration had done by counsellors in administration of psychological tests and in all above mentioned activities. Majority of trainees considered guidance and demonstration provided in above mentioned activities as relevant and effective. But every trainee did not prepare time-table, school budget, record and report at stipulated time and norm nor they submitted it at properly.

They will prepare themselves for active participation in all above mentioned activities. The course materials found to be highly relevant and effective by majority trainees. Efforts need to be directed towards studying the SLM before counselling and identify weak areas for discussion during workshops. Identify the practical problems and areas that need special attention. Be prompt for fulfilling the requirements of the programmes. Read student teachers' hand book thoroughly before starting to study, that will help to clear most of the doubts about the programme and save the time. Develop good study habits to interact with course materials regularly. Write assignments in time to get timely feedback with the help of SLM correlate and apply the learning day-to-day practice to enhance the skills.

5.4 Suggestions for Further Studies

This research is an eye opener for being acquainted with empirical evidences on teaching training very much specific to B.Ed. training programme. There is a scope to enlarge the study and explore the association of different factors processes dynamics of B.Ed. training.

The present study was conducted on processes of B.Ed. programmes of open universities. The samples for the present study were mostly chosen from state level. Same study can be undertaken from country level open universities.

There is also a scope for indepth and qualitative studies on exploring context specific experience based evidences in the context of organization of practical processes.

There is also a scope for qualitative studies of the B.Ed. processes of various (More than two) open universities.

There is scope to comparative study of process of study centres of distance B.Ed. programme of any open university.

There is scope to study practical process in traditional and open universities.

There are scope to study the relevance and effectiveness of such process of B.Ed. programmes in state and central universities.

A case study can be undertaken on the given component in order to know ground reality in depth.

The present study should be conducted on a large scale and replicated on a large sample.

A study to identify various factors influencing attitude and practices of distance B.Ed. trainees may be conducted.

A correlation study may help to identify the relationship between knowledge skills, practices and attitudes of trainees after completing the programme.

A comparative study of distance vs. traditional system should be conducted to assess their effectiveness.

Appendices

Appendix-I

Questionnaire for Trainees

SECTION-A
Exploring Processes

I. Preparation for Teaching: The processes adopted during B.Ed. training through Open University to make you an affective teacher is presented into nine parts (I to IX) before you. Questions related to such processes are kept in this first part which has been further divided into three parts (A, B & C).

(A) Micro Teaching: In this section some questions related to micro teaching are kept. Put a (✓) mark at the appropriate correct option and write your experiences in the space provided.

1. **How many micro-teaching plans have you made/taught in each of the teaching skill?**

Skills	*Number of skill Plan*					
	1	2	3	4	5	Other
1. Introduction skill						
2. Objective writing skill						
3. Questioning skill						
4. Stimulus variation skill						
5. Reinforcement skill						
6. Illustration with example skill						
7. Explanation skill						
8. Blackboard writing skill						
9. Demonstration skill						
10. Lesson closure skill						
Total						

2. How many skills have been demonstrated by the counsellor?

   (i) One ( ) (ii) 2-5 ( ) (iii) 6-10 ( ) (iv) Not done

3. How are the teaching skills demonstrated?

   (i) Taught by the counsellor ( )

   (ii) By video cassette ( )

(iii) Not done ( )
(iv) Other.....................

4. Who had provided feed-back during micro teaching?
   (i) Counsellor ( )
   (ii) Peer trainees ( )
   (iii) Both Counsellors and Peer trainees ( )
   (iv) None ( )
5. State the problems you experienced during micro-teaching
   (i) ....
   (ii) ....
   (iii) ....
   (iv) ....

(B) Practice Teaching: Few questions related to practice teaching are presented before you in this part. Put a (✓) mark in front of the right option and write your experiences, if required, in the space provided.

1. **How many lesson plans have you prepared in each of the teaching subject?**
   (a) In the first teaching subject:
   (i) 1-5 ( ) (ii) 6-10 ( )
   (iii) 11-15 ( ) (iv) 16-20 ( )
   (b) In the Second teaching subject:
   (i) 1-5 ( ) (ii) 6-10 ( ) (iii) 11-15 ( ) (iv) 16-20 ( )
2. **How many lesson plans have been checked before teaching/presentation?**
   (a) In the First teaching subject:
   (i) 1-5 ( ) (ii) 6-10 ( ) (iii) 11-15 ( ) (iv) 16-20
   (b) In the Second teaching Subject:
   (i) 1-5 ( ) (ii) 6-10 ( ) (iii) 11-15 ( ) (iv) 16-20
3. **Who has checked the lesson plans before teaching/presentation?**
   (i) Mentor ( ) (ii) Peer trainees ( )
   (iii) None ( ) (iv) other ....
4. **How many lesson plans have you taught in each of the teaching subjects?**
   (a) In the first teaching subject:
   (i) 1-5 ( ) (ii) 6-10 ( ) (iii) 11-15 ( ) (iv) 16-20
   (b) In the Second teaching subject:
   (i) 1-5 ( ) (ii) 6-10 ( ) (iii) 11-15 ( ) (iv) 16-20

5. **During Practice teaching who has usually observed your class presentation?**
   (i) Mentor ( ) (ii) Peer trainees ( )
   (iii) Counsellor ( ) (iv) Other...........
6. **Mention the problems you came across during practice teaching.**
   (i) ....
   (ii) ....
   (iii) ....
   (iv) ....

(C) Unit Plan: Few questions related to Unit-Plan are presented before you in this part. Put a (✓) mark in front of the right option and write your experiences if required in the space provided.

1. **Whether training for preparing Unit-Plan is provided?**
   (i) Regularly provided ( ) (ii) Sometimes ( )
   (iii) Never provided ( ) (iv) Other ....
2. **What is informed about preparation of Unit-plans in the workshop?**
   (i) ....
   (ii) ....
   (iii) ....
   (iv) ....

II. Preparation of teaching aids and its use: In this section few questions related to the preparation of teaching aids and its appropriate utilization are presented. Put a (✓) mark in front of the right option and mention your experiences if required in the space provided.

1. **During teaching to what extent do you use the following aids?**

S. No.	*Teaching aid*	*Large extent*	*Less extent*	*Do not use*
1.	Chart			
2.	Artificial/Readymade Model			
3.	Natural objects (Flower, leaf plant, stone etc.)			
4.	I.C.T. based (Computer, T.V. Radio etc.)			

2. **Whose help do you take for the preparation of teaching aids?**
   (i) Mentor ( ) (ii) Peer trainees ( )
   (iii) Counsellor ( ) (iv) Other.............. ( )

3. **During teaching state the problems you come across in reference of the use of teaching aids?**
   (i) ....
   (ii) ....
   (iii) ....
   (iv) ....
4. **State how do you resolved the problems you came across, in the use of aids during teaching**
   (i) ....
   (ii) ....
   (ii) ....
   (iv) ....

III. Class-room teaching motivation: In this section few question are presented for motivating students during class-room teaching. Put a (✓) mark in front of the right option and write your experiences if required in the space provided.

1. **State the measures in which you are been trained in the workshops to motivate your students in class.**
   (i) ....
   (ii) ....
   (iii) ....
   (iv) ....
2. **Who has guided you as how to motivate the students of your class?**
   (i) Mentor ( ) (ii) Peer trainees ( )
   (iii) Counsellor ( ) (iv) other ....

IV. Class-room Communication: In this section question related to classroom communication is presented before you, write your experiences in the space provided.

1. **What is taught to you to make classroom communication effective?**
   (i) ....
   (ii) ....
   (iii) ....
   (iv) ....

V. Student Evaluation: In this section questions related to students evaluation are presented before you in two part (competency development related to evaluation and competency development related to assignment). Put a (✓) mark in front of the choiced option and write your experiences in the space provided.

(A) Competency Development related to Evaluation:

1. **How do the mentors assist you in increasing/developing abilities related to evaluation?**
   - (i) By helping in the preparation of blue print/question paper. ( )
   - (ii) By helping in the evaluation of achievement (answer copy) of students ( )
   - (iii) By helping in the preparation of progress report/result of students. ( )
   - (iv) All of the above ( )
2. **How do the counsellors assist you in developing abilities related to evaluation?**
   - (i) By assisting in the successful completion of assignments. ( )
   - (ii) By assisting in the administration of Psychological test. ( )
   - (iii) Via group discussion. ( )
   - (iv) All of the above. ( )
3. **What do the counsellors do to make you capable of making examination question paper?**
   - (i) They demonstrate the method of preparing question paper. ( )
   - (ii) They provide feedback during the preparation of question paper during the workshops. ( )
   - (iii) Do not put any effort. ( )
   - (iv) Other.................
4. **What do the counsellors do to make you capable of making psychological test?**
   - (i) They demonstrate the method of preparation and administration of psychological test. ( )
   - (ii) They provided feedback in the preparation of psychological tests during the workshops. ( )
   - (iii) Both of the above. ( )
   - (iv) Do not put any effort. ( )
   - (v) Other..........................
5. **How do the following assist you in solving problems faced during evaluation of students in classroom?**

   (a) Mentor:
   - (i) By helping in evaluation work. ( )
   - (ii) By providing important points for problem solving. ( )
   - (iii) Both of the above ( )
   - (iv) Other................................

(b) Peer trainees:

(i) By discussing about problems. ( )

(ii) By helping in evaluation work. ( )

(iii) Both of the above. ( )

(iv) Other............................

(B) Competency development related to Assignment:

1. How do you present the assignment?

(i) By taking help of the counsellor. ( )

(ii) By reading book. ( )

(iii) With the help of library. ( )

(iv) By reading old assignments. ( )

(v) All of the above. ( )

(vi) Other.......................

VI. School Management and Planning: In this section questions related to school management and planning are presented before you. Put a (✓) mark in front of the right option and write your experience in the space provided.

1. How do the following assist you in making time-table?

(a) Mentor:

(i) By giving important information regarding periods. ( )

(ii) By commenting the faults in the time-table developed. ( )

(iii) Both of the above. ( )

(iv) Do not take any initiative. ( )

(v) Other.......................

(b) Counsellors:

(i) By giving appropriate examples. ( )

(ii) By assisting us in making the time-table in the workshop and providing due feedback. ( )

(iii) Both of the above. ( )

(iv) Do not take any initiative. ( )

(v) Other ....

(c) Peer Trainees:

(i) By discussing self-experiences. ( )

(ii) Assist in making it together. ( )

(iii) By providing feedback. ( )

(iv) Other ....

2. How do the following help you in preparing school record/register?

(a) Mentor:

(i) By providing us right information regarding school activities. ( )

(ii) By amending the already prepared register by you. ( )
(iii) Both of the above ( )
(iv) Do not take any initiative. ( )
(v) Other ....

(b) Counsellor:

(i) By providing example in the workshop. ( )
(ii) By amending and providing feedback of the already prepared register. ( )
(iii) Both of the above. ( )
(iv) Do not take any initiative. ( )
(v) Other ....

(c) Peer Trainees:

(i) By discussing self-experiences. ( )
(ii) Assist in making the register. ( )
(iii) By providing feedback. ( )
(iv) Other ....

3. **How do the following help you in preparing school budget?**

(a) Mentor:

(i) By providing right information about school's income and expenditure. ( )
(ii) By amending the already prepared school budget. ( )
(iii) Both of the above. ( )
(iv) Do not take any initiative. ( )
(v) Other ....

(b) Counsellor:

(i) By providing examples of school budget. ( )
(ii) By preparing and providing feedback in the workshop. ( )
(iii) Both of the above. ( )
(iv) Do not take any initiative. ( )
(v) Other................................

(c) Peer Trainees:

(i) By discussing self-experiences. ( )
(ii) Assist in making it. ( )
(iii) By amending already prepared school budget. ( )
(iv) Other ....

4. **(a) Have you done action research?**

(i) Yes ( ) (ii) No ( )

(b) On what Subject/Topic have you done action research?

....

....

5. **How do the following assist you ın doing action research?**

(a) Mentor:

(i) By selecting the problem. ( )
(ii) By resolving the problem in research work. ( )
(iii) Both of the above. ( )
(iv) Do not take any initiative. ( )
(v) Other..............................

(b) Peer trainees:

(i) By discussing self-experiences. ( )
(ii) In selection of problem. ( )
(iii) By showing their report of action research. ( )
(iv) Do not take any initiative. ( )
(v) Other..............................

(c) Counsellor:

(i) By providing theoretical knowledge. ( )
(ii) By giving feedback on our weakness during workshop. ( )
(iii) By providing help from library. ( )
(iv) Do not take any initiative. ( )
(v) Other..............................

6. **What is taught to you to make assembly/prayer knowledgeable, attractive and interesting?**

(i) Thought presentation by students. ( )
(ii) Daily news presentation by students. ( )
(iii) To honour intellectual (Gifted) students in assembly. ( )
(iv) All of the above ( )
(v) Others..........................

VII. Community Participation: In this section question related to community participation is presented before you. Put a (✓) mark in front of the right option and write your experiences in the space provided.

1. **(a) Do activities related to community participation organized during workshop?**

(i) Yes ( ) (ii) No ( )

(b) If yes, then which activities related to community participation are organised?

(i) Health education related. ( )
(ii) Community work and survey. ( )
(iii) Both of the above. ( )
(iv) Other ....

2. **How do you resolve the problems related to the**

implementation of activities concerned with community participation in school?

(i) With the help of mentor. ( )
(ii) With the help of peer trainees. ( )
(iii) Both of the above ( )
(iv) Other ....

VIII. Co-curricular Activities: In this section questions related to co-curricular activities are presented before you. Put a (✓) mark in front of the right option and write your experiences in the space provided.

1. **(a) Are co-curriculum activities organised during workshop?**
   (i) Regularly ( ) (ii) Some-times ( ) (iii) Never ( )

   (b) Which co-curricular activities are organized during workshop?
   (i) Educational tour. ( )
   (ii) Sports and game. ( )
   (iii) Debate competition. ( )
   (iv) Seminar. ( )
   (v) Functions related to school. ( )

2. **What types of activities are organized in the workshop for the development of competency related to organization of co-curricular activities?**
   (i) Group Discussion. ( )
   (ii) Presentation of report. ( )
   (iii) Cultural programme during inaugural and validatory session ( )
   (iv) All of the above. ( )
   (v) Other ....

IX. Self-Learning Materials: In this section questions related to self-learning material and student teacher handbook (provided by Open University) are presented before you. Put a (✓) mark in front of the right option and write your experiences in the space provided.

1. **What type of help do you receive from Self-learning materials?**
   (i) Selection of appropriate teaching methods. ( )
   (ii) In the development of teaching learning skills. ( )
   (iii) In preparing Lesson Plan. ( )
   (iv) To write assignments properly ( )
   (v) All of the above ( )

2. **What type of help do you received by student-teacher hand-book?**
   (i) Provide information about theoretical paper. ( )
   (ii) Provide information about practical programmes. ( )
   (iii) Provide information about workshop-based activities. ( )
   (iv) It works like a silent guide. ( )
   (v) All of the above. ( )
3. **To what extent you feel correlation between the lessons of self-learning materials and training provided during the workshop.**
   (i) To large extent. ( ) (ii) To average extent. ( )
   (iii) To less extent. ( ) (iv) Not at all. ( )
4. **How does student-teacher handbook help you in the practical programmes?**
   (i) ....
   (ii) ....
   (iii) ....
   (iv) ....

SECTION-B
Relevance of Processes

Select the level of relevance by putting a (✓) mark in front of the appropriate alternative on the training processes adopted by open universities.

Sl. No.	Relevance Question/Statement	*Level of Relevance*		
		Highly Agree	**Agree**	**Disagree**
1.	Preparing micro lesson plans is related to the development of teaching competency.			
2.	Demonstration of micro lesson plan by counsellors is related to your subject-teaching.			
3.	Feedback provided during micro teaching is in accordance to your competency.			
4.	Preparing lesson plans for practice teaching is related to your school teaching.			

(Contd.)

5.	Practice teaching vitalizes you in your school teaching.			
6.	Guidance provided during workshop for preparing Unit Plan is must for completing durinal syllabus timely.			
7.	Training for the use of teaching aids is in accordance to the B.Ed. syllabus.			
8.	Training given for preparing teaching aids is related to the available resources at schools.			
9.	Home work given by counselors for preparing question paper is related to your teaching competence.			
10.	Activities related to psychological test are helpful in understanding the students.			
11.	Assignment given to you is according to your syllabus.			
12.	Assignment given to you is activity oriented.			
13.	Assignment given to you is related to your experience.			
14.	Training given for the preparation of school time-table is in accordance with the time-table prepared at your school.			
15.	Training given for the maintenance of register work is related to the work given by principal in your school.			
16.	Guidance provided for conducting action research is in accordance to problem resolution at your school.			
17.	Training given to make school assembly interesting and meaningful is according to your school's environment.			
18.	Community work conducted in the workshop is related to surrounding environment of your school.			
19.	Seminar conducted during workshop is related to your school activities.			
20.	Organization of group discussion during workshop is related to skill development in you.			
21.	Self-learning materials given to you by open University is related to teaching learning syllabus			
22.	Student-teachers' handbook is related with the activities being performed by you.			

SECTION-C
Effectiveness of the Process

Select the level of effectiveness by putting a (✓) mark in front of the appropriate alternative on the training processes adopted by Open Universities.

Sl. No.	Effectiveness Question	Level of Effectiveness		
		More extent	Some extent	Least
1.	By preparing micro lesson plans to what extent following teaching skills are developed in you? (i) To write correct introduction. (ii) To write correct objective. (iii) To write questions correctly. (iv) To decide stimulus variation. (v) To decide re-inforcement (vi) To decide illustration with example. (vii) To explain correctly. (viii) To decide matter to be written on black board. (ix) To decide material for demonstration. (x) For lesson closure. (xi) To decide homework.			
2.	To what extent feedback given during micro teaching assist you in the development of following skills? (i) Introductory lesson skill. (ii) Objective writing skill. (iii) Questioning skill. (iv) Stimulus variation skill. (v) Reinforcement skill. (vi) Illustration with example skill. (vii) Explanation skill. (viii) Blackboard writing skill. (ix) Demonstration skill. (x) Lesson closure skill.			

(Contd.)

3.	To what extent lesson plan prepared for practice teaching assist you in obtaining competence on the following points? (i) In writing instructional objectives. (ii) In writing subject-matter correctly (iii) In writing questions appropriately.			
4.	By practice teaching to what extent you obtain competence in the following points? (i) To create appropriate situation for introducing the lesson in class-room. (ii) To state introduction of the lesson effectively. (iii) Acceptance of student response appropriately. (iv) In explanation of facts appropriately. (v) In presentation of appropriate example. (vi) In selection of appropriate teaching aids. (vii) To provide reinforcement to student. (viii) To make classroom communication effective. (ix) In appropriate lesson closure.			
5.	To what extent the guidance provided during the workshops for unit plan assist you in developing competence for the preparation of unit plan in your own teaching subject?			
6.	To what extent the training provided for preparation of teaching aids assist you in the development of competence for the preparation and utilization of teaching aids? (i) In the successful utilization of teaching aids. (ii) To prepare teaching aid by waste materials. (iii) To make classroom teaching interesting.			
7.	To what extent the training provided during the workshops developed your competence in the evaluation of students' in the following areas:			

(*Contd.*)

	(i) In making good question paper. (ii) In the preparation of progress report of students. (iii) In the administration of psychological test.			
8.	To what extent assignments assist you in the following points? (i) To know self-progress. (ii) To improve your own demerits. (iii) In the preparation of examination. (iv) Readiness in undertaking teaching related activities.			
9.	To what extent training related to school management and planning assist you in the development of competencies in the following areas: (i) In the preparation of school time-table. (ii) In the preparation of school records. (iii) In making school budget directed by principal.			
10.	To what extent guidance provided in action research assist you in the development of competencies in the following areas: (i) In the relation to the conduction of action research. (ii) Presentation of research report.			
11.	To what extent training provided to make school assembly interesting and meaningful assist you in the development of competencies in the following activities? (i) In the organization of appropriate assembly. (ii) In the inclusion of various activities in assembly.			
12.	To what extent organisation of community participation related activities during the workshops assist you in the development of skills in the following points? (i) To reduce pollution by plantation. (ii) In maintain cleanness near school.			

(Contd.)

	(iii) To enrich participation of students in Pulse Polio Programme. (iii) To motivate students and guardians for the success of adult education.			
13.	To what extent the efforts during workshop imparted for enhancing competencies related to co-curricular activities assisted you in the following points? (i) Implementing sports and cultural programme in the school. (ii) To organize educational tour successfully. (iii) To enrich participation of students in sports and cultural programme.			
14.	To what extent self-learning material provided by open university assist you in the following points? (i) In the selection of appropriate teaching-methods. (ii) In the development of teaching learning skills. (iii) In preparing lesson plan. (iv) In writing assignments correctly.			
15.	To what extent student teacher hand book provided for your assistance assist you in the following points? (i) To maintain correlation between training and theoretical subjects. (ii) To understand subject matter related to teaching competency.			

Appendix-II

Questionnaire for Counsellors

Name of Counsellor: ....
Educational Qualification: ....
Designation: Prof./Reader/Lecturer/Principal ....
Nature of Job: Regular/Adhoc/Self-finance. ....
Name of University/College (where you are working): ....
Teaching Experience as Teacher Educator: ....
Subject in which you have mastery: ....
Name of the B.Ed. Study Centre: ....
Name of the Affiliated University: (IGNOU/UPRTOU) ....
Have you got training in Distance Education: (Yes/No) ....
Have you got training for being a B.Ed. Counsellor: (Yes/No) ....
Since how many years you are providing your service to B.Ed. trainees of Open Universities: ....

SECTION-A
Exploring Processes

I. Preparation for Teaching: The processes adopted during B.Ed. training through Open University is presented into nine parts (I to IX) before you. Questions related to such processes are kept in this first part which has been further divided into three parts (A, B & C).

(A) Micro Teaching: In this section some questions related to micro teaching are kept. Put a (✓) mark at the appropriate correct option and write your experiences in the space provided.

1. **How do you demonstrate on teaching skills?**
   (i) Teaching personally ( ) (ii) By video-cassettes ( )
   (iii) Both i & ii ( ) (iv) Other ....
2. **State the problems you experienced during micro-teaching.**
   (i) .... (ii) ....
   (iii) .... (iv) ....

(B) Practice Teaching: In this section, questions related to practice teaching are presented before you. Put a (✓) mark in front of the right option and write your experiences, if required, in the space provided.

1. How many lesson plans were prepared by trainees in each of the teaching subject?

(a) In the first teaching subject:

(i) 1-5 ( ) (ii) 6-10 ( )
(iii) 11-15 ( ) (iv) 16-20 ( )

(b) In the Second teaching subject:

(i) 1-5 ( ) (ii) 6-10 ( )
(iii) 11-15 ( ) (iv) 16-20 ( )

2. Who has observed the classes of trainees during practice teaching?

(i) Mentor ( ) (ii) Peer trainees ( ) (iii) Subject teacher
(iv) None ( ) (v) Other ....

3. How many lesson plans have been observed by mentors of B.Ed. trainees during practice teaching?

(i) 1-5 ( ) (ii) 6-10 ( )
(iii) 11-15 ( ) (iv) 16-20

4. Who has checked the lesson plans before teaching/ presentation?

(i) Mentor ( ) (ii) Peer trainees ( )
(iii) Subject teacher ( ) (iv) None .... (v) Other ......

5. How many lesson plans have been observed by counsellors/teacher-educators of B.Ed. trainees during practice teaching?

(i) 1-5 ( ) (ii) 6-10 ( )
(iii) 11-15 ( ) (iv) 16-20 ( )

(C) Unit Plan: Few questions related to Unit-Plan are presented before you in this part. Put a (✓) mark in front of the right option and write your experiences if required in the space provided.

1. Whether training for preparing Unit-Plan is provided by you?

(i) Regularly provided ( )
(ii) Sometimes ( )
(iii) Never provided ( )
(iv) Other..........

2. How you have trained B.Ed. trainees for preparing Unit-Plan?

(i) ....
(ii) ....
(iii) ....
(iv) ....

II. Preparation of teaching aids and its uses: In this section few questions related to the preparation of teaching aids and its appropriate utilization are presented. Put a (✓) mark in front of the right option and mention your experiences if required in the space provided.

1. **Where do B.Ed. trainees prepare teaching-aids?**
   - (i) Their own school ( )
   - (ii) In workshops ( )
   - (iii) Both i & ii ( )
   - (iv) Not prepared ( )
2. **How many teaching aids were prepared by B.Ed. trainees during workshops?**
   - (i) 1-5 ( )
   - (ii) 6-10 ( )
   - (iii) 11-15 ( )
   - (iv) They prepared at home and submit it during the workshops.

III. Class-room teaching motivation: In this section a question is presented for motivating students during class-room teaching and space provided in fornt the question for answer. Write your experiences in the space provided.

1. **State the process you have adopted during the workshops for making B.Ed. trainees trained to motivate their students in class.**
   - (i) ....
   - (ii) ....
   - (iii) ....
   - (iv) ....

IV. Class-room communication: In this section question related to classroom communication is presented before you. Write your experiences in the space provided.

1. **What is taught by you to B.Ed. trainees that they make classroom communication effective?**
   - (i) ....
   - (ii) ....
   - (iii) ....
   - (iv) ....

V. Students' Evaluation: In this section questions related to students' evaluation are presented before you in two parts (competency development related to evaluation and competency development related to assignment). Put a (✓) mark in front of the choice option and write your experiences in the space provided.

(A) Competency Development related to Evaluation:

1. **Which type of help is provided by you to B.Ed. trainees for development of abilities related to students' evaluation?**
   (i) Helping in the preparation of blue print/question paper. ( )
   (ii) By administrating psychological test. ( )
   (iii) By providing theoretical knowledge. ( )
   (iv) All of the above ( )
   (v) Other ....
2. **What do you do to make competent B.Ed. trainees in making question paper?**
   (i) State the example of examination question paper. ( )
   (ii) Provide feedback during the preparation of examination question paper by trainees during the workshops. ( )
   (iii) Both of the above. ( )
   (iv) Do not take any initiative. ( )
   (v) Other ....
3. **What do you do to make B.Ed. trainees competent in administration of psychological test?**
   (i) State the method of preparation and administration of psychological test. ( )
   (ii) Provide feedback during the preparation of psychological test during the workshops. ( )
   (iii) Both of the above. ( )
   (iv) Do not take any initiative. ( )
   (v) Other ....

(B) Competency development related to Assignment:

1. **How do you help B.Ed. trainees in the assignments?**
   (i) By providing theoretical knowledge. ( )
   (ii) By providing feedback in prepared assignment by B.Ed. trainees. ( )
   (iii) Both of the above. ( )
   (iv) Do not take any initiative. ( )
   (vi) Other .... ( )

VI. School Management and Planning: In this section questions related to school management and planning are presented before you. Put a (✓) mark in front of the right option and write your experience in the space provided.

1. **How do you help B.Ed. trainees in preparing time table?**
   (i) By giving theoretical knowledge. ( )

(ii) By preparing during the workshops and giving feedback. ( )
(iii) Both of the above. ( )
(iv) Other........................

2. **Do you make B.Ed. trainees prepare the school record/ register?**
(i) Yes ( ) (ii) No ( ) (iii) Not required ( )

3. **What do you do for making competent B.Ed. trainees in preparing school records/register?**
(i) By giving assignment. ( )
(ii) By preparing during the workshops and giving feedback. ( )
(iii) Both of the above. ( )
(iv) Other................................

4. **What do you do for making competent B.Ed. trainees in preparing school budget?**
(i) By giving example. ( )
(ii) By preparing during the workshops and giving feedback. ( )
(iii) Both of the above. ( )
(iv) Other...............................

5. **How do you make B.Ed. trainees learn to conduct action research successfully?**
(i) By providing theoretical knowledge. ( )
(ii) By providing feedback for their shortcomings during workshops. ( )
(iii) Both of the above. ( )
(iv) Other ....

VII. Community Participation: In this section question related to community participation is presented before you. Put a (✓) mark in front of the right option and write your experiences in the space provided.

1. **Which type of activities related to community participation were organised during workshops by you?**
(i) Related to health education. ( )
(ii) Community work and survey ( )
(iii) Both of the above ( )
(iv) Other ....

2. **How do you make B.Ed. trainees competent in organization of activities concerned with community participation?**

(i) By providing detailed theoretical knowledge on study centre. ( )
(ii) By organization of such type activities during the workshops. ( )
(iii) Both of the above ( )
(iv) Other ....

VIII. Co-curricular Activities: In this section questions related to co-curricular activities are presented before you. Put a (✓) mark in front of the right option and write your experiences in the space provided.

1. **Which type of co-curricular activities are organized during workshop?**
   (i) Educational tour. ( )
   (ii) Sports and game. ( )
   (iii) Debate competition. ( )
   (iv) Seminar. ( )
   (v) Functions related to school. ( )
   (vi) All of the above. ( )
2. **What type of activities are organised during the workshops for the development of competency related to organization of co-curricular activities?**
   (i) Group discussion. ( )
   (ii) Presentation of report. ( )
   (iii) Cultural programme during inaugural and valedictory session ( )
   (iv) All of the above. ( )
   (v) Other ....

IX. Self-Learning Materials: In this section questions related to self-learning material and student teacher handbook (provided by Open University) are presented before you. Put a (✓) mark in front of the right option and write your experiences in the space provided.

1. **What type of help is received by B.Ed. trainees from Self-learning materials?**
   (i) Selection of appropriate teaching methods. ( )
   (ii) In the development of teaching learning skills. ( )
   (iii) In preparing Lesson Plan. ( )
   (iv) To write assignments properly. ( )
   (v) All of the above. ( )
2. **What type of help is received by B.Ed. trainees from student-teachers' handbook?**

(i) It provides information about theoretical paper. ( )
(ii) It provides information about practical programmes. ( )
(iii) It provides information about workshops based activities. ( )
(iv) It works like a guide. ( )
(v) All of the above. ( )

3. **To what extent correlation exists between the lessons of self-learning materials and training provided by you during the workshops.**
(i) To large extent. ( ) (ii) To average extent. ( )
(iii) To less extent. ( ) (iv) Not at all. ( )

SECTION-B
Relevance of Processes

Select the level of relevance by putting a (✓) mark in front of the appropriate alternative on the training processes of distance B.Ed. curriculum adopted by you.

Sl. No.	*Relevance Question/Statement*	*Level of Relevance*		
		Highly Agree	**Agree**	**Disagree**
1.	Demonstration of micro teaching skills by you is related to competency development of B.Ed. trainees.			
2.	Lesson plans prepared by B.Ed. trainees are related to their school teaching.			
3.	Feedback provided to B.Ed. trainees during practice teaching is in accordance to their competency development.			
4.	Guidance provided by you for preparing unit plan is assisting B.Ed. trainees in completion of daily syllabus timely.			

(Contd.)

5.	Training given to B.Ed. trainees by you for preparation of teaching aids is in accordance to their B.Ed. syllabus.			
6.	Training given to B.Ed. trainees by you for the use of teaching aids is in accordance to their school resources.			
7.	Home-work given to B.Ed. trainees by you for preparing question paper is related to their teaching competency.			
8.	Assignment given to B.Ed. trainees by you is in accordance to their syllabus.			
9.	Assignment given to B.Ed. trainees by you is activity oriented.			
10.	Assignment given to B.Ed. trainees by you is related to their experience.			
11.	Training given to B.Ed. trainees by you for preparation of school time-table is related to their school's time table.			
12.	Training given to B.Ed. trainees by you for preparation of school record is related to their own school work given by their principal.			
13.	Guidance provided to B.Ed. trainees by you for conducting action research is in accordance to their school problems.			
14.	Training given to B.Ed. trainees by you to make school assembly interesting and knowledgeable is according to their own school environment.			
15.	Community work conducted by you is related to surrounding environment of school of B.Ed. trainees.			
16.	Seminar conducted by you during the workshops is related to school activities of B.Ed. trainees.			

(Contd.)

17.	Conduction of the debate by you is related to skills development of B.Ed. trainees.			
18.	Organisation of group discussion by you during the workshops is related to skill development of B.Ed. trainees.			
19.	Self-learning material given by open universities is related to teaching learning and B.Ed. syllabus of trainees.			
20.	Student-teachers' handbook provided to B.Ed. trainees is according to activities performed by them.			

SECTION-C
Effectiveness of the Process

Select the level of effectiveness by putting a (✓) mark in front of the appropriate alternative on the training processes adopted by Open Universities.

Sl. No.	***Effectiveness Question***	**Level of Effectiveness**		
		More extent	**Some extent**	**Least**
1.	After getting training during the workshops by preparing micro lesson plans to what extent following teaching skills are developed in B.Ed. trainees? (i) To write correct introduction. (ii) To write correct objective. (iii) To write questions correctly. (iv) To decide stimulus variation. (v) To decide re-inforcement (vi) To decide illustration with example. (vii) To explain correctly. (viii) To decide matter to be written on blackboard.			

(Contd.)

	(ix) To decide material for demonstration. (x) For lesson closure. (xi) To decide homework.			
2.	To what extent feedback given by you during micro teaching assist B.Ed. trainees in the development of following skills? (i) Introductory lesson skill. (ii) Objective writing skill. (iii) Questioning skill. (iv) Stimulus variation skill. (v) Reinforcement skill. (vi) Illustration with example skill. (vii) Explanation skill. (viii) Blackboard writing skill. (ix) Demonstration skill. (x) Lesson closure skill.			
3.	To what extent lesson plans prepared by B.Ed. trainees for practice teaching assist them in obtaining competence on the following points? (i) In writing instructional objectives. (ii) In writing subject-matter correctly (iii) In writing questions appropriately.			
4.	By practice teaching to what extent B.Ed. trainees obtain competence in the following points? (i) To create appropriate situation for introducing the lesson in classroom. (ii) To state introduction of the lesson effectively. (iii) Acceptance of student response appropriately. (iv) In explanation of facts appropriately. (v) In presentation of appropriate example.			

(Contd.)

	(vi) In selection of appropriate teaching aids. (vii) To provide reinforcement to student. (viii) To make classroom communication effective. (ix) In appropriate lesson closure.			
5.	To what extent the guidance provided during the workshops for unit plan assist B.Ed. trainees in developing competence for the preparation of unit plan in their own teaching subject?			
6.	To what extent the training provided for preparation of teaching aids assist B.Ed. trainees in the development of competence for the preparation and utilization of teaching aids? (i) In the successful utilization of teaching aids. (ii) To prepare teaching aid by waste materials. (iii) To make classroom teaching interesting.			
7.	To what extent the training provided during the workshops developed competence of B.Ed. trainees in the evaluation of students in the following areas: (i) In making good question paper. (ii) In the preparation of progress report of students. (iii) In the administration psychological test.			
8.	To what extent assignments given by you to B.Ed. trainees assist them in the following points? (i) To know self-progress. (ii) To improve your own demerits.			

(Contd.)

	(iii) In the preparation of examination. (iv) Readiness in undertaking teaching related activities.			
9.	To what extent training given by you to B.Ed. trainees regarding school management and planning assist them in the development of competencies in the following areas: (i) In the preparation of school time-table. (ii) In the preparation of school records. (iii) In making school budget directed by principal.			
10.	To what extent guidance provided to B.Ed. trainees by you for making competent in action research assist them in the development of competencies in the following areas: (i) In the relation to the conduction of action research. (ii) Presentation of research report.			
11.	To what extent training provided to B.Ed. trainees by you to make school assembly interesting and meaningful, assist them in the development of competencies in the following activities? (i) In the organization of appropriate assembly. (ii) In the inclusion of various activities in assembly.			
12.	To what extent organization of community participation related activities by you during the workshops assist B.Ed. trainees in the development of skills in the following points? (i) To reduce pollution by plantation. (ii) In maintain cleanness near school. (iii) To enrich participation of students in Pulse Polio Programme.			

(Contd.)

	(iv) To motivate students and guardians for the success of adult education			
13.	To what extent your efforts during the workshops imparted for enhancing competencies related to co-curricular activities assisted B.Ed. trainees in the following points? (i) Implementing sports and cultural programme in the school. (ii) To organize educational tour successfully. (iii) To enrich participation of students in sports and cultural programme.			
14.	To what extent self-learning material provided by open University assist B.Ed. trainees in the following points? (i) In the selection of appropriate teaching methods. (ii) In the development of teaching-learning skills. (iii) In preparing lesson plan. (iv) In writing assignments correctly.			
15.	To what extent student teachers' hand-book provided by open universities assist B.Ed. trainees in the following points? (i) To maintain correlation between training and theoretical subjects. (ii) To understand subject matter related to teaching competency.			

Appendix-III

Interview Schedule for Counsellor

(I) Preparation for Teaching:

1. How do you make train B.Ed. trainees for preparing micro teaching lesson plans?
2. How do B.Ed. trainees do micro teaching practice?
3. How do you provide feedback to B.Ed. trainees of distance mode in micro teaching practice?
4. How do micro teaching assist B.Ed. trainees of distance mode?
5. How are the skills of B.Ed. trainees affected by micro teaching practice?
6. What is the provision of practice teaching in workshops for B.Ed. trainees of distance mode?
7. Who provide feedback in practice teaching to B.Ed. trainees of distance mode?
8. How do the model lesson plans presented by you assit B.Ed. trainees of distance mode for preparing lesson plan of practice teaching?
9. How is practice teaching related with development of competency of distance mode B.Ed. trainees?
10. How is competency of distance mode B.Ed. trainees effected by practice teaching?

(II) Preparation of Teaching Aids and its Use:

1. What types of help is provided by you to B.Ed. trainees of distance mode in the preparation of teaching aids?
2. What types of help is provided by you to B.Ed. trainees of distance mode for appropriate use of library/laboratory/media and other teaching aids in the schools?
3. Motivation for the utilization of which type of I.C.T. based teaching aids is provided to B.Ed. trainees by you?
4. How useful is the help provided by you to B.Ed. trainees of distance mode for the preparation and appropriate utilization of teaching aids?

(III) Classroom-teaching Motivation:

1. How do you train B.Ed. trainees of distance mode for maintaining discipline in the class?
2. How do you help B.Ed. trainees of distance mode for improvement of teacher-student interaction in the class?
3. How do group discussion organized by you develop competency in B.Ed. trainees of distance mode?

(IV) Students' Evaluation:

1. What type of activities do you conduct for development of competency related to students' evaluation among B.Ed. trainees of distance mode?
2. How do you learn B.Ed. trainees of distance mode learn administration of psychological tests, preparation and administration of achievement test?
3. What is the provision of action research in B.Ed. programme of distance mode?
4. How do you resolve problems of distance mode B.Ed. trainees related to action research?
5. Hów do action research is related to development of competency of distance mode B.Ed. trainees?

(V) School Management and Planning:

1. How do you help B.Ed. trainees of distance mode in the preparation of school records and registers?
2. How do you help B.Ed. trainees of distance mode in the preparation of school time-table and school-budget?
3. How useful is the help provided by you to B.Ed. trainees of distance mode in the preparation of school records and time-table?

(VI) Community Participation:

1. How do you train B.Ed. trainees of distance mode in the execution of activities related to health education?
2. What type of social work and community survey do you make B.Ed. trainees of distance mode to undertake?

3. How are the health education and social survey conducted by you useful for B.Ed. trainees of distance mode?

(VII) Co-curricular Activities:

1. How do you develop competency related to sports and other cultural programmes among B.Ed. trainees of distance mode?
2. How do seminar conducted by you during the workshops assist B.Ed. trainees of distance mode?

Appendix IV

Interview Schedule for Mentor

(I) Preparation for Teaching:

1. How do you help B.Ed. trainees of distance mode in resolving problems encountered during preparation of unit plan?
2. How do you help B.Ed. trainees of distance mode in resolving problems encountered during preparation of lesson plan?
3. How do you help B.Ed. trainees of distance mode during practice teaching?
4. How do the B.Ed. trainees of distance mode take advantage of the feedback provided by you during practice teaching?

(II) Preparation of Teaching Aids and its Use:

1. How do you help B.Ed. trainees of distance mode in the preparation of teaching aids?
2. What are the various problems faced by B.Ed. trainees of distance mode in the utilization of teaching aids (mode of communication and localized material)?
3. How do you help B.Ed. trainees of distance mode in resolving problems in the utilization of teaching aids (mode of communication and localized material)?
4. What are the problems faced by B.Ed. trainees of distance mode in the utilization of library and laboratory?
5. How do you help B.Ed. trainees of distance mode in resolving the problems related to the utilization of library and laboratory?

(III) Classroom-Teaching Motivation:

1. How do you help B.Ed. trainees of distance mode in problems related to classroom discipline?
2. What are the problems faced by B.Ed. trainees of distance mode in establishing interaction with students in the class?

3. How do you help B.Ed. trainees of distance mode in resolving problems related to establishing interaction with the students in the class?
4. State the competencies in which you find B.Ed. trainees of distance mode lacking while teaching in the class.
5. What measures do you take while teaching in the class to overcome the deficiencies observed by you in B.Ed. trainees of distance mode?

(IV) Students' Evaluation:

1. What are the processes adopted by B.Ed. trainees of distance mode to evaluate their students?
2. What are the problems faced by B.Ed. trainees of distance mode while evaluating their students?
3. How do you help B.Ed. trainees of distance mode in resolving problems related to evaluation?

(V) School Management and Planning:

1. What help do you extend to B.Ed. trainees of distance mode in the preparation of school records, registers, school budget and time-table?
2. What are the problems encountered by B.Ed. trainees of distance mode in the activities related to action research?
3. How do you help B.Ed. trainees of distance mode in resolving problems related to action research?

(VI) Community Participation:

1. State the activities related to health education, social and community work being executed at school level by B.Ed. trainees of distance mode?
2. How do the B.Ed. trainees of distance mode execute activities related to health education and social and community work at school level?
3. What are the problems faced by B.Ed. trainees of distance mode in the execution of activities related to health education and social and community work?

4. How do you help B.Ed. trainees of distance mode in the execution of activities related to health education and social and community work?

(VII) Co-curricular Activities:

1. In the organization of which co-curricular activities do the B.Ed. trainees of distance mode actively participate?
2. What are the problems faced by B.Ed. trainees of distance mode in the execution of educational tour, sports and other cultural activities?
3. How do you help B.Ed. trainees of distance mode in resolving problems related to the execution of educational tour, sports and other cultural activities?

Appendix-V

Observation Schedule

SECTION: A
Regarding Resources/Equipment

Name of Study Centre ....

Name of concern University: IGNOU/UPRTOU ....

(A) Space Requirement:

Sl. No.	*Resources*	*Availability*		*Condition*	
		Yes	*No*	*Very good*	*Good*
1.	Main office/Information cell				
2.	Admission Office				
3.	Computer Lab				
4.	Number of class-room............				
5.	Arrangement of library:				
	a. Available only for regular students of the institute				
	b. Available only for IGNOU/ UPRTOU students				
6.	Store Room				
7.	Others				

(B) Resources/Equipment:

Sl. No.	*Resources*	*Availability*		*Condition*	
		Yes	*No*	*Very good*	*Good*
1.	Basic office equipments				
2.	Notice Board				

3.	Adequate furniture				
	a. Bench-Desk				
	b. Chair-Table				
	c. Others if available				
5.	Books of Hindi and English medium available according to the curriculum				
6.	Reference books				
7.	Number of computer				
8.	Facility of internet				
9.	Multimedia equipment				
	a. Television				
	b. Audio-video recorder				
	c. V.C.R./D.V.D. Player				
	d. L.C.D.				
	e. OHPs				
10.	Others				

(C) Required Staff:

Sl. No.	*Staff*	*Availability*		*Condition*	
		Yes	*No*	*Very good*	*Good*
1.	Programme incharge				
2.	Counsellors at the reception counter				
3.	Office assistant				
4.	Others				

(D) Administrative/Academic Resources:

Sl. No.	*Resources*	*Availability*		*Condition*	
		Yes	*No*	*Very good*	*Good*
1.	Number of trained and competent counselors				

2.	Distribution of course materials				
3.	Record and register:				
	a. Enquiry register				
	b. Admission register				
	c. Students attendance register				
	d. Counsellors attendance register				
	e. Course materials distribution register				
	f. Library books distribution register				
	g. Assignment submission register				

SECTION: B
In Reference to Counsellors/Academic Faculty

(1) Presentation of Model lesson plans by counselors:
   (i) Presented.
   (ii) Presented in all teaching subjects.
   (iii) Presented model lesson plans are effective.
   (iv) Others ....

(2) Preparation of micro teaching lesson plans by the subject expert:
   (i) Prepared.
   (ii) Prepared in all teaching subjects.
   (iii) Prepared in some specific teaching subjects.

(3) Practices of micro teaching:
   (i) Practiced during the workshops.
   (ii) Practice had been done in all teaching subjects.
   (iii) Practice had been done in all teaching skills.
   (iv) Practice had been done in some specific teaching skills.

(4) Demonstration of teaching skills by counsellors.
   (i) Demonstration had been done by counsellors.
   (ii) Demonstration had been done by counsellors in some specific skills.
   (iii) Demonstration had been done by counsellors in all skills.

(5) Preparation of lesson plans during the workshops.
   (i) Lesson plans had been prepared.
   (ii) Lesson plans had been prepared in some specific skills.
   (iii) Others ....

(6) Feedback provided for improvement in teaching behaviour of the trainees.

(i) Regularly. (ii) Often.
(iii) Never. (iv) Others ....

(7) Use of teaching aids by counsellors during the demonstration of lessons.

(i) Counsellors used teaching aids.
(ii) Teaching aids were used by all the counsellors during demonstration.
(iii) Teaching aids were used by very few number of counsellors during demonstration.
(iv) Others (if any)...

(8) Use of different kind of teaching aids by counsellors during the demonstration of lessons.

(i) Chart and readymade aids were used.
(ii) Natural objects were used.
(iii) ICT-based teaching aids were used.
(vi) Others ....

Sl. No.	*Activities of counsellors*	*Very Effective*	*Effective at Average Extent*	*Least Effective*	*Not Effective*
9.	Counsellors presented a model of school budget.				
10.	Counsellors presented a model lesson plan.				
11.	Organization of activities related to health education during the workshops.				
12.	Organization of debate competition during the workshops.				
13.	Trainees were made to learn the administration of psychological test by the counsellors.				

14.	Trainees were made to learn the organisation of co-curricular activities by the counsellors.				
15.	Trainees were made to learn how to use library by the counsellors.				
16.	Trainees were made to learn use of laboratory by the counsellors.				

(17) Make to learn use of technological equipment (TV, Computer, OHP etc.) by the counsellors.
(i) Make to learn taught. (ii) Taught by practical
(iii) Verbally. (iv) Theoretical.

(18) Make to learn preparation of register by counsellors.
(i) Make learn to prepare fees collection register.
(ii) By presenting model.
(iii) Through preparation during the workshops.

(19) Trainees were taught to prepare fees collection register by the counsellors.
(i) Make learn.
(ii) By presenting model.
(iii) By preparing during the workshops.

(20) Counsellors taught how to prepare question paper.
(i) Make learn
(ii) By presenting model.
(iii) By preparing blue-print.
(iv) By presenting model and preparing blue-print during the workshops.

SECTION: C
In Reference to B.Ed. Trainees

Name of the trainee: ....
School/College of trainees: ....

(1) Lesson plans were prepared by trainees.
(i) Yes (ii) No

(2) Trainees taught with the help of the lesson plans.
(i) Yes (ii) No

(3) Classroom management of trainees during practice teaching.
(i) Highly effective (ii) Effective at average level
(iii) Least effective (iv) Not effective

(4) Help of trainees to their students in the library.
(i) Highly effective (ii) Effective at average level
(iii) Least effective (iv) Not effective

(5) School budget had been prepared by trainees.
(i) Yes (ii) No

(6) School budget prepared by the trainees was:
(i) Highly effective (ii) Effective at average level
(iii) Least effective (iv) Not effective

(7) Trainees participated in the seminar during the workshops.
(i) Yes (ii) No

(8) Seminar presentation of trainees was:
(i) Highly effective. (ii) Effective at average level.
(iii) Least effective. (iv) Not effective.

(9) Trainee had done project work during the workshops.
(i) Highly effective. (ii) Effective at average level.
(iii) Least effective. (iv) Not effective.

(10) Lesson plans has been prepared by trainee during the workshops.
(i) By actively participating. (ii) With average participation.
(iii) With less participation. (iv) Without participating.

(11) Report of action research had been submitted by trainees during the workshops.
(i) Yes (ii) No

(12) Report presentation of action research by trainees during the workshops was:
(i) Highly effective. (ii) Effective at average level.
(iii) Least effective. (iv) Not effective.

(13) Psychological test had been administered by trainee at their school.
(i) Yes (ii) No

(14) Methods of administration of psychological test by trainee was:
(i) Highly effective. (ii) Effective at average level.
(iii) Least effective. (iv) Not effective.

(15) Trainee had prepared question paper.

(i) Yes (ii) No

(16) Trainee cooperate in sports during the workshops.

(i) By actively participating. (ii) With average participation.

(iii) With less participation. (iv) Without participating.

Appendix-VI

List of B.Ed. Study Centres of UPRTOU in U.P.

Sl. No.	*Name of Study Centres*
1.	Chaudhary Tulasi Ram Yadav Mahavidyalaya, Dhosra, Allahabad.
2.	D.J.P.G. College, Baghpat, Baraut.
3.	Deen Dayal Upadhyay Gorakhpur University, Gorakhpur.
4.	Hindu College, Moradabad.
5.	R.B.S. College, Agra.
6.	Shivali National Post Graduate College Azamgarh.
7.	Shyamlal Saraswati Mahavidyalaya, Shikarpur, Bulandshahr.
8.	T.D. College, Jaunpur.
9.	Upardaha Degree College, Baraut, Allahabad.
10.	V.S.S.D. College, Kanpur.

Appendix-VII

List of B.Ed. Study Centres of IGNOU in U.P.

Sl. No.	*Name of Study Centres*
1.	A.K. College, Shikohabad.
2.	Aligarh Muslim University, Aligarh.
3.	Bareilly College, Bareilly.
4.	Dayanand Womens Training College, Kanpur.
5.	Deen Dayal Upadhyay Gorakhpur University, Gorakhpur.
6.	E.C.C. Allahabad.
7.	Education Department, B.H.U. Kamaccha, Varansi.
8.	Firoj Gandhi College, Rai Bareilly.
9.	Hindu College Moradabad.
10.	J.N.P.G. College Lucknow.
11.	J.N.P.G. College, Banda.
12.	K.N.I. Sultanpur.
13.	K.N.P.G. College, Gyanpur.
14.	K.S. Saket Post Graduate College, Ayodhya, Faizabad.
15.	M.D.P.G. College, Pratapgarh.
16.	M.L.K.P.G. College, Balrampur.
17.	Satish Chandra College, Balia.
18.	St. John's College, Agra.
19.	Sukhdevanand P.G. College, Shahjahanpur.
20.	U.P. College, Varansi.
21.	University of Lucknow.

Bibliography

Books

Admiraal, W.F., *et al.* (1998). Computer-Mediated Communication Environments in Teacher Education: Computer Conferencing and Supervision of In-service Teachers. *Learning Environments Research*, 1, 59-74.

Agrawal, Y.P. (2007). *The Science of Educational Research: A Source Book.* Kurukshetra: Nirmal Book Agency.

Angelo, T. and Cross, P. (1993). *Classroom Assessment Techniques: A Handbook for College Teachers*. San Francisco: Josey-Bass Publishers.

Bates, A.W. (1984). *The Role of Technology in Distance Education*. London: Croom Helm.

Beeby, C.E. (1966). *The Quality of Education in Developing Countries.* Cambridge, MA: Harvard University Press.

Best, J.W. and Kahan, J.V. (2009). *Research in Education*, New Delhi: Prentice-Hall of India.

Brink, P. and Wood, M.J. (1989). *Advanced Designs to Nursing Research.* Sage Publication, Inc.

Calvert (1986). Quoted by Dash, N.K. in Mukhopadhyay, M. (1993). *Optimizing Human Learning*. Delhi: Amar Prakashan.

Creswell, J.W. (1998). *Qualitative Inquiry and Research Design-Choosing Among Five Traditions*. New Delhi: SAGE Publications.

Crookes, P.A. and Sue, D. (1998). *Research into Practice.* Glasgow: Bell and Bain Ltd.

Dash, N.K. (1998). Research Possibilities in Distance Education. In Mukhopadhyay, M. (Ed.). *Optimizing Human Learning*. Delhi: Amar Prakashan.

Gakhar, S.C. (2009). *Micro teaching, Macro teaching, Unit Planning.* Hariyana: N.M. Publication.

Garrett, H.E. (2006). *Statistics in Psychology and Education.* Delhi: Suraj Publication.

Gay, L.R. (1987). *Educational Research Competencies for Analysis and Application.* USA: Marrill Publishing Company.

Harichandan, D. (2010). *A study of Teacher Education Programmes Offered Through Distance Education Mode in Indian Universities.* In Teacher Education Through Distance Education. New Delhi: Deep and Deep Publication Pvt. Ltd.

Hiemstra, R., (Ed.) (1982). *Self-Directed Adult Learning: Some Implications for Practice*. Occasional Paper. Syracuse, NY: Adult Education Programme, School of Education.

Hollloway, R.E. and Ohler, J. (1991). Distance Education in the Next Decade. In G.J. Anglin, (Ed). *Instructional Technology Past, Present and Future.* Englewood, Co: Libraries Unlimited, 259-266.

Holmberg, B. (1977). *Distance Education: A Survey and Bibliography.* London: Kogan Page.

Holmberg, B. (1982). *Essentials of Distance Education (a Distance-Study Course Based on a Handbook and a Reader)*. German version: Groundage des Fernstudium. Hagen: Fern Universidad.

Holmberg, B. (1982). *Recent Research in Distance Education.* Hagen: Fern Universidad, Vol. 1-2.

Holmberg, B. (1985). Communication in Distance Study. *In Status and Trends of Distance Educational*, Lund, Sweden: Lector Publishing.

Holmberg, B. (1986). *Growth and Structure of Distance Education.* London: Croom-Helm.

Holmberg, B. (1989). *Theory and Practice of Distance Education.* New York: Routledge.

Holmbes, D.R. *et al.* (1993). Radio Education in Nepal. In H. Perraton (Ed.). *Distance Education for Teacher Training*, New York: Routledge, 136-195.

Keegan, D. (1990). *Foundations of Distance Education.* 2nd Edition, London: Routledge.

Khan, M.S. (1983). *Teacher Education in India and Abroad*, New Delhi: Ashish Publication.

Kumar, J.P. *et al.*(..). *Open University, Student Support Services.* New Delhi: Discovery Publishing House.

Kundu, C.L. (1988). *Indian Yearbook on Teacher Education.* New Delhi: Sterling Publication Pvt. Ltd.

Miles, M.B. (1983). Qualitative Data as an Attractive Nuisance: The Problem of Analysis. In J. Van Maanen (Ed.), *Qualitative Methodology.* Beverly Hill, CA: Sage.

Miles, M.B. and Huberman, A.M. (1984). *Qualitative Data Analysis: A Source Book of New Methods.* London: Sage Publication.

Moore, M. and Kersley, G. (1996). Belmont, CA: Wadsworth Publishing Company.

Oliveira, J. and Orivel, F. (1993). Logos II in Brazil. In H. Perraton (Ed.) *Distance Education for Teacher Training.* New York: Routledge, 69-94.

Patton, M.Q. (1980). *Qualitative Evaluation Methods.* England: SAGE Publications.

Polit, D.F. and Hungler, B.H. (1995). *Nursing Research Principles and Methods.* Philadelphia: J.B. Lippin Cott. Company.

Prawat, R.S. and Floden, R.W. (1994). Philosophical Perspectives on Constructivist Views of Learning. *Education Psychology*, 29.37-48.

Robinson, B. (1997). Distance Education for Primary Teacher Training in Developing Countries. In Lynch, J. *et al.* (ed.) *Innovations in Delivering*

Primary Education. Vol. III of Education and Development: Tradition and Innovation. London: Cassell.

Ronnie Carr, Yuonne Fung and Shui Kin Chan (2002). *"Distance Education for Teacher Education: Hong Kong experience".*

Rubin, H.J. and Rubin, I.S. (1995). *Qualitative Interviewing: The Art of Hearing Data.* Thousand Oaks, CA: Sage.

Sahoo, P.K. (1994). *Open Learning System.* New Delhi: Uppal.

Seidman, I.E. (1998). *Interviewing as Qualitative Research: A Guide for Researchers in Education and the Social Sciences.* New York: Teacher's College Press.

Siddiqui, M.A. (1991). *In-service Teacher Education.* New Delhi: Ashish Publishing House.

Singh, A.K. (2001). *Research Methods in Psychology Sociology And Education.* New Delhi: Shri Jainendra Press.

Singh, B. (1995). *New Horizons in Distance Education.* New Delhi: Uppal Publishing House.

Steinar, K. (1996). *Interviews: An Introduction to Qualitative Research Interviewing.* Thousand Oaks, CA: Sage.

Verduin, J.R. and Clark, T.A. (1991). *Distance Education: The Foundations of Effective Practice.* San Francisco, CA: Jossey-Bass Publishers.

Willis, B. (1993). *Distance Education: A Practical Guide.* Englewood Cliffs, NJ: Educational Technology Publications.

Wood, M.J. (1994). *Basic steps in planning Nursing Research* (4th ed.). Boston: Mass, Jones and Barlett.

Proceedings

Gunawardena, C. (2000). Using Technology for Quality Improvement of Teacher Education in OUSL: Problems and Possibilities. In Das, N.K. and Menon, S.B., Training *of Professionals Through Distance Education South Asia (Proceeding).* New Delhi, IGNOU, Pp. 108-114.

Kabir, S. (2000). Teacher Education in Bangladesh Through Distance Mode and Possibilities for Collaboration Between Bangladesh Open University and IGNOU and Allama Iqbal Open University. In Das, N.K. and Menon, S.B., *Training of Professionals Through Distance Education South Asia (Proceeding).* New Delhi, IGNOU, Pp. 115-124.

Rasid, M. (2000). Teacher training through Distance Education in Pakistan. In Das, N.K. and Menon, S.B., *Training of Professionals Through Distance Education South Asia (Proceeding).* New Delhi, IGNOU, pp. 125-134.

Parajuli, C.R. (2000). Teacher Training Through Distance Teaching. In Das, N.K. and Menon, S.B., *Training of Professionals Through Distance Education South Asia (Proceeding).* New Delhi, IGNOU, pp. 158-164.

Joshi, V. (2000). In-Service Training of Primary School Teachers Through Distance Mode: IGNOU Experience. In Das, N.K. and Menon, S.B., *Training of Professionals Through Distance Education South Asia (Proceeding).* New Delhi, IGNOU, pp. 165-175.

Phalachandra, B. and Veena, S. (2000). Efficacy of Interactive Television Technique in the Training of Primary School Teachers. In Das, N.K. and Menon, S.B., *Training of Professionals Through Distance Education South Asia (Proceeding)*. New Delhi, IGNOU, pp. 176-190.

Pradhan, B. (2000). Effect of Cooperative Peer Learning Strategies on Attitude of Student Teachers and Primary School Pupils and Their Perception towards Teaching and Learning. In Das, N.K. and Menon, S.B., *Training of Professionals Through Distance Education South Asia (Proceeding)*. New Delhi, IGNOU, pp. 220-223.

Government Publication/National and International Reports

Arora, G.L. and Singh, A. (1998). *Training Needs of Primary Teachers—A Pilot Study*. New Delhi: NCERT (Mimeo).

Bhushan, A. and Bhushan, M.A. (1999). *Distance teacher education—Self Instructional Material (Planning, Design and Development)*. New Delhi: IGNOU-UNESCO Chair. (mimeo).

Chivore, B.R.S. (1992). *"Pre-Service Teacher Education at a Distance: The Case of Zimbabwe"*, Report to World Bank.

Hodes, C. (1995). *Delivery System Preferences of Nontraditional Learners*. ERIC document ED368337.

Kenneth M.Z. (1993). Traditions of Practice in U.S. Preservice Teacher Education Programmes. *Teaching and Teacher Education*, 9(1), 1-13.

Khan, A.W. (2001). *Information and Communication Technology for Professional Development of Primary Education Personnel-Professional Development with Learning Technologies*. New Delhi: DEP-DPEP, IGNOU.

Menon, M.B. (1997). Primary Teacher Training Through Distance Mode. *DPEP Calling*, New Delhi: DPEP, 1 (12), 24-32.

MHRD (1986). *National Policy on Education—1986 (with Modifications Undertaken in 1992)*. New Delhi: MHRD.

Ministry of Education. (1966). *Education and National Development Report of the Education Commission 1964-66*. New Delhi: MHRD.

Moore, M.G. ***et al.*** (1990). The Effects of Distance Learning: A Summary of the Literature. *In Research Monograph* No. 2. University Park, P.A.: American Center for the Study of Distance Education, The Pennsylvania State University.

NCERT (1995). *Training Manual for Special Orientation Programme for Primary School Teachers*. New Delhi: NCERT.

NCTE (1998). *Curriculum Framework for Quality Teacher Education*. New Delhi: NCTE.

NCTE (1998). *In-service Teacher Education, Curriculum Framework for Quality Teacher Education*. New Delhi: NCTE.

Passi, B.K. (1998). *Envisioning Research Path*. New Delhi: IGNOU-UNESCO Chair, IGNOU. (mimeo).

Passi, B.K. (2000). *Formative Research for Video Production—A Seminar Report.* New Delhi: IGNOU-UNESCO Chair, IGNOU.

Phalachandra, B. (1998). Training Primary Teachers Through Satellite. *DPEP Calling*, 2(3), 24-41.

Reddy, U.V. (1998). *A Critical Evaluation of Research Methods Commonly Used in Educational Media Research.* New Delhi: IGNOU-UNESCO Chair, IGNOU. (mimeo).

S., *et al.* (Ed) (2001). *Information and Communication Technology for Professional Development of Primary Education Personnel-International Workshop.* New Delhi: DEP-DPEP, IGNOU.

Singh, R.P. (1999). *Distance Teacher Education—Face-to-Face-vis-à-vis Distance Mode (an Enquiry into the B.Ed. Programmes of Indian Universities).* New Delhi: IGNOU-UNESCO Chair, IGNOU. (mimeo).

Sinha, A., *et al.* (1994). Interactive Communication for Distance Education: *An Evaluative Study of ISRO-IGNOU Experiment. ISRO, Ahmedabad and IGNOU, New Delhi.*

UGC-NCTE-DEC (1999). *Norms and Standards for B.Ed. Programme Through Distance Mode (An Extract). In IGNOU-UNESCO Chair: Appendix II.* New Delhi: IGNOU-UNESCO Chair, IGNOU.(mimeo)

UNESCO (1990). What is a Study Center? The Range of Possible Functions. *In Handbook on the Organization and Management of Distance Education Study Centers.* Bangkok: UNESCO, 7-20, 30.

UNESCO (2002). *Teacher Education Guidelines: Using Open and Distance Learning Technology-Curriculum-Cost-Evaluation Paris*: UNESCO.

Journal/Bulletin/Newspapers

Balasubramaniam, S. (1986). The Status of Correspondence Courses in India. *University News.* New Delhi: Association of Indian Universities, 24 (42).

Basu, S. (1996). Regular Telecasts by IGNOU: Feedback from Students. *Indian Journal of Open Learning.* New Delhi: Indira Gandhi National Open University, 5(1), 34-43.

Beare, P.L. (1989). The Comparative Effectiveness of Videotape, Audiotape, and Telelecture. *The American Journal of Distance Education*, PA, USA: Pennsylvania State University, 3(2), 57-66.

Berge, Z.L. and Mrozowski, S. (2001). Review of Research in Distance Education, 1990 to 1999. *The American Journal of Distance Education*, PA, USA: Pennsylvania State University, 15(3), 5-19.

Bischoff, W.R., *et al.* (1996). Transactional Distance and Interactive Television in the Distance Education of Health Professionals. *The American Journal of Distance Education*, PA, USA: Pennsylvania State University, 10 (3).

Burge, E.J. and Howard, J.L. (1990). Audio-Conferencing in Graduate Education: A Case Study. *The American Journal of Distance Education*, PA, USA: Pennsylvania State University, 4 (2), 3-13.

Chen, Y.J. and Willits. F.K. (1999). Dimensions of Educational Transactions in a Videoconferencing Learning Environment. *The American Journal of*

Distance Education, PA, USA: Pennsylvania State University, 13 (1). 45-59.

Clark, T. (1993). Attitudes of Higher Education Faculty Toward Distance Education: A National Survey. *The American Journal of Distance Education*, PA, USA: Pennsylvania State University, 7(2), 19-31.

Coldeway, D.O. (1988). Methodological issues in Distance Educational Research. *The American Journal of Distance Education*, PA, USA: Pennsylvania State University, 2(3)

Cragg, C.E. Betty (1987). Nurses Experiences of a Distance Course by Correspondence and Audio teleconference. *Journal of Distance Education/Revue de I'enseignement distance*, 2(2).

Daresh, J.C. (1987). Research Trends in Staff Development and In-Service Education. *Journal of Teaching*, 13 (1), 3-11.

Das, N. (1997). Reactions of Primary School Teachers Towards Training Through Interactive Television. *Indian Journal of Open Learning*, Vol. 6, Nos. 1&2,

Egan, M.W., ***et al.*** (1992). Learner's Perceptions of Instructional Delivery Systems: Conventional and Television. *The American Journal of Distance Education*, PA, USA: Pennsylvania State University, 6(2)

Evans, T. (2000). The Strategic Importance of Institutional Research in Open Universities. *Indian Journal of Open Learning*, New Delhi: IGNOU, 9(1), 1-12.

Fulford, C.P. and Zhang, S. (1993). Perception of Interaction: The Critical Predictor in Distance Education. *The American Journal of Distance Education*, PA, USA: Pennsylvania State University, 7(3), 8-21.

Graham, G. (2003). Teacher Education Through Open and Distance Learning, open learning. *The Journal of Open and Distance Learning*, Vol. 18, No. 182, U.K. centre for higher education practice Open University.

Guawardena, C. (1995). Social Presence Theory and Implications for Interaction and Collaborative Learning in Computer Conferencing. *International Journal of Educational Telecommunications*, VA, USA: Association for the Advancement of Computing in Education, 1(2-3), 147-166.

Guba E.G. and Lincoln, Y.S. (1982). Epistemological and Methodological Bases of Naturalistic Inquiry. *Educational Communication and Technology Journal*, 30 (4), 233-252.

Guba, E.G. (1981). Criteria for Assessing the Trustworthiness of Naturalistic Enquiries. *Educational Communication and Technology Journal*, 29(2). 75-91.

Gupta, S.P. (2006). Distance Teacher Education. *Apear in Journal of Education*, Allahabad: APEAR, Vol. 6, No. 1, pp. 1-6.

Hillman, D.C. A., ***et al.*** (1994). Learner-Interface Interaction in Distance Education: An Extension of Contemporary Models and Strategies for Practitioners. *The American Journal of Distance Education*, PA, USA: Pennsylvania State University, 8 (2).

Holmberg, B. (1986). A Discipline of Distance Education. *Journal of Distance Education/Revue de I'enseignement distance. 1(1)*

Holstein, J.A. (1992). Making the Written Word "Speak" Reflections on the Teaching of Correspondence Courses. *The American Journal of Distance Education*, PA, USA: Pennsylvania State University, 6(3).

Keegan, D. (1988). Problems in Defining the Field of Distance Education. *The American Journal of Distance Education*, PA, USA: Pennsylvania State University, 2 (2), 4-11.

Kember, D. and Harper, G. (1992). Approaches to Studying Research and its Implications for the Quality of Learning From Distance Education. *Journal of Distance Education/Revue de' I enseignement distance,* 7(1).

Kember, D. *et al.* (1990). Naturalistic Evaluation of Distance Learning Courses. *Journal of Distance Education,* 5 (1).

Kirby, D.M. and Chugh, U. (1992). A Comparison of the Perceptions of Students and instructors of Elements in the Audio-Teleconferencing Environment. *Journal of Distance Education/Revue de I' enseignement distance*. 7 (2).

Kumar, S. (2018). *Study of Practice Teaching Processes Adopted for Development of Teaching Competencies Through ODL Mode,* International Journal of Creative Research Thoughts (IJCRT), ISSN:2320-2882, Volume.6, Issue 1, (Impact Factor: 5.97), pp. 723-735, Available at: http://www.ijcrt.org/IJCRT1872118.pdf

Kumar, S. (2018). Micro Teaching Practices Adopted for Development of Teaching Competencies Among Teacher Trainees Through ODL Mode, *International Journal of Research in Economics and Social Sciences (IJRESS)*, Vol. 8 Issue 2, ISSN(o): 2249-7382 (Impact Factor: 6.939), pg. 393-413, **Available at:** http://euroasiapub.org/category/ijress/current-ijress/page/4/?

Kumar, S. (2013). A Study of Process of B.Ed. Programmes in Open Universities, Researchs and Studies, *A Journal of Department of Education,* University of Allahabad, Allahabad, IISN : 0084 – 621X, Vol. 65, pp. 28-33.

Lundin, R. (1998). Being Unreal: Epistemology, Ontology and Phenomenology in a Virtual Educational World. *The American Journal of Distance Education*, PA, USA: Pennsylvania State University, 12(3).

Machtmes, K. and Asher, J.W. (2000). A Meta-Analysis of the Effectiveness of Telecourses in Distance Education. *The American Journal of Distance Education*, PA, USA: Pennsylvania State University, 14 (1).

Maheshwari, A. (2006). Teacher Education Via open Distance Learning: A Democratic Alternative. In *University News, A weekly journal of Higher Education*. New Delhi: AIU House, pp. 1-5.

Mandal, S. and Shah, A. (1992). Use of Modern and Conventional Media for Distance Education—An Experiment. *Kakatiya Journal of Distance Education,* 1(2), 46-57.

Martin, E.E. and Rainey, L. (1993). Student Achievement and Attitude in a Satellite-Delivered High School Science Course. *The American Journal of Distance Education,* PA, USA: Pennsylvania State University, 7 (1) 54-61.

McCleary, I.D. and Egan, M.W. (1989). Programme Design and Evaluation: Two-way Interactive Television. *The American Journal of Distance Education*. PA, USA: Pennsylvania State University, 3 (1), 50-60.

McDonald, J. and Gibson, C.C. (1998). Interpersonal Dynamics and Group Development in Computer Conferencing. *The American Journal of Distance Education.* PA, USA: Pennsylvania State University, Vol. 12. (1), 7-25.

Mishra, S. (2000). In-service Teacher Education Through Distance Mode: An Innovative Model. *University News*, New Delhi: Association of Indian Universities, 38(13).

Misra, K.S. *et al.* (2009). Research and studies. *A Journal of Department of Education.* Allahabad: University of Allahabad.

Mohanty, J. and Behera, S.C. (1985). Teacher Education Programme under INSAT, *EPA Bulletin*, Vol. 8. Nos. 1 & 2.

Moore, M.G. (1989) (Ed.) Three of Interaction. *The American Journal of Distance Education.* PA, USA: Pennsylvania State University, 3(2).

Moore, M.G. (1995) (Ed.). The 1995 Distance Education Research Symposium: A Research Agenda. *The American Journal of Distance Education*, PA, USA: Pennsylvania State University, 9(2).

Moore, M.G. (1996). Media Options. *The American Journal of Distance Education*, PA, USA: Pennsylvania State University, 10(3).

Moore, M.G. (1997) (Ed). Quality in Distance Education: Four cases. *The American Journal of Distance Education*, PA, USA: Pennsylvania State University, 11(3).

Morgan, A. (1984). A Report on Qualitative Methodogies in Research in Distance Education. *Distance Education: An International Journal*, 5 (2), 252-267.

Murali M.K. (1996). *Distance education Theory and Practice*, Volume 1V, Distance Education Research in India, Hyderabad: Open Learning Society (Dr. B.R. Ambedkar Open University).

Murugan, K. (1996). Selection as an Input for Counselor Training: Some Reflections. *In Indian Journal of Open Learning*, 5 (2).

Naidu, S. (1994). Applying Learning and Instructional Strategies in Open and Distance Learning. *Distance Education*, 15 (1), 23-41.

Owens, R. (1982). Methodogical Rigor in Naturalistic Inquiry: Some Issues and Answers. *Educational Administration Quarterly*, 18(2), 1-21.

Passi, B.K. (2000). Using Action Research for Professional Development. *Indian Journal of Open Learning*, New Delhi: IGNOU, 9(2), 165-168 (mimeo).

Passi, B.K. and Mishra, S. (2000). Research Operations in Open Universities. *Indian Journal of Open Learning*, New Delhi: IGNOU, 9(1), 113-118.

Pittman, V.V., Jr. (1987). The Persistence of Print: Correspondence Study and the New Media. *The American Journal of Distance Education*, PA, USA: Pennsylvania State University. 1(1).

Powar, K.B. (2001). Research in Indian University. In *Supervision of Research in Universities*, New Delhi: Association of Indian Universities.

Prahar, M. (1999). Pedagogical Analysis of Instructional Material in School Education. *Indian Journal of open Learning,* New Delhi: Indira Gandhi National Open University, 8(1), 85-101.

Senapaty, H.K. (1999). *Professional Needs of Elementary School Teachers*: A Case Study IGNOU, UNESCO chair project.

Singh, L.C., and Singh, A. (1999). *Paradigm for Teacher Development through Distance Education*. IGNOU, UNESCO chair project.

Singh, R.P. and Rana, G. (1999). *An Inquiry into the B.Ed. Programme of Indian Universities Face to Face Vis-a-vis distant modes*. IGNOU, UNESCO chair project.

Upreti, D.C. (1988). *Impact of Teacher Training Through Correspondence Courses (B.Ed. SSCCC) on upward occupational mobility of the elementary teachers in the western region*. Bhopal: RCE, Project.

Thesis, Research Studies, Abstract and Survey

Agrawal, I. (2000). *Distance Education: Prospects and Problems*. Ph.D. (Edu.) Dr. B. R. Ambedkar University.

Aiholi, V.D. (1996). *Forecasting Needs and Resource Potentials for in-Service Education for Secondary School Teachers of Karnataka State towards 2005*. Unpublished Ph.D. Education Thesis, Indore: DAVV.

Albright, M.J. (1988). *A Conceptual Framework for the Design and Delivery of a University-level Credit Course by Communications Satellite*. Ph.D. Diss., Iowa City: Iowa State University.

Alkin, M.C. (1992). *Encyclopedia of Educational Research, sixth edition*, Vol-12, New York: Macmillan Publishing Company.

Ansari, M.M. and Dash, N.K. (----). "Managing and Financing Teacher education using distance mode: A study", *Journal of Distance Education*, Volume X, No. 12003, D.D.E. University of Jummu.

Arun, Renu (1990) *A study of success in Distance Learning System in Relation to Some Key Learner and Institutional Variables*, Doctoral Dissertation, Kurukshetra University, Kurukshetra.

Benekanal, V.A. (1996). *Forecasting Needs and Resource Potentials for in-Service Education for College Teachers of Karnataka State towards 2005*. Unpublished Ph.D. Education Thesis, Indore: DAVV.

Biswal, B.N. (1979). *A Study of Correspondence Education in India*. Ph.D., (Edu.) Baroda: The Maharaja Sayajirao University of Baroda.

Boondao, S. (2005). *How Assignment Affect Students Studying Mathmatics in A Distance Education System in Thiland*. ICDE International Conference, Abstracts of Papers. Nov. 19-23, New Delhi, IGNOU, pp. 116.

Chandhok, S. (1995). Role of Libraries in Distance Learning Universities: A Study of Students' Problem. In Panda, S.K. and Sharma, R.C. (Eds). *Indian Distances Education: Contemporary Research*. New Delhi, 33-34.

Coldeway, D.O., *et al.* (1980). *Distance Education from the Learner's Perspective: The Results of Individual Learner Tracking* at Athabasca University. Edmonton, Alberta: Athabasca University.

Ganesan, S. (1996). Teacher Education through Formal and Distance Education in the University of Madras. Unpublished Ph.D. thesis, Madras: Institute of Correspondence Education University.

Gupta, M.L. (1985). *Indian Economy and Higher Education with Reference to Correspondence Education.* Rajasthan: Institute of Correspondence Studies, Univ. of Rajasthan.

Husen, T. and Postlethwaite, T.N. (1994). *The International Encyclopedia of Education, Second Edition.* Vol-3, Great Britain: BPC Weatons Ltd., Exeter.

Kapoor, B.K. (1997). *Development and Validation of In-Service Education, Curriclum for Primary School Head Masters of Delhi.* Ph.D. Education Work in Progress, Kota: Kota Open University.

Kaul, L. (1997). Open and Distance Education. In *Fifth Survey of Educational Research 1988-92, Trend Reports*. New Delhi: NCERT.

Kaushal, S. (2002). *Functioning of Distance Education Institutions in Delhi.* Unpublished Ph.D. Thesis, Delhi: University of Delhi.

Khan, M. (1999). A Study of In-Service Teacher Education Programmes through Distance Education in M.P. Unpublished Ph.D. Thesis, Indore: DAVV.

Khan, N. (1991). Effectiveness of DE Programme with Reference to the Teachers Training Course. Unpublished Ph.D. Thesis, Srinagar: University of Kashmir.

Koul, L. (1997). *Open and Distance Education in Fifth Survey of Research in Education (1988-92)*. New Delhi: NCERT.

Kumar, S. (2011). A study of processes of B.Ed. Progammes in open universities, D. Phil. Thesis, U.P.: University of Allahabad, Allahabad.

Manjrekar, N. (1999). Learning One's Gender in the Primary School A Study of Curriculum. Unpublished Ph.D. thesis, Baroda: The M.S. University of Baroda.

Mavin, C.A. (1992). *Encyclopedia of Educational Research, Sixth Edition,* Vol. 1, American Educational Research Association.

Mishra, S. (2002). Study of the Process-issues for Organizing Research And Training in Distance Teacher Education. Unpublished Ph.D. thesis, Orissa: Utkal University, Beni Vihar Bhubaneswar.

Mohamad, S.J.A.N.S., *et al.* (2005). Analysis of Learning Styles of Distance Learners At the Institute of Education Development, University Technology Mora Malaysia. *ICDE International Conference, Abstracts of Papers.* Nov. 19-23, New Delhi, IGNOU, pp. 84-85.

Nagar, D. and Mahapatra, B.C. (2005). Skills for Development: A Case Study of Special Educational Programme Through Distance Mode. *ICDE International Conference, Abstracts of Papers.* Nov. 19-23, New Delhi, IGNOU, pp. 139-140.

Peng, L. and Yanhui, L. (2004). Survey on the Requirement of Support Service for Distance Learners. *The 18th AAOU Annual Conference, Abstracts of Papers. Nov. 28-30, China, Shanghai, pp. 22.*

Piyuan, Z. and BaoHong, L. (2004). Analysis of Distance Learners' Study Habit. *The 18th AAOU Annual Conference, Abstracts of Papers. Nov. 28-30, China, Shanghai, p. 108.*

Pradhan, K. (2002). *A Comparative Study of the Effectiveness of Traditional versus Correspondence B.Ed. Programmes of The Universities of Orissa.* Unpublished Ph.D. Thesis, Orissa: Utkal University Benivihar Bhubaneshwar.

Pugalenthi, N. (1998). *An evaluation of Distance Education Teaching with specific reference to certain selected Universities in the State of Tamil Nadu.* Ph.D. (Edu.), Bharathiyar University.

Pugazhenthi, G. (1991). *A Study of Teacher Education Programme Through the Correspondence System in Madurai Kamraj University.* Ph.D. Edu., Baroda: The Maharaja Sayajirao University of Baroda.

Qining, Y. (2004). Training English Teachers aboard The Necessity and Feasibility Research. *The 18th AAOU Annual Conference, Abstracts of Papers. Nov. 28-30,* China, Shanghai, pp. 196-197.

Rahayu, U. Ratnaningsih, A. and Lryani, K. (2004). The Study of learning Materials and the Implementation of Practical Work of Biology in Indonesian Open University. *The 18th AAOU Annual Conference, Abstracts of Papers. Nov. 28-30,* China, Shanghai, p. 130.

Prasad, Rajendra, D. and John, E.A. (1992). Development of skills through teaching practice — a comparative study of the attitudes of B.Ed. trainees of distance and conventional institutions, *Kakatiya Journal of Distance Education,* 1(2), 80-91.

Sahoo, S.N. (1999). *Exploring Needs for In-Service Education for Primary School Teachers of Tribal Districts of Orissa.* Ph.D. Education Work in Progress, Kota: Kota Open University.

Sahoo, P.K. and Tripathi, A.K. (2004). Study of Networking of Institutions in Promoting Quality of Students Support Services in Open Universities. *The 18th AAOU Annual Conference, Abstracts of Papers. Nov. 28-30,* China, Shanghai, pp. 201-202.

Sahu, B.N. (2005). *A Study of the Distance Education System in Orissa as an Alternative Channel.* Unpublished Ph.D. Thesis, Orissa: Utkal University, Vanivihar, Bhubaneswar.

Sesharatnam, C. (1994). *Multimedia Instructional System in Distance Education: A Case Study of Dr. B.R. Ambedker Open University.* Doctoral Diss., Hyderabad: Osmania University.

Srinivas, Rashmi (1992). *Teacher training through the Distance Mode: An Approach to the Teaching of Grammar,* M. Litt. Dissertation, Central Institute of English and Foreign Language, Hyderabad.

Srinivasan, T.R. (2004). *Developing and Validating a Training Package to Promote Distance Teaching Activity Through Tutor Comments on the Learners Assignment Responses of IGNOU B.Ed. Programme in Tamilnad.* Ph. D. (Edu.) Alagappa University Karaikudi.

Teacher's Encyclopedia, Thirty-six Contributors, America: The Prentice-Hall Editorial staff, 8883-X.

Tianjing, L. and Jingtao, L. (2004). Exploration of Instructional Staff Training Model in Rural Distance Education: Case Study of Instructional Staff Training Of TCP Project. *The 18th AAOU Annual Conference, Abstracts of Papers. Nov. 28-30,* China, Shanghai, p. 22.

Yadav, D. and Sahoo, P.K. (2004). University Teachers' Perception About Future of ICT in Education. *The 18th AAOU Annual Conference, Abstracts of Papers. Nov. 28-30,* China, Shanghai, p. 169.

Yadav, G. (2009). *Study of problems related to practice teaching of B.Ed. students of distance mode.* Unpublished M.Ed. Dissertation. Allahabad: University of Allahabad.

Seminar and Conference Paper/Reports

Behera, S.C. (1991). *An Investigation into the Impact of ETV Programmes on the Competency of the Teachers of Elementary Schools.* Paper presented in AIAET Annual Conference, Dec., Bhubaneswar.

Cookson, P.S. (2000). *Access and Equity in Distance Education: Research and Development and Quality Concerns.* Keynote Address in Annual Conference of the Asian Association of Open Universities, 22-26 February 2002, New Delhi.

Egan, M.W., ***et al.*** (1991). Effective Television Teaching: *Perceptions of Those Who Count Most...Distance Learners.* Proceedings of the Rural Education Symposium, Nashville, T.N.

Jones, P.K. (1989). *Report on the 1989 Research Assessment Exercise.* London: University Funding Council.

Maheshwari, A.N. and Raina V.K. (1996). *INSET Through Interactive Video Technology: An Innovative Indian Experience—A Paper*: New Delhi: NCERT.

Mukhopadhyay, M. (1999). *Alternative Strategies in Teacher Education* paper presented in National Seminar on Teacher Education organised by DEP-DPEP, IGNOU, March 22-24.

Sahoo, P.K. and Kumar, A. (2004). *Study of Networking of Institutions in Promoting Quality of Students Support Services in Open Universities.*

Sahoo, P.K. (..).*Alternative Forms of Teacher Education: A seminar paper Baroda,* C.A.S.E., M.S. University.

Sahoo, P.K. (..). Perspectives of Research in Distance Education and Professional Development of teachers, Paper presented.

Sahoo, P.K. (2001). Perspectives of Research in Distance Education and Professional Development of Teachers. In Jena.

Unesco, Bangkok (1987). *In-Service Training and Tomorrow's Primary Education,* Report.

Willis, B. (1992). Instructional Development for Distance Education. *ERIC Digest* (ED351007 Nov 92).

Websites

Chen, T.C.J. (1998). *Chapter Four Focus Paper: Research on Effectiveness.* <http://seamonkey.ed.asu.edu/~mcisaac/disted/week1/4focustc.html

Dr. B.R. Ambedkar Open University: www.braou.ac.in<http://www.braou.ac.in>

Emporia State University (1997). Doctor o. Philosophy (Ph.D.). School of Library and Information Management, Emporia State University. http://slim.emporia.edu/program/phd/doctoral.htm.

Government of India, Ministry of Education (2001). List of Institutions offering course on Distance Mode and Open Universities in India (As in January 2001). http://www.education.nic.in/htmlweb/dist _inst.htm

http://www.athabascau.ca/html/staff/admin/cookson/AAOU_keynote.doc

http://www.ihets.org/consortium/ipse/fdhandbook/inst_dd.html.

http://www.ihets.org/consortium/ipse/fdhandbook/resrch.html

http://www.irrodi.org/content/v1.1/farhad.pdf.

http://www.stat.go.jp/english/iaos/paper/bregar.pdf

http://www1.worldband.org/disted/Teaching/Support/cent-01.html

Indira Gandhi National Open University: www.ignou.edu<http://www.ignou.edu>

Jegede, O. and Zhang, W.Y. (2000). Conference on 'Research in Distance and Adult Learning in Asia' (CRIDALA 2000). *Global E-Journal of Open, Flexible and Distance Education.* http://www.ignou.edu/

Kota Open University: http://www.koukota.com/programmes.htm

Madhukar, N.S. (1998). Natworking of Indian Open Universities: A Proposal. http://www.ouhk.edu.hk/~AAOUNet/round/madhukar.pdf

McBride, R. and Schostak, J. (----). Chapter 2: Qualitative Versus Quantitative Research. In *An Introduction to Qualitative Research.* Enquiry Learning Unit (ELU), School of Education and Professional Development http://www,uea.ac.uk/edu/, University of East Anglia, Norwich. http://www.uea.ac.uk/care/elu/Issues/Research/Res1Ch2.html.

Mohapi, M. and Taole, N. (1999). *Information for Enhancement of Life: Dissemination of Research Results in Lesotho.* http://boleswa97.tripod.com/mohapi _taole.htm.

Morgan, A. (1984), quoted in Jeffries, M. (2000). *IPSE-Research in Distance Education.* http://www.ihets.org/consortium/ipse/fdhandbook/resrch.html.

NCTE (----): *Norms and Standards for Teacher Education Institutions (B.Ed. Distance Education Including Correspondence) (Secondary).* http://www.ncte-in.org/ norms/bed_dst0.htm.

Nelson, H.A. (1996). Short Thesis on Supervision. In *Supervision of Research Students: Three Papers*, The Australian National University. http://www.anu.edu.au/graduate/pubs/occasional-papers/gs96_2.html.

OUHK (1999). *A Report of the OUHK 10th Anniversary Specialized Workshop on Institutional Research in Open and Distance Learning Held on Wednesday, 13 October 1999.* http://www.ouhk.edu.hk/cridal/10th.thm

Perration, H. (1997). The Cost effectiveness of Distance Education for Primary Teacher Training http://www.colorg/consultancies/97primeteach.htm.

Perraton, H and Potashnik, M. (1997). *Teacher Education at a Distance.* http://wbln0018.worldbank.org/HDNet/HDdocs.nsf/C11FBFF6C1B77F998 5256686006DC949/18AF6A7F0846CA5085256755005D3501/$FILE/v2n2 .pdf

Sherry, L. (1996). Issues in Distance Learning. *International Journal of*

Education Telecommunications, 1(4), 337-365. http://carbon.cudenver.edu~lsherry/pubs/issues. html

Teacher Education and Special Education, Albany, NY: Boyd Printing Company, Inc. Vol. 15, 62-86. <http:/www.tese.uc.edu/>

World Bank (...). Learner support..What is a Study Centre and Why is it Needed?
http://www1.worldbank.org/disted/Teaching/Support/studycenters.html

Yashwantrao Chavan Maharashtra Open University: www.ycmou.com

Yes Pakistan.com Staff Writer (2002). AIOU's Successful Distance Teacher Education. Program. http://www.yespakistan.com/education/successful_DTE.aspd
http://www.wbnsou.ac.in/NSOU%20conceptDE.htm

Index